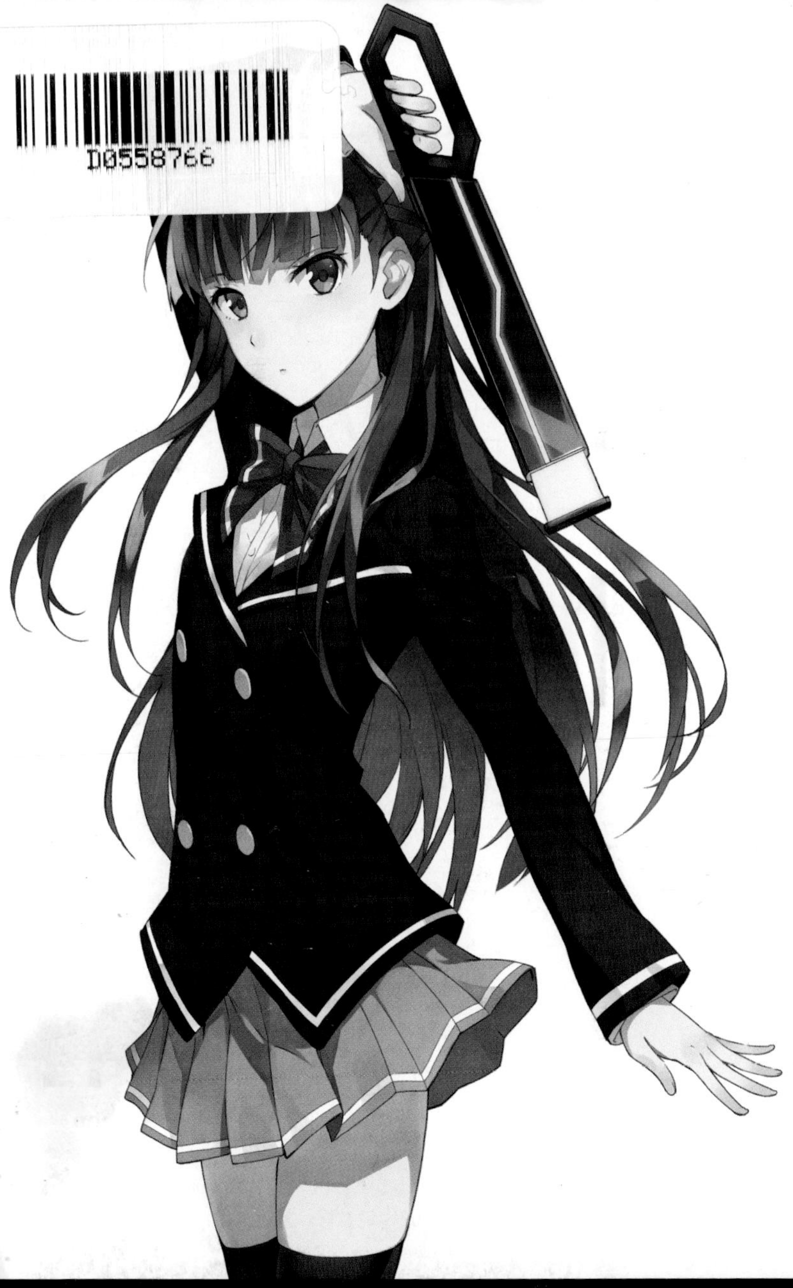

THE ISOLATOR

realization of
absolute solitude

CONTENTS

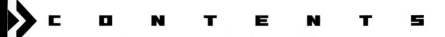

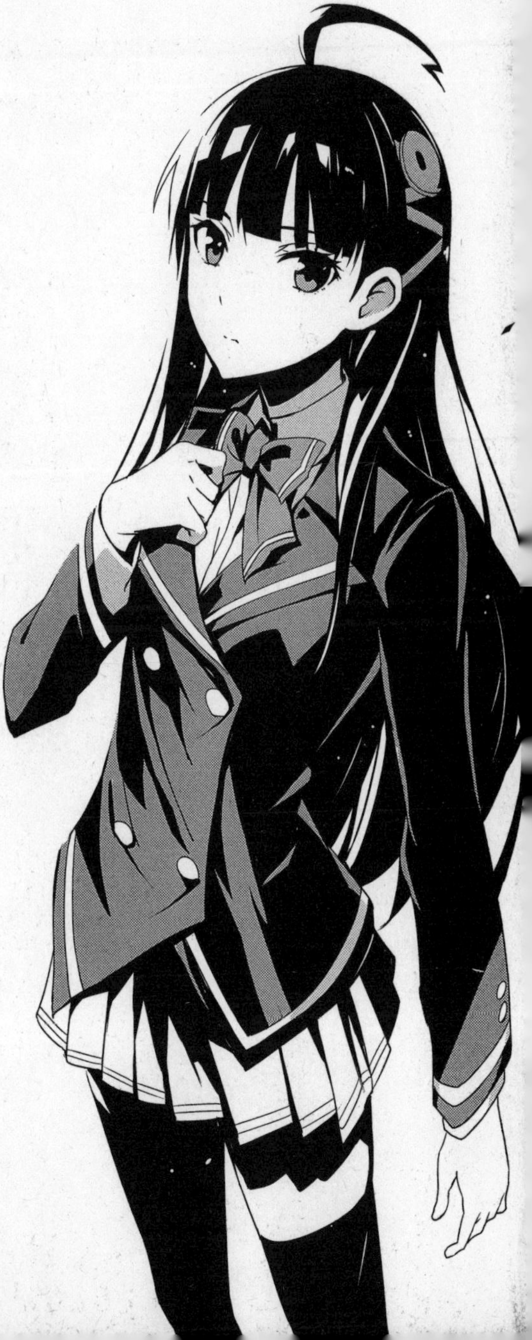

Sect.007

LONGING FOR PEACE

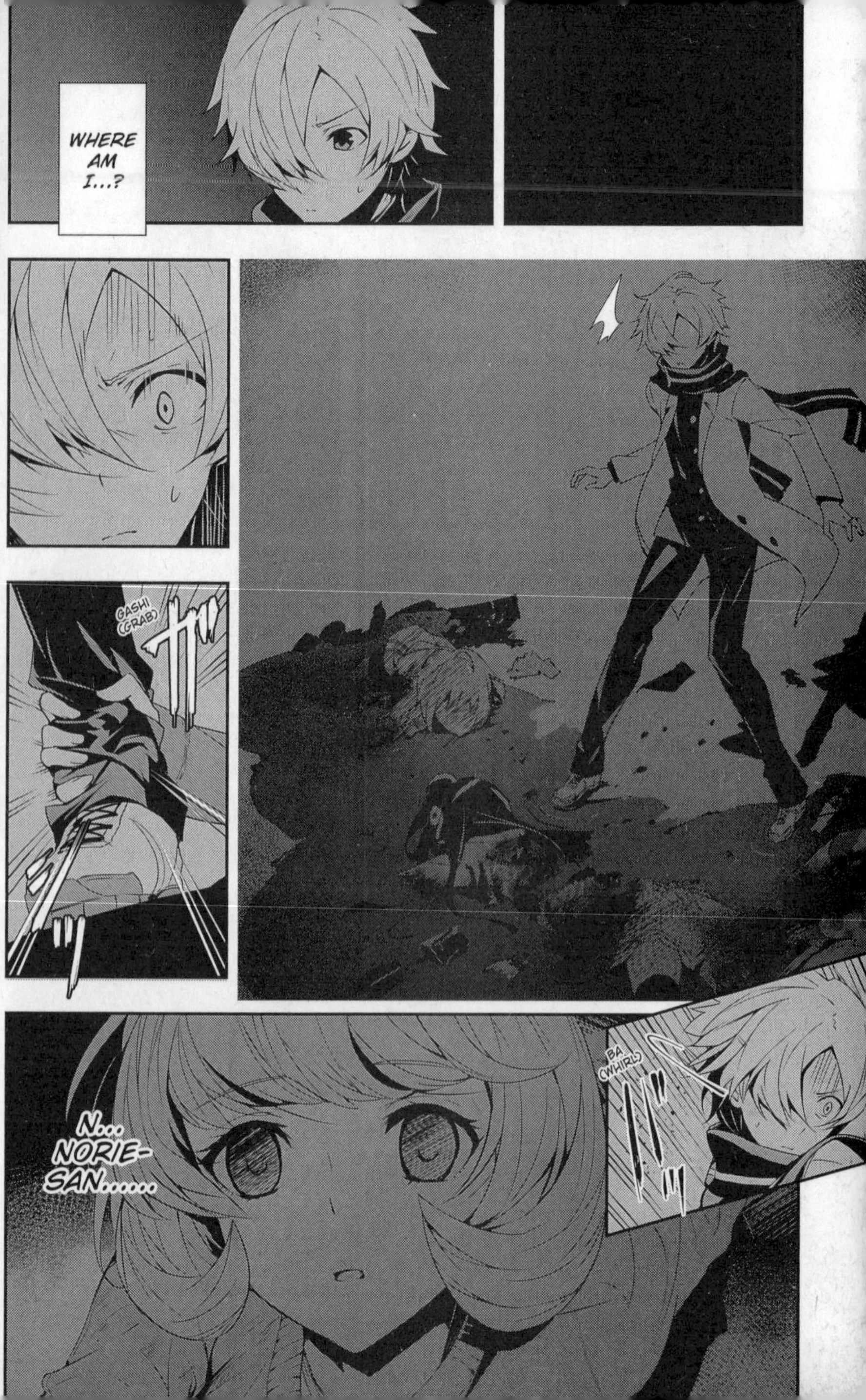
WHERE AM I...?
GASHI (GRAB)
BA (WHIRL)
N... NORIE-SAN......

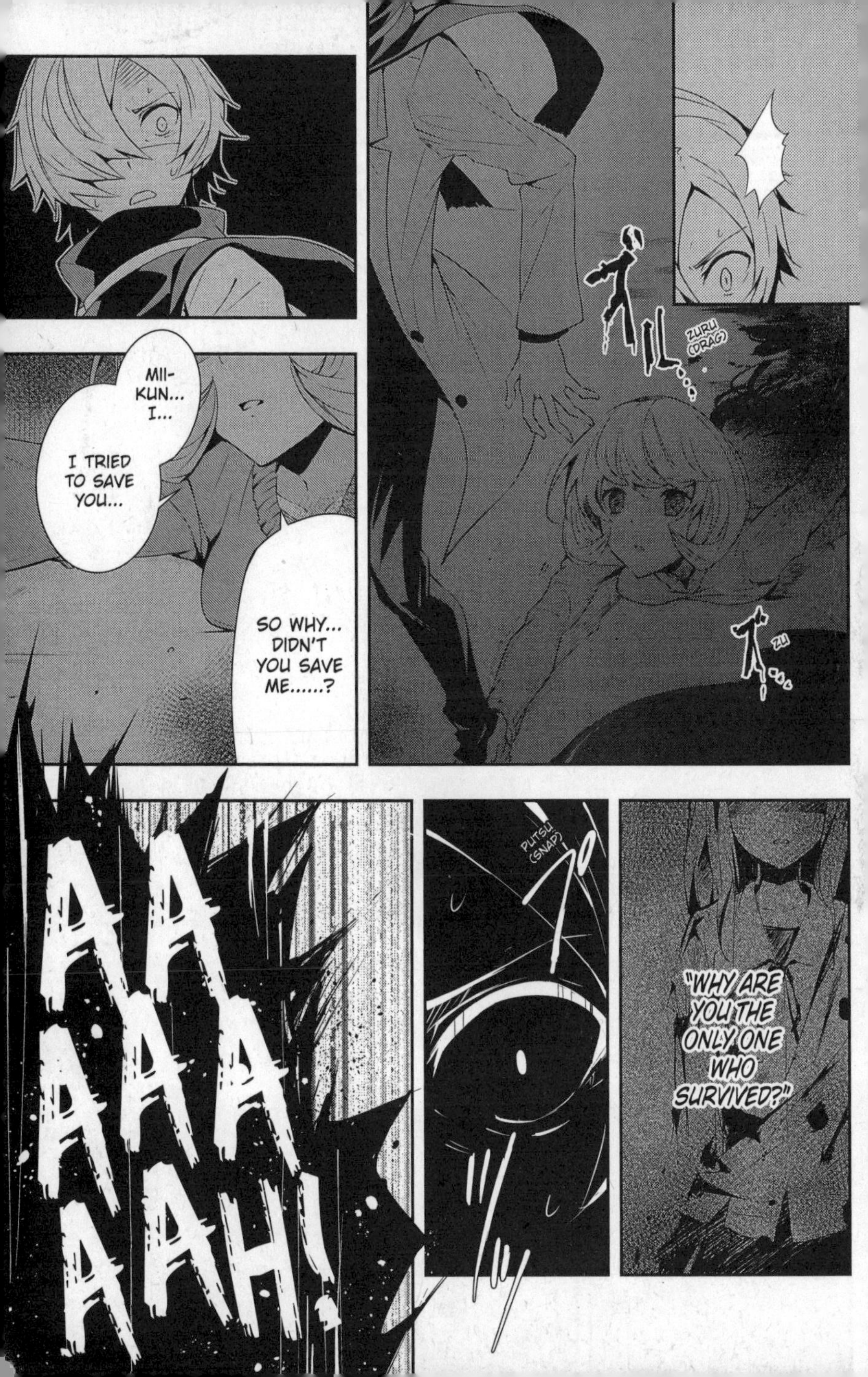
ZURU (DRAG)
ZU
MII-KUN... I...
I TRIED TO SAVE YOU...
SO WHY... DIDN'T YOU SAVE ME......?
"WHY ARE YOU THE ONLY ONE WHO SURVIVED?"
PUTSU (SNAP)
AAAAAAAH!

GABA
(BOLT)

HFF!
HAH!
HFF!
HFF! HAH!
HAH!

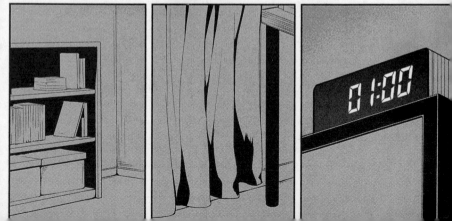

01:00

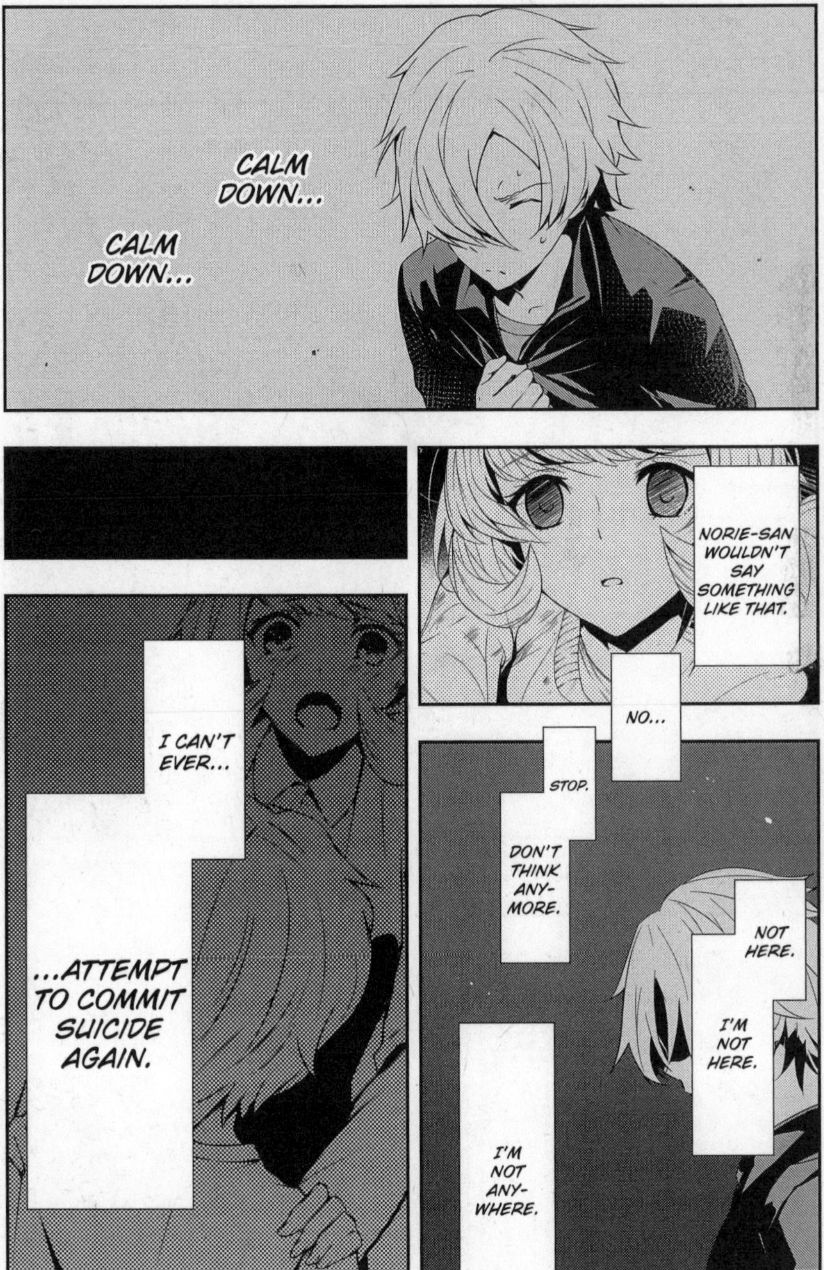
CALM DOWN...
CALM DOWN...
NORIE-SAN WOULDN'T SAY SOMETHING LIKE THAT.
NO...
STOP.
DON'T THINK ANY-MORE.
NOT HERE.
I'M NOT HERE.
I'M NOT ANY-WHERE.
I CAN'T EVER...
...ATTEMPT TO COMMIT SUICIDE AGAIN.

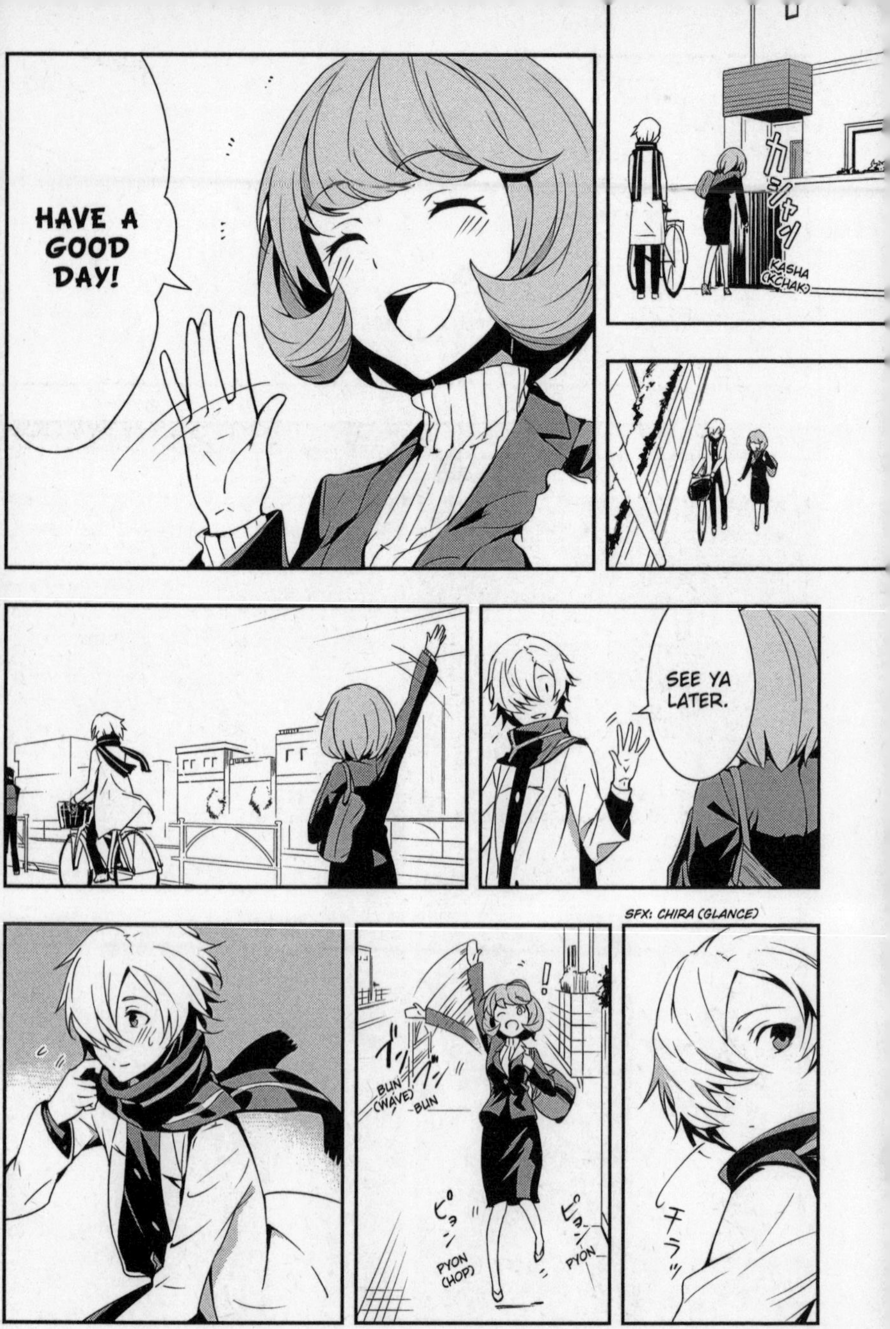
KASHA (KCHAK)
HAVE A GOOD DAY!
SEE YA LATER.
SFX: CHIRA (GLANCE)
BUN (WAVE) BUN
PYON (HOP) PYON

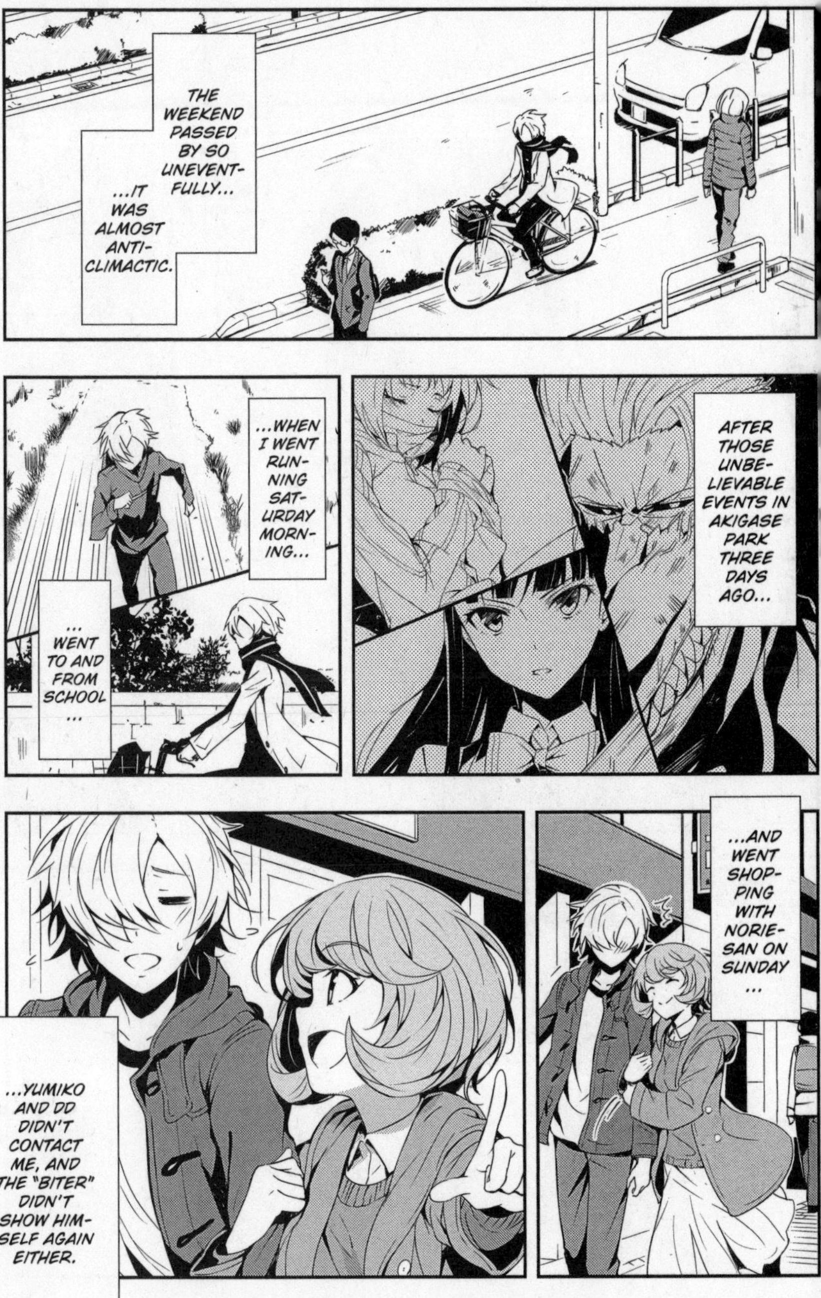
THE WEEKEND PASSED BY SO UNEVENTFULLY...
...IT WAS ALMOST ANTI-CLIMACTIC.
AFTER THOSE UNBELIEVABLE EVENTS IN AKIGASE PARK THREE DAYS AGO...
...WHEN I WENT RUNNING SATURDAY MORNING...
...WENT TO AND FROM SCHOOL...
...AND WENT SHOPPING WITH NORIE-SAN ON SUNDAY...
...YUMIKO AND DD DIDN'T CONTACT ME, AND THE "BITER" DIDN'T SHOW HIMSELF AGAIN EITHER.

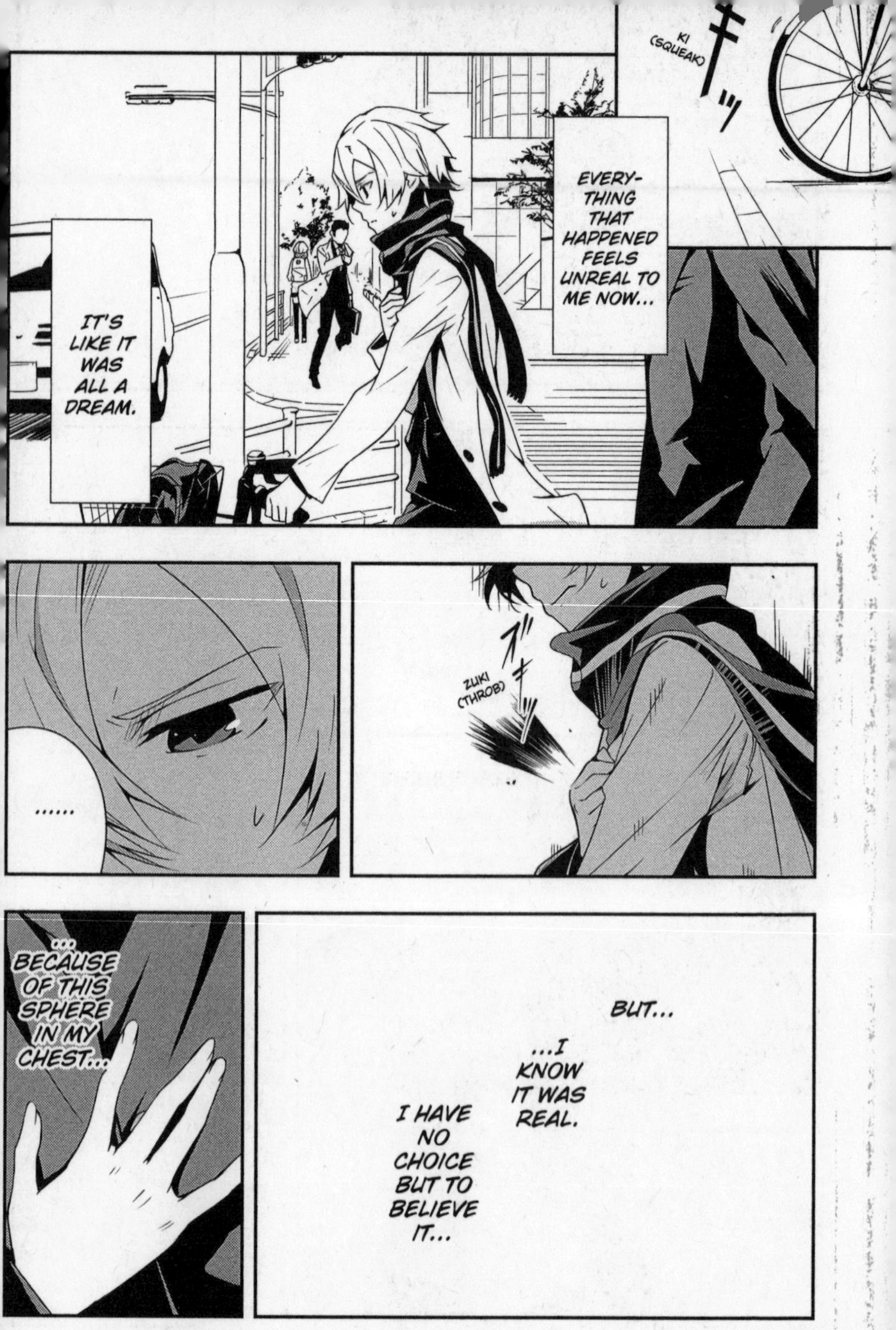
KI (SQUEAK)
EVERYTHING THAT HAPPENED FEELS UNREAL TO ME NOW...
IT'S LIKE IT WAS ALL A DREAM.
ZUKI (THROB)
......
BUT...
...I KNOW IT WAS REAL.
I HAVE NO CHOICE BUT TO BELIEVE IT...
...BECAUSE OF THIS SPHERE IN MY CHEST...

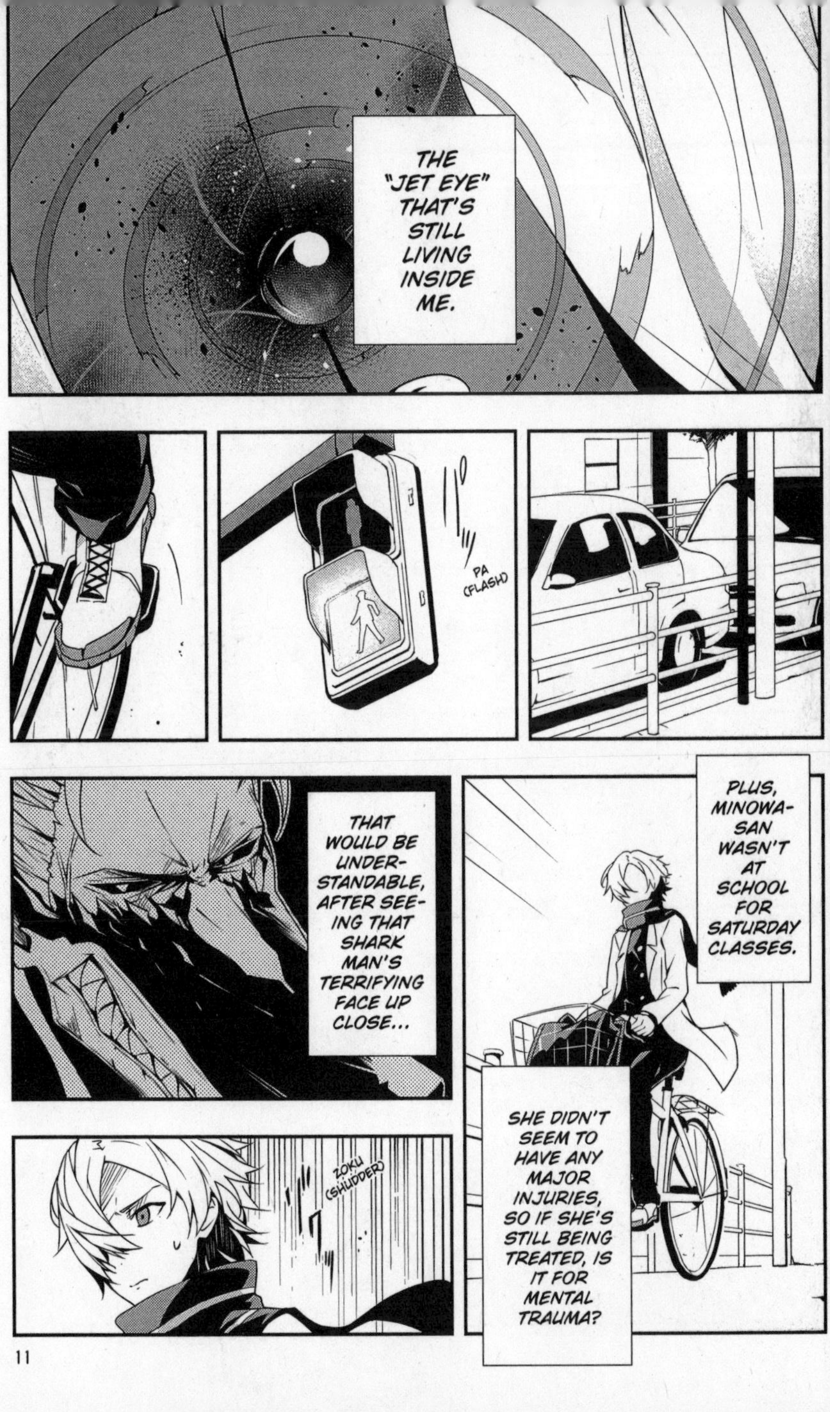
THE "JET EYE" THAT'S STILL LIVING INSIDE ME.
PA (FLASH)
PLUS, MINOWA-SAN WASN'T AT SCHOOL FOR SATURDAY CLASSES.
SHE DIDN'T SEEM TO HAVE ANY MAJOR INJURIES, SO IF SHE'S STILL BEING TREATED, IS IT FOR MENTAL TRAUMA?
THAT WOULD BE UNDER-STANDABLE, AFTER SEE-ING THAT SHARK MAN'S TERRIFYING FACE UP CLOSE...
ZOKU (SHUDDER)

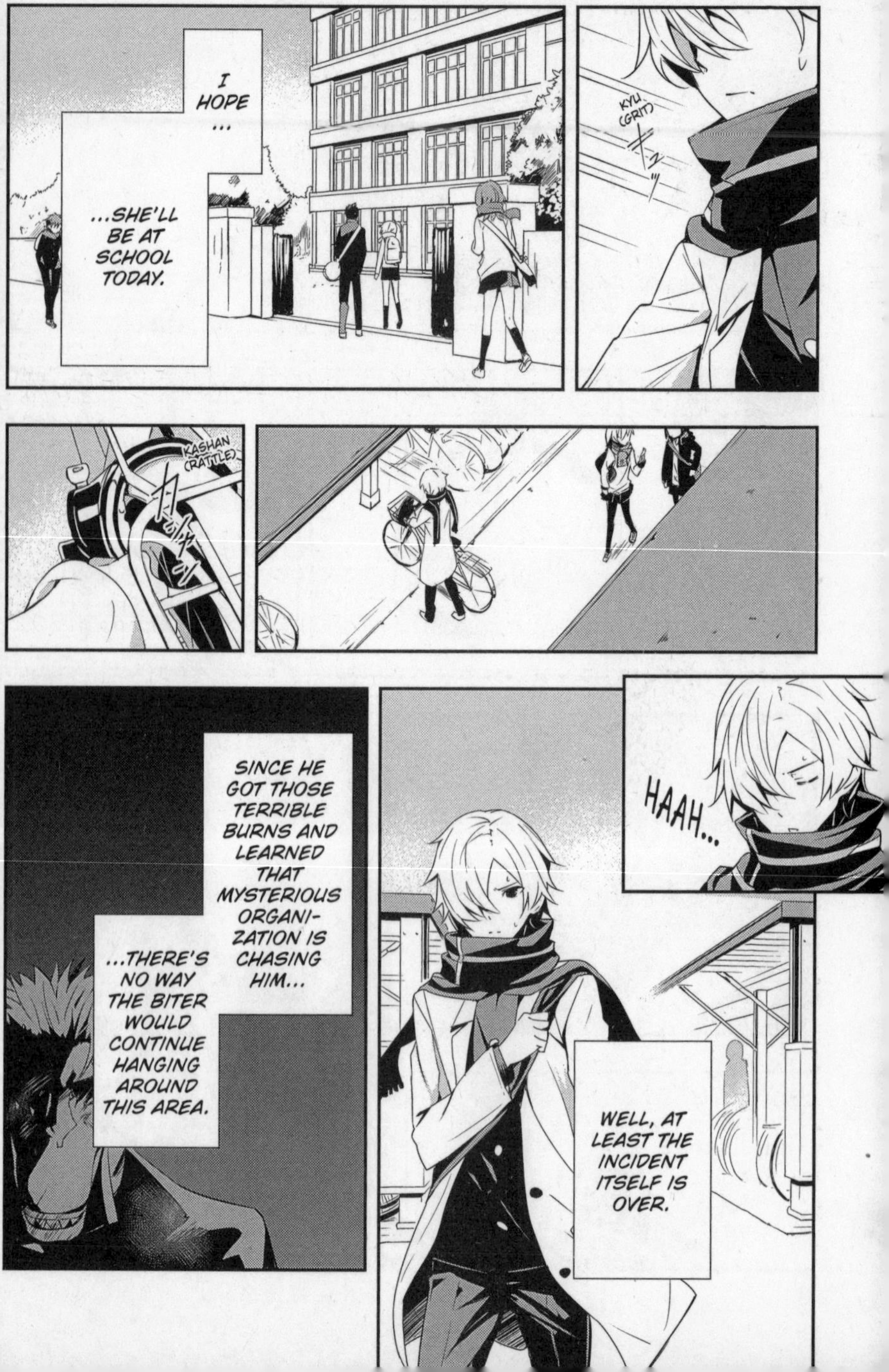
KYU (GRIT)
I HOPE...
...SHE'LL BE AT SCHOOL TODAY.
KASHAN (RATTLE)
HAAH...
WELL, AT LEAST THE INCIDENT ITSELF IS OVER.
SINCE HE GOT THOSE TERRIBLE BURNS AND LEARNED THAT MYSTERIOUS ORGANI-ZATION IS CHASING HIM...
...THERE'S NO WAY THE BITER WOULD CONTINUE HANGING AROUND THIS AREA.

GOOD MORNIIING!

GOOD MORNIIING!

GOOD MORNING.

I'M SURE HE FLED SOMEWHERE FAR AWAY ALREADY, AND YUMIKO AND THE OTHERS ALL FOLLOWED HIM.

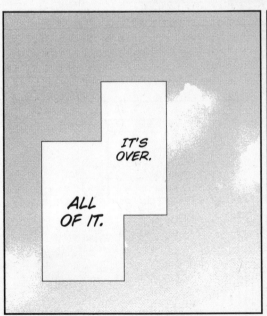

IT'S OVER.

ALL OF IT.

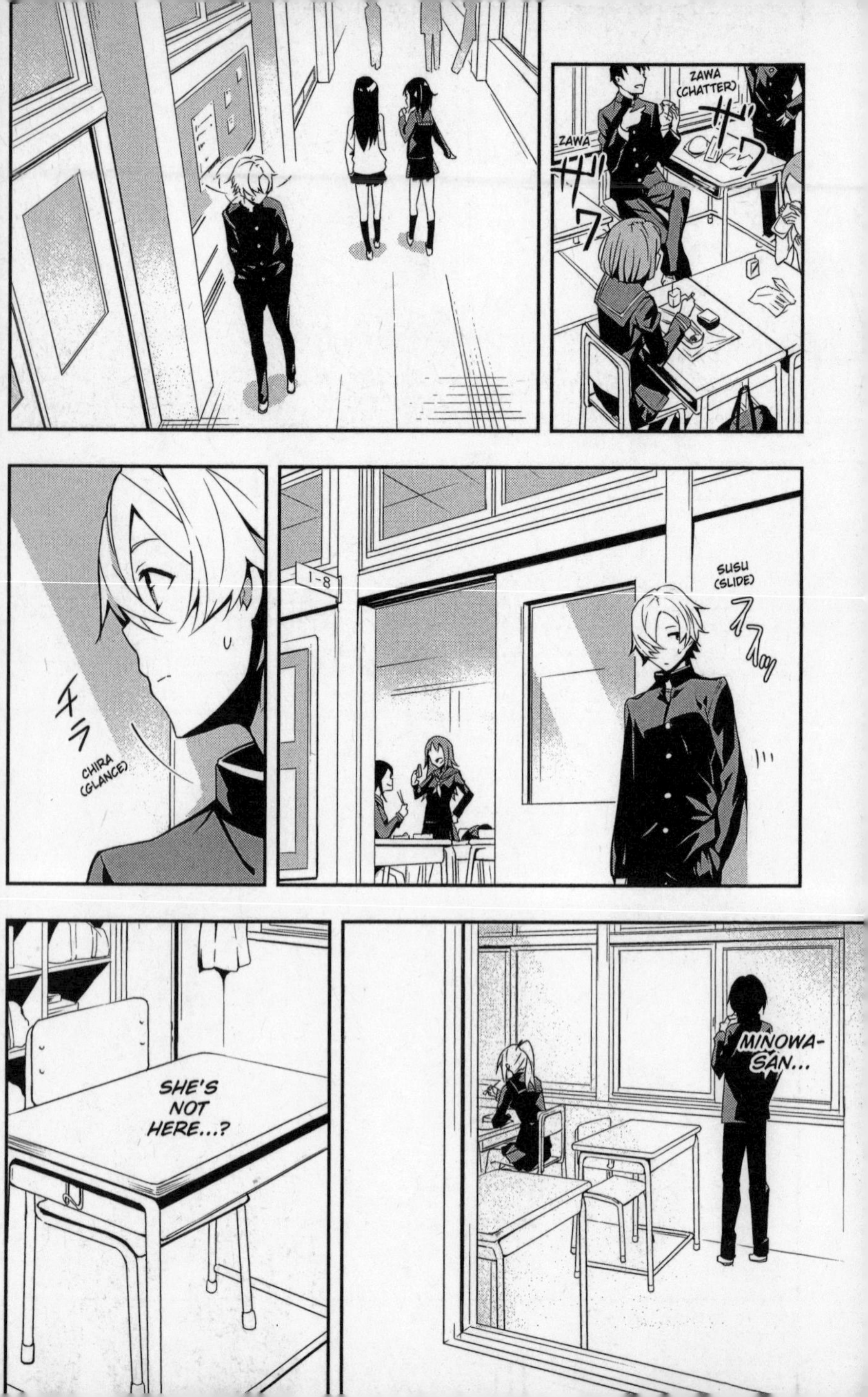

ZAWA (CHATTER)
ZAWA
SUSU (SLIDE)
CHIRA (GLANCE)
MINOWA-SAN...
SHE'S NOT HERE...?

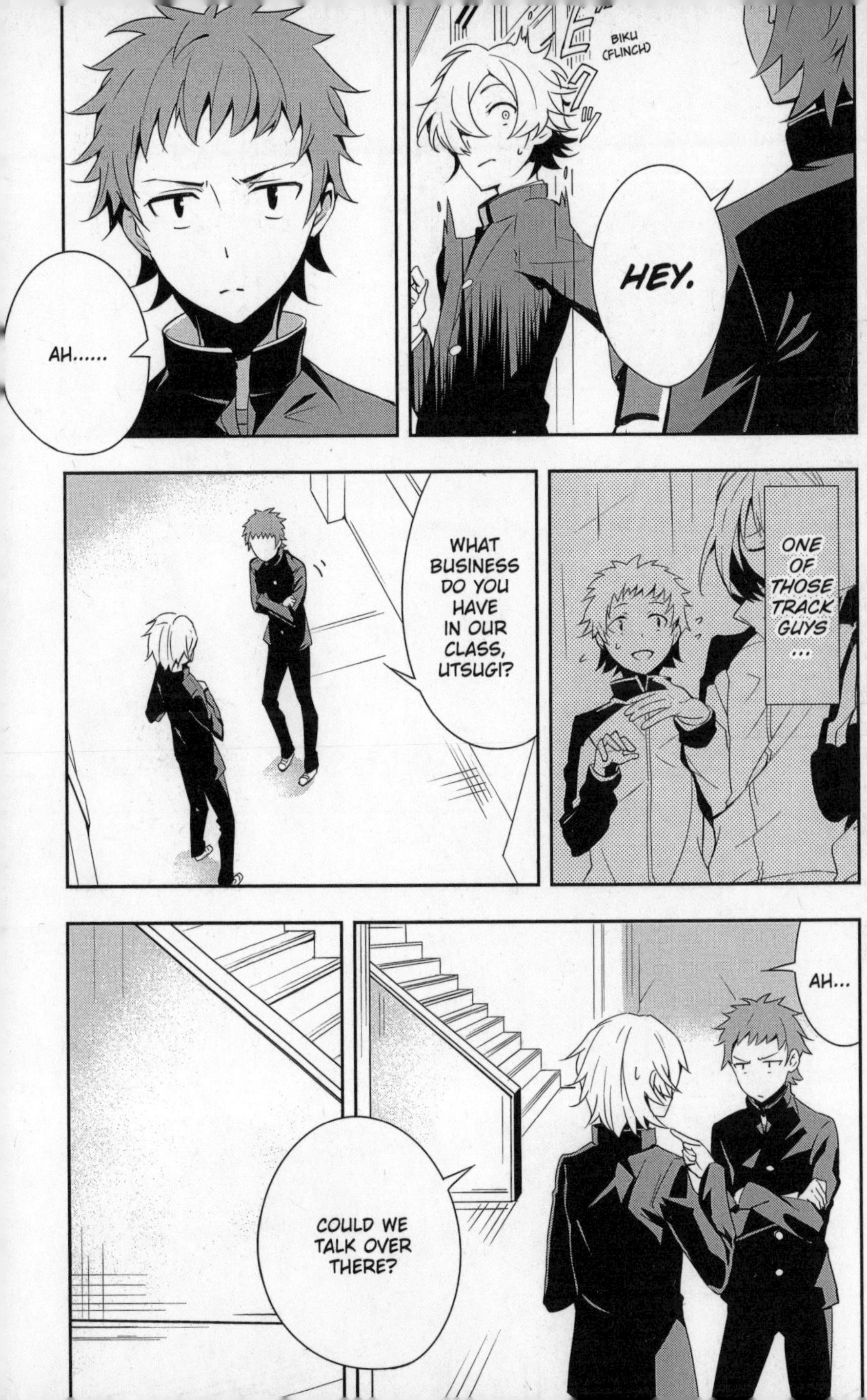
BIKU (FLINCH)
HEY.
AH......
ONE OF THOSE TRACK GUYS ...
WHAT BUSINESS DO YOU HAVE IN OUR CLASS, UTSUGI?
AH...
COULD WE TALK OVER THERE?

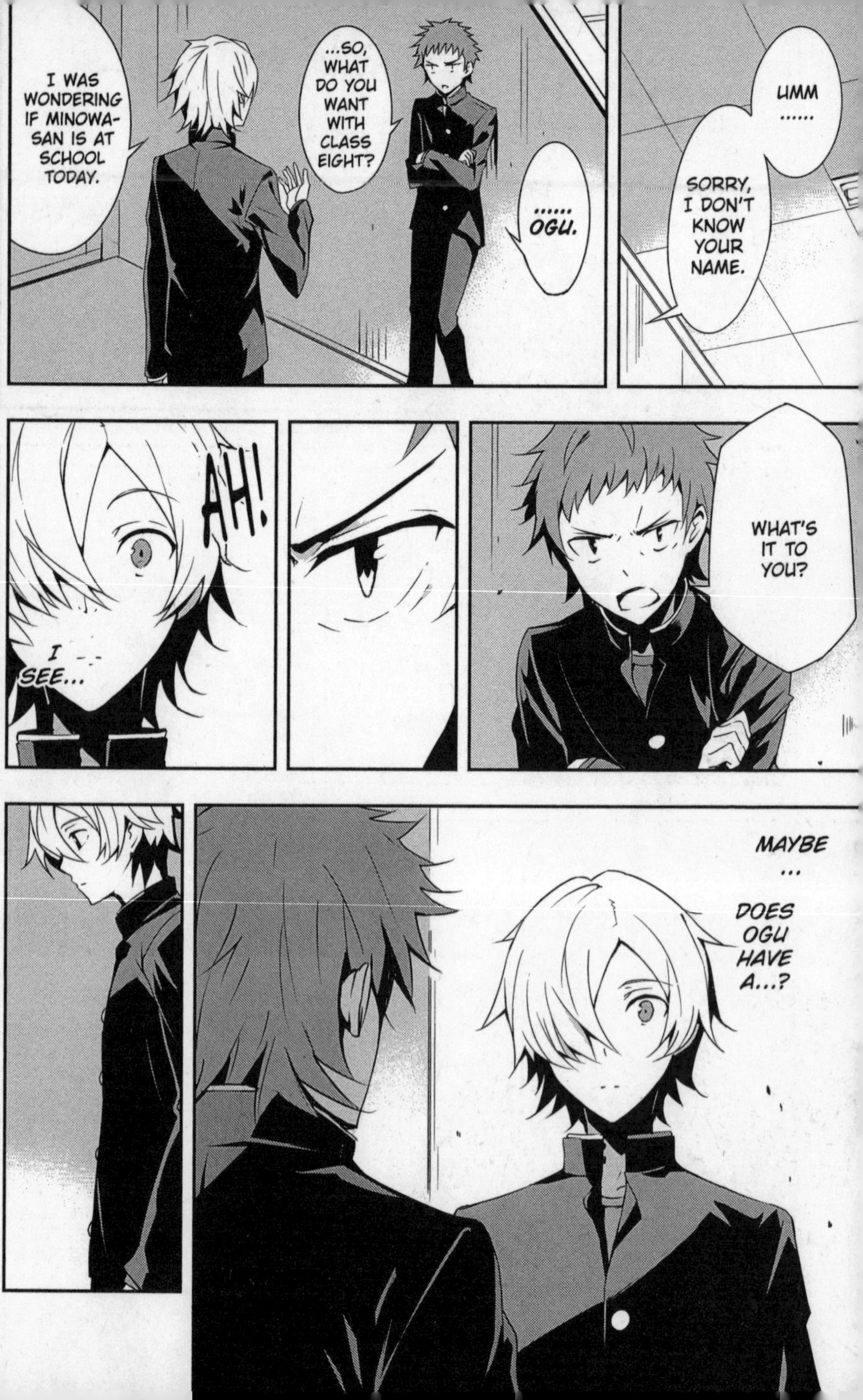
UMM ......
SORRY, I DON'T KNOW YOUR NAME.
...... OGU.
...SO, WHAT DO YOU WANT WITH CLASS EIGHT?
I WAS WONDERING IF MINOWA-SAN IS AT SCHOOL TODAY.
WHAT'S IT TO YOU?
AH!
I SEE...
MAYBE ...
DOES OGU HAVE A...?

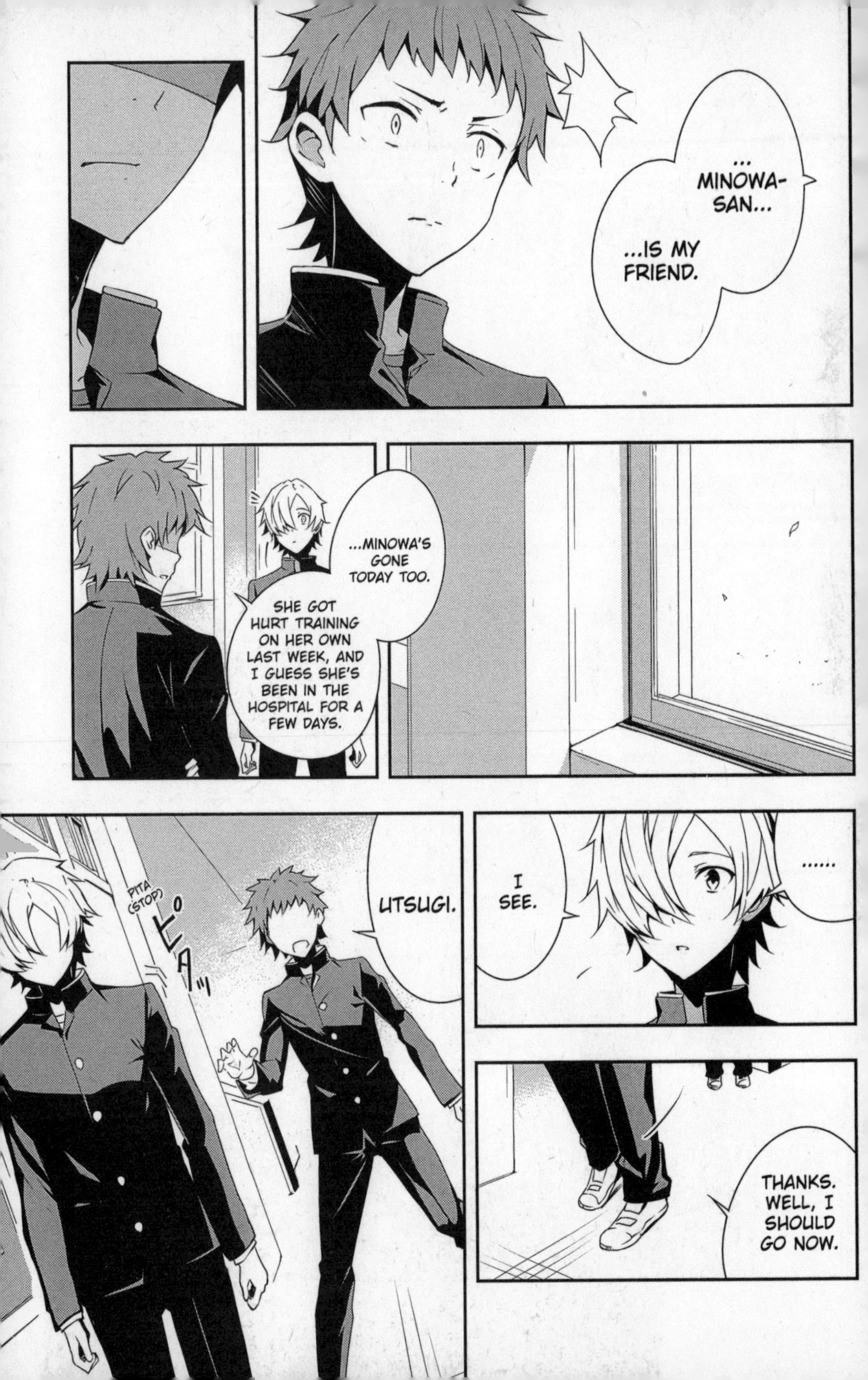
... MINOWA-SAN...
...IS MY FRIEND.
...MINOWA'S GONE TODAY TOO.
SHE GOT HURT TRAINING ON HER OWN LAST WEEK, AND I GUESS SHE'S BEEN IN THE HOSPITAL FOR A FEW DAYS.
......
I SEE.
THANKS. WELL, I SHOULD GO NOW.
UTSUGI.
PITA (STOP)
ピタッ

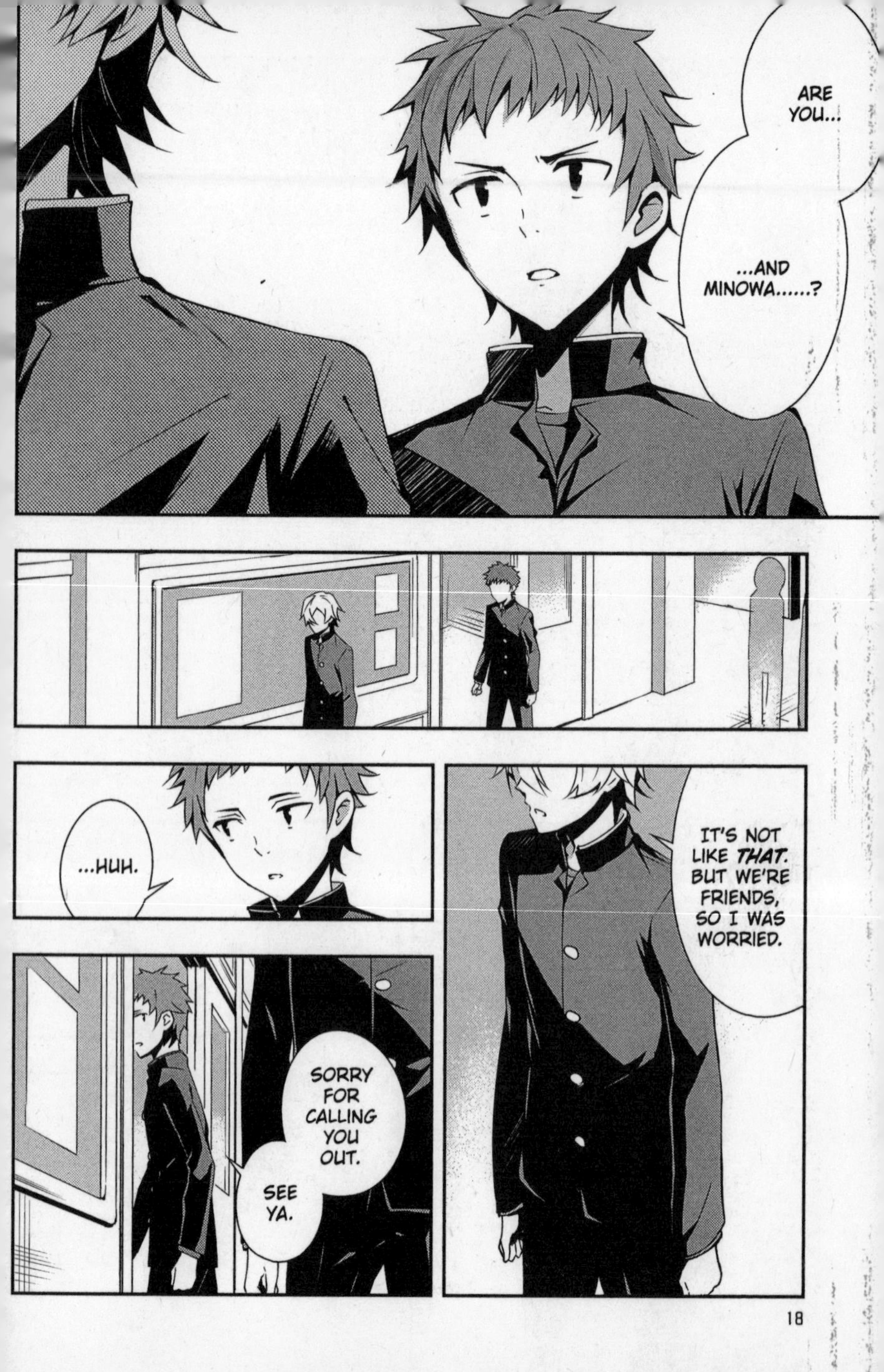
ARE YOU...
...AND MINOWA......?
IT'S NOT LIKE *THAT*. BUT WE'RE FRIENDS, SO I WAS WORRIED.
...HUH.
SORRY FOR CALLING YOU OUT.
SEE YA.

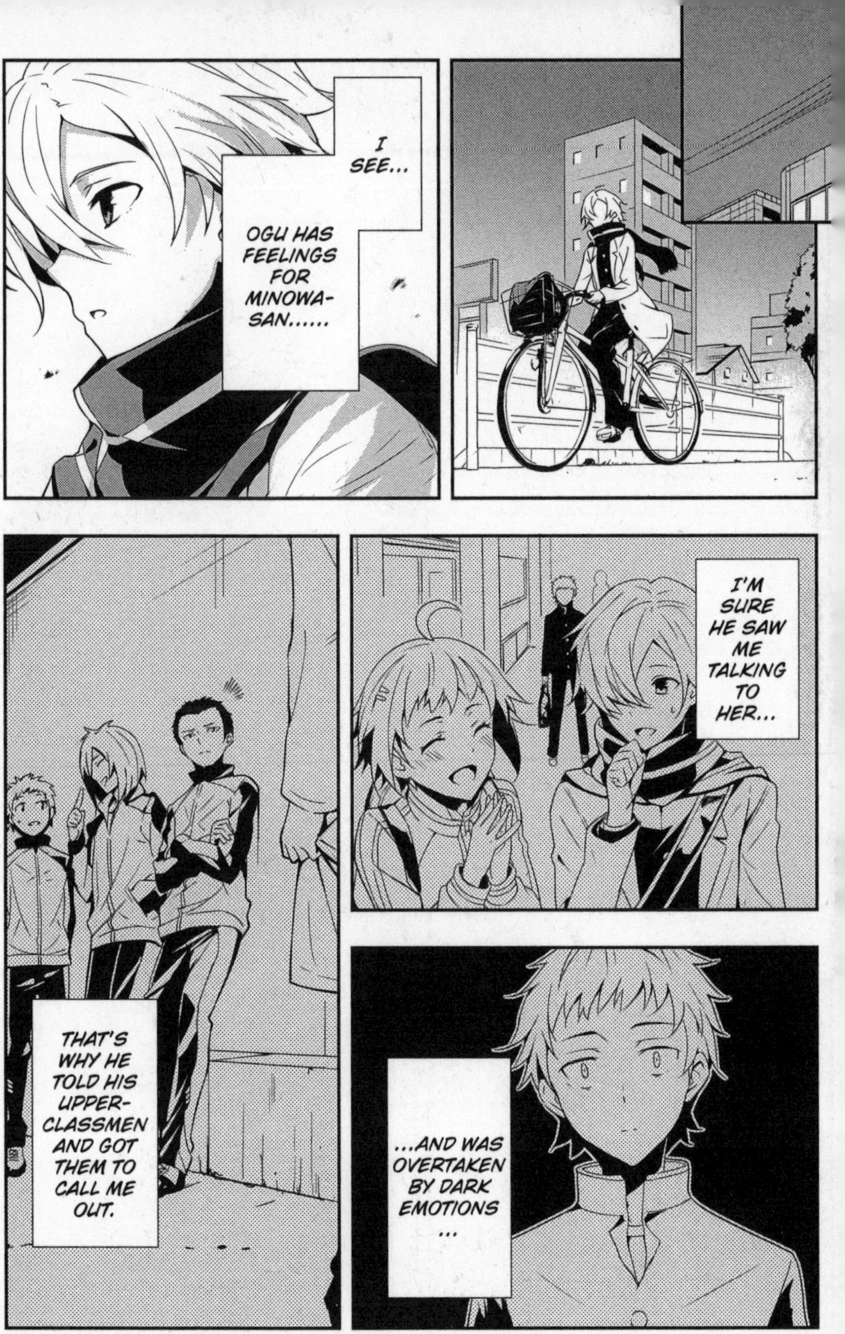
I SEE...
OGU HAS FEELINGS FOR MINOWA-SAN......
I'M SURE HE SAW ME TALKING TO HER...
...AND WAS OVERTAKEN BY DARK EMOTIONS...
THAT'S WHY HE TOLD HIS UPPER-CLASSMEN AND GOT THEM TO CALL ME OUT.

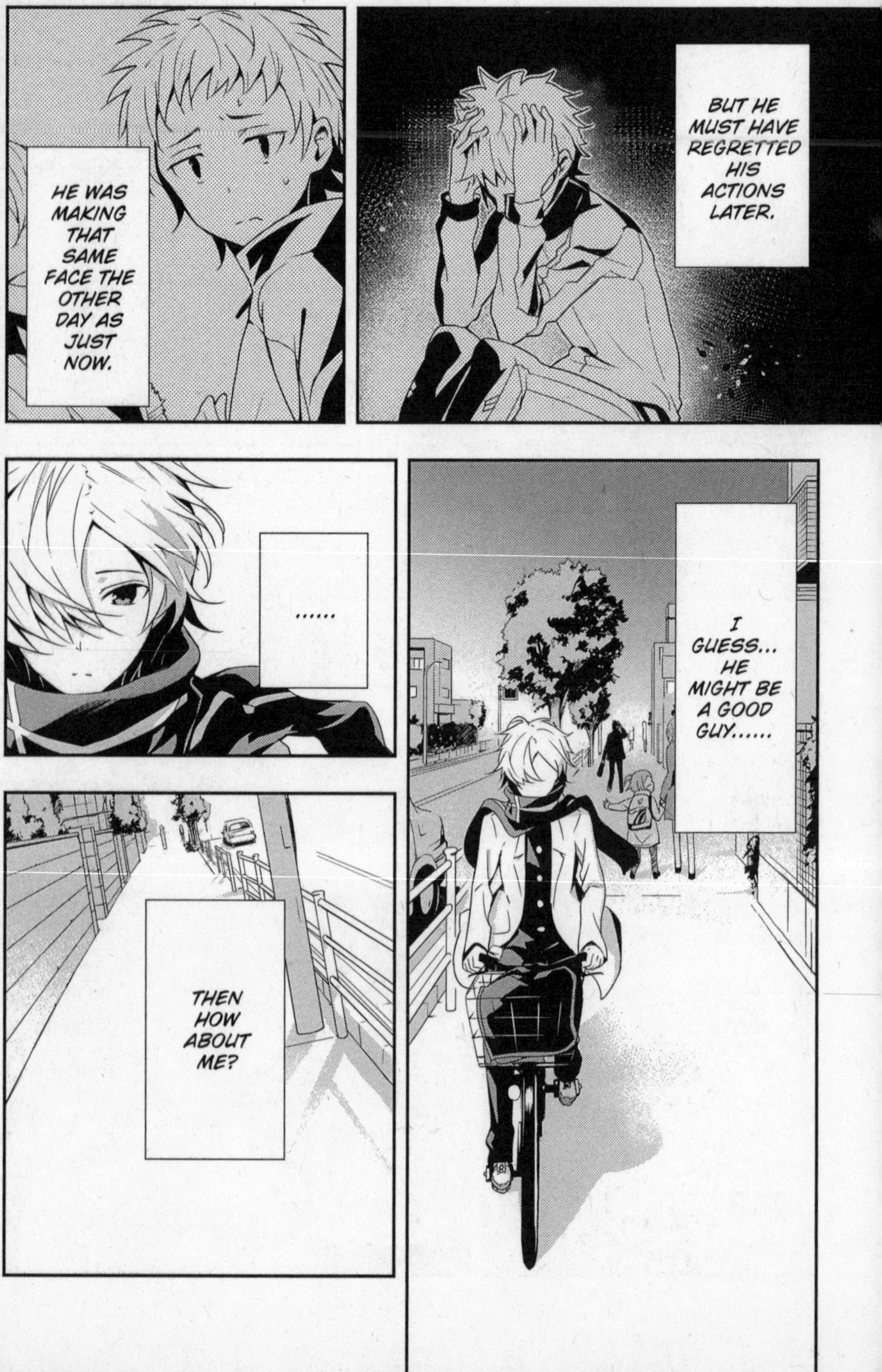
BUT HE MUST HAVE REGRETTED HIS ACTIONS LATER.
HE WAS MAKING THAT SAME FACE THE OTHER DAY AS JUST NOW.
I GUESS... HE MIGHT BE A GOOD GUY......
......
THEN HOW ABOUT ME?

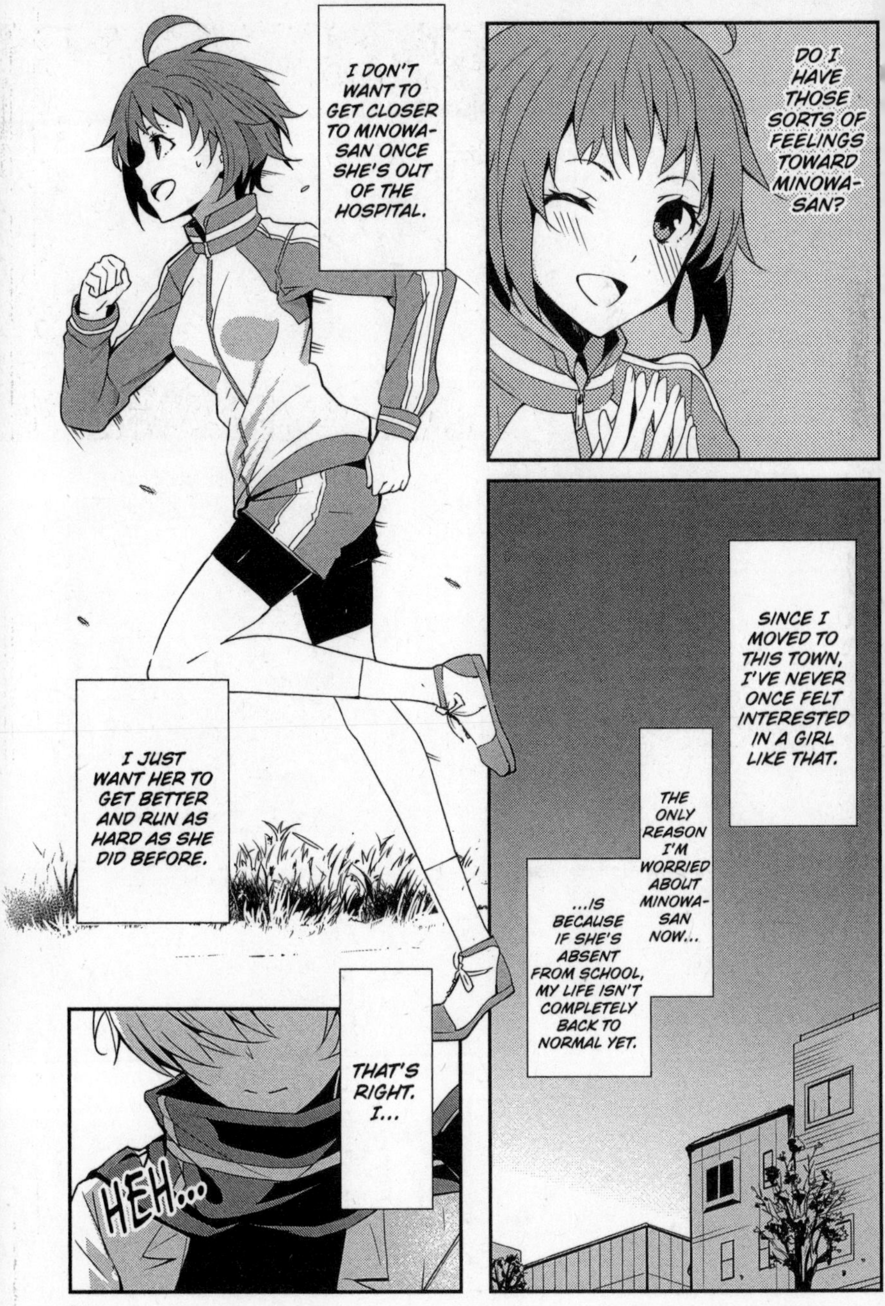
DO I HAVE THOSE SORTS OF FEELINGS TOWARD MINOWA-SAN?
SINCE I MOVED TO THIS TOWN, I'VE NEVER ONCE FELT INTERESTED IN A GIRL LIKE THAT.
THE ONLY REASON I'M WORRIED ABOUT MINOWA-SAN NOW...
...IS BECAUSE IF SHE'S ABSENT FROM SCHOOL, MY LIFE ISN'T COMPLETELY BACK TO NORMAL YET.
I DON'T WANT TO GET CLOSER TO MINOWA-SAN ONCE SHE'S OUT OF THE HOSPITAL.
I JUST WANT HER TO GET BETTER AND RUN AS HARD AS SHE DID BEFORE.
THAT'S RIGHT. I...
HEH...

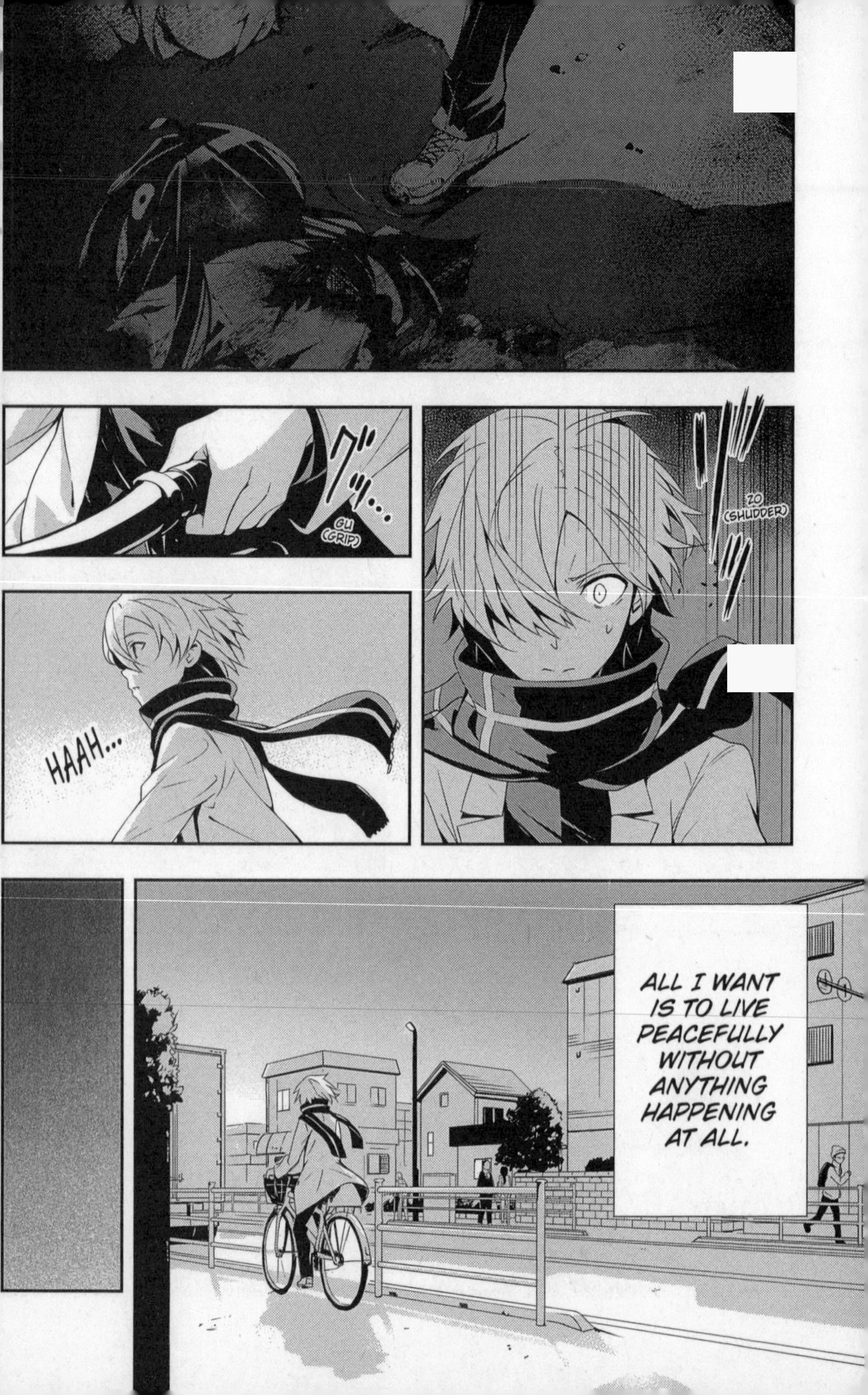
ZO (SHUDDER)
GU (GRIP)
HAAH...
ALL I WANT IS TO LIVE PEACEFULLY WITHOUT ANYTHING HAPPENING AT ALL.

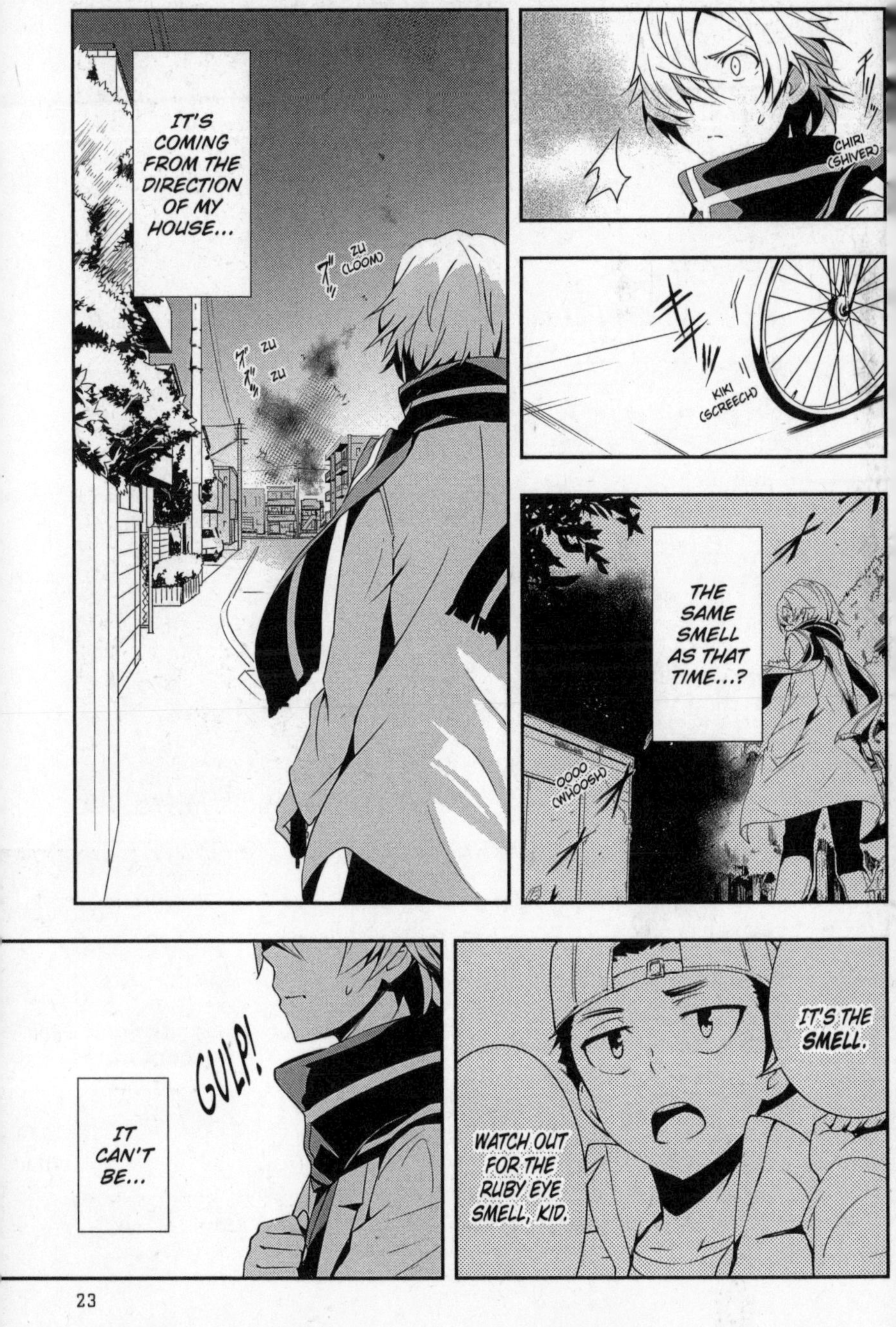
CHIRI (SHIVER)
KIKI (SCREECH)
THE SAME SMELL AS THAT TIME...?
OOOO (WHOOSH)
IT'S COMING FROM THE DIRECTION OF MY HOUSE...
ZU (LOOM)
ZU ZU
IT'S THE SMELL.
WATCH OUT FOR THE RUBY EYE SMELL, KID.
GULP!
IT CAN'T BE...

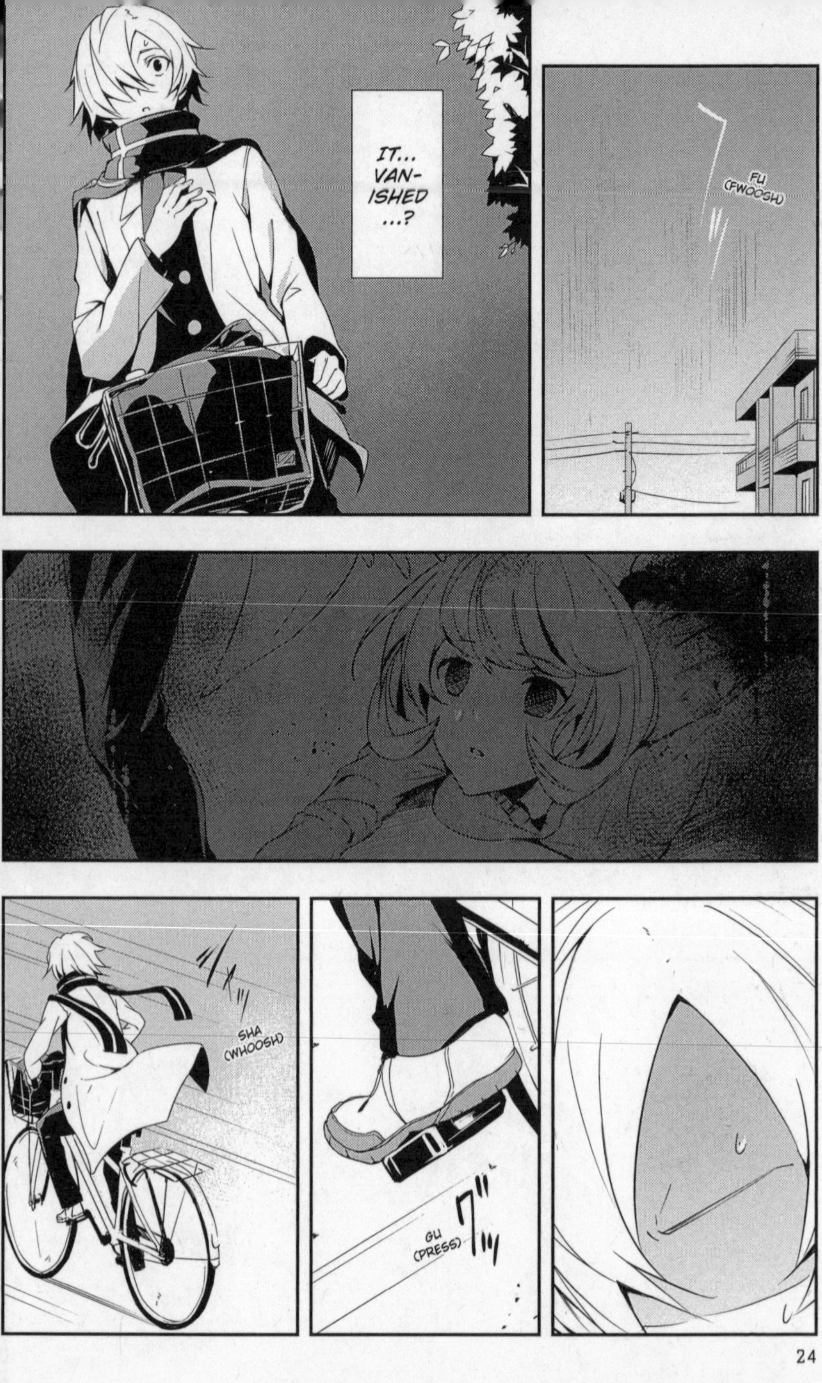
FU (FWOOSH)
IT... VAN-ISHED ...?
GU (PRESS)
SHA (WHOOSH)

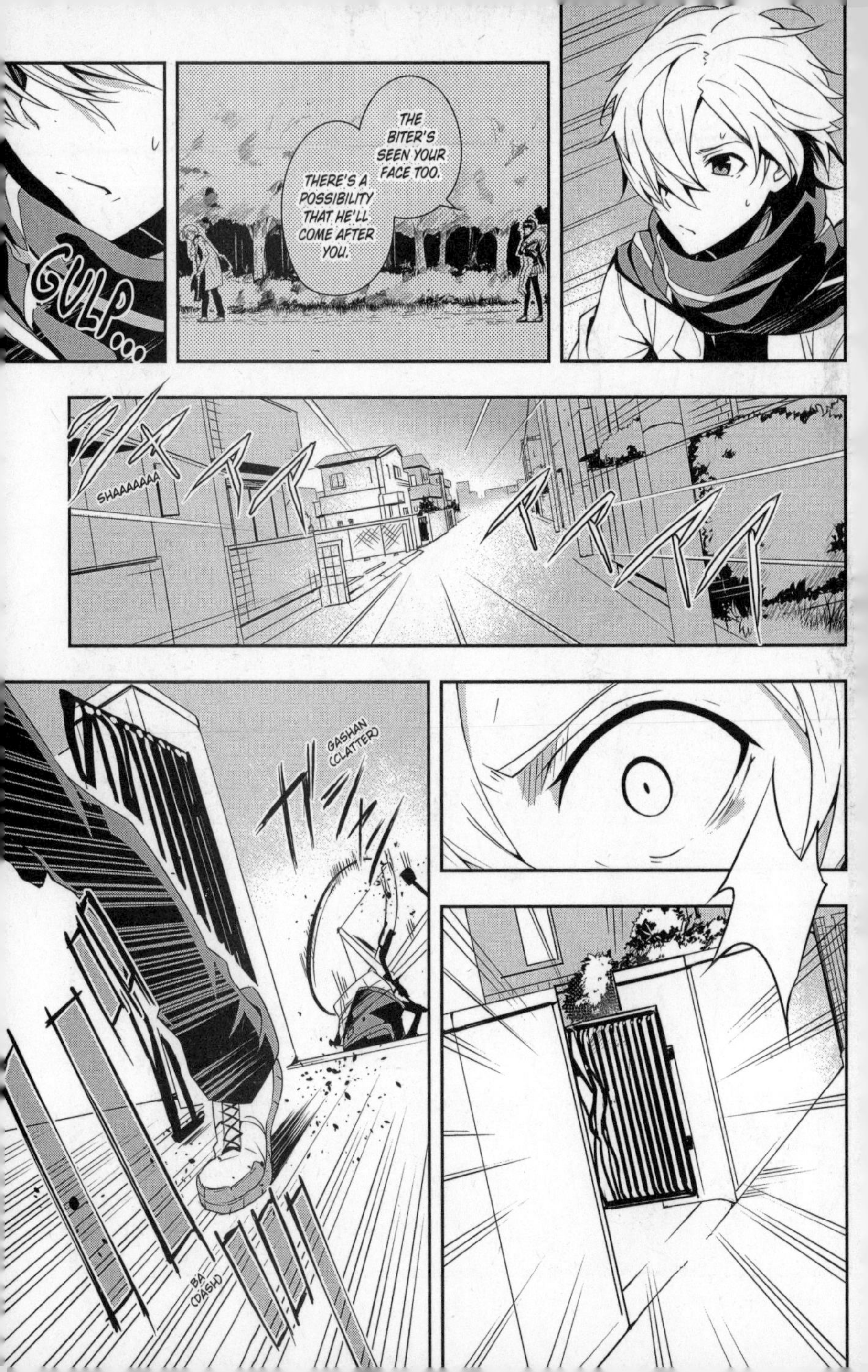
THE BITER'S SEEN YOUR FACE TOO.
THERE'S A POSSIBILITY THAT HE'LL COME AFTER YOU.
GULP...
SHAAAAAAA
GASHAN (CLATTER)
BA (DASH)

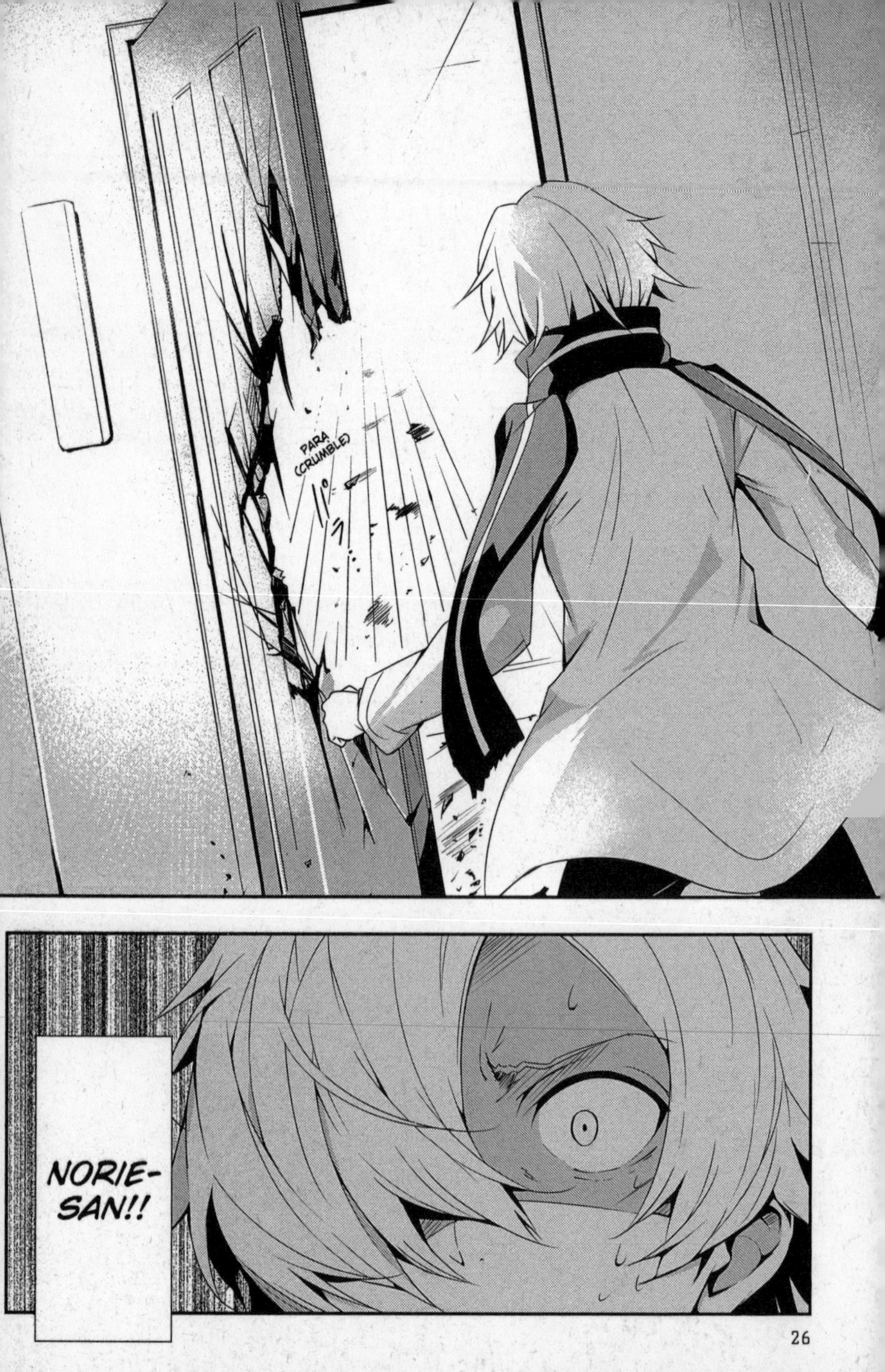
PARA (CRUMBLE)
NORIE-SAN!!

THE ISOLATOR
realization of
absolute solitude

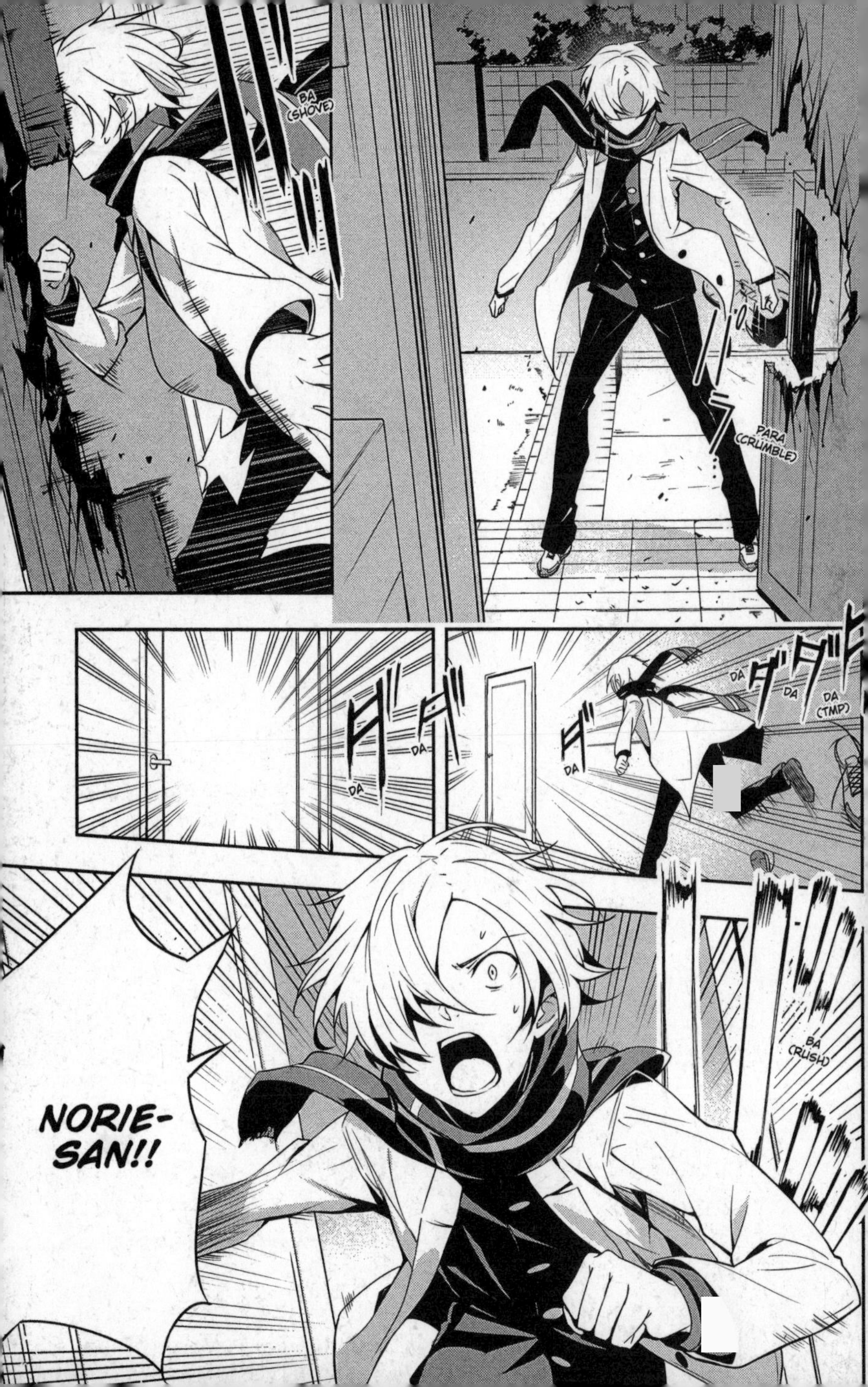
PARA
(CRUMBLE)
BA
(SHOVE)
DA
DA
DA
(TMP)
DA
DA
DA
NORIE-
SAN!!
BA
(RUSH)

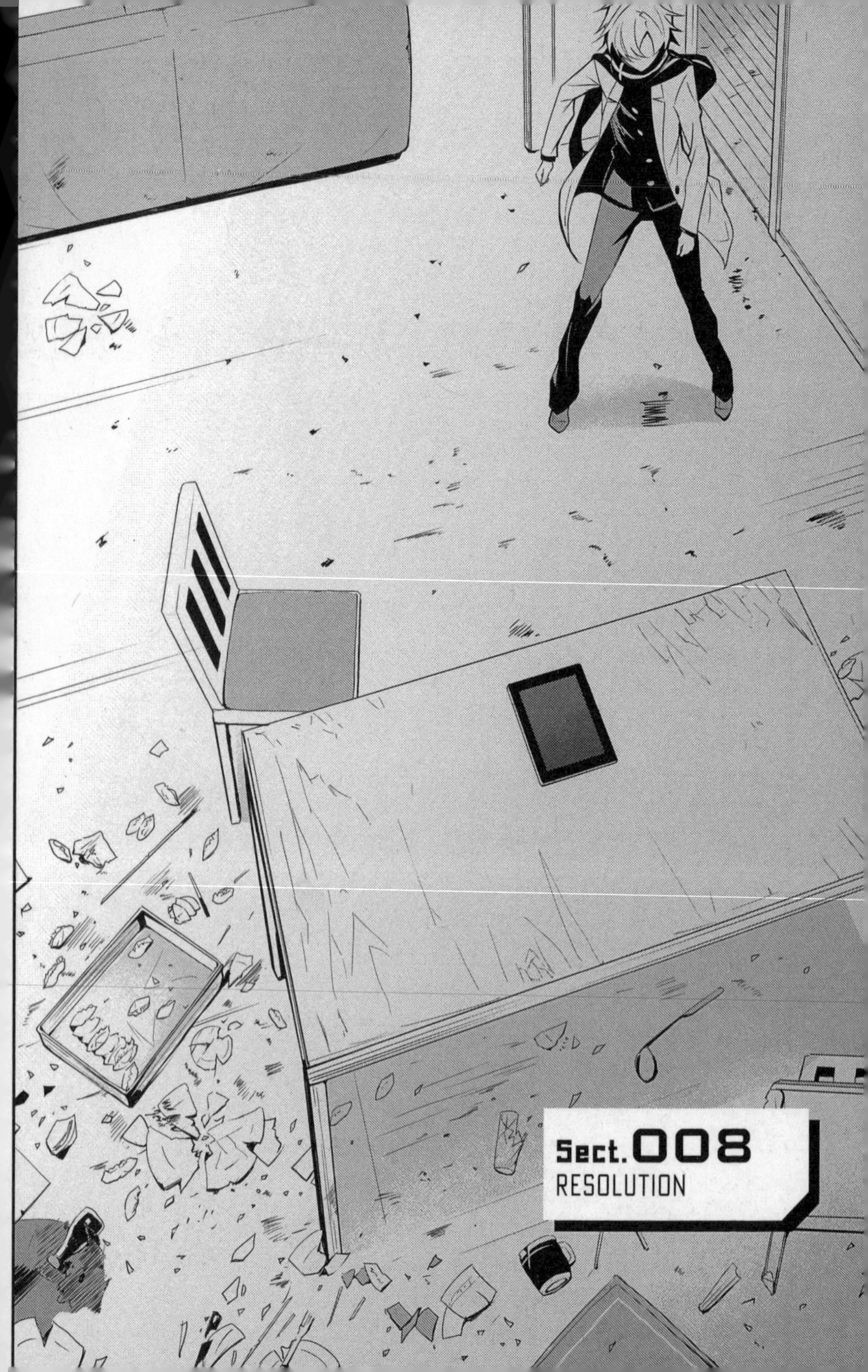
Sect.008
RESOLUTION

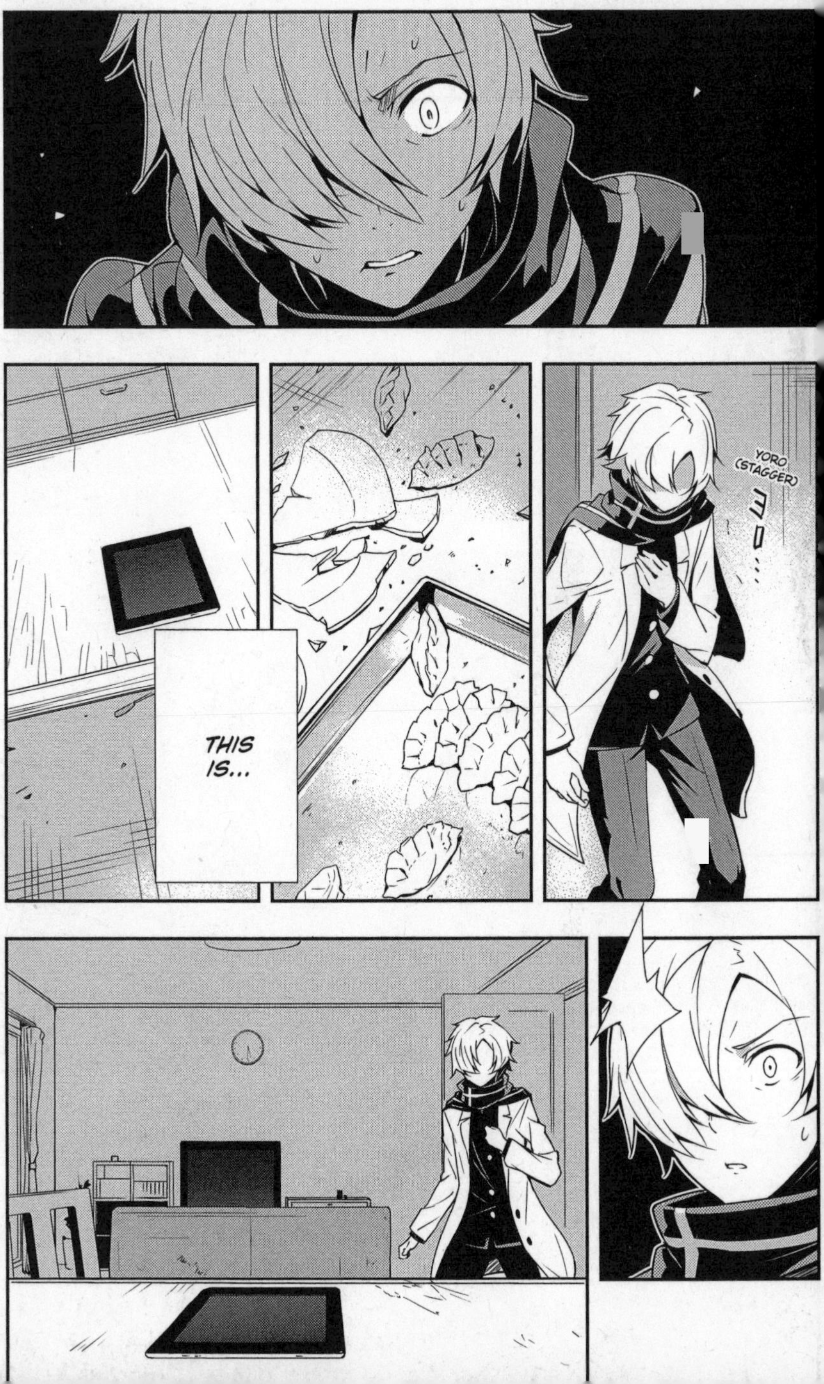
YORO (STAGGER)
ヨロ…
THIS IS...

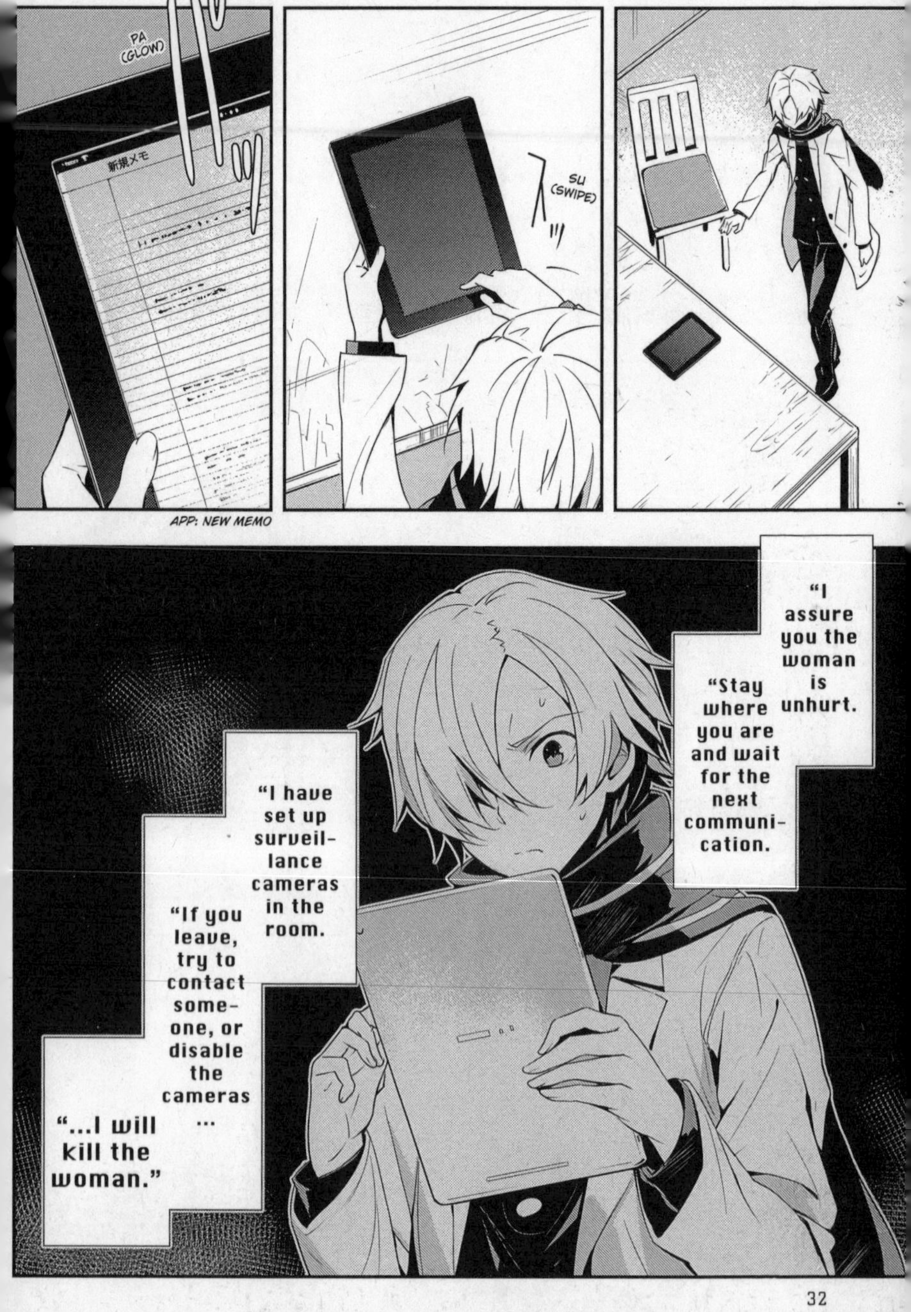
SU (SWIPE)
PA (GLOW)
新規メモ
APP: NEW MEMO
“I assure you the woman is unhurt.
“Stay where you are and wait for the next communication.
“I have set up surveillance cameras in the room.
“If you leave, try to contact someone, or disable the cameras…
“…I will kill the woman.”

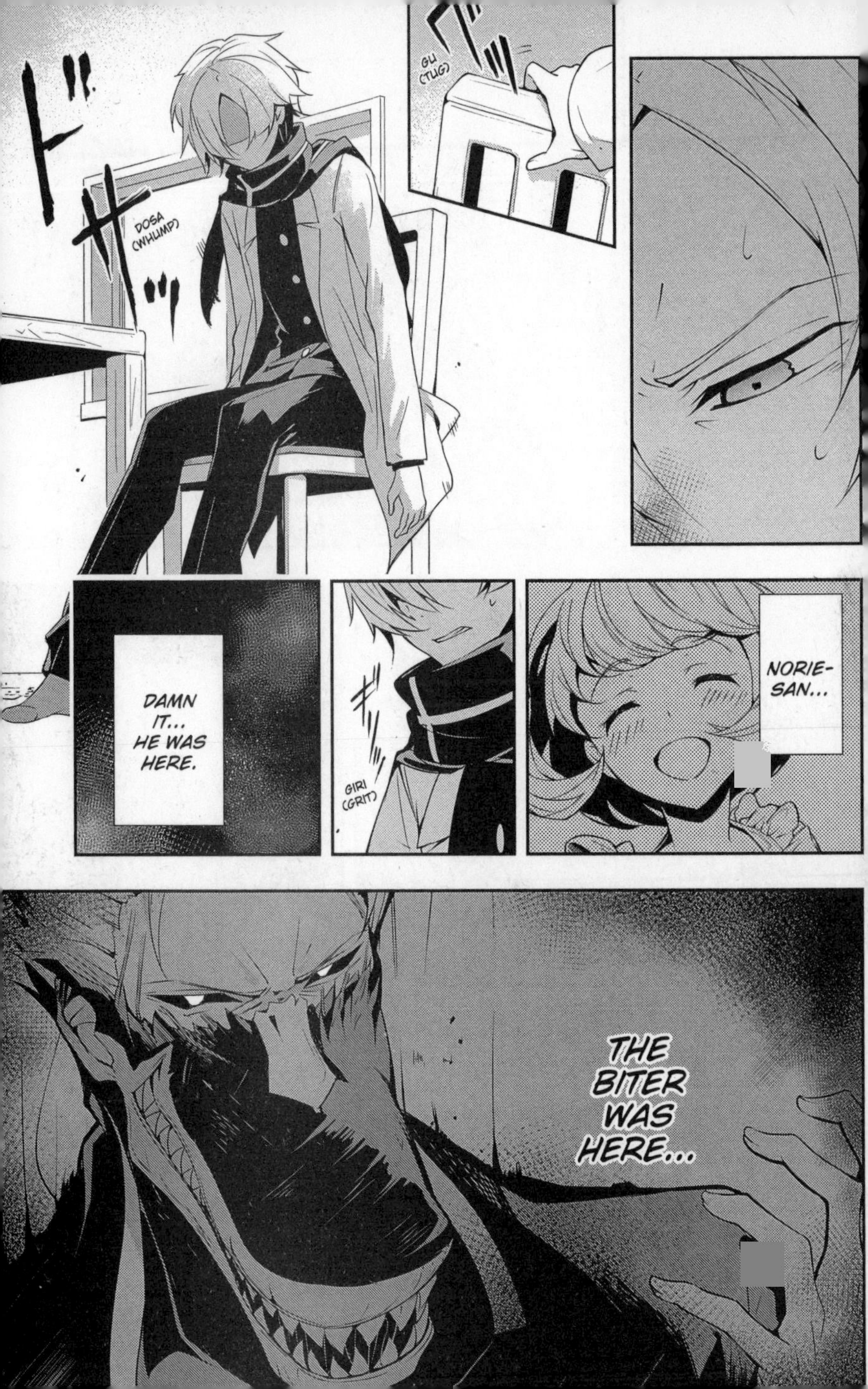
GU (TUG)
DOSA (WHUMP)
NORIE-SAN...
GIRI (GRIT)
DAMN IT... HE WAS HERE.
THE BITER WAS HERE...

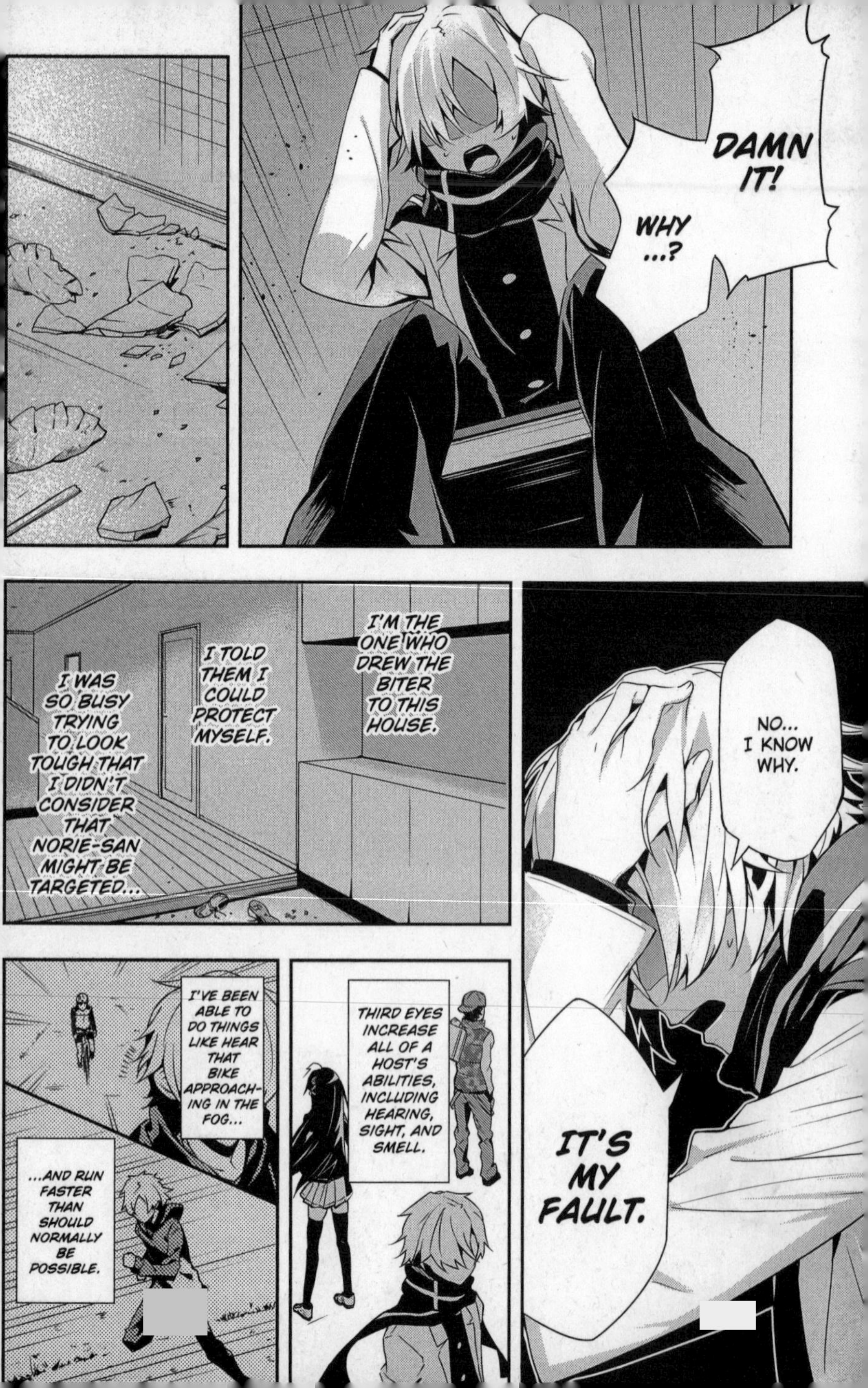
DAMN IT!
WHY ...?
NO... I KNOW WHY.
IT'S MY FAULT.
I'M THE ONE WHO DREW THE BITER TO THIS HOUSE.
I TOLD THEM I COULD PROTECT MYSELF.
I WAS SO BUSY TRYING TO LOOK TOUGH THAT I DIDN'T CONSIDER THAT NORIE-SAN MIGHT BE TARGETED...
THIRD EYES INCREASE ALL OF A HOST'S ABILITIES, INCLUDING HEARING, SIGHT, AND SMELL.
I'VE BEEN ABLE TO DO THINGS LIKE HEAR THAT BIKE APPROACH-ING IN THE FOG...
...AND RUN FASTER THAN SHOULD NORMALLY BE POSSIBLE.

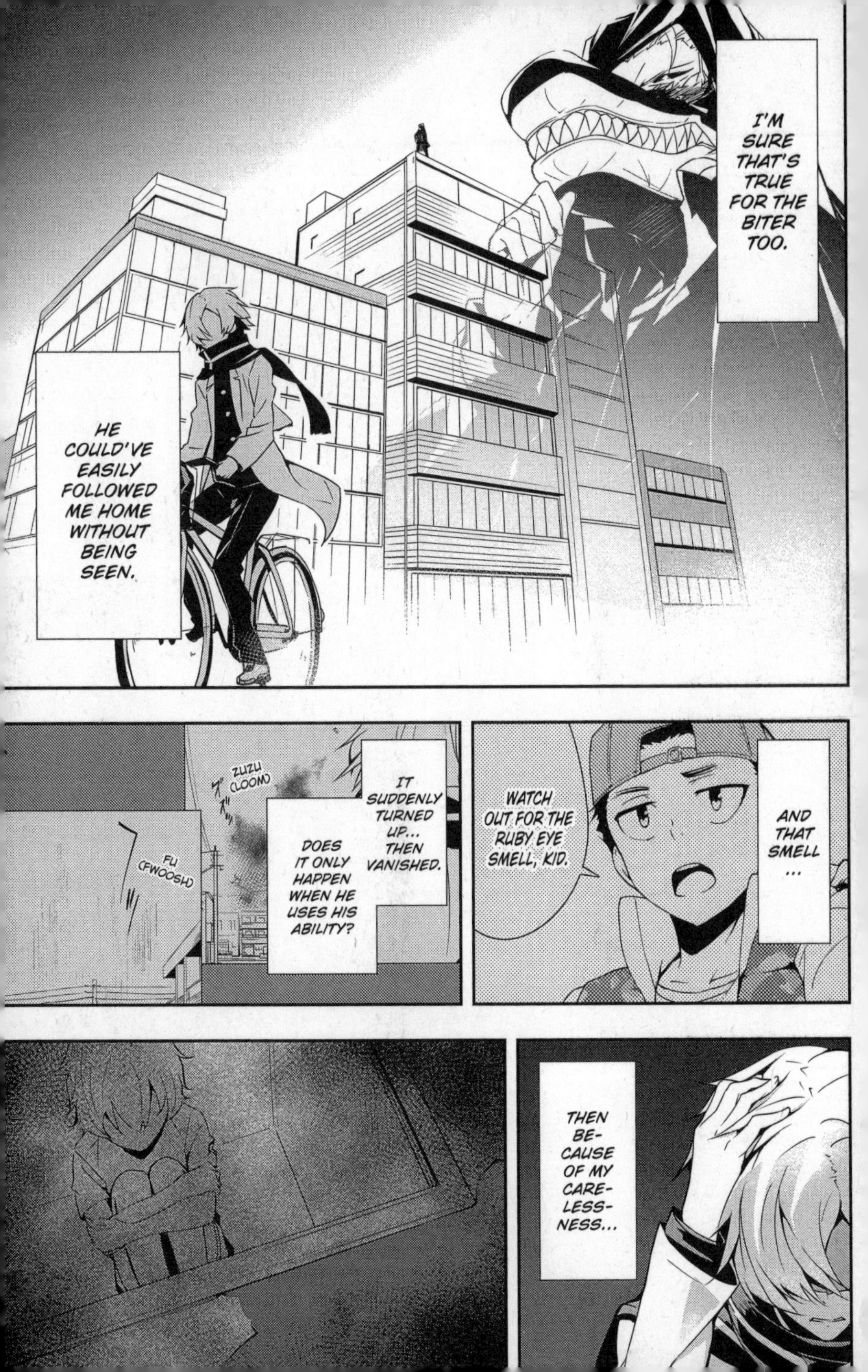
I'M SURE THAT'S TRUE FOR THE BITER TOO.
HE COULD'VE EASILY FOLLOWED ME HOME WITHOUT BEING SEEN.
AND THAT SMELL ...
WATCH OUT FOR THE RUBY EYE SMELL, KID.
IT SUDDENLY TURNED UP... THEN VANISHED.
ZUZU (LOOM)
DOES IT ONLY HAPPEN WHEN HE USES HIS ABILITY?
FU (FWOOSH)
THEN BE-CAUSE OF MY CARE-LESS-NESS...

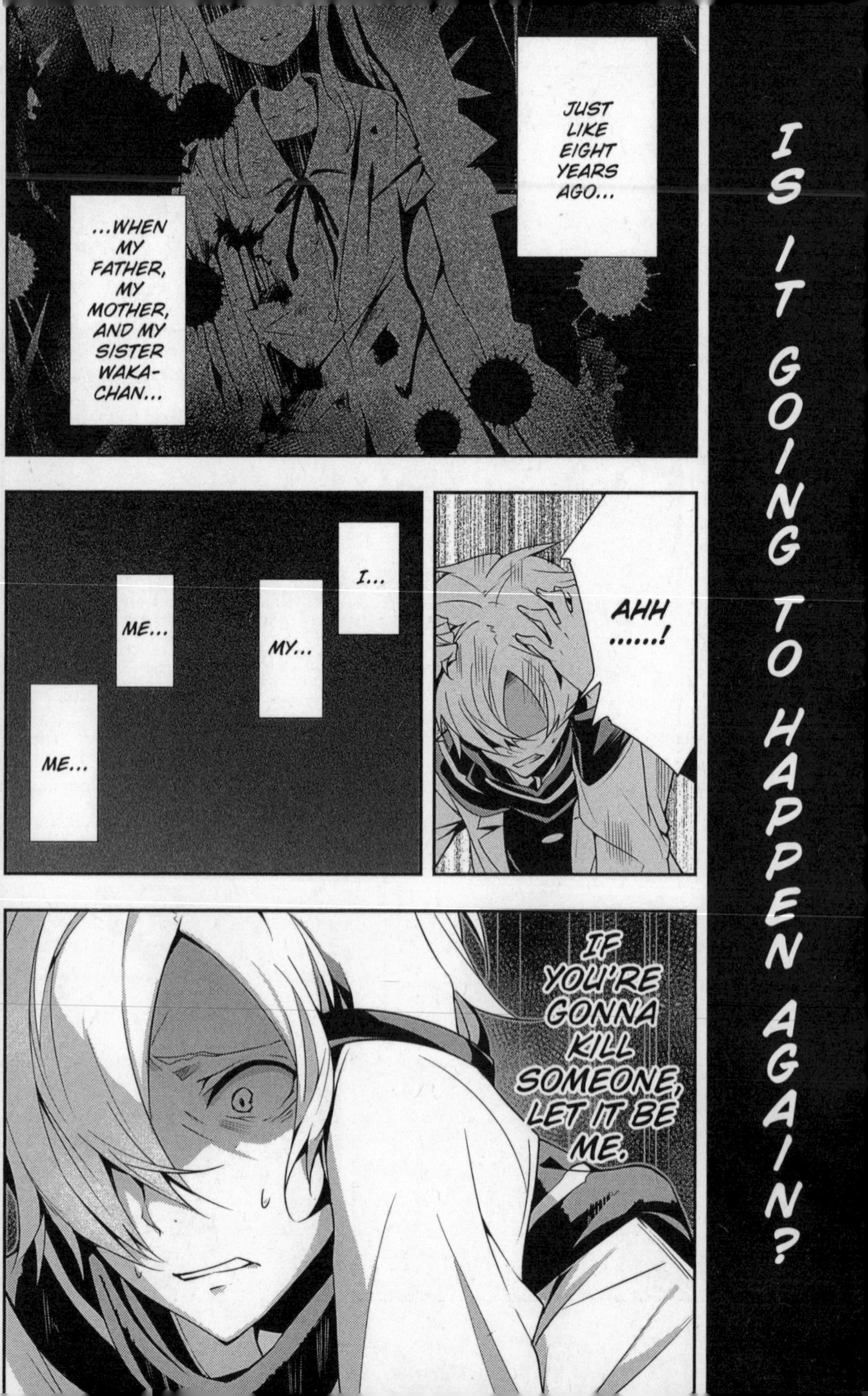
IS IT GOING TO HAPPEN AGAIN?
JUST LIKE EIGHT YEARS AGO...
...WHEN MY FATHER, MY MOTHER, AND MY SISTER WAKA-CHAN...
AHH ......!
I...
MY...
ME...
ME...
IF YOU'RE GONNA KILL SOMEONE, LET IT BE ME.

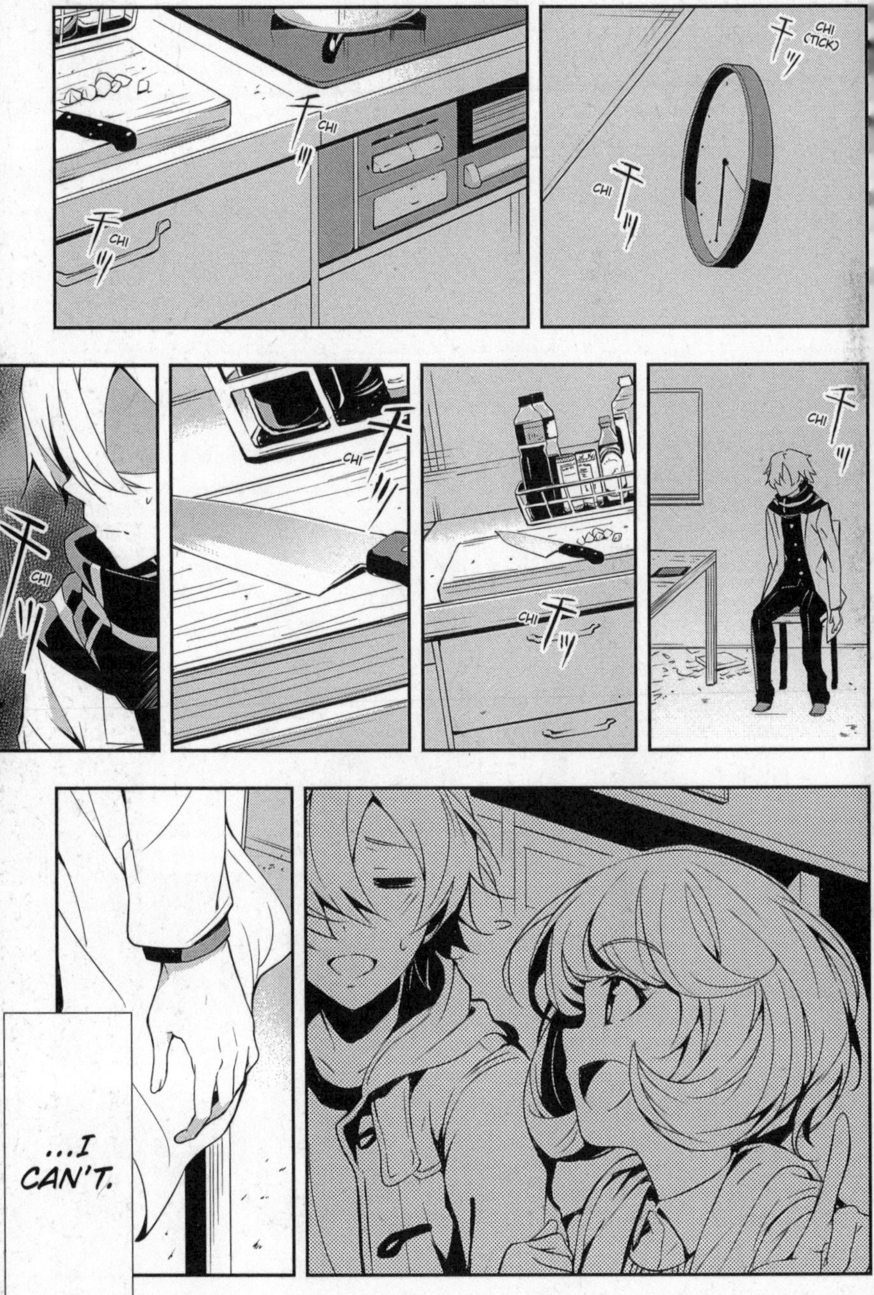
チッ
CHI (TICK)
チッ
CHI
チッ
CHI
チッ
CHI
チッ
CHI
チッ
CHI
チッ
CHI
チッ
CHI
...I CAN'T.

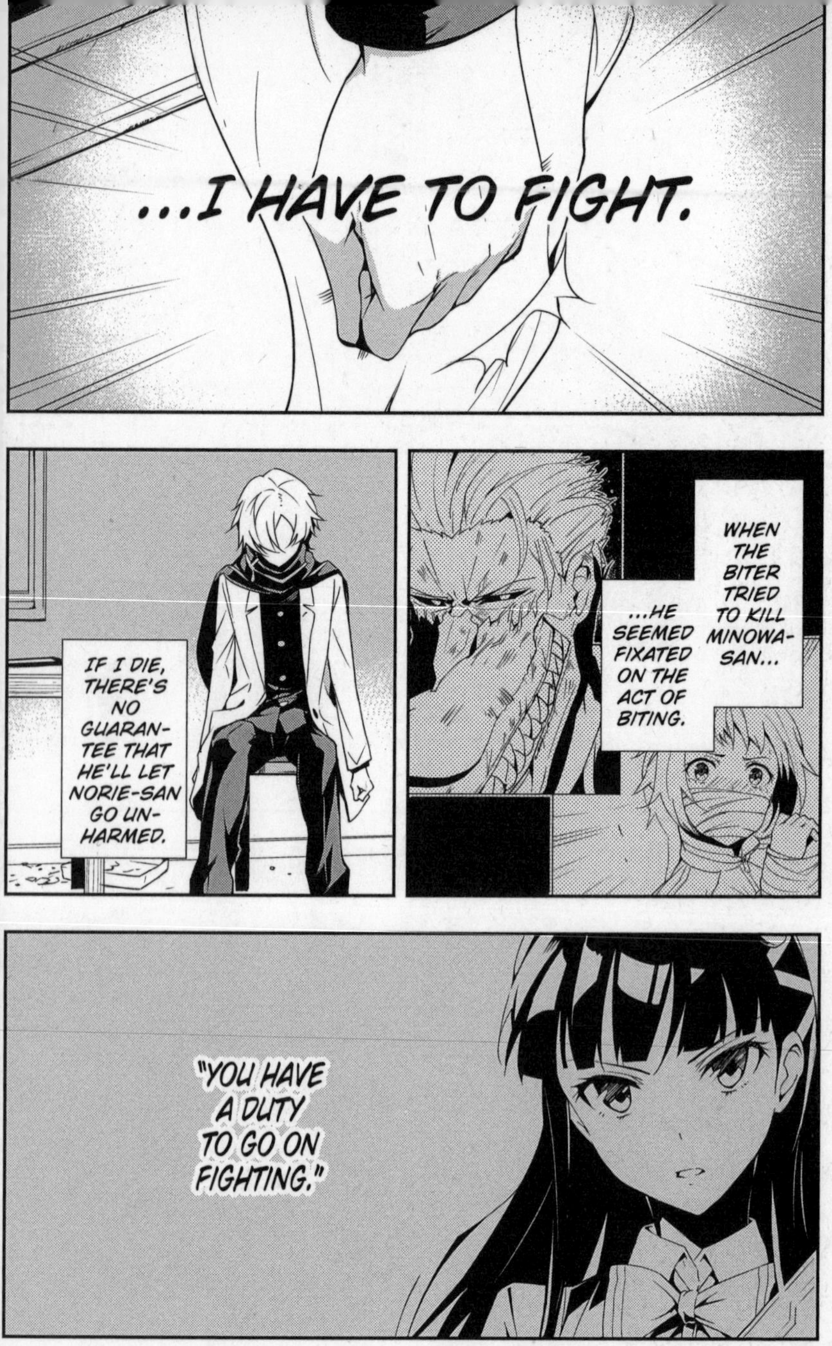
...I HAVE TO FIGHT.
WHEN THE BITER TRIED TO KILL MINOWA-SAN...
...HE SEEMED FIXATED ON THE ACT OF BITING.
IF I DIE, THERE'S NO GUARANTEE THAT HE'LL LET NORIE-SAN GO UNHARMED.
"YOU HAVE A DUTY TO GO ON FIGHTING."

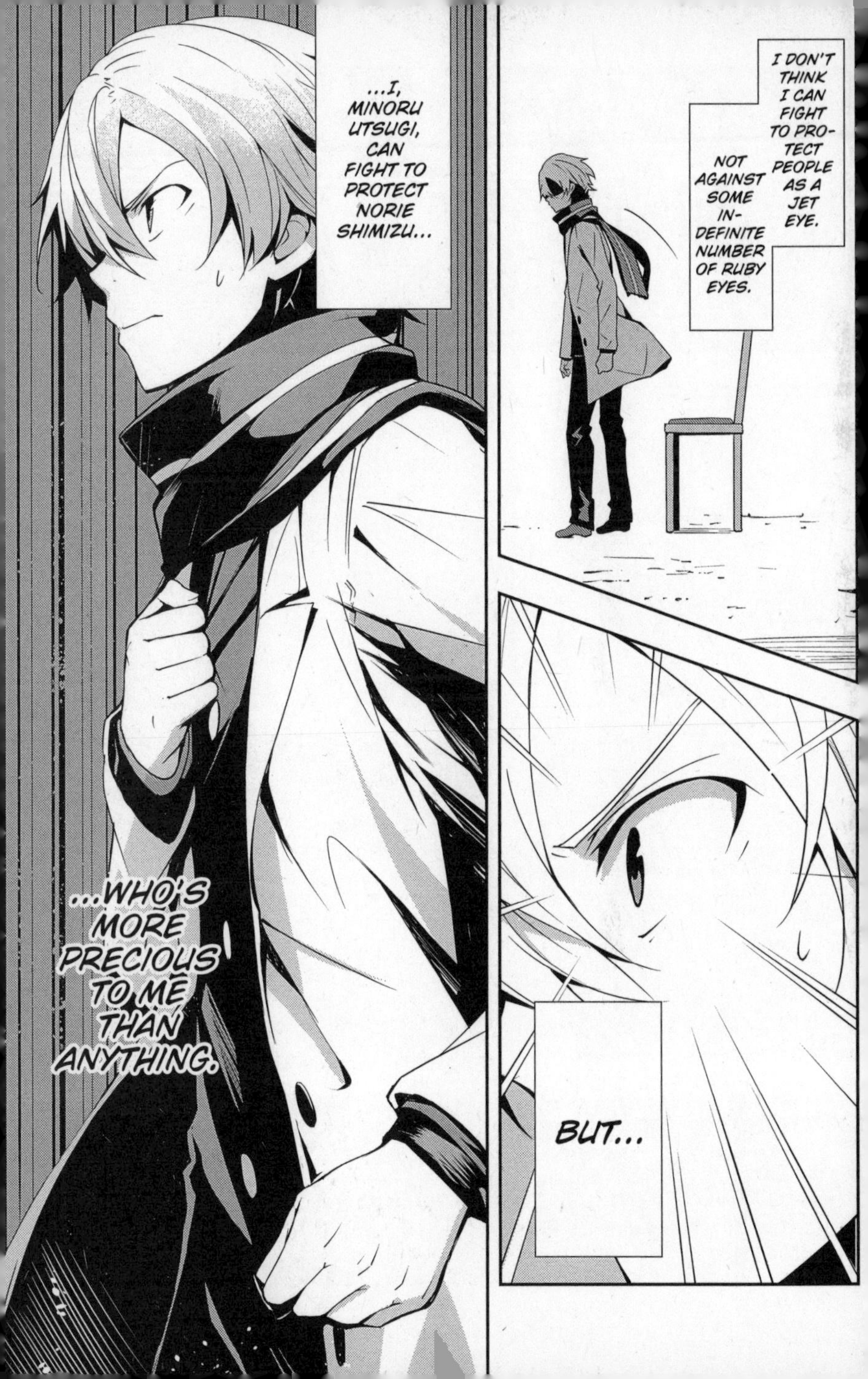
I DON'T THINK I CAN FIGHT TO PROTECT PEOPLE AS A JET EYE.
NOT AGAINST SOME INDEFINITE NUMBER OF RUBY EYES.
BUT...
...I, MINORU UTSUGI, CAN FIGHT TO PROTECT NORIE SHIMIZU...
...WHO'S MORE PRECIOUS TO ME THAN ANYTHING.

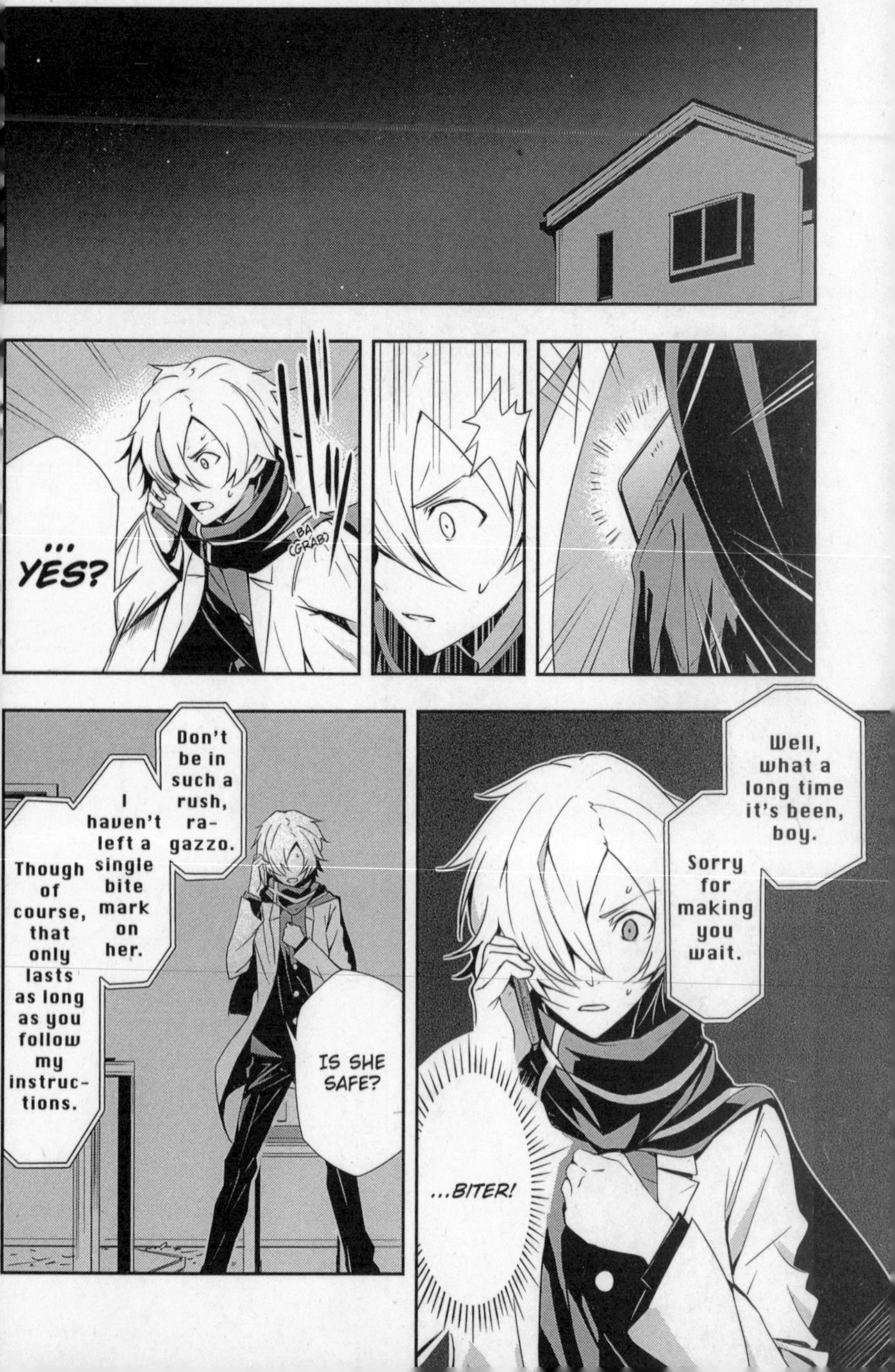
BA (GRAB)
...YES?
Well, what a long time it's been, boy.
Sorry for making you wait.
...BITER!
IS SHE SAFE?
Don't be in such a rush, ragazzo.
I haven't left a single bite mark on her.
Though of course, that only lasts as long as you follow my instructions.

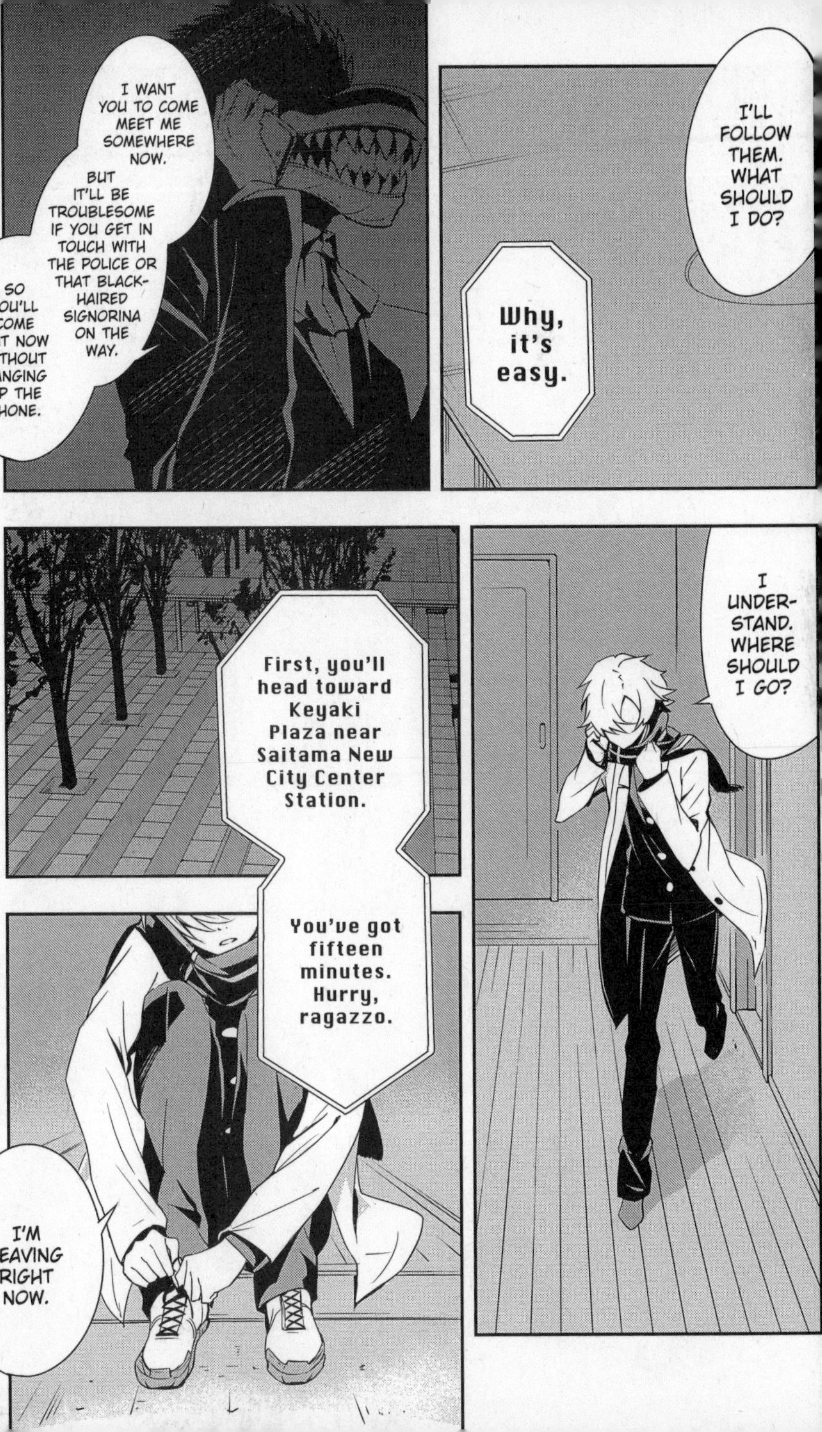
I'LL FOLLOW THEM. WHAT SHOULD I DO?
Why, it's easy.
I WANT YOU TO COME MEET ME SOMEWHERE NOW.
BUT IT'LL BE TROUBLESOME IF YOU GET IN TOUCH WITH THE POLICE OR THAT BLACK-HAIRED SIGNORINA ON THE WAY.
SO YOU'LL COME OUT NOW WITHOUT HANGING UP THE PHONE.
I UNDER-STAND. WHERE SHOULD I GO?
First, you'll head toward Keyaki Plaza near Saitama New City Center Station.
You've got fifteen minutes. Hurry, ragazzo.
I'M LEAVING RIGHT NOW.

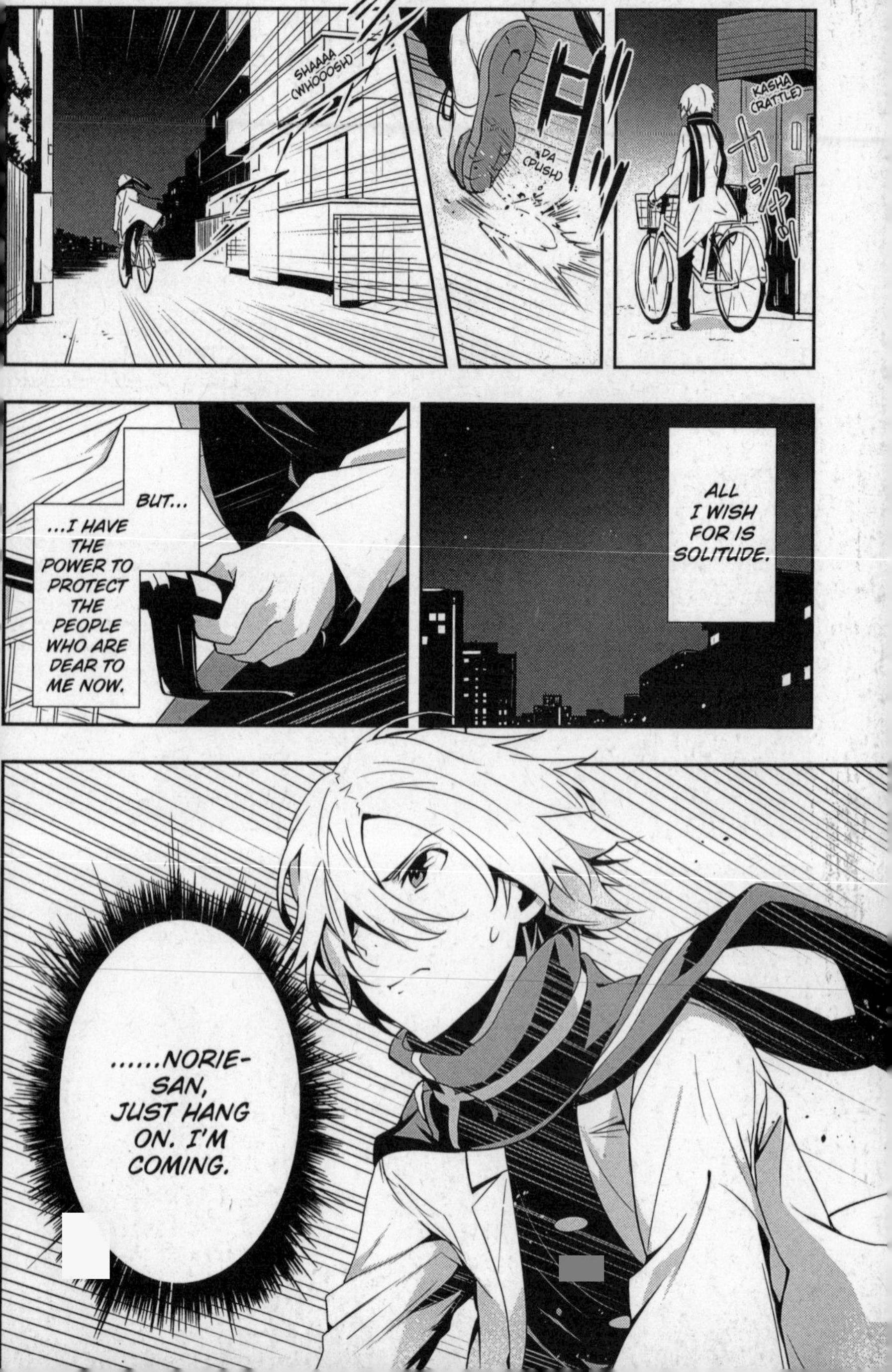
KASHA (RATTLE)
DA (PUSH)
SHAAAA (WHOOOSH)
ALL I WISH FOR IS SOLITUDE.
BUT...
...I HAVE THE POWER TO PROTECT THE PEOPLE WHO ARE DEAR TO ME NOW.
......NORIE-SAN, JUST HANG ON. I'M COMING.

THE ISOLATOR
realization of
absolute solitude

Sect. 009
SHARK

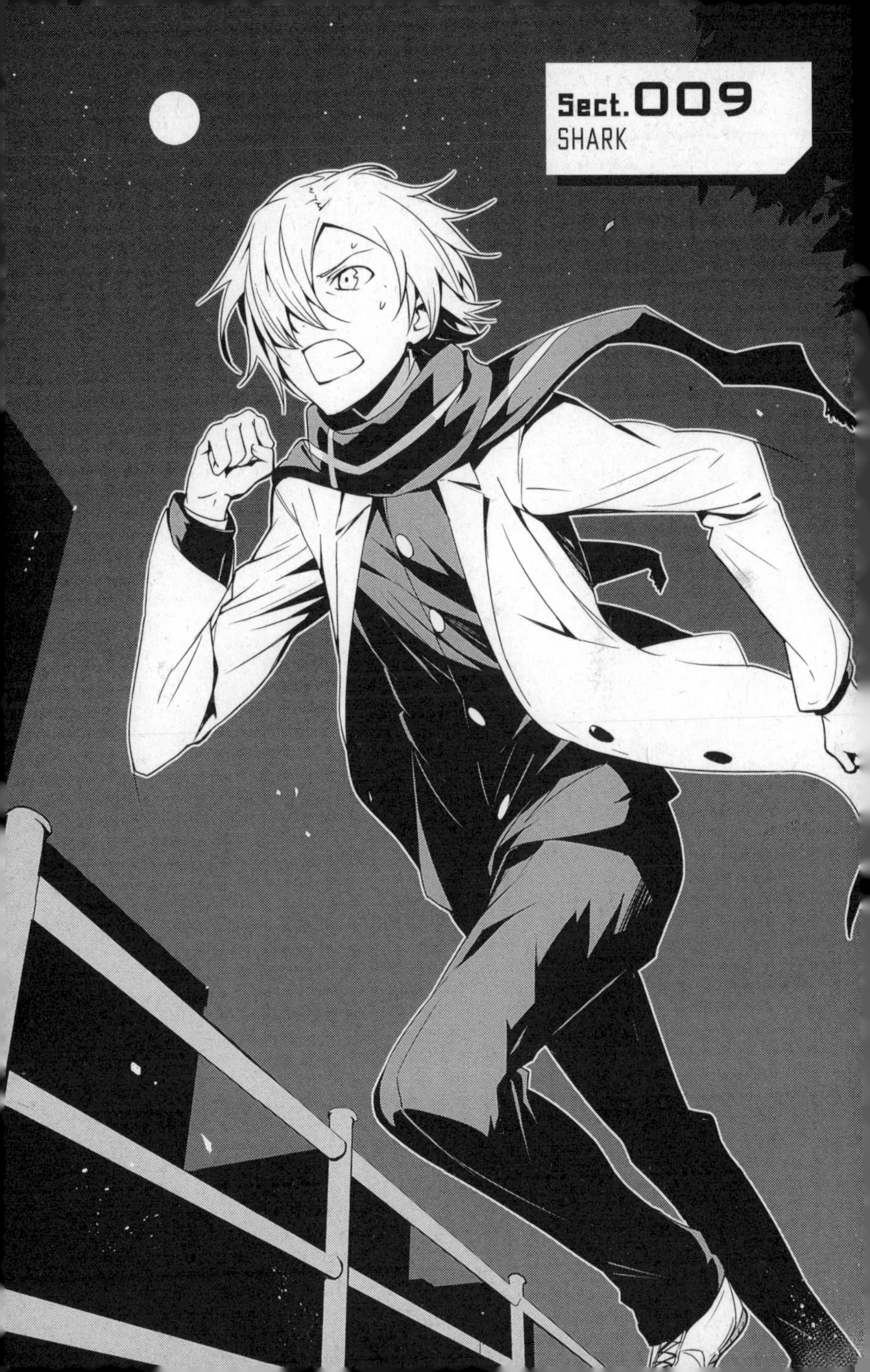

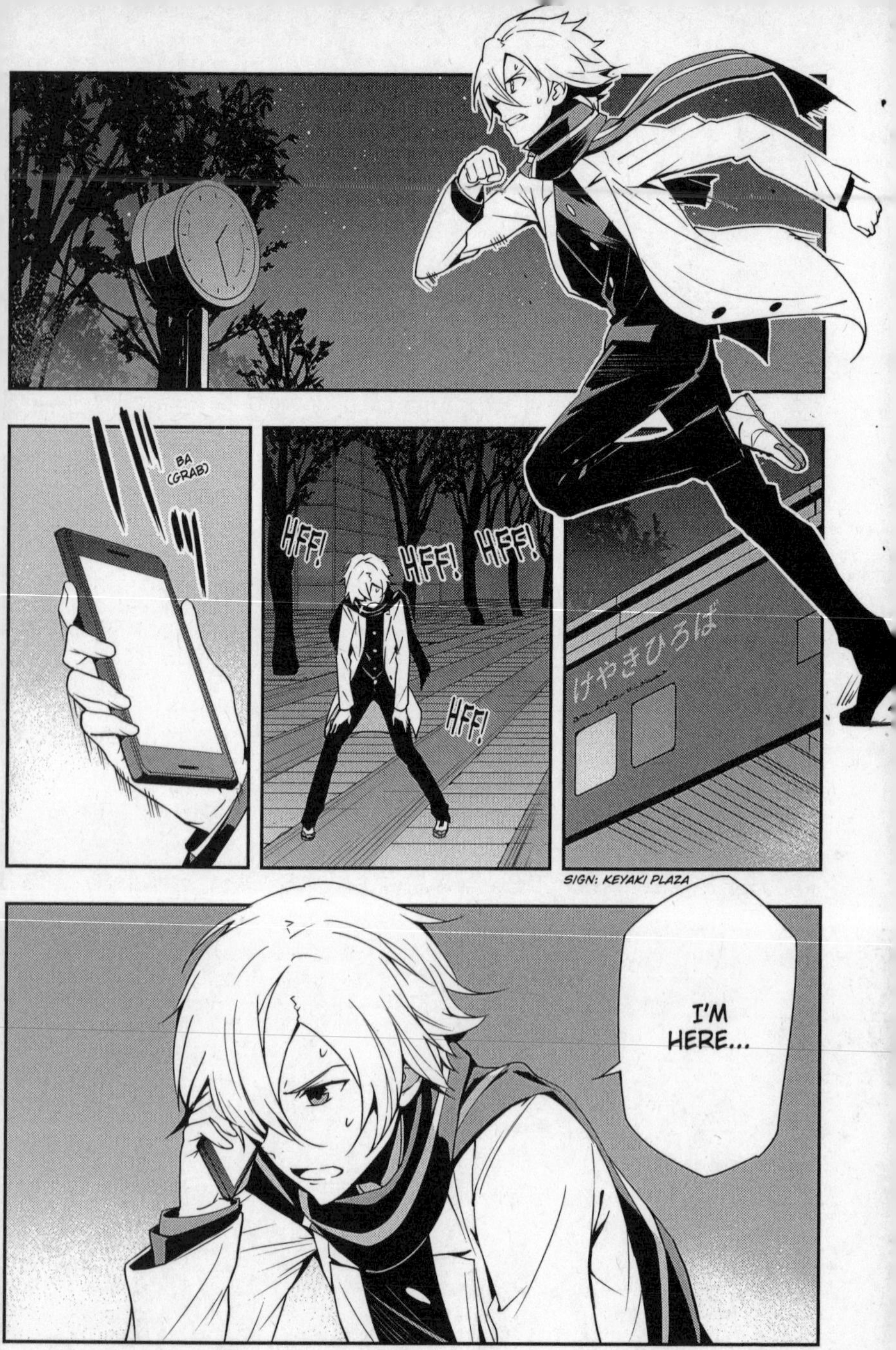

けやきひろば
SIGN: KEYAKI PLAZA
HFF!
HFF! HFF!
HFF!
BA (GRAB)
I'M HERE...

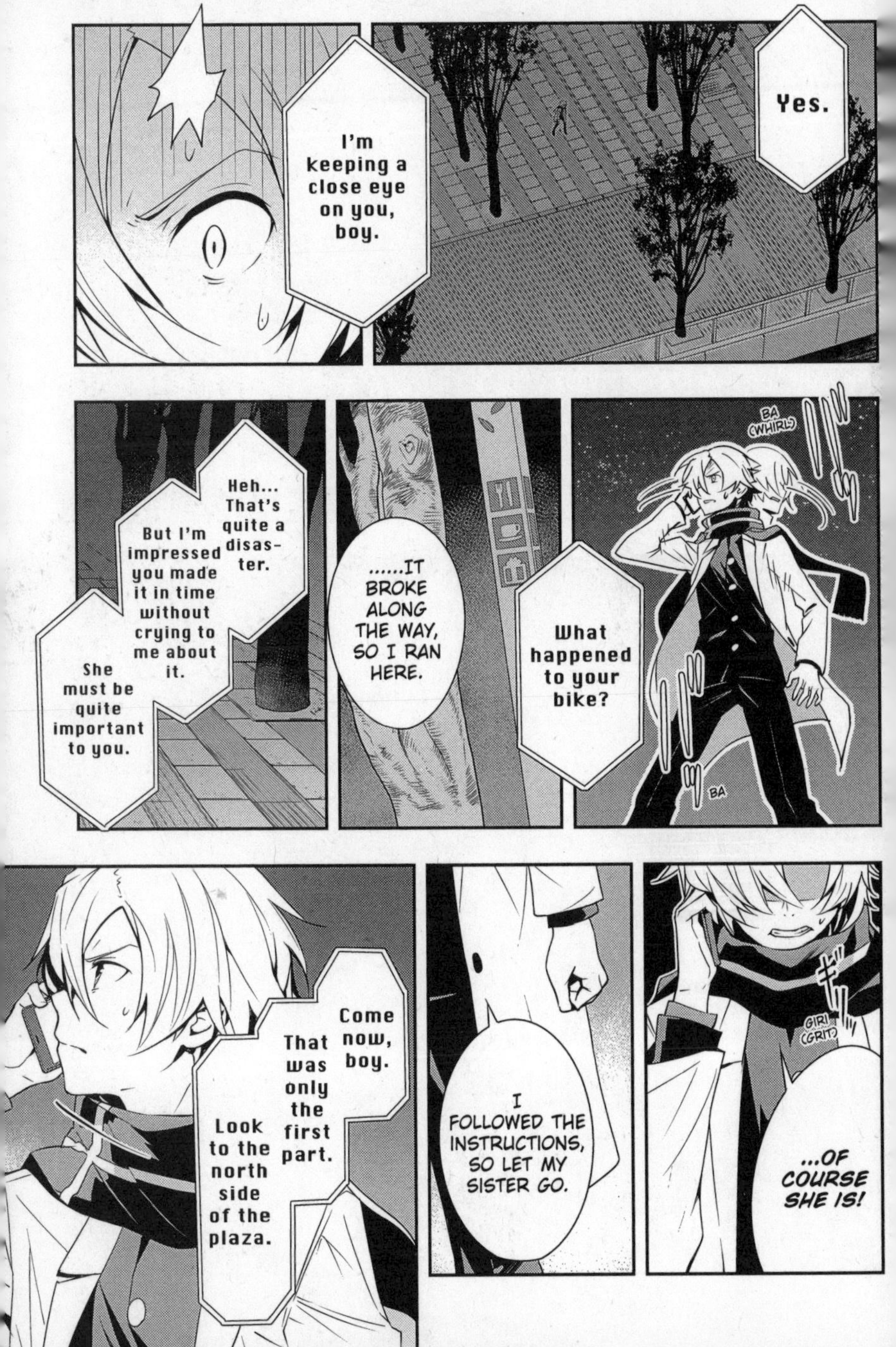
Yes.
I'm keeping a close eye on you, boy.
BA (WHIRL)
What happened to your bike?
BA
......IT BROKE ALONG THE WAY, SO I RAN HERE.
Heh... That's quite a disaster.
But I'm impressed you made it in time without crying to me about it.
She must be quite important to you.
GIRI (GRIT)
...OF COURSE SHE IS!
I FOLLOWED THE INSTRUCTIONS, SO LET MY SISTER GO.
Come now, boy.
That was only the first part.
Look to the north side of the plaza.

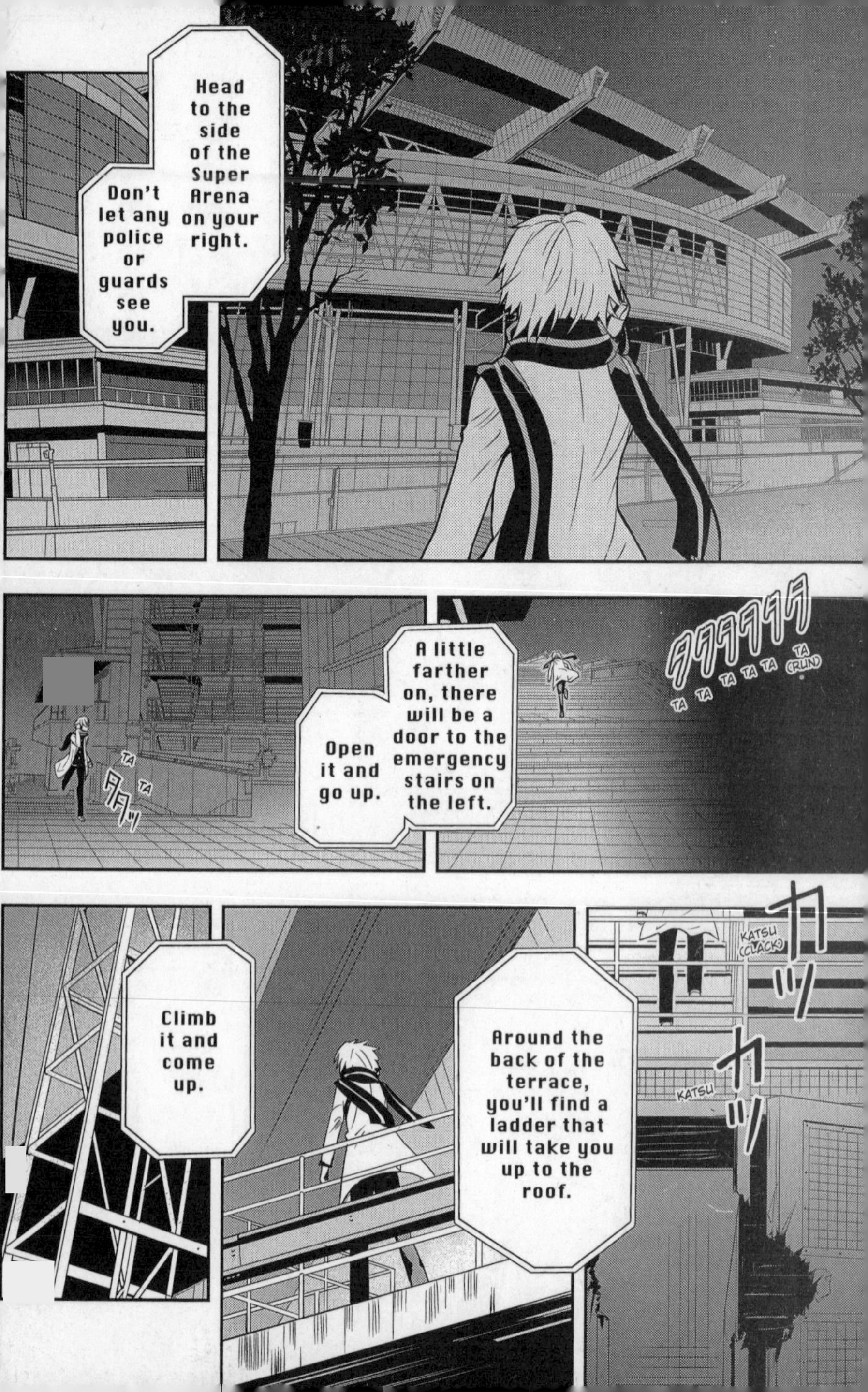
Head to the side of the Super Arena on your right.
Don't let any police or guards see you.
TA TA TA TA TA TA (RUN)
A little farther on, there will be a door to the emergency stairs on the left.
Open it and go up.
TA TA
KATSU (CLACK)
KATSU
Around the back of the terrace, you'll find a ladder that will take you up to the roof.
Climb it and come up.

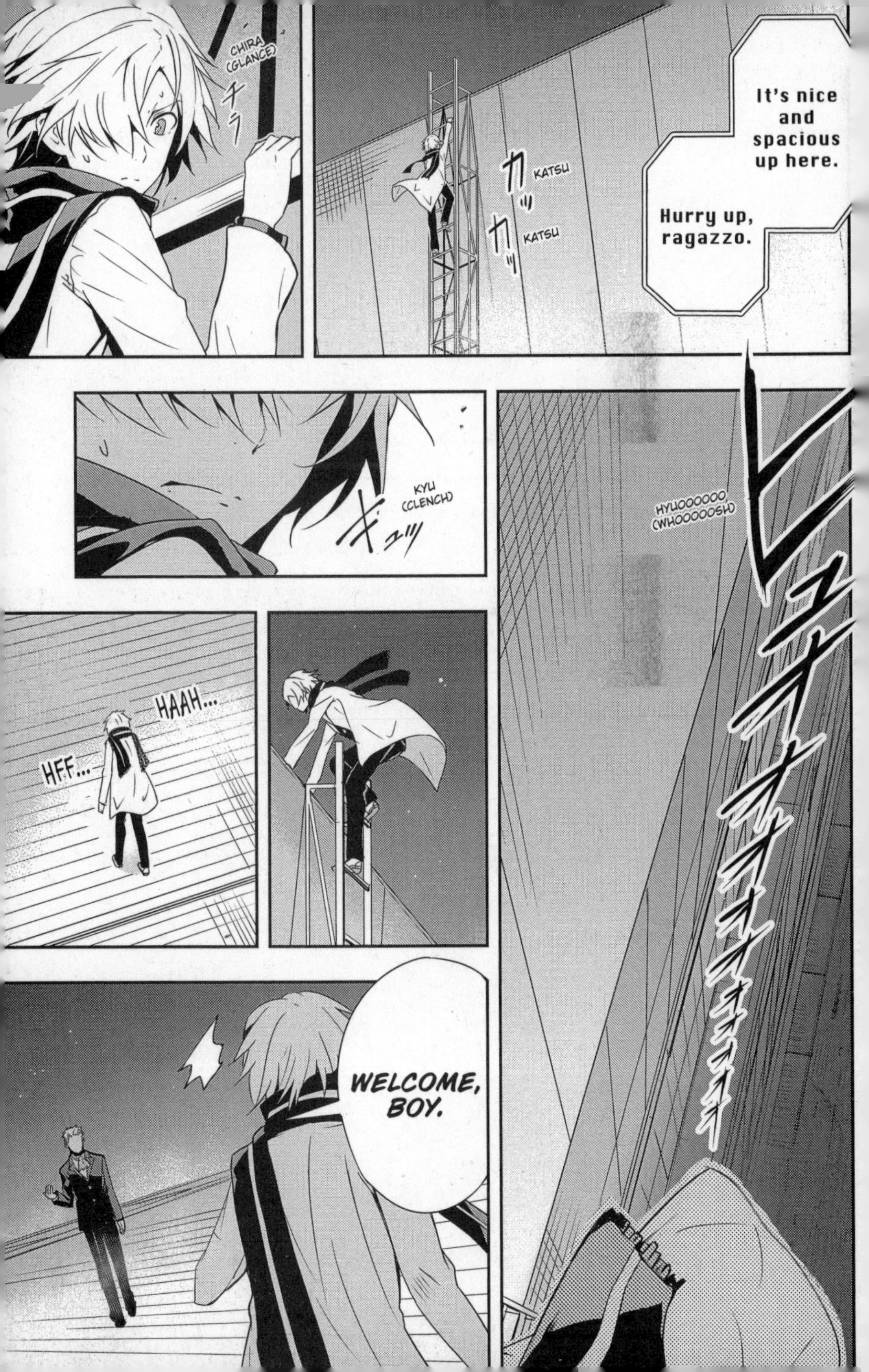
It's nice and spacious up here.
Hurry up, ragazzo.
カッ KATSU
カッ KATSU
CHIRA (GLANCE)
チラ
HYUOOOOOO (WHOOOOOSH)
KYU (CLENCH)
ギュッ
HAAH...
HFF...
WELCOME, BOY.

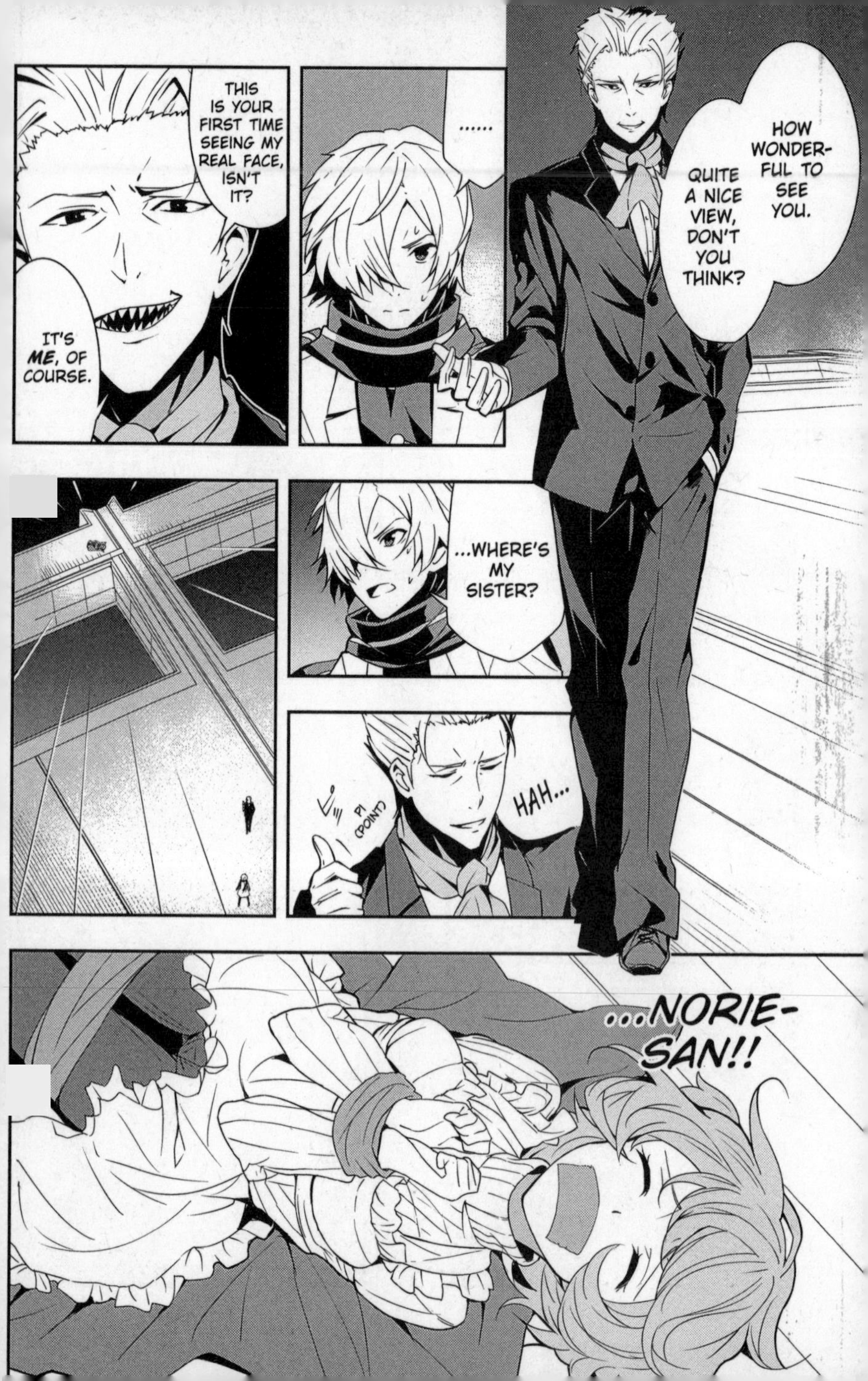
HOW WONDERFUL TO SEE YOU.
QUITE A NICE VIEW, DON'T YOU THINK?
......
THIS IS YOUR FIRST TIME SEEING MY REAL FACE, ISN'T IT?
IT'S *ME*, OF COURSE.
...WHERE'S MY SISTER?
HAH...
PI (POINT)
...NORIE-SAN!!

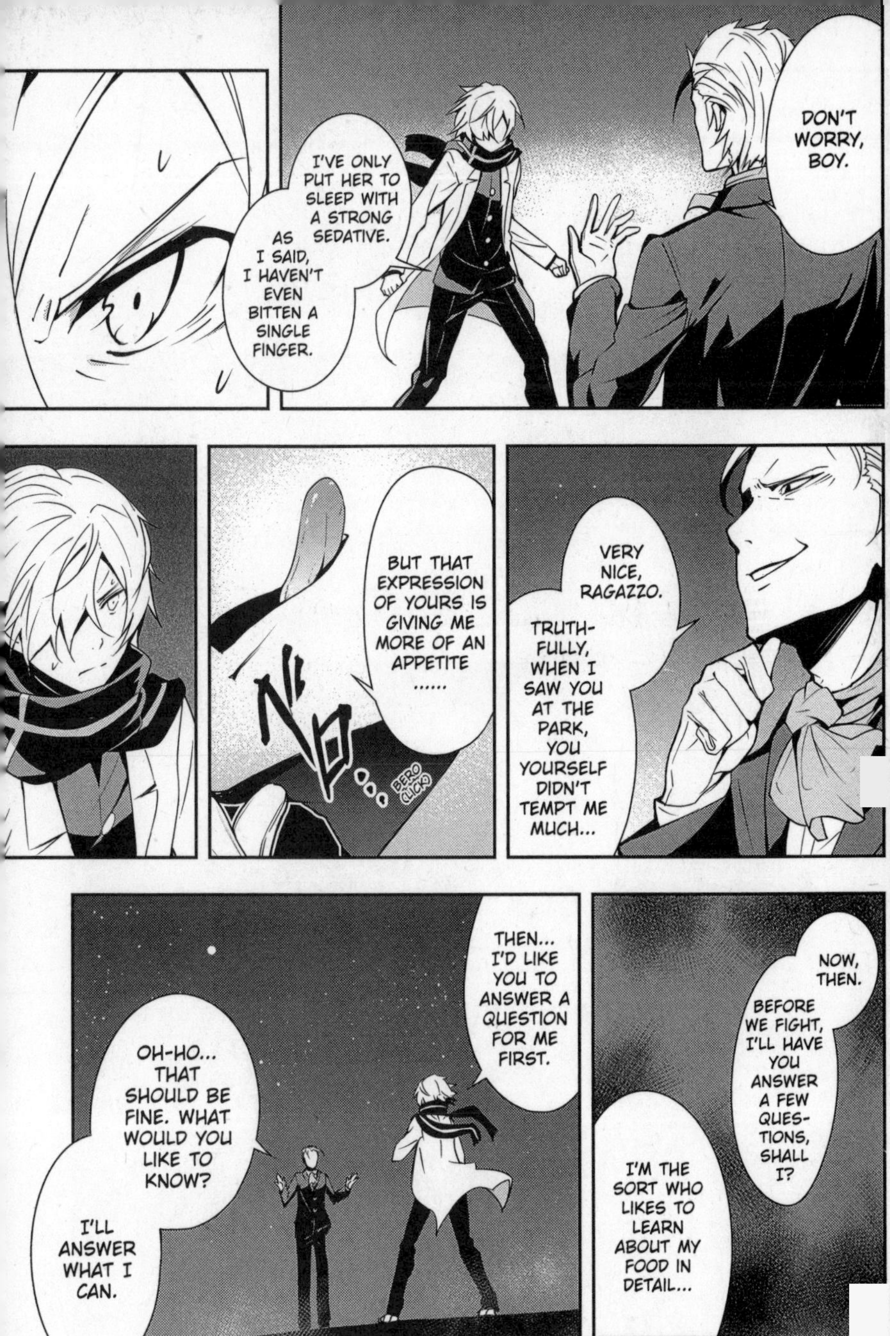
DON'T WORRY, BOY.
I'VE ONLY PUT HER TO SLEEP WITH A STRONG SEDATIVE.
AS I SAID, I HAVEN'T EVEN BITTEN A SINGLE FINGER.
VERY NICE, RAGAZZO.
TRUTH-FULLY, WHEN I SAW YOU AT THE PARK, YOU YOURSELF DIDN'T TEMPT ME MUCH...
BUT THAT EXPRESSION OF YOURS IS GIVING ME MORE OF AN APPETITE ......
BERO (LICK)
NOW, THEN.
BEFORE WE FIGHT, I'LL HAVE YOU ANSWER A FEW QUES-TIONS, SHALL I?
I'M THE SORT WHO LIKES TO LEARN ABOUT MY FOOD IN DETAIL...
THEN... I'D LIKE YOU TO ANSWER A QUESTION FOR ME FIRST.
OH-HO... THAT SHOULD BE FINE. WHAT WOULD YOU LIKE TO KNOW?
I'LL ANSWER WHAT I CAN.

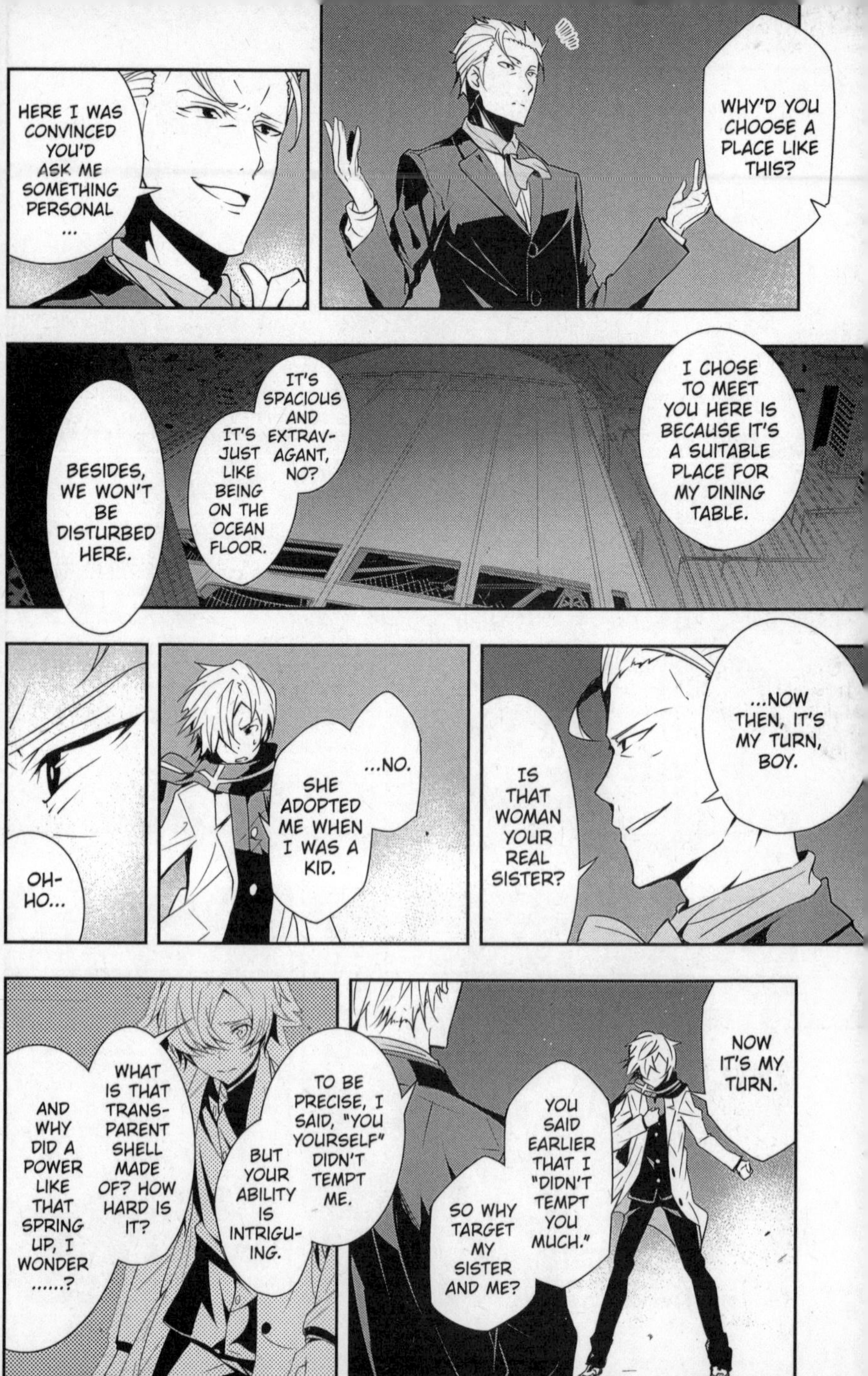
WHY'D YOU CHOOSE A PLACE LIKE THIS?
HERE I WAS CONVINCED YOU'D ASK ME SOMETHING PERSONAL...
I CHOSE TO MEET YOU HERE IS BECAUSE IT'S A SUITABLE PLACE FOR MY DINING TABLE.
IT'S SPACIOUS AND EXTRAVAGANT, NO?
IT'S JUST LIKE BEING ON THE OCEAN FLOOR.
BESIDES, WE WON'T BE DISTURBED HERE.
...NOW THEN, IT'S MY TURN, BOY.
IS THAT WOMAN YOUR REAL SISTER?
...NO.
SHE ADOPTED ME WHEN I WAS A KID.
OH-HO...
NOW IT'S MY TURN.
YOU SAID EARLIER THAT I "DIDN'T TEMPT YOU MUCH."
SO WHY TARGET MY SISTER AND ME?
TO BE PRECISE, I SAID, "YOU YOURSELF" DIDN'T TEMPT ME.
BUT YOUR ABILITY IS INTRIGUING.
WHAT IS THAT TRANSPARENT SHELL MADE OF? HOW HARD IS IT?
AND WHY DID A POWER LIKE THAT SPRING UP, I WONDER......?

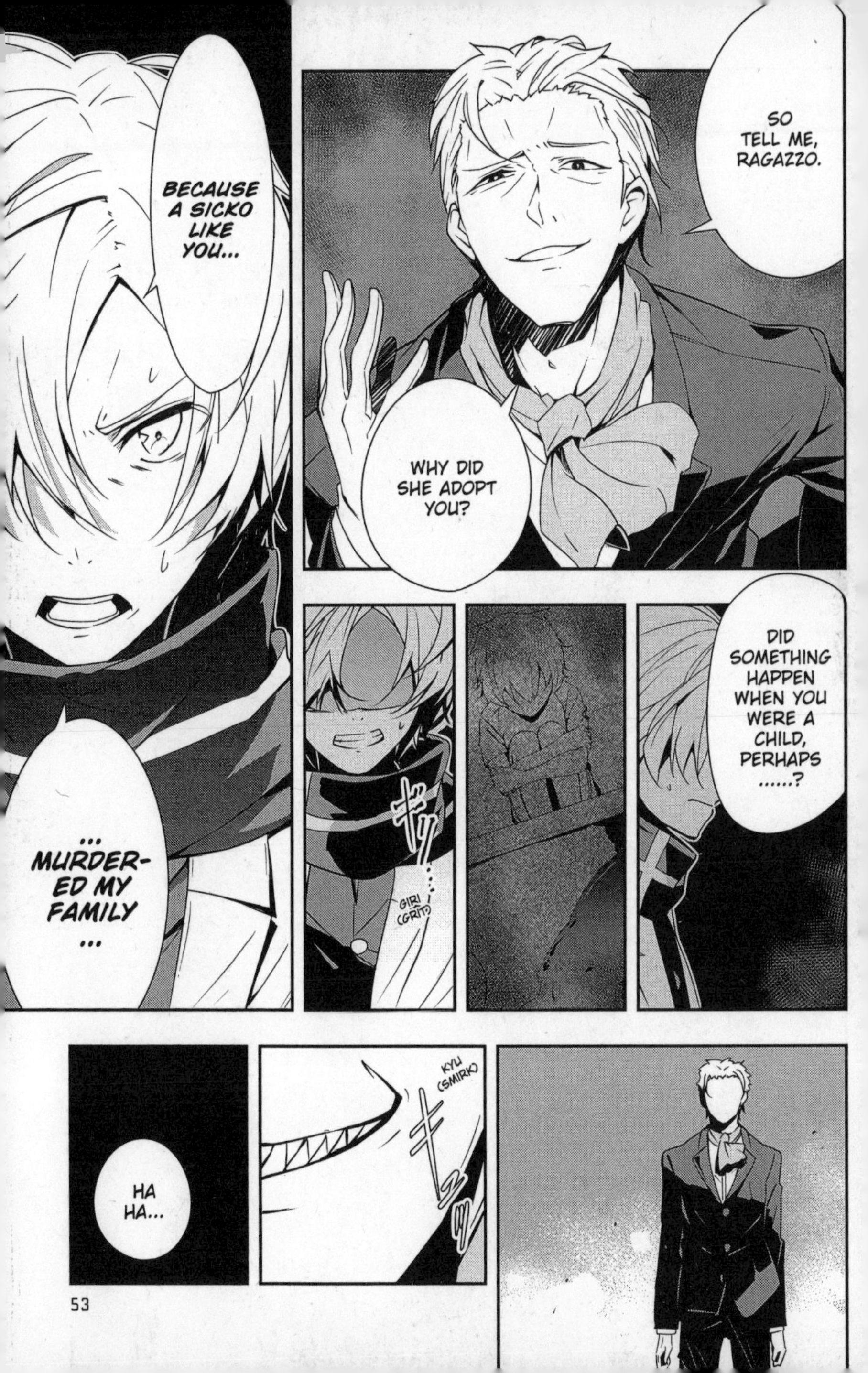
SO TELL ME, RAGAZZO.
WHY DID SHE ADOPT YOU?
DID SOMETHING HAPPEN WHEN YOU WERE A CHILD, PERHAPS ......?
GIRI (GRIT)
BECAUSE A SICKO LIKE YOU...
... MURDER-ED MY FAMILY ...
KYU (SMIRK)
HA HA...

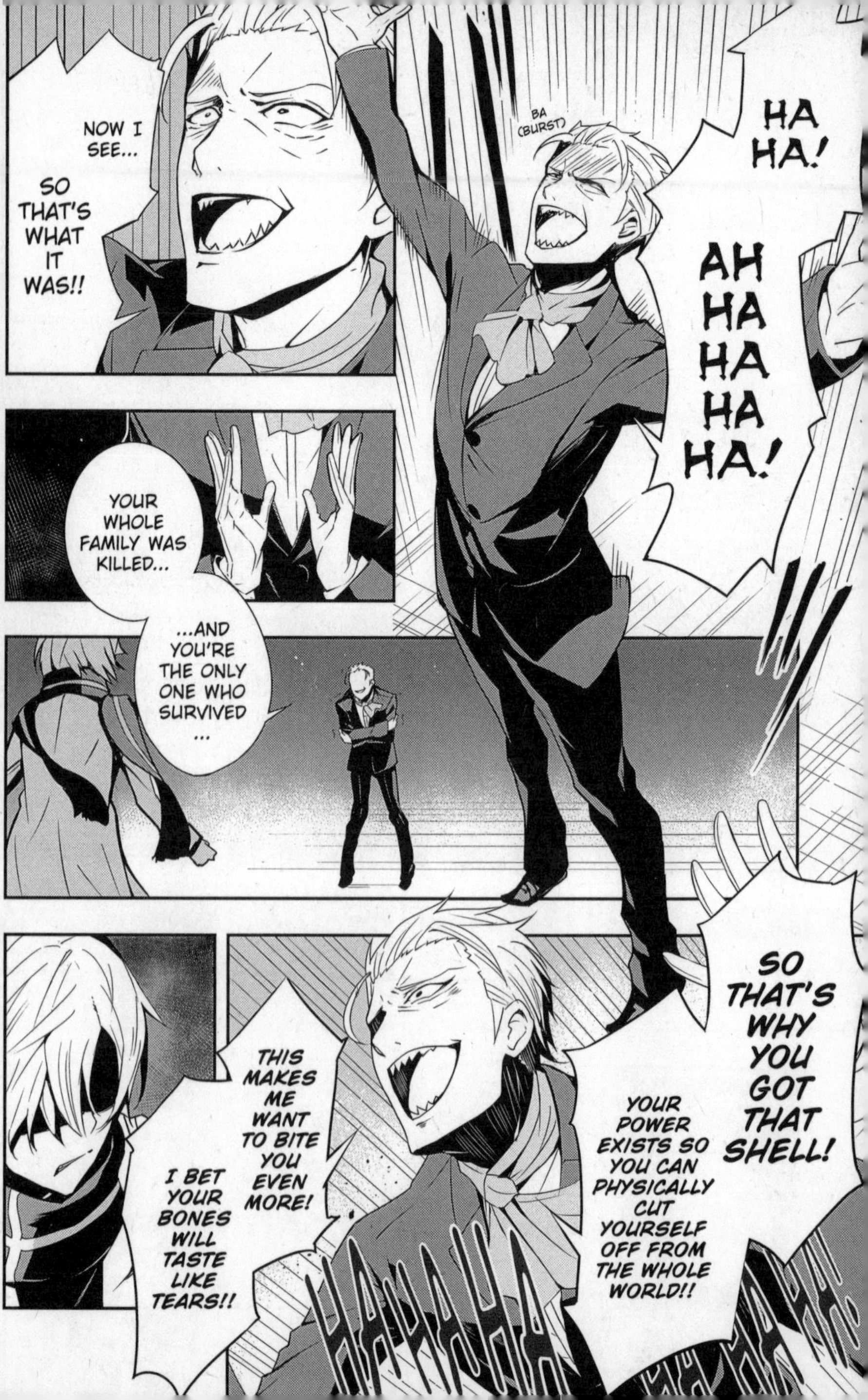
BA (BURST)
HA HA!
AH HA HA HA HA!
NOW I SEE...
SO THAT'S WHAT IT WAS!!
YOUR WHOLE FAMILY WAS KILLED...
...AND YOU'RE THE ONLY ONE WHO SURVIVED...
SO THAT'S WHY YOU GOT THAT SHELL!
YOUR POWER EXISTS SO YOU CAN PHYSICALLY CUT YOURSELF OFF FROM THE WHOLE WORLD!!
THIS MAKES ME WANT TO BITE YOU EVEN MORE!
I BET YOUR BONES WILL TASTE LIKE TEARS!!

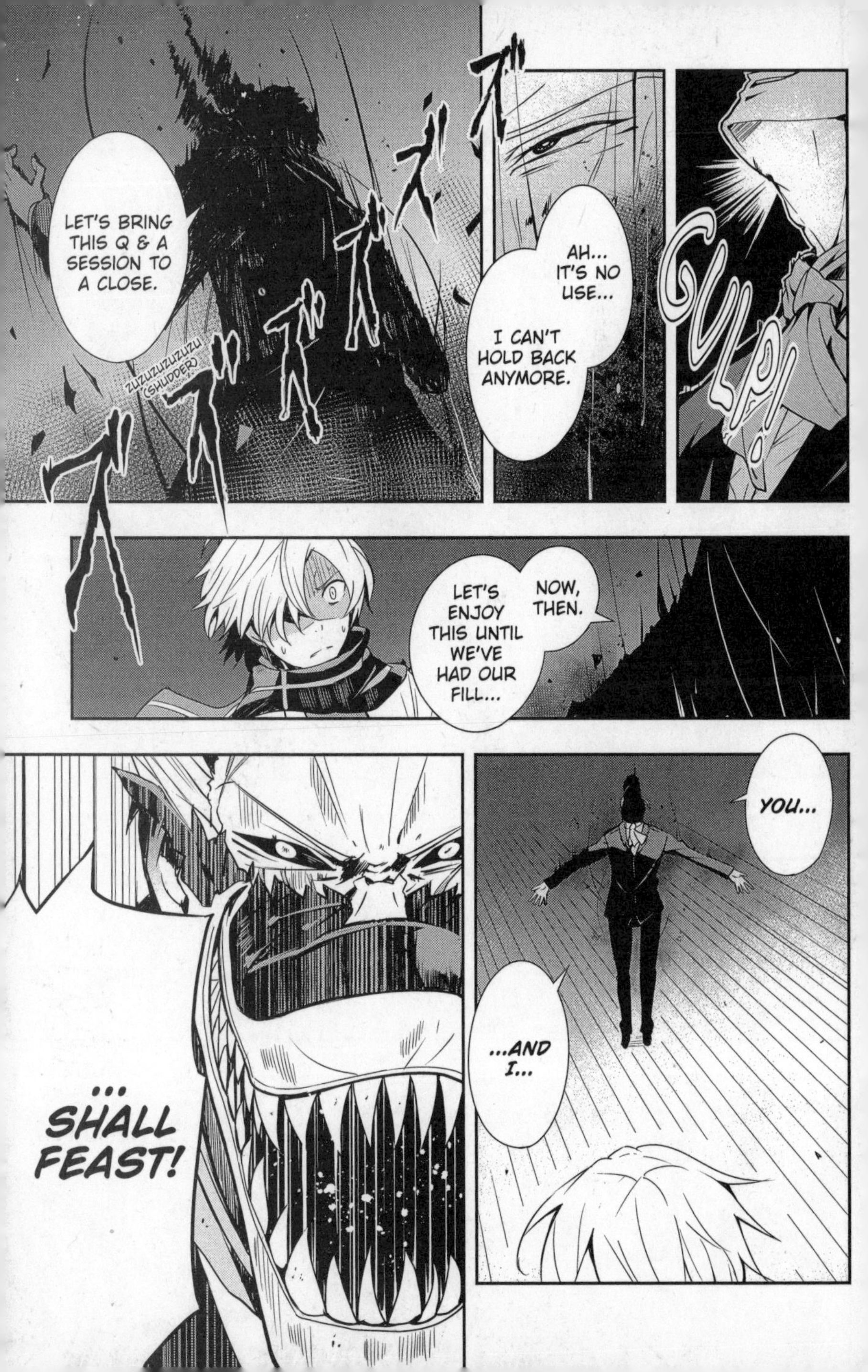
GULP!
AH... IT'S NO USE...
I CAN'T HOLD BACK ANYMORE.
LET'S BRING THIS Q & A SESSION TO A CLOSE.
ZUZUZUZUZUZU (SHUDDER)
NOW, THEN.
LET'S ENJOY THIS UNTIL WE'VE HAD OUR FILL...
YOU...
...AND I...
...SHALL FEAST!

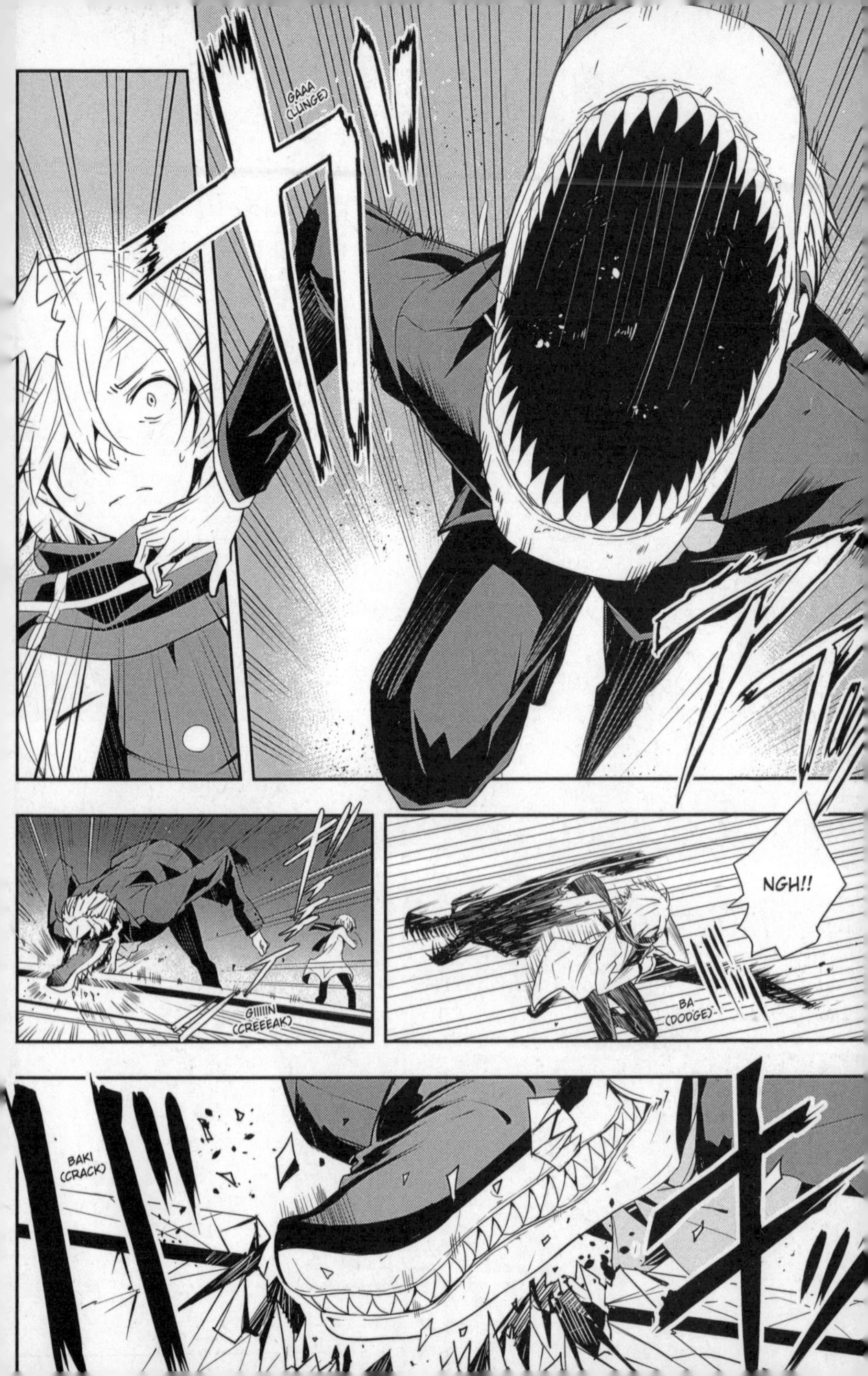
GAAA
(LUNGE)
NGH!!
BA
(DODGE)
GIIIIN
(CREEEAK)
BAKI
(CRACK)

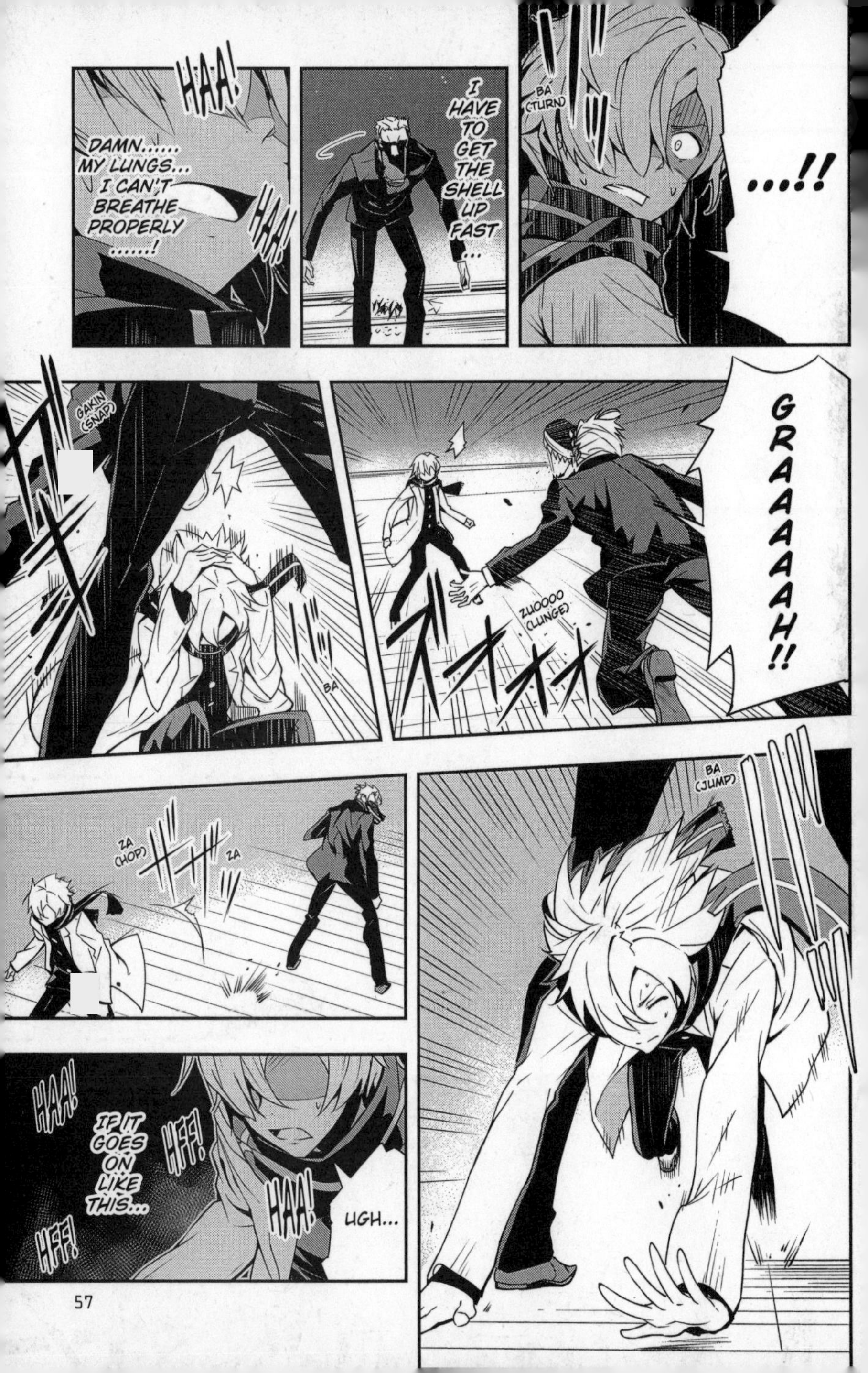
BA (TURN)
...!!
I HAVE TO GET THE SHELL UP FAST...
HAA!
DAMN...... MY LUNGS... I CAN'T BREATHE PROPERLY......!
HAA!
GRAAAAAAH!!
ZUOOOO (LUNGE)
GAKIN (SNAP)
BA
BA (JUMP)
ZA (HOP)
ZA
HAA!
IF IT GOES ON LIKE THIS...
HFF!
HAA!
UGH...
HFF!

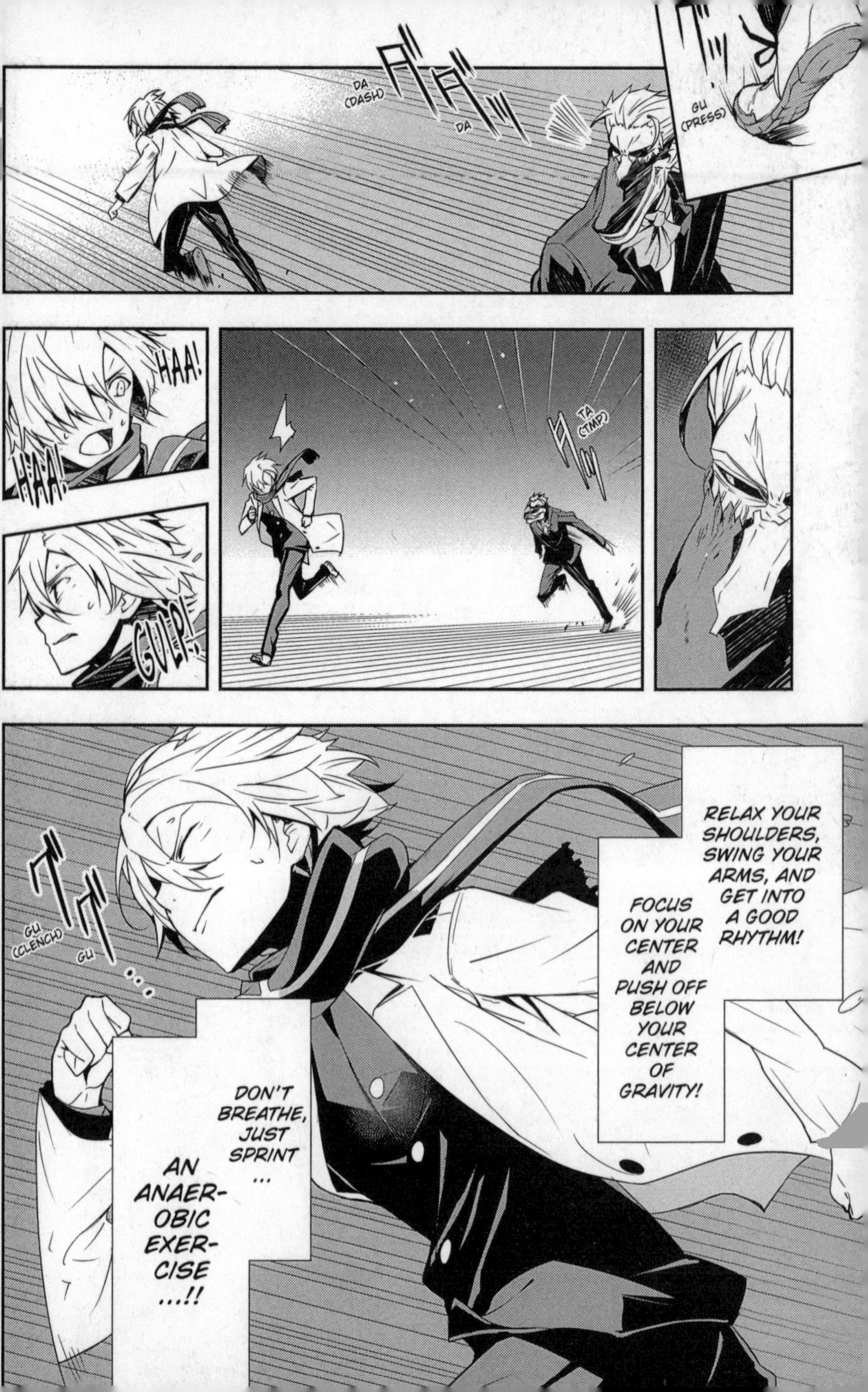
GU (PRESS)
DA (DASH)
DA
TA (TMP)
HAA! HAA!
GULP!
RELAX YOUR SHOULDERS, SWING YOUR ARMS, AND GET INTO A GOOD RHYTHM!
FOCUS ON YOUR CENTER AND PUSH OFF BELOW YOUR CENTER OF GRAVITY!
GU (CLENCH)
GU
...
DON'T BREATHE, JUST SPRINT...
AN ANAER-OBIC EXER-CISE...!!

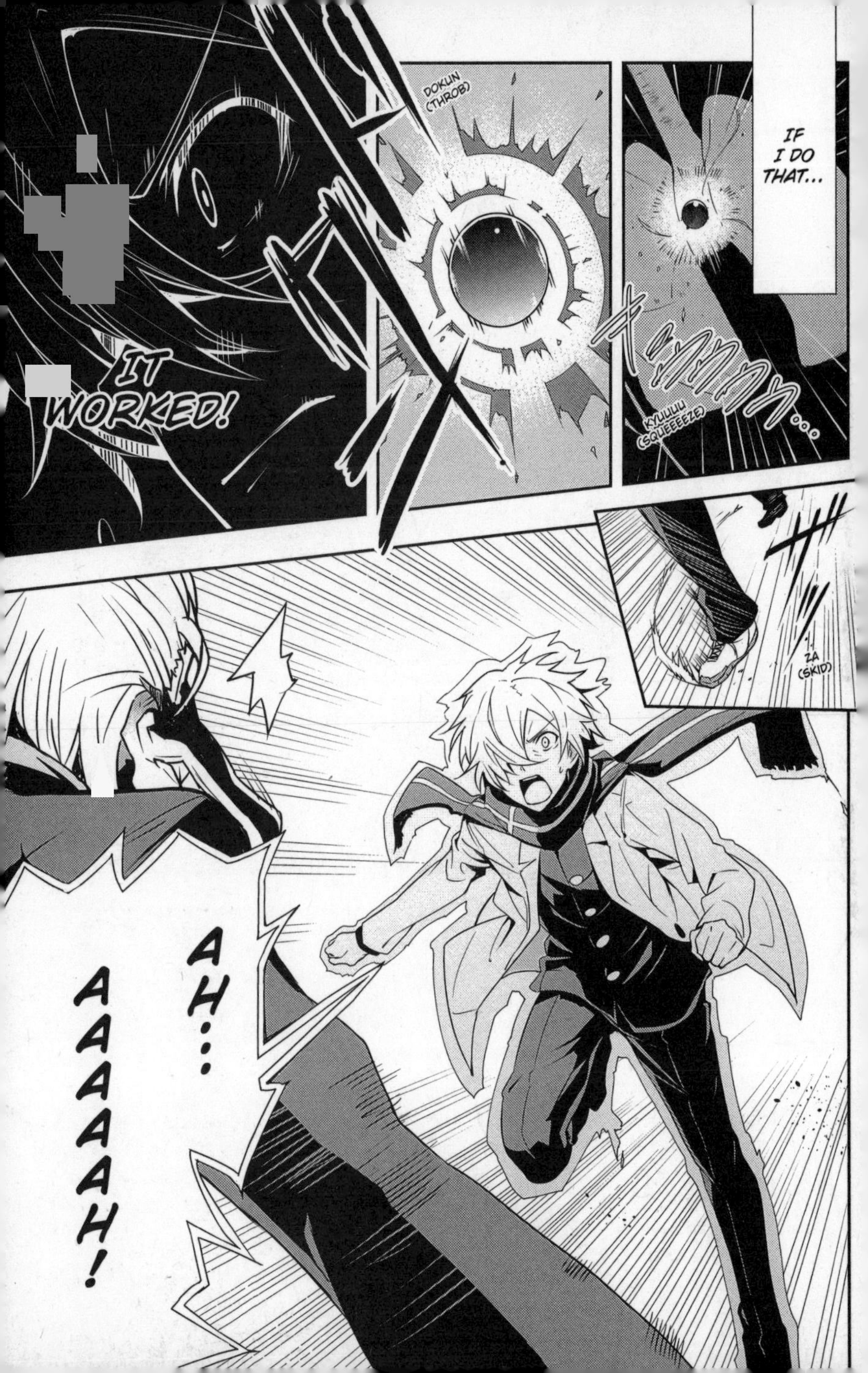
IF I DO THAT...
KYUUUU (SQUEEEEZE)
DOKUN (THROB)
IT WORKED!
ZA (SKID)
AH...
AAAAAAH!

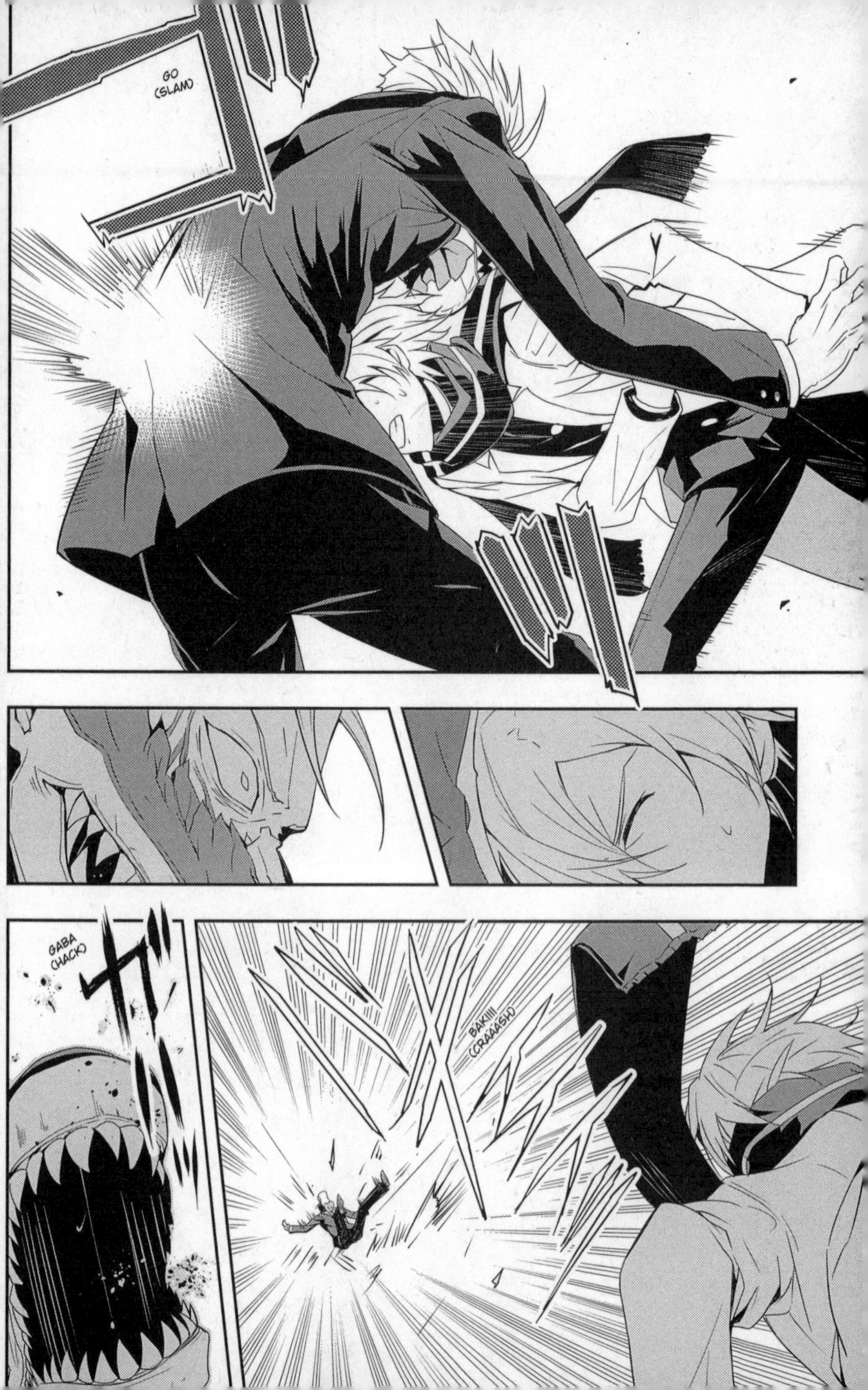
GO (SLAM)
BAKI!!!! (CRAAASH)
GABA (HACK)

DAN
(STOMP)

BA
(LEAP)

DO
(WHUD)

GAKI
(CRACK)

BYU
(WHOOSH)

DOGO
(THUMP)

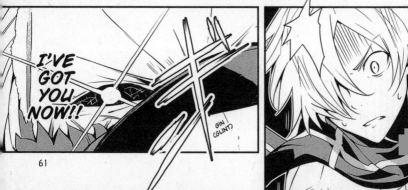

I'VE GOT YOU NOW!!

GIN
(GLINT)

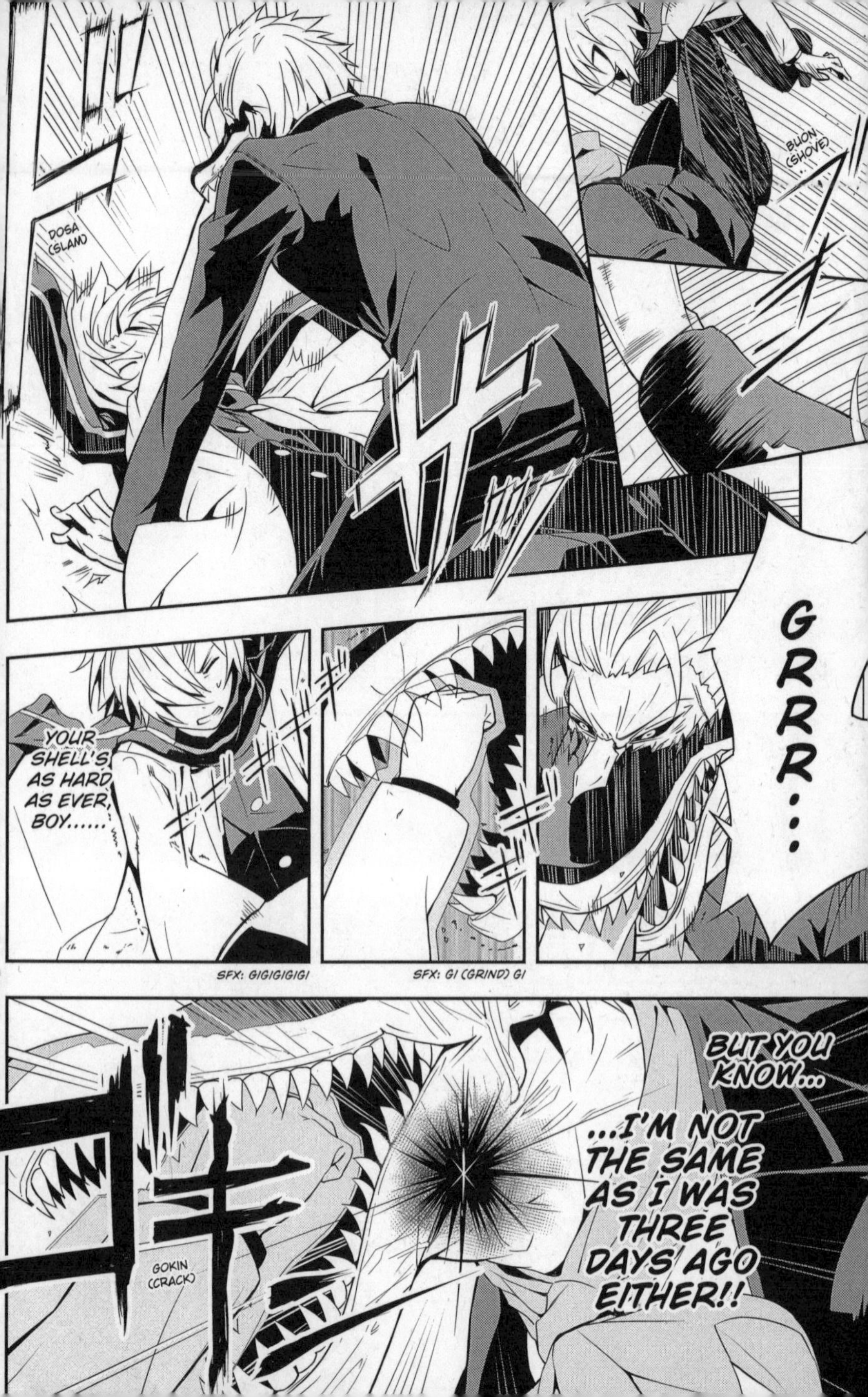
BUON (SHOVE)
DOSA (SLAM)
GRRR...
SFX: GI (GRIND) GI
YOUR SHELL'S AS HARD AS EVER, BOY......
SFX: GIGIGIGIGI
BUT YOU KNOW...
...I'M NOT THE SAME AS I WAS THREE DAYS AGO EITHER!!
GOKIN (CRACK)

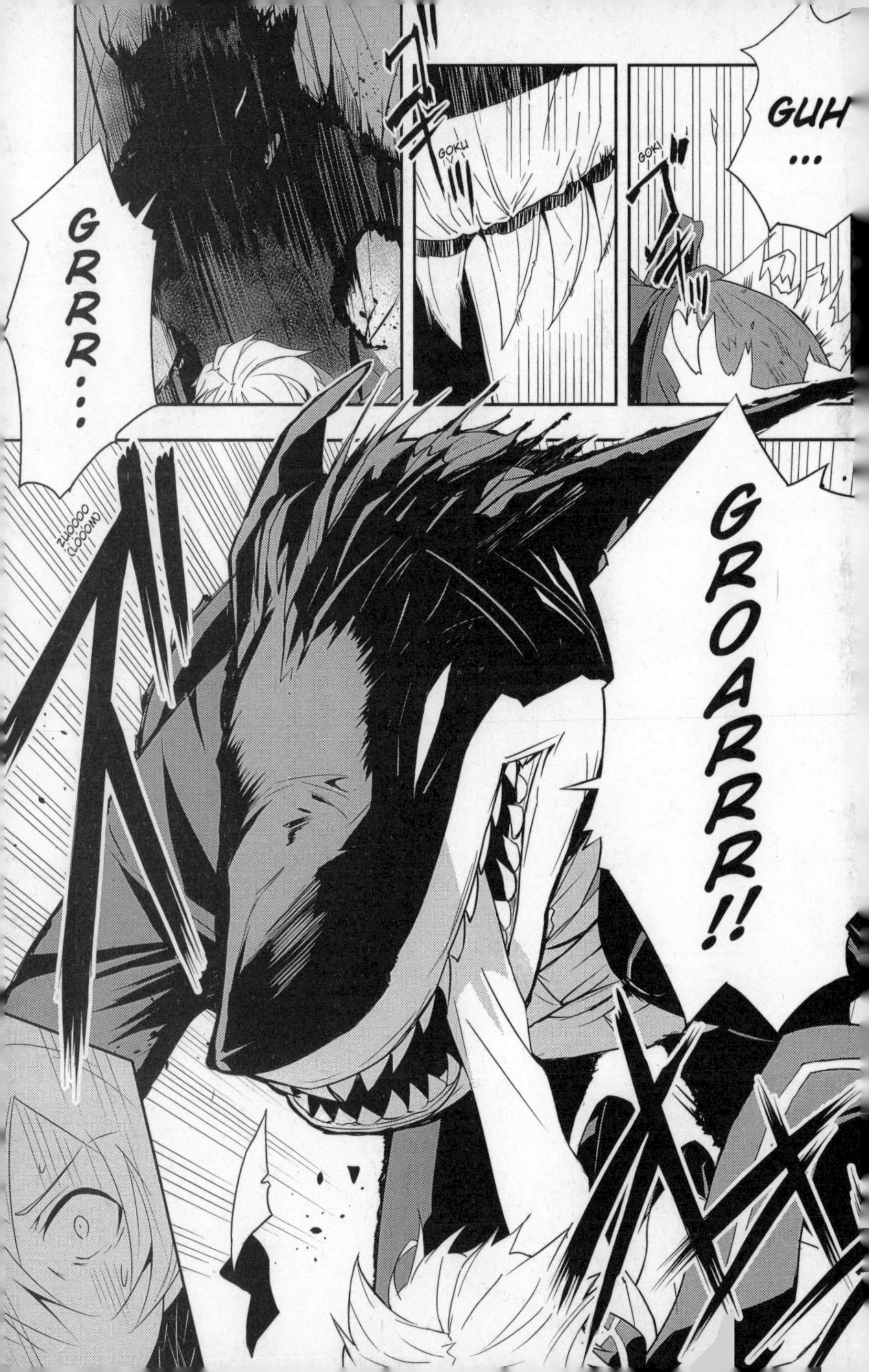
GUH ...
GOKI
GOKU
GRRR...
GROARRRR!!
ZUOOOO (CLOOOM)

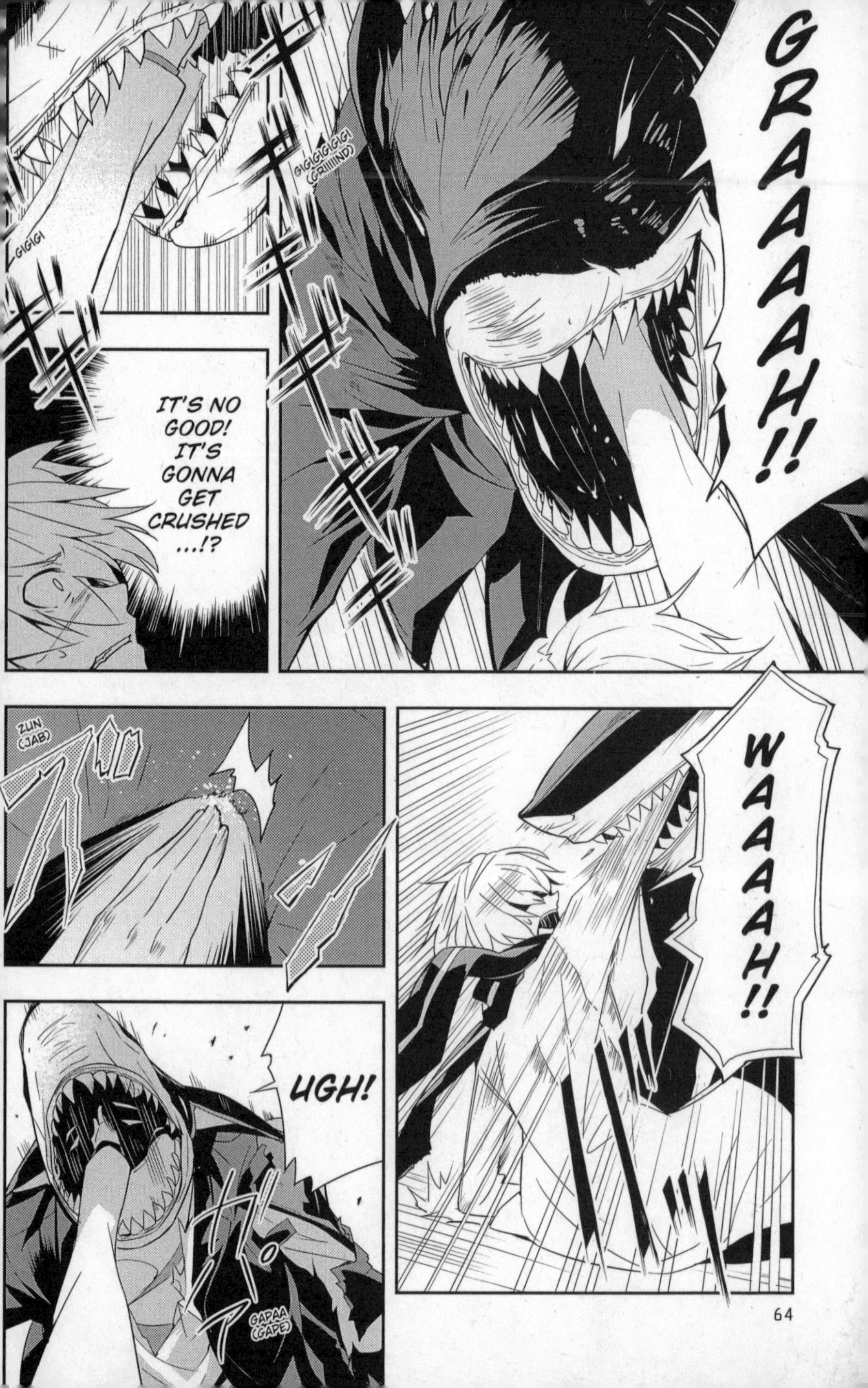
GRAAAAAH!!
GIGIGIGIGI
(GRIIIIIND)
GIGIGI
IT'S NO GOOD! IT'S GONNA GET CRUSHED ...!?
WAAAAAH!!
ZUN
(JAB)
UGH!
GAPAA
(GAPE)

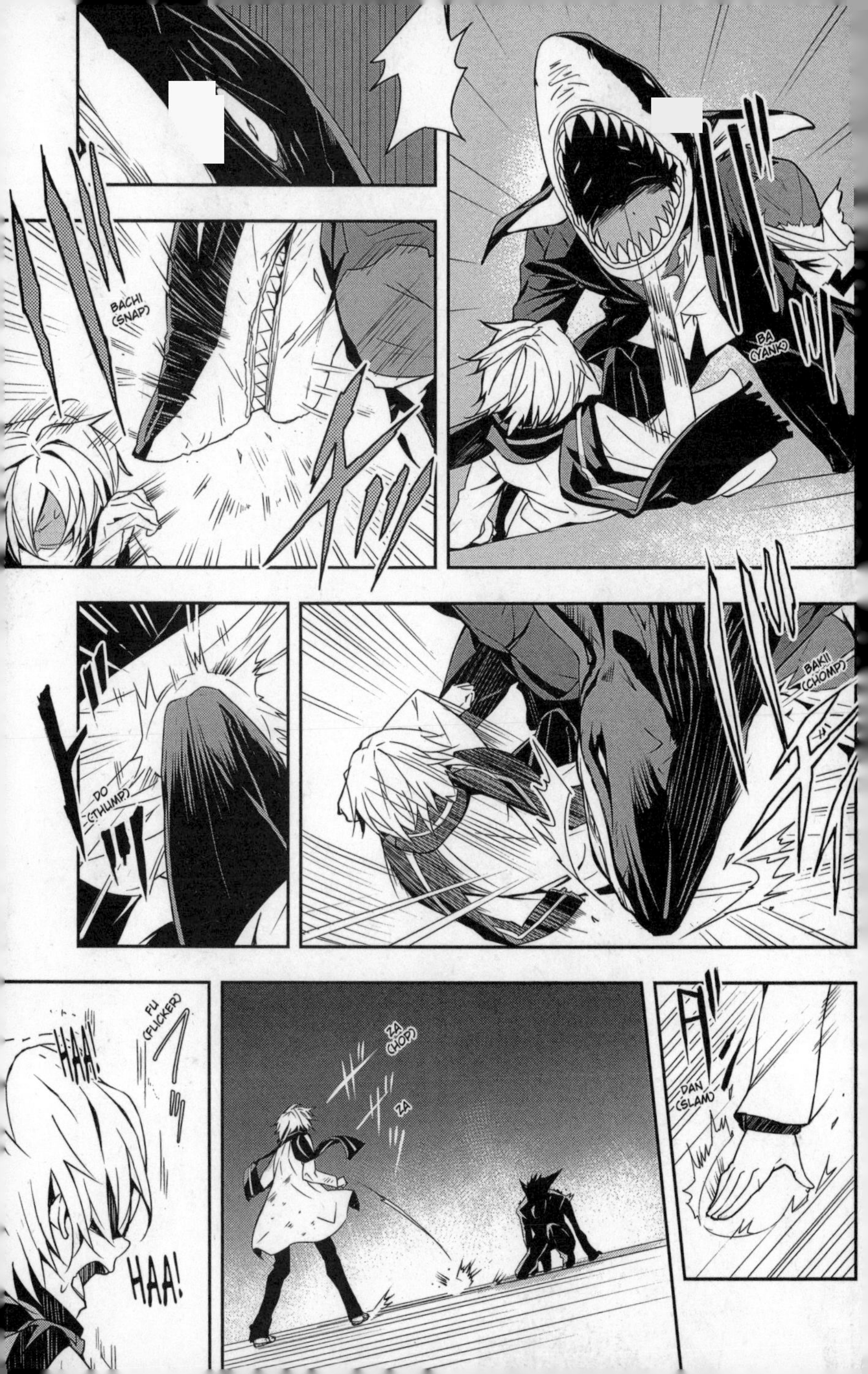
BA (YANK)
BACHI (SNAP)
BAKI (CHOMP)
DO (THUMP)
DAN (SLAM)
ZA (CHOP)
ZA
FU (FLICKER)
HAA!
HAA!

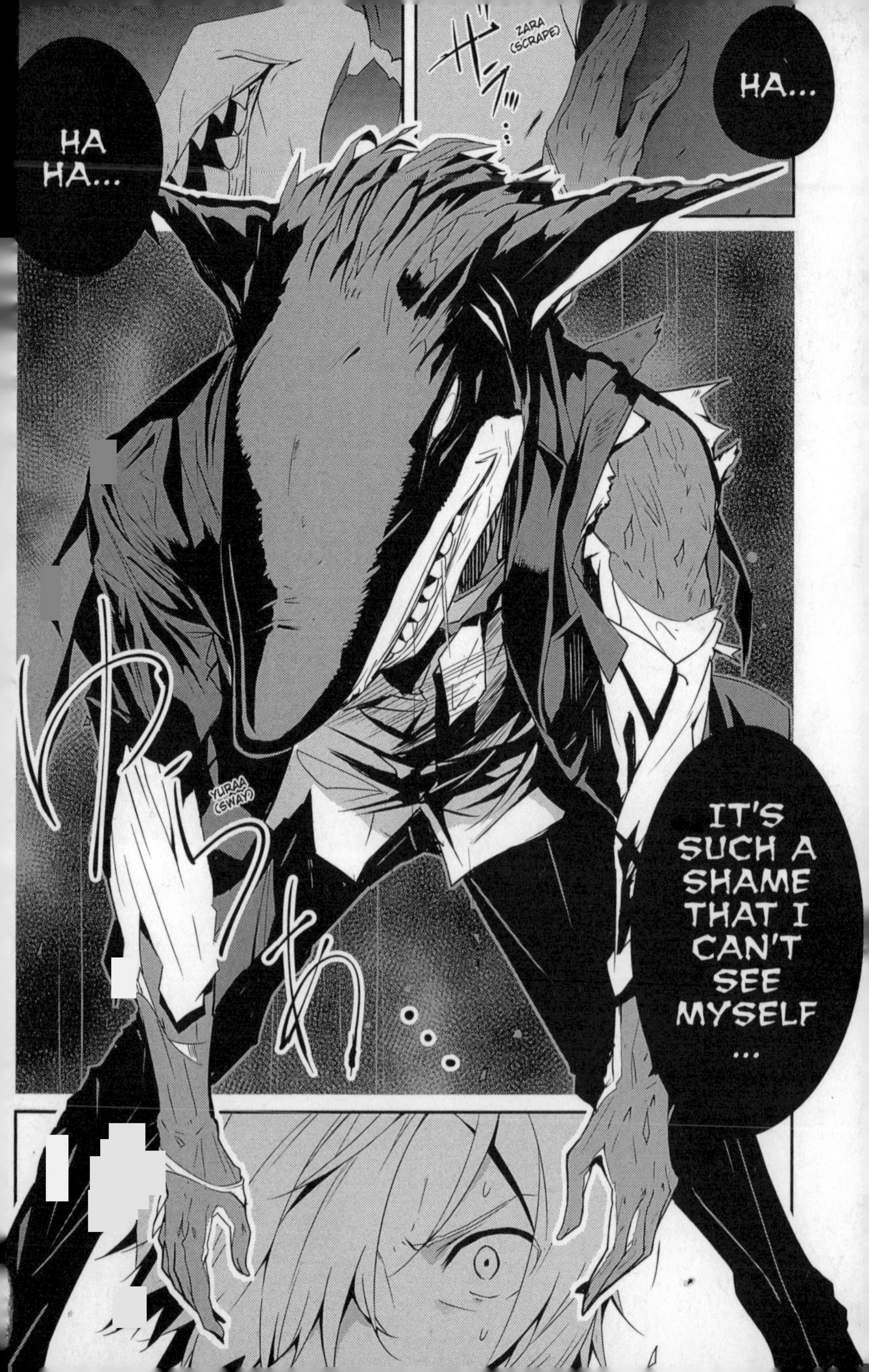
HA...
ZARA (SCRAPE)
HA HA...
IT'S SUCH A SHAME THAT I CAN'T SEE MYSELF ...
YURAA (SWAY)

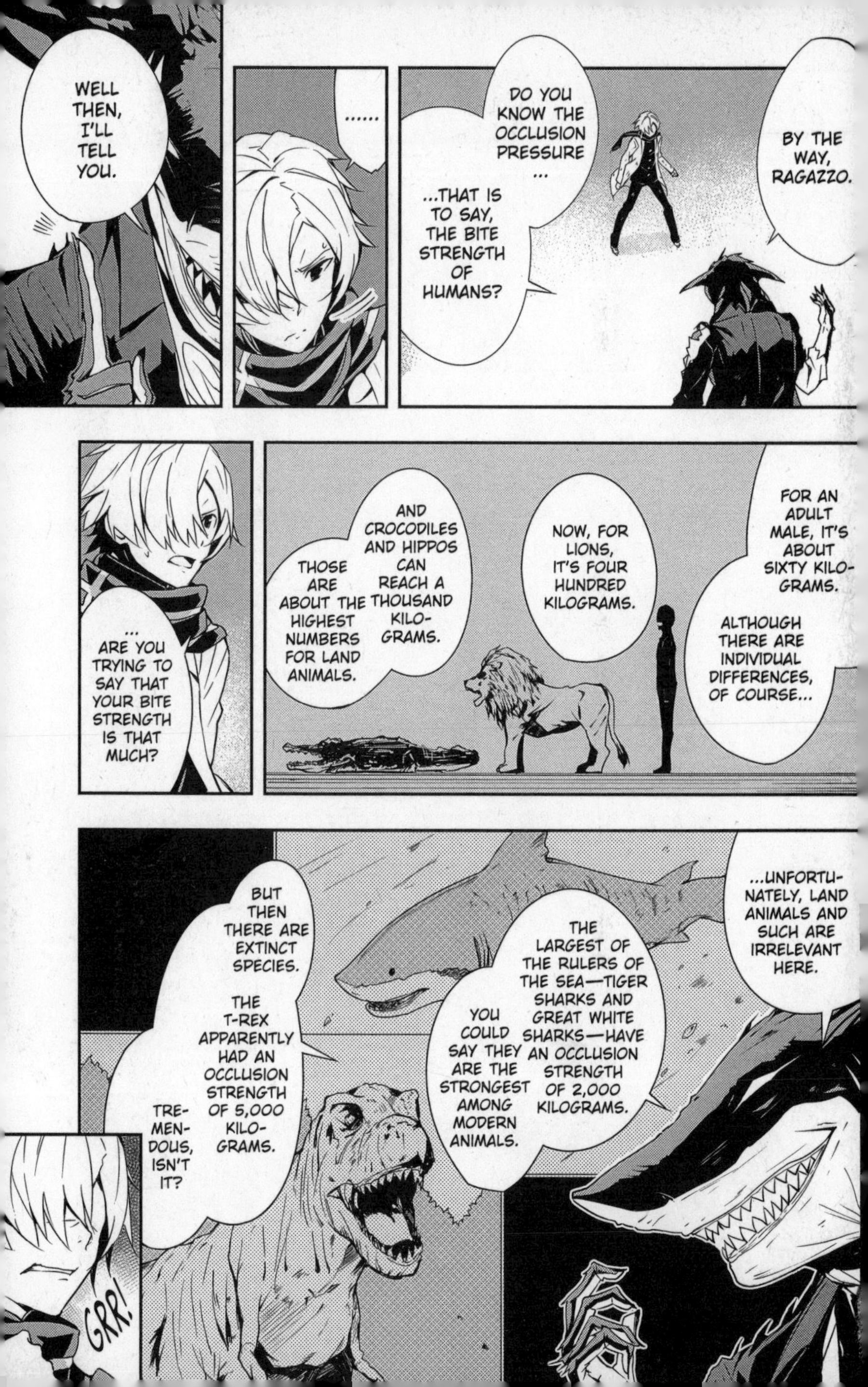
BY THE WAY, RAGAZZO.
DO YOU KNOW THE OCCLUSION PRESSURE ...
...THAT IS TO SAY, THE BITE STRENGTH OF HUMANS?
......
WELL THEN, I'LL TELL YOU.
FOR AN ADULT MALE, IT'S ABOUT SIXTY KILO-GRAMS.
ALTHOUGH THERE ARE INDIVIDUAL DIFFERENCES, OF COURSE...
NOW, FOR LIONS, IT'S FOUR HUNDRED KILOGRAMS.
AND CROCODILES AND HIPPOS CAN REACH A THOUSAND KILO-GRAMS.
THOSE ARE ABOUT THE HIGHEST NUMBERS FOR LAND ANIMALS.
... ARE YOU TRYING TO SAY THAT YOUR BITE STRENGTH IS THAT MUCH?
...UNFORTU-NATELY, LAND ANIMALS AND SUCH ARE IRRELEVANT HERE.
THE LARGEST OF THE RULERS OF THE SEA—TIGER SHARKS AND GREAT WHITE SHARKS—HAVE AN OCCLUSION STRENGTH OF 2,000 KILOGRAMS.
YOU COULD SAY THEY ARE THE STRONGEST AMONG MODERN ANIMALS.
BUT THEN THERE ARE EXTINCT SPECIES.
THE T-REX APPARENTLY HAD AN OCCLUSION STRENGTH OF 5,000 KILO-GRAMS.
TRE-MEN-DOUS, ISN'T IT?
GRR!

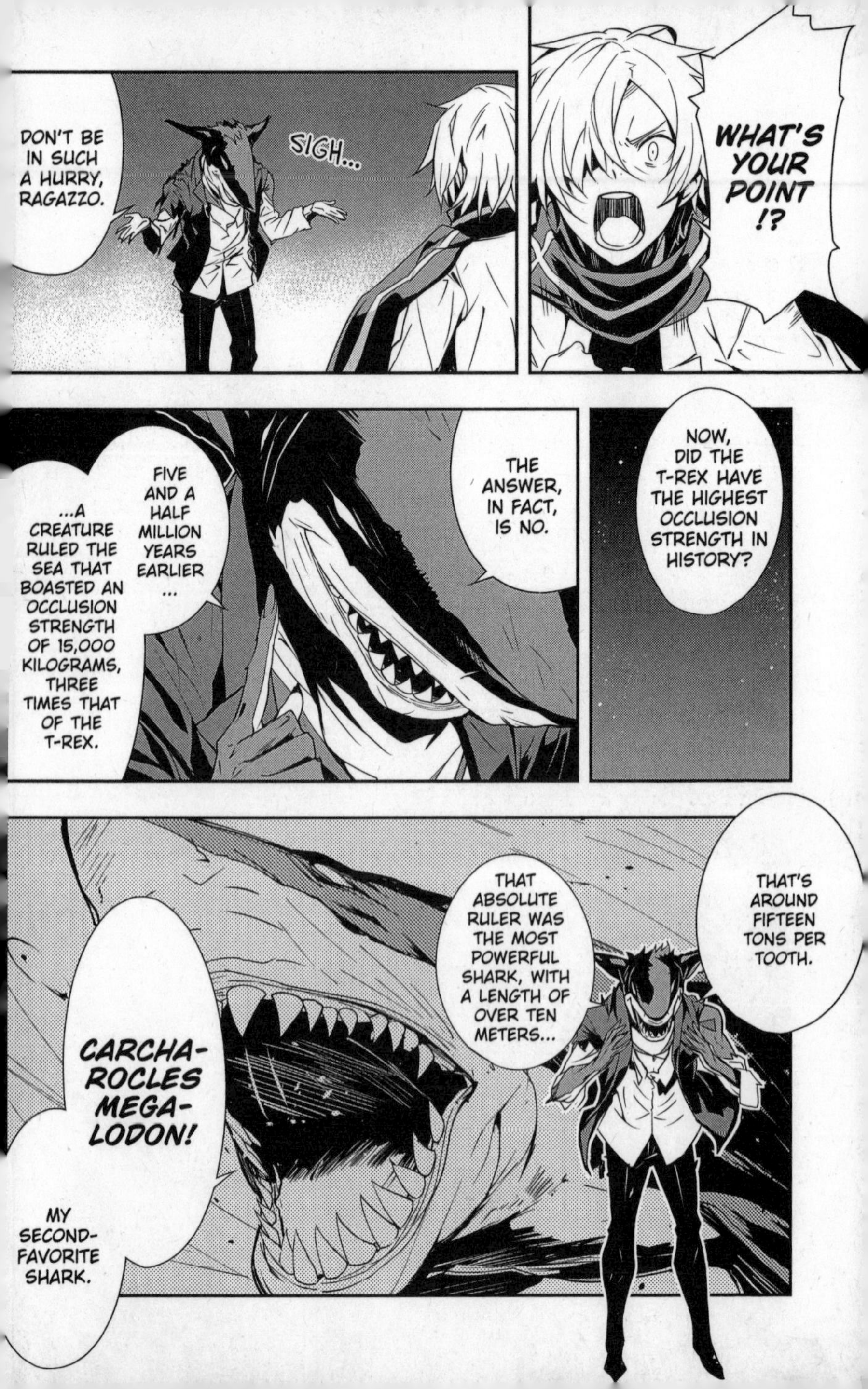
WHAT'S YOUR POINT !?
SIGH...
DON'T BE IN SUCH A HURRY, RAGAZZO.
NOW, DID THE T-REX HAVE THE HIGHEST OCCLUSION STRENGTH IN HISTORY?
THE ANSWER, IN FACT, IS NO.
FIVE AND A HALF MILLION YEARS EARLIER ...
...A CREATURE RULED THE SEA THAT BOASTED AN OCCLUSION STRENGTH OF 15,000 KILOGRAMS, THREE TIMES THAT OF THE T-REX.
THAT'S AROUND FIFTEEN TONS PER TOOTH.
THAT ABSOLUTE RULER WAS THE MOST POWERFUL SHARK, WITH A LENGTH OF OVER TEN METERS...
CARCHA-ROCLES MEGA-LODON!
MY SECOND-FAVORITE SHARK.

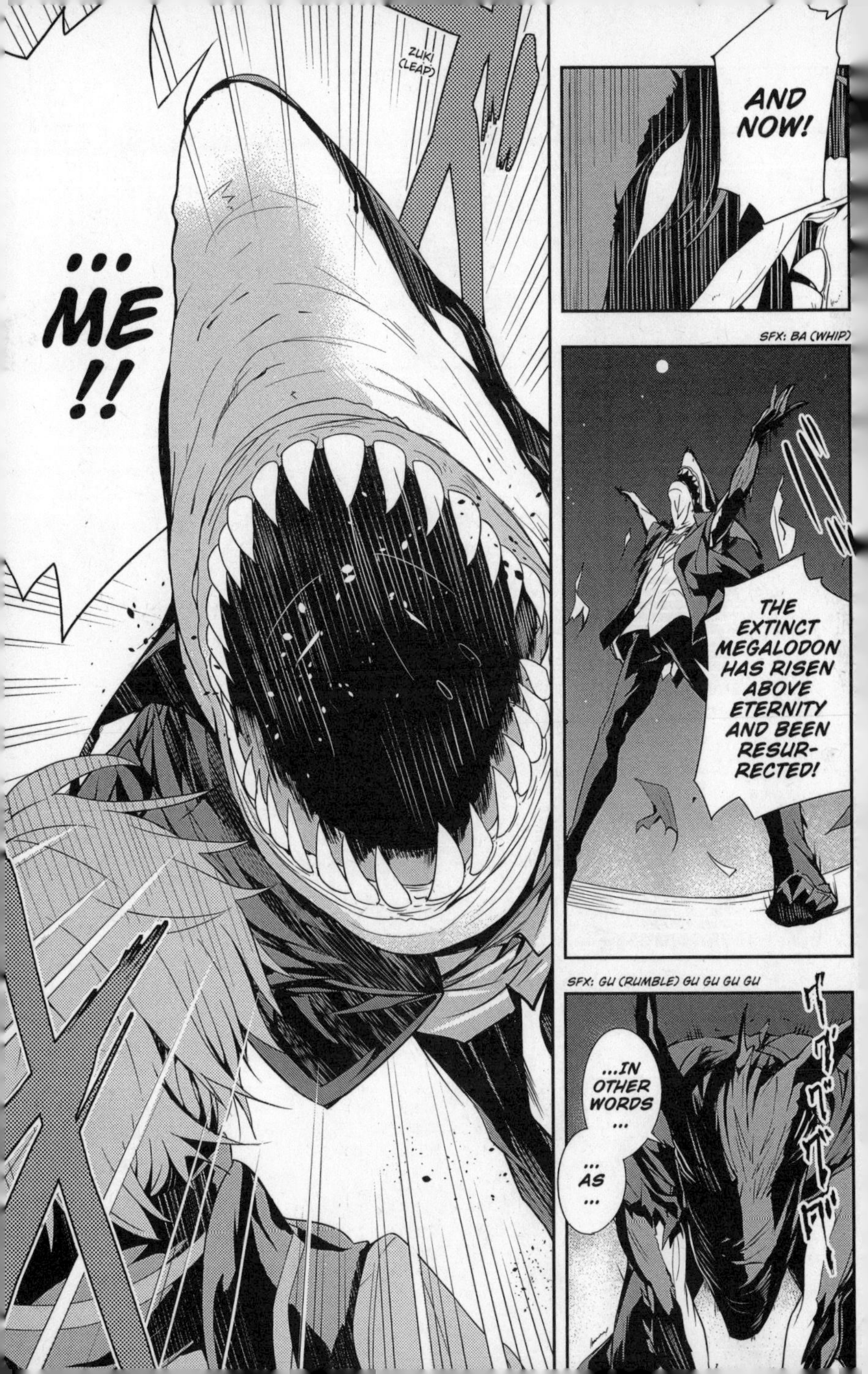
AND NOW!
SFX: BA (WHIP)
THE EXTINCT MEGALODON HAS RISEN ABOVE ETERNITY AND BEEN RESUR-RECTED!
SFX: GU (RUMBLE) GU GU GU GU
...IN OTHER WORDS...
...AS...
ZUKI (LEAP)
...ME!!

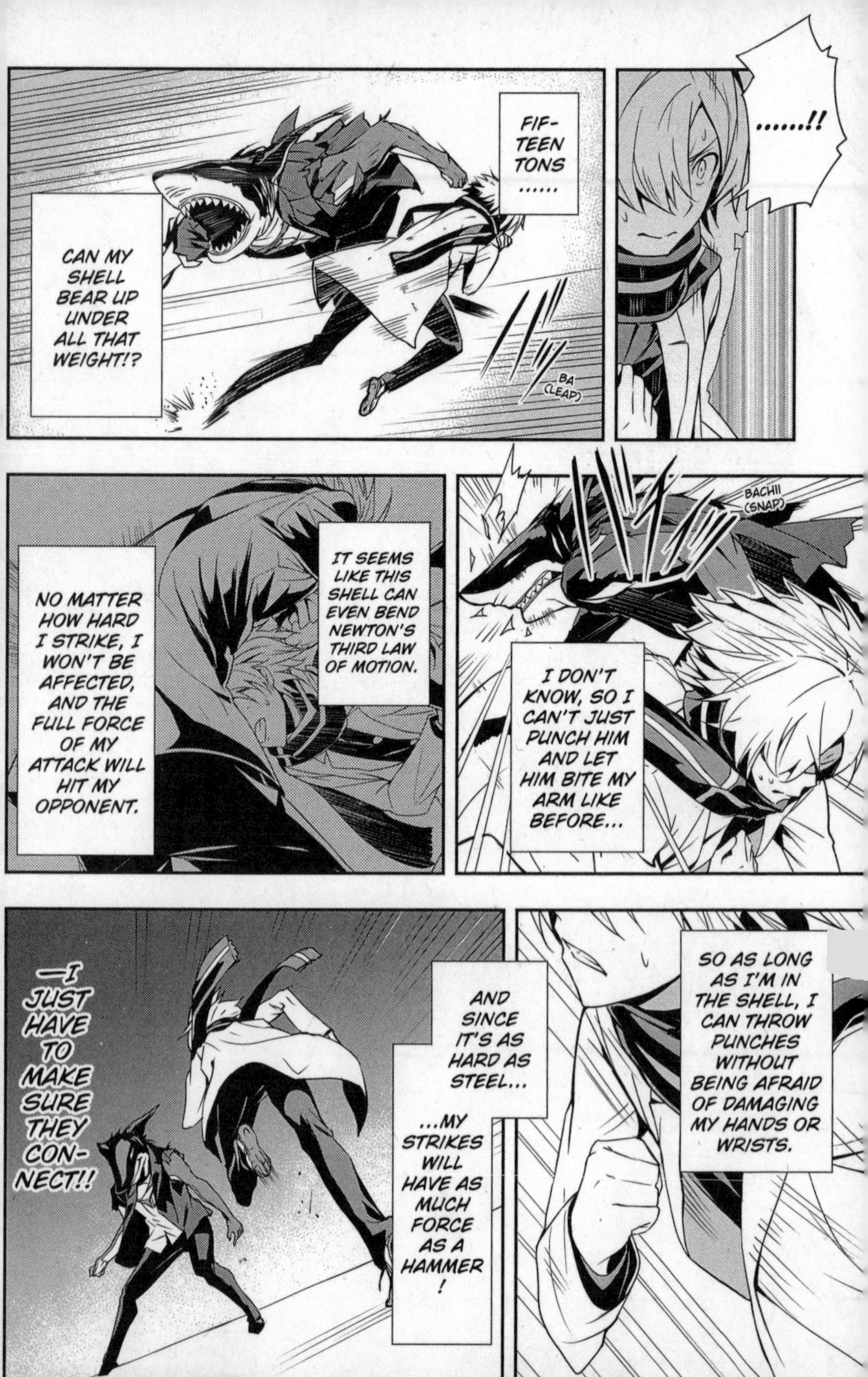
......!!
FIFTEEN TONS......
CAN MY SHELL BEAR UP UNDER ALL THAT WEIGHT!?
BA (LEAP)
BACHII (SNAP)
I DON'T KNOW, SO I CAN'T JUST PUNCH HIM AND LET HIM BITE MY ARM LIKE BEFORE...
IT SEEMS LIKE THIS SHELL CAN EVEN BEND NEWTON'S THIRD LAW OF MOTION.
NO MATTER HOW HARD I STRIKE, I WON'T BE AFFECTED, AND THE FULL FORCE OF MY ATTACK WILL HIT MY OPPONENT.
SO AS LONG AS I'M IN THE SHELL, I CAN THROW PUNCHES WITHOUT BEING AFRAID OF DAMAGING MY HANDS OR WRISTS.
AND SINCE IT'S AS HARD AS STEEL...
...MY STRIKES WILL HAVE AS MUCH FORCE AS A HAMMER!
—I JUST HAVE TO MAKE SURE THEY CONNECT!!

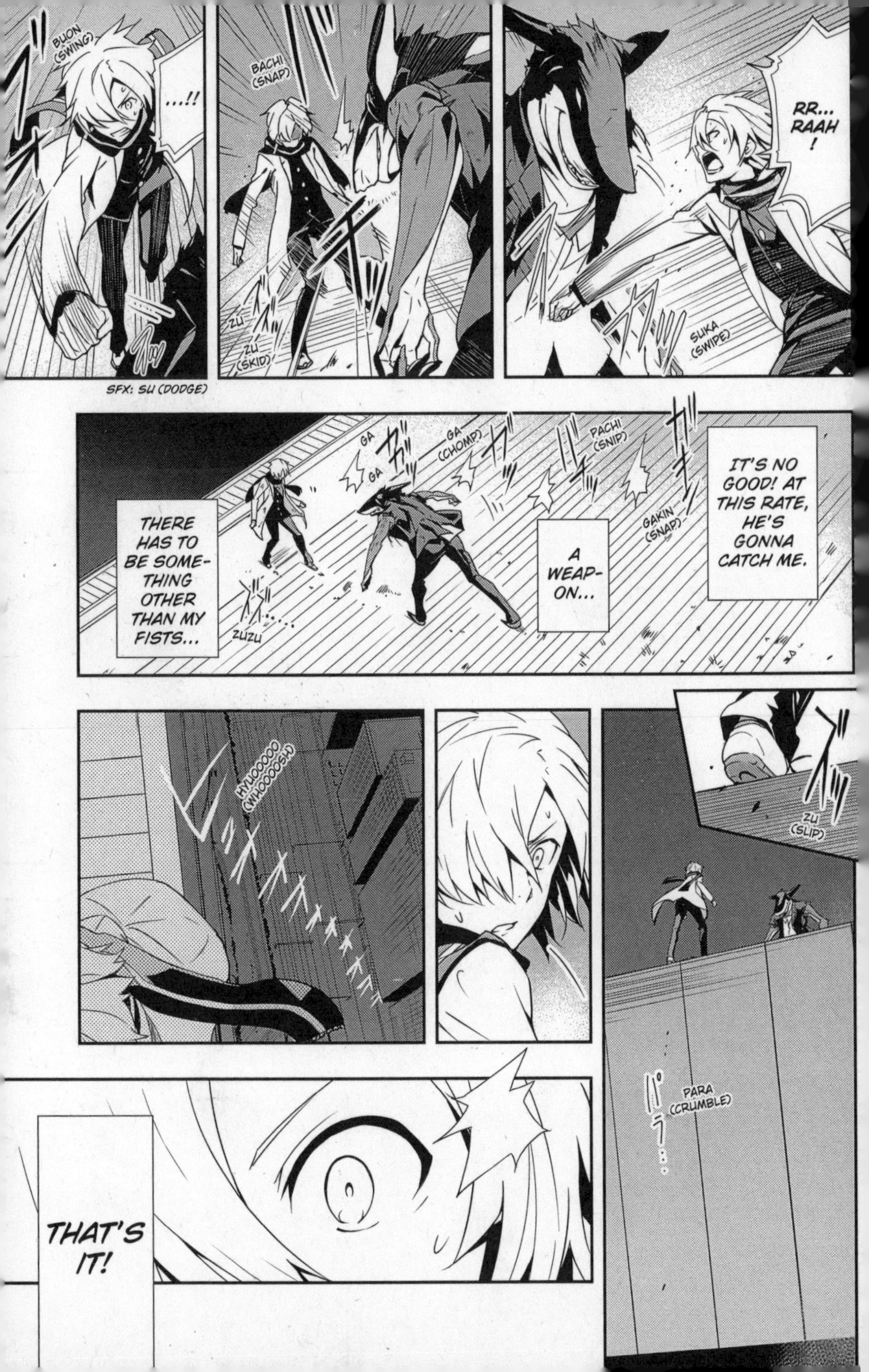
RR... RAAH!
SUKA (SWIPE)
BACHI (SNAP)
ZU ZU (SKID)
BUON (SWING)
...!!
SFX: SU (DODGE)
IT'S NO GOOD! AT THIS RATE, HE'S GONNA CATCH ME.
GAKIN (SNAP)
PACHI (SNIP)
GA (CHOMP)
GA GA
A WEAP-ON...
THERE HAS TO BE SOME-THING OTHER THAN MY FISTS...
ZUZU
ZU (SLIP)
PARA (CRUMBLE)
HYUOOOOO (WHOOOOSH)
THAT'S IT!

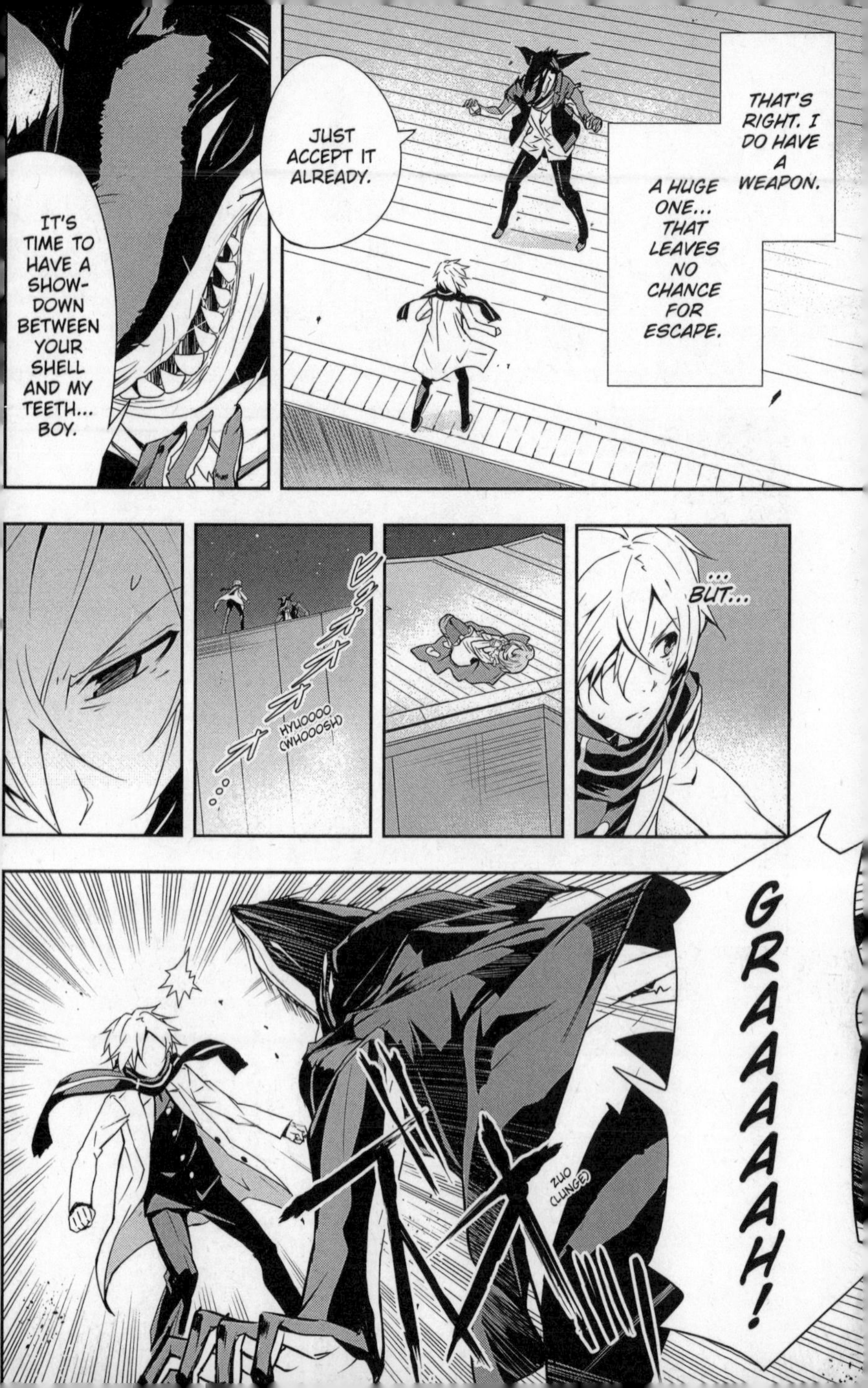
THAT'S RIGHT. I DO HAVE A WEAPON.
A HUGE ONE... THAT LEAVES NO CHANCE FOR ESCAPE.
JUST ACCEPT IT ALREADY.
IT'S TIME TO HAVE A SHOW-DOWN BETWEEN YOUR SHELL AND MY TEETH... BOY.
...BUT...
HYUOOOO (WHOOOSH)
GRAAAAAH!
ZUO (LUNGE)

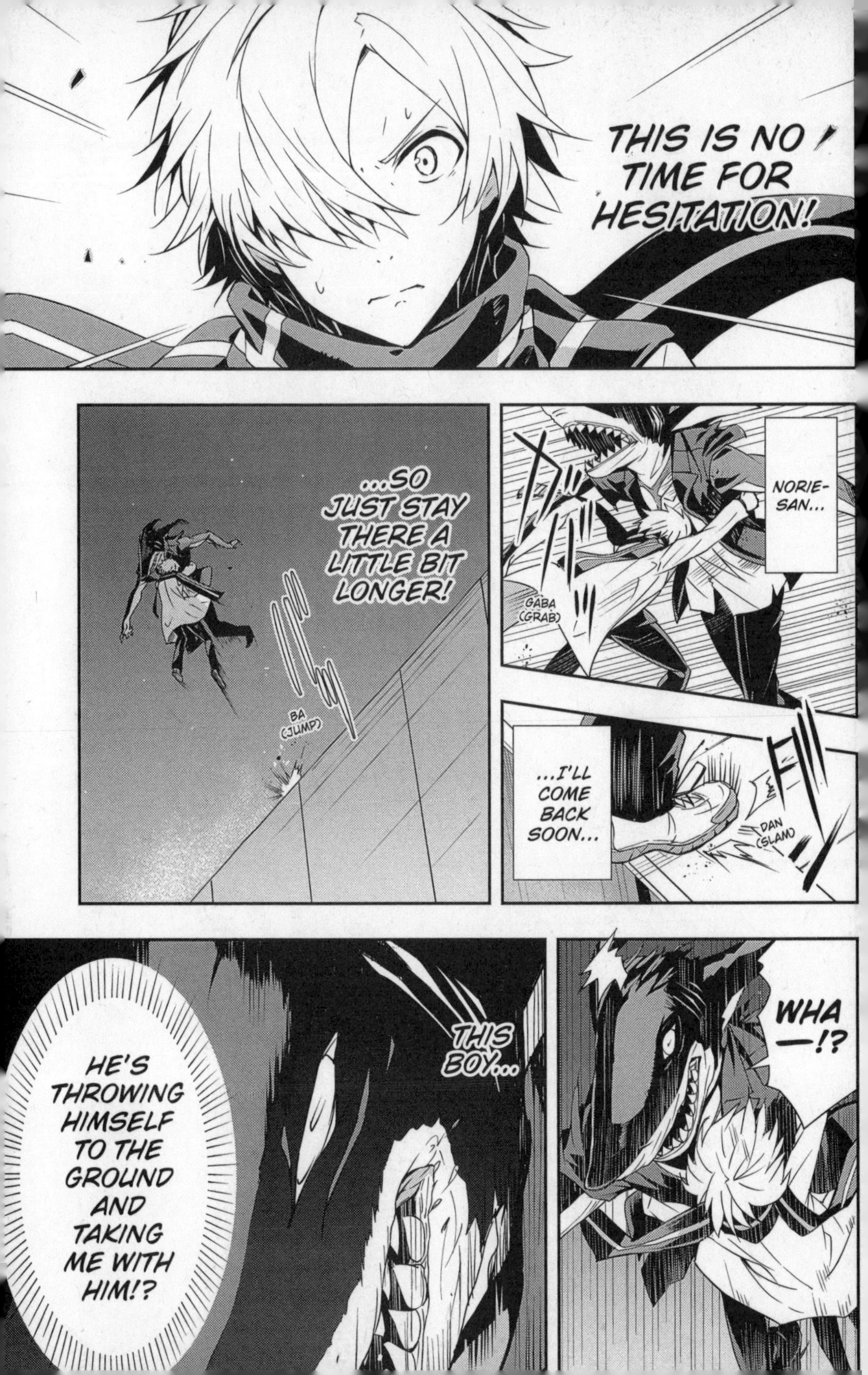
THIS IS NO TIME FOR HESITATION!
NORIE-SAN...
GABA (GRAB)
...I'LL COME BACK SOON...
DAN (SLAM)
...SO JUST STAY THERE A LITTLE BIT LONGER!
BA (JUMP)
WHA—!?
THIS BOY...
HE'S THROWING HIMSELF TO THE GROUND AND TAKING ME WITH HIM!?

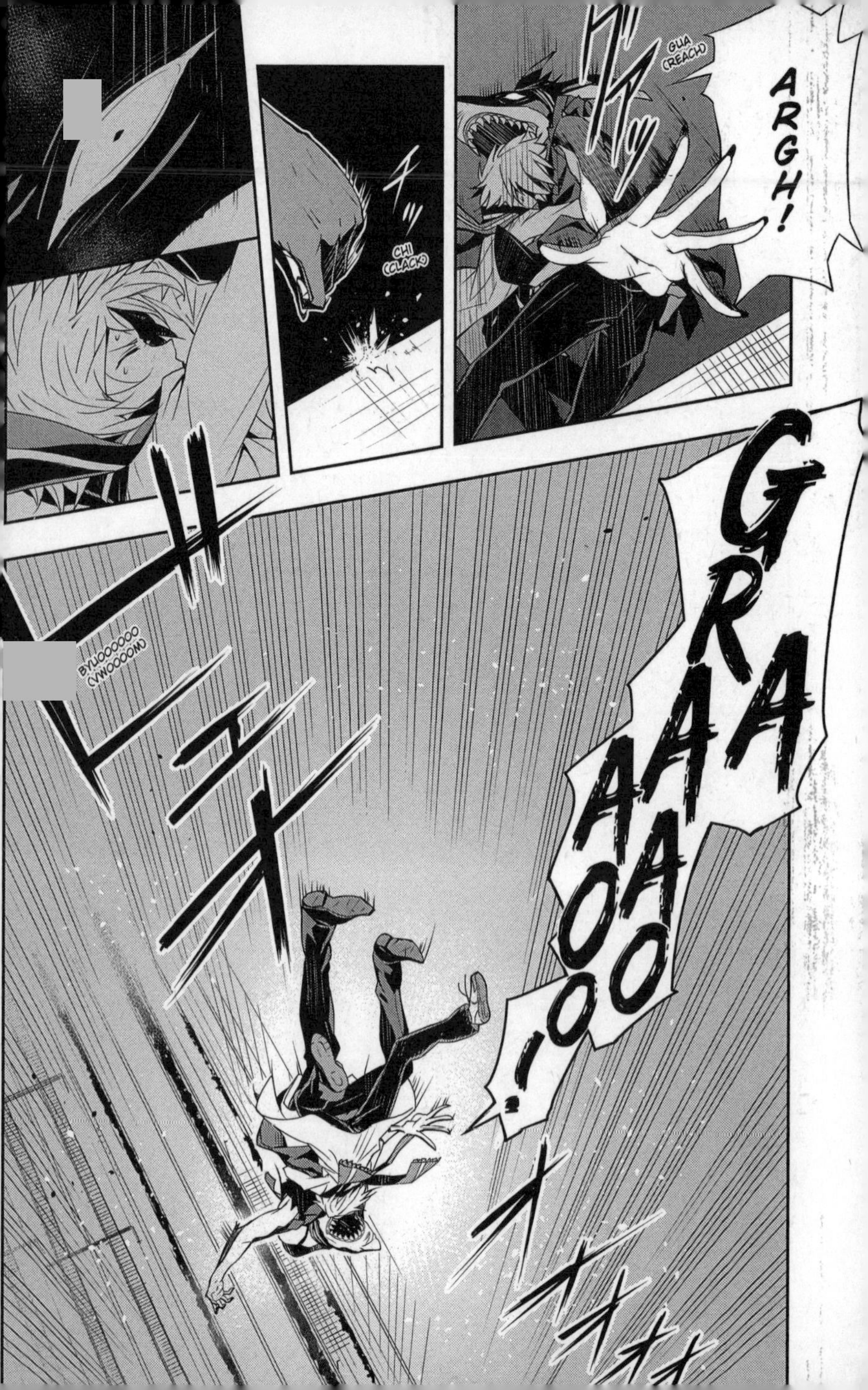
GUA (REACH)
ARGH!
CHI (CLACK)
GRAAAAAOAOOO!
BYUOOOOOO (VWOOOOM)

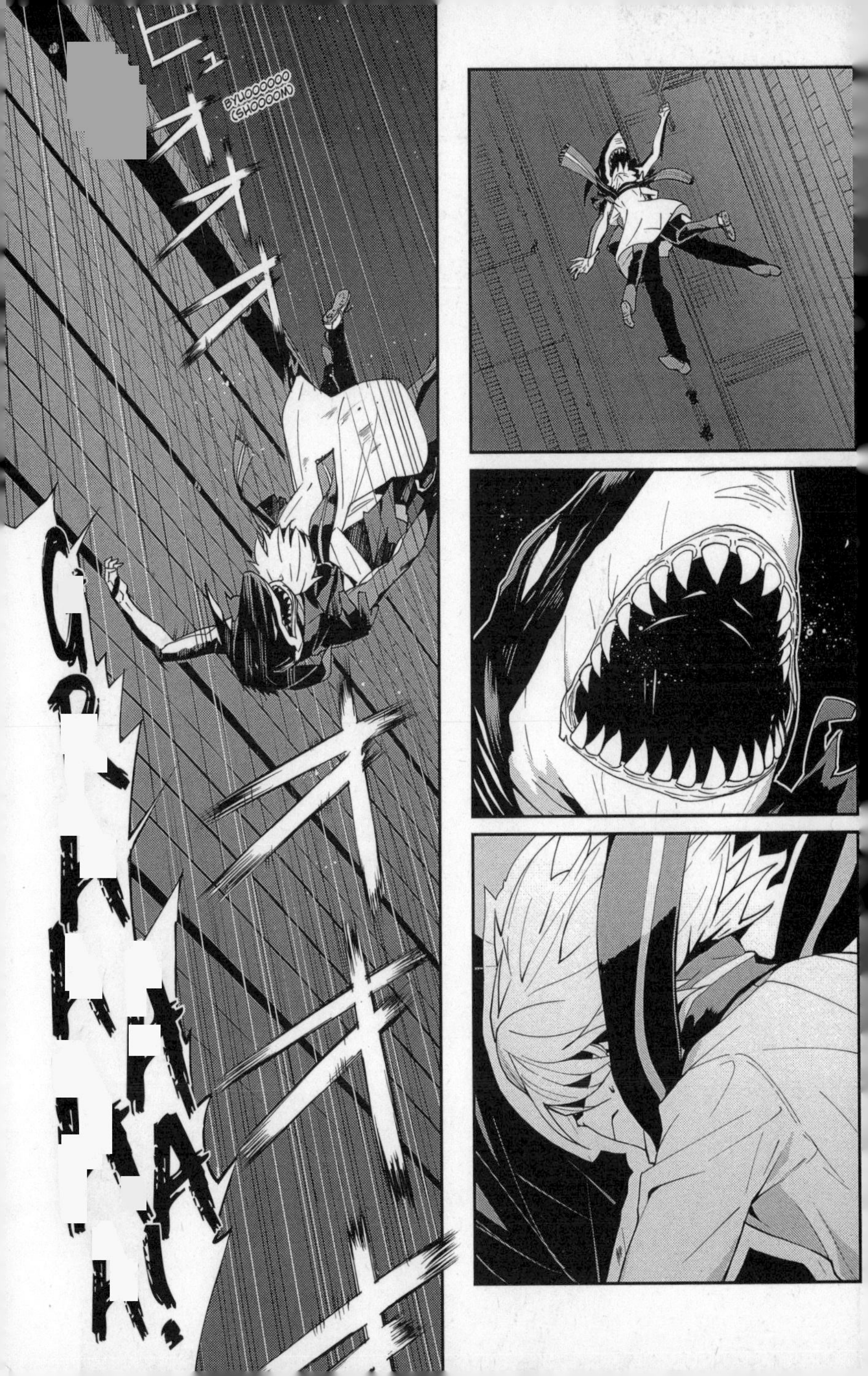
BYUOOOOO
(SHOOOOM)

Sect. 010
KILLING INTENT

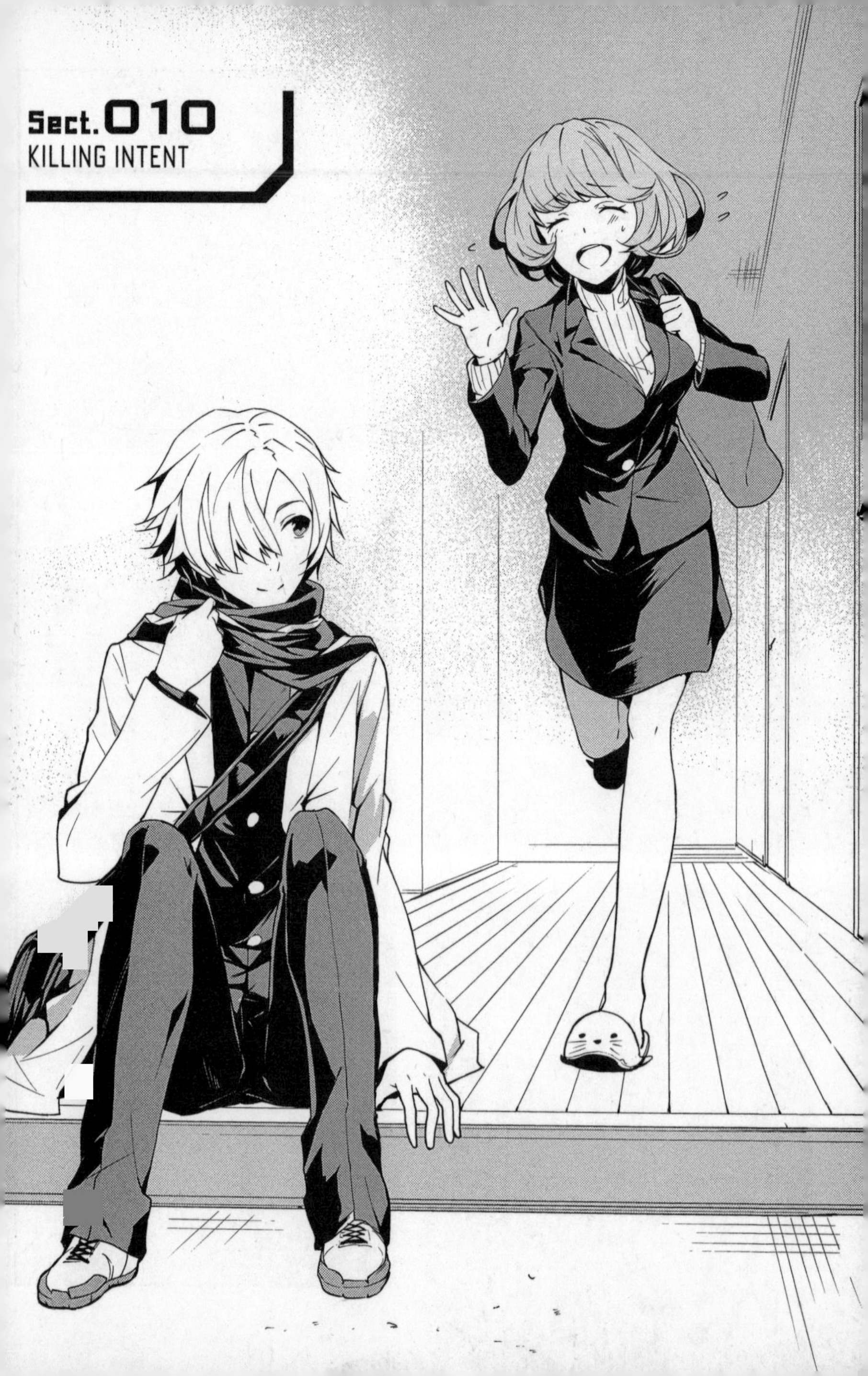

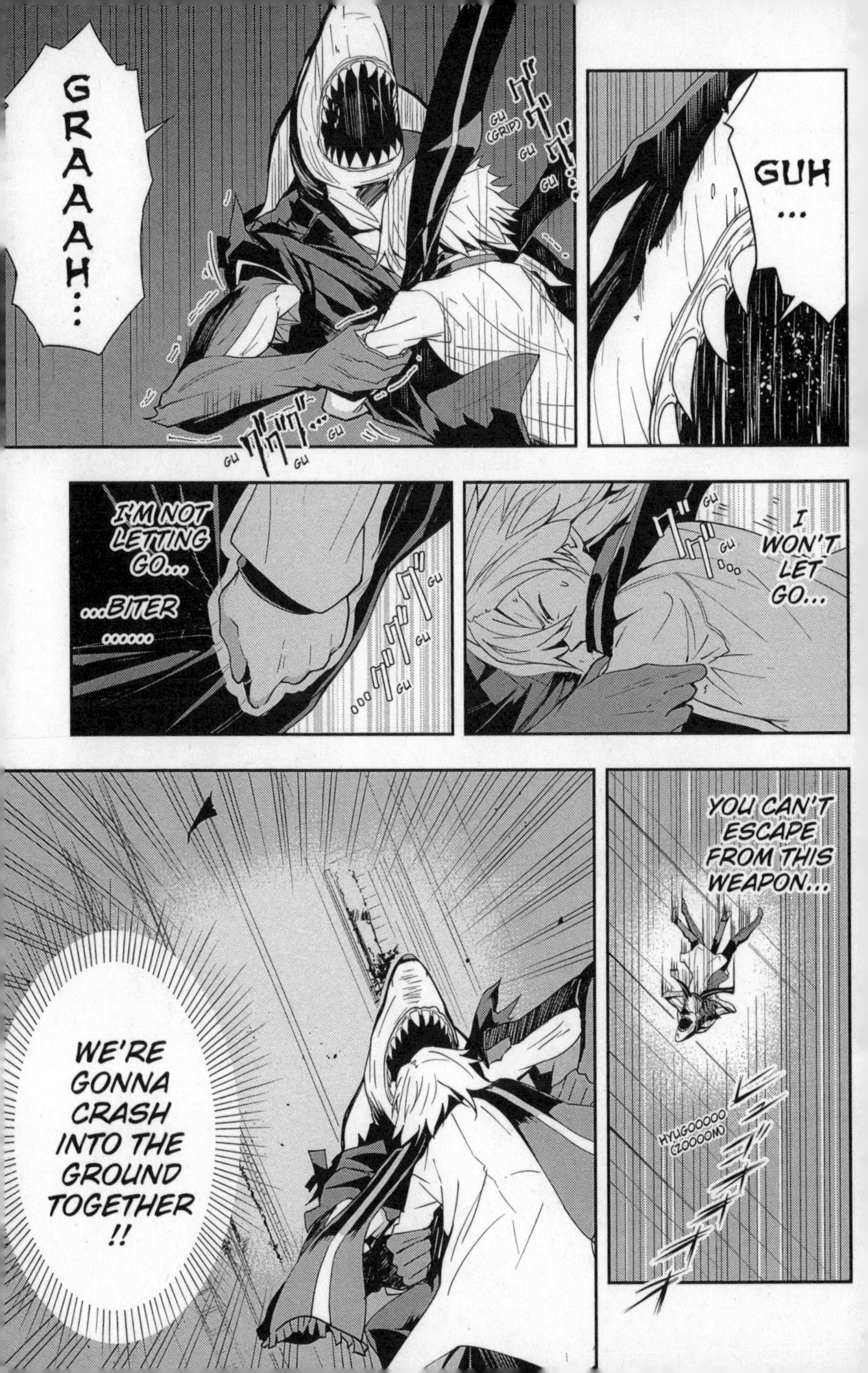
GUH ...
GRAAAH...
GU (GRIP)
GU
GU
GU
GU
I WON'T LET GO...
GU
GU
I'M NOT LETTING GO...
...BITER ......
GU
GU
GU
YOU CAN'T ESCAPE FROM THIS WEAPON...
HYUGOOOOO (ZOOOOM)
WE'RE GONNA CRASH INTO THE GROUND TOGETHER !!

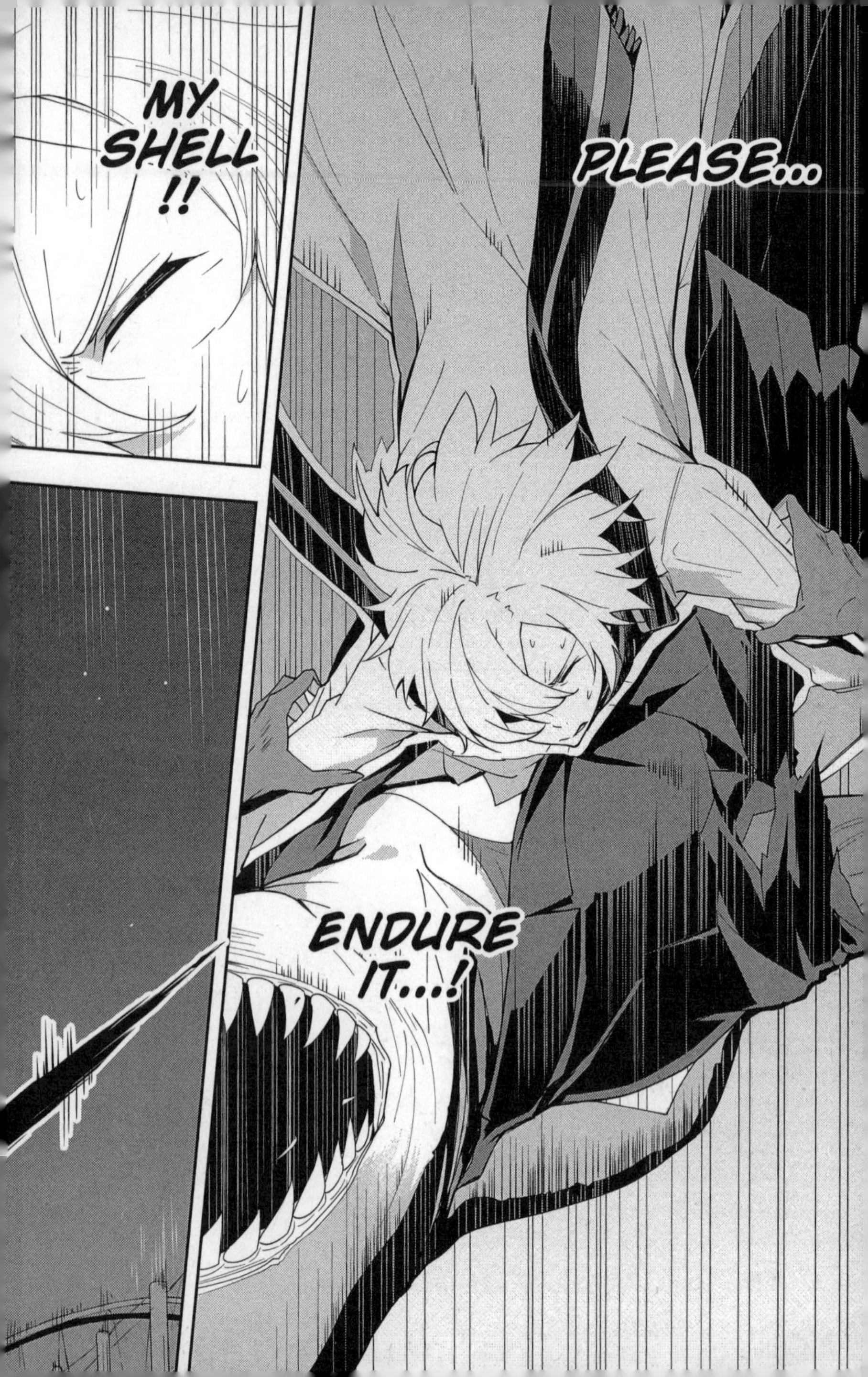
PLEASE...
ENDURE IT...!
MY SHELL!!

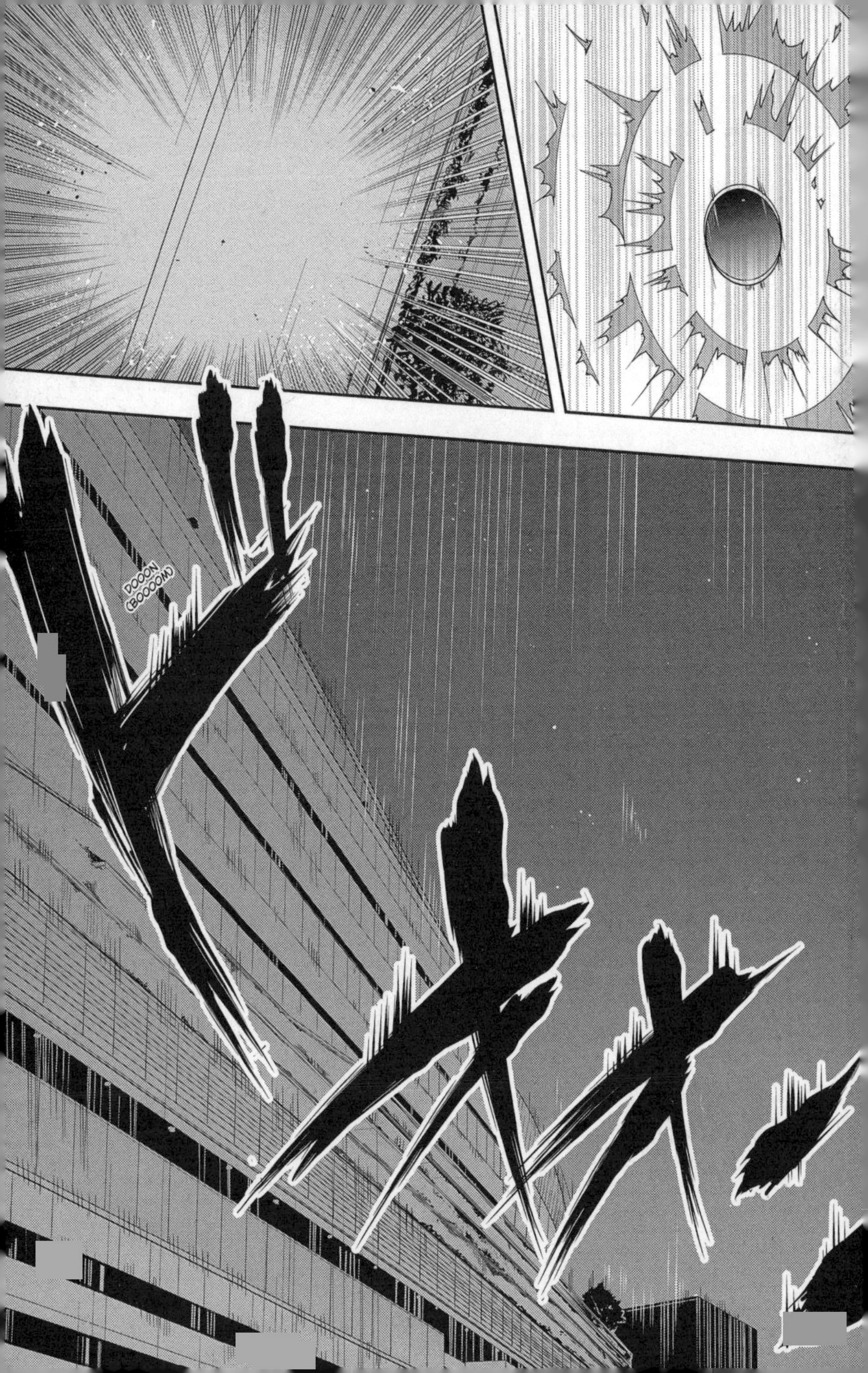
DOOON
(BOOOOM)

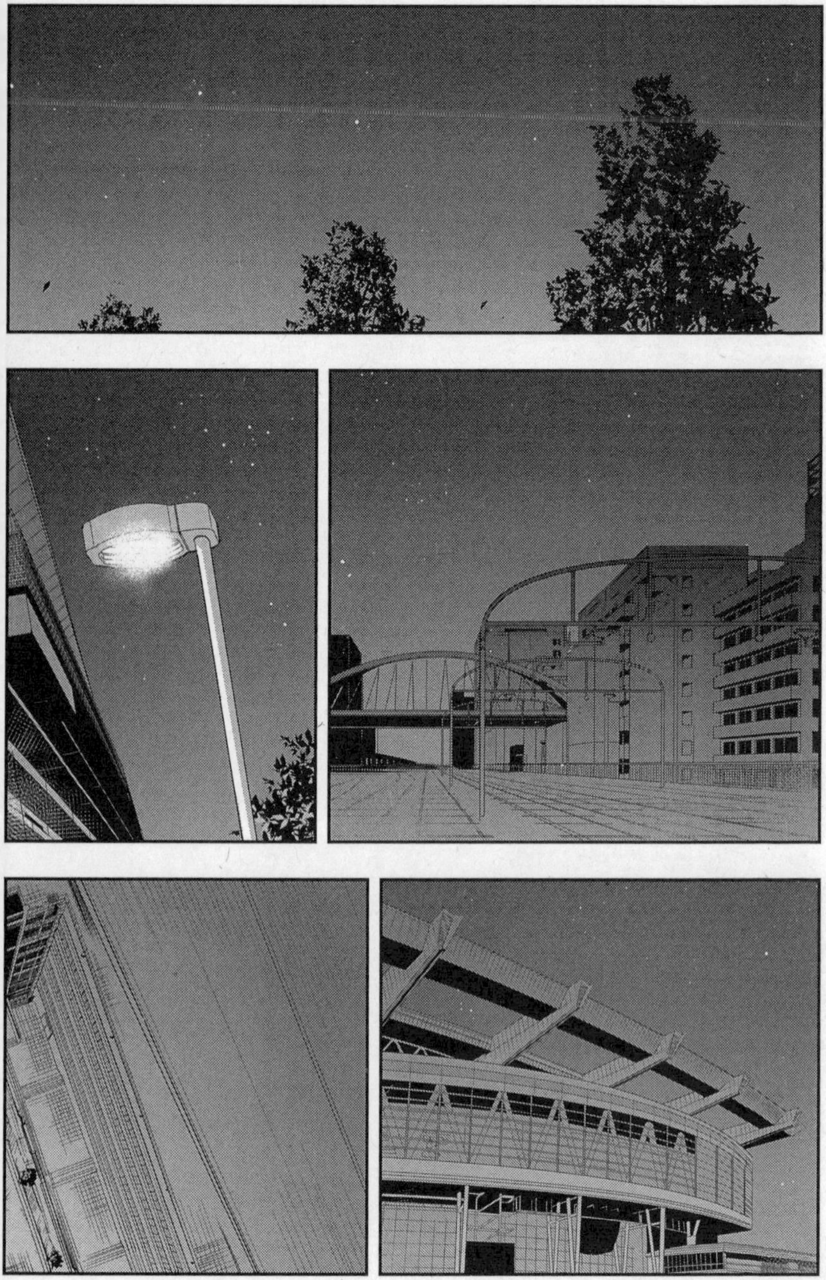

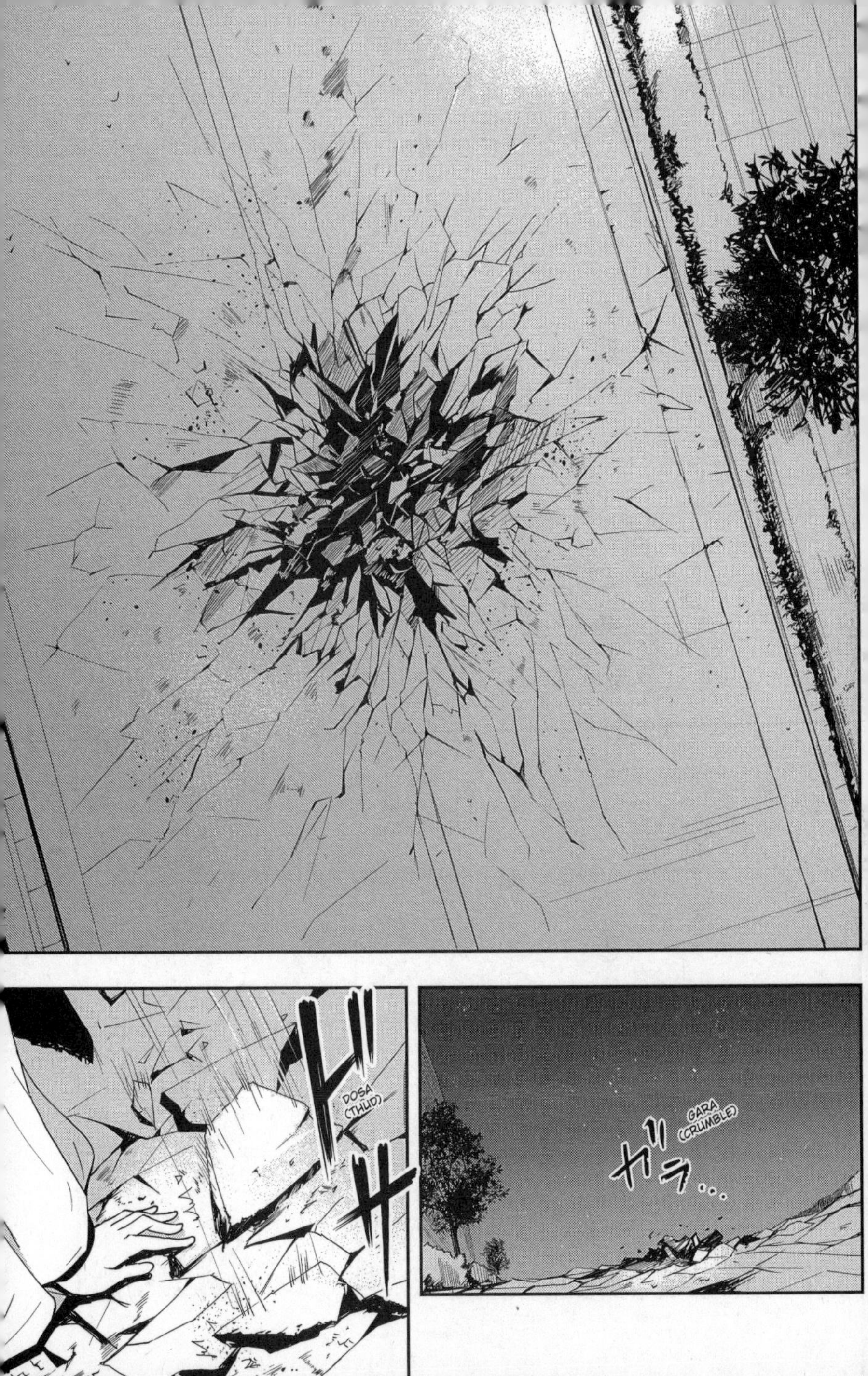
ガラ…
GARA (CRUMBLE)
ドサ
DOSA (THUD)

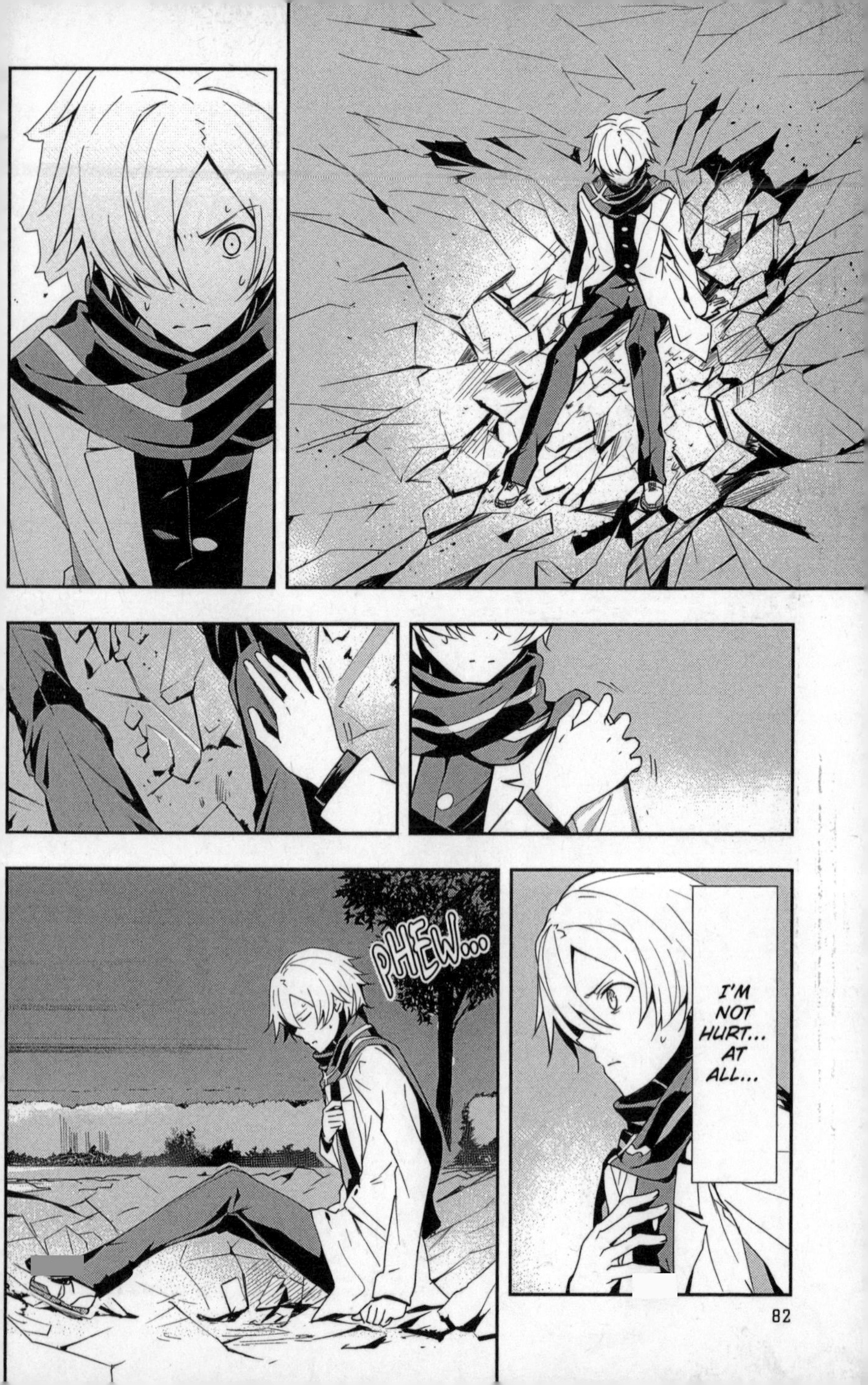
I'M NOT HURT... AT ALL...
PHEW...

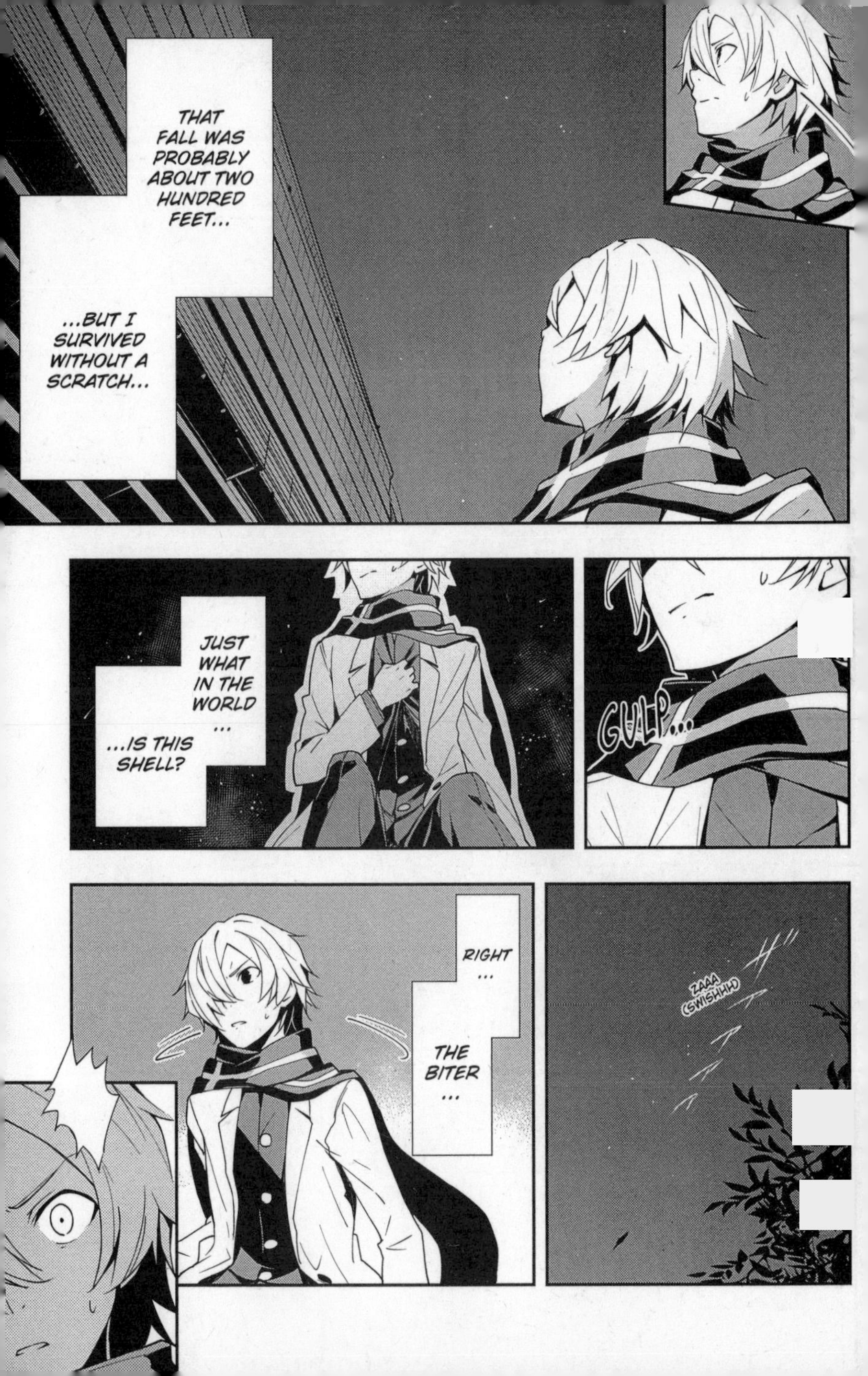
THAT FALL WAS PROBABLY ABOUT TWO HUNDRED FEET...
...BUT I SURVIVED WITHOUT A SCRATCH...
GULP...
JUST WHAT IN THE WORLD...
...IS THIS SHELL?
ZAAA (SWISHHH)
RIGHT...
THE BITER...

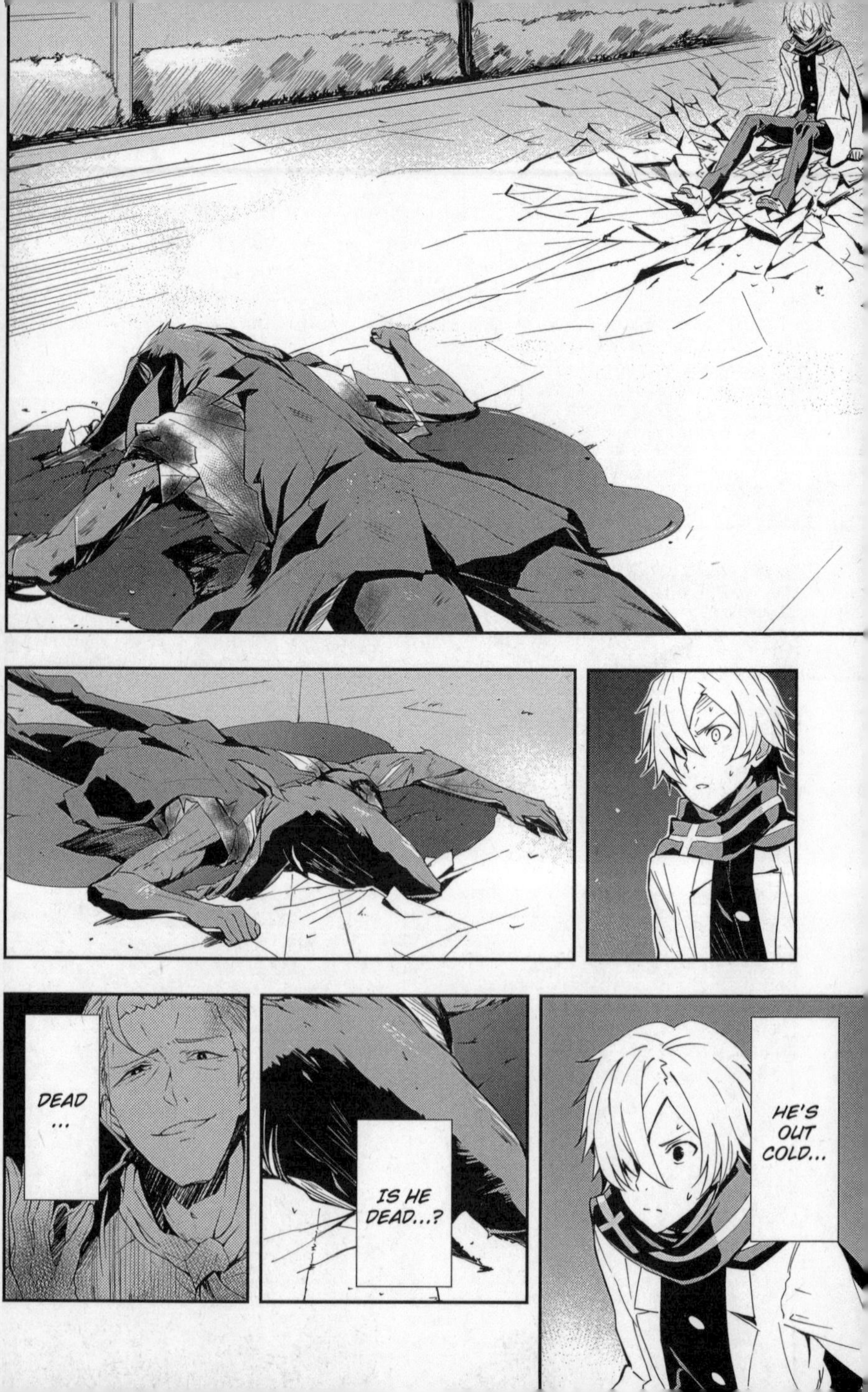
HE'S OUT COLD...
IS HE DEAD...?
DEAD...

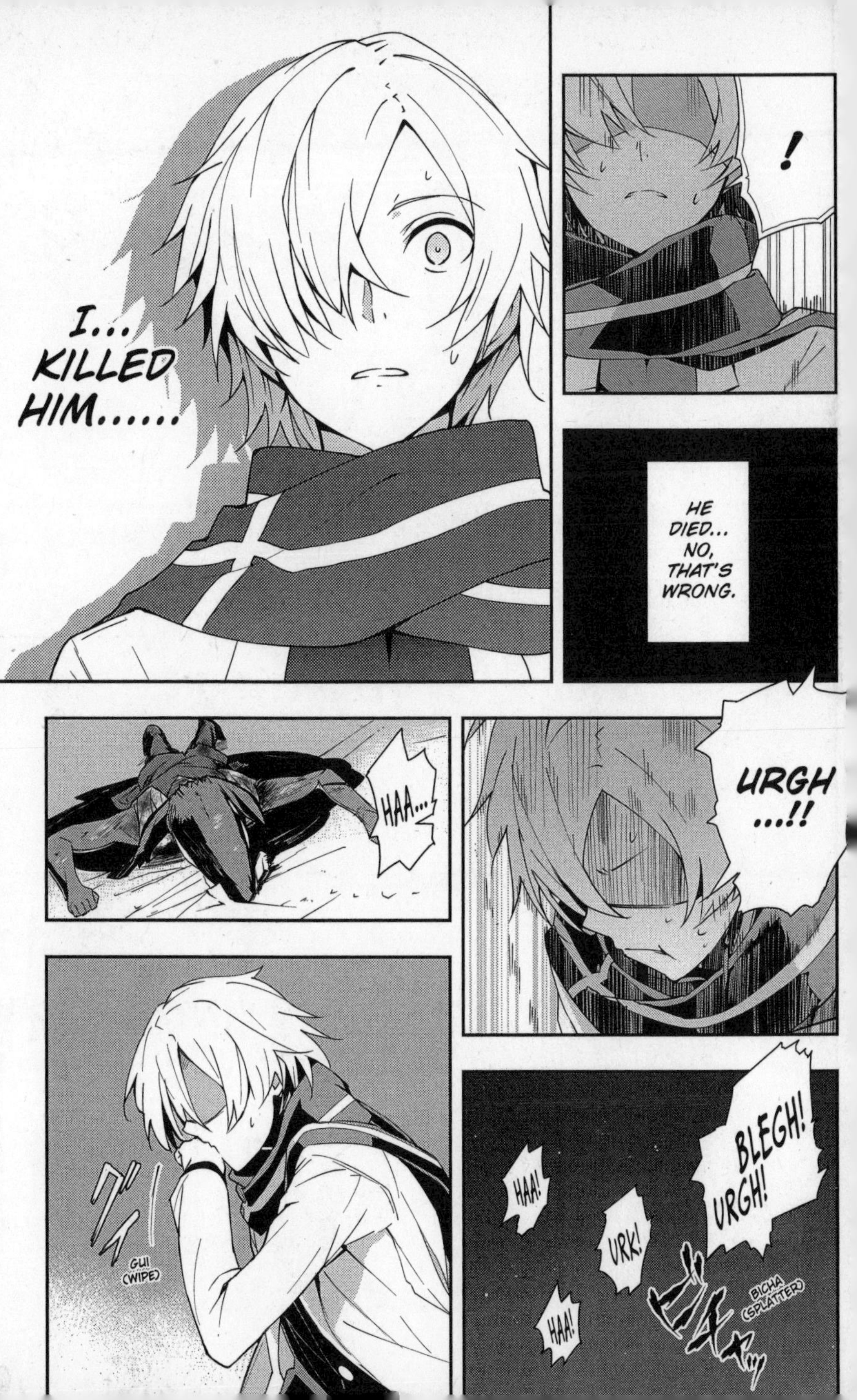
!
HE DIED... NO, THAT'S WRONG.
I... KILLED HIM......
URGH ...!!
HAA...
BLEGH! URGH!
HAA!
URK!
BICHA (SPLATTER)
HAA!
GUI (WIPE)

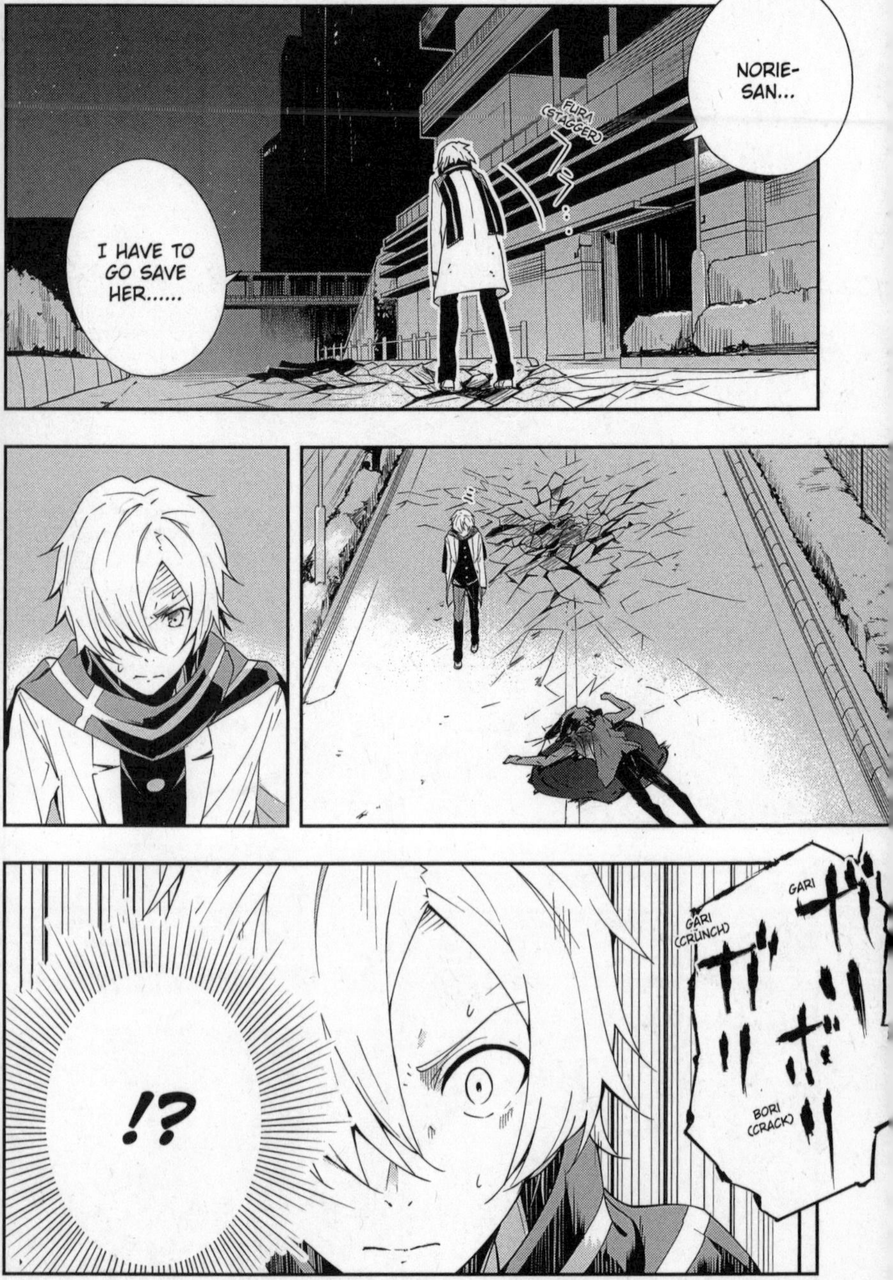
NORIE-SAN...
FURA (STAGGER)
I HAVE TO GO SAVE HER......
GARI
GARI (CRUNCH)
BORI (CRACK)
!?

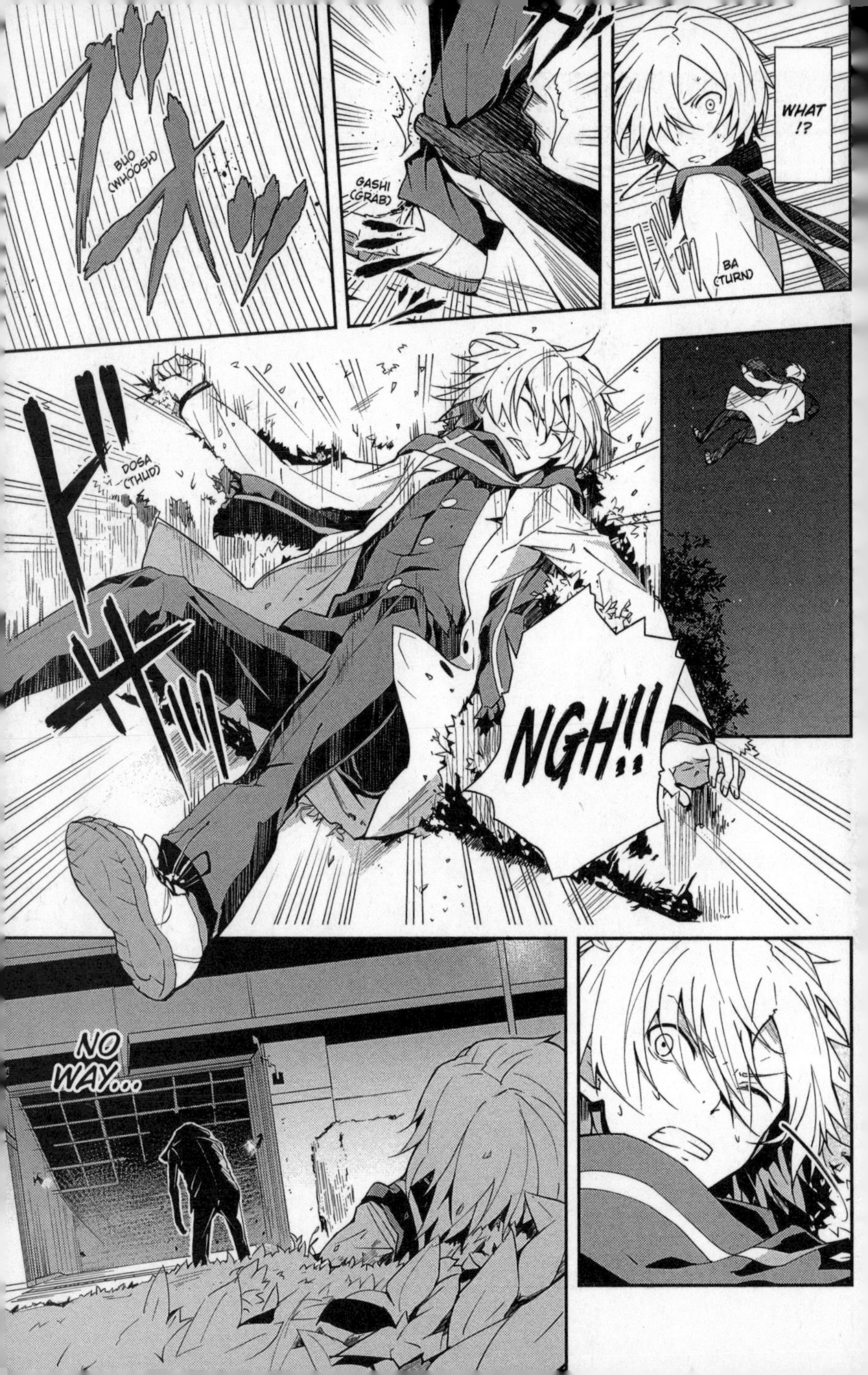
WHAT !?
BA (TURN)
GASHI (GRAB)
BUO (WHOOSH)
DOSA (THUD)
NGH!!
NO WAY...

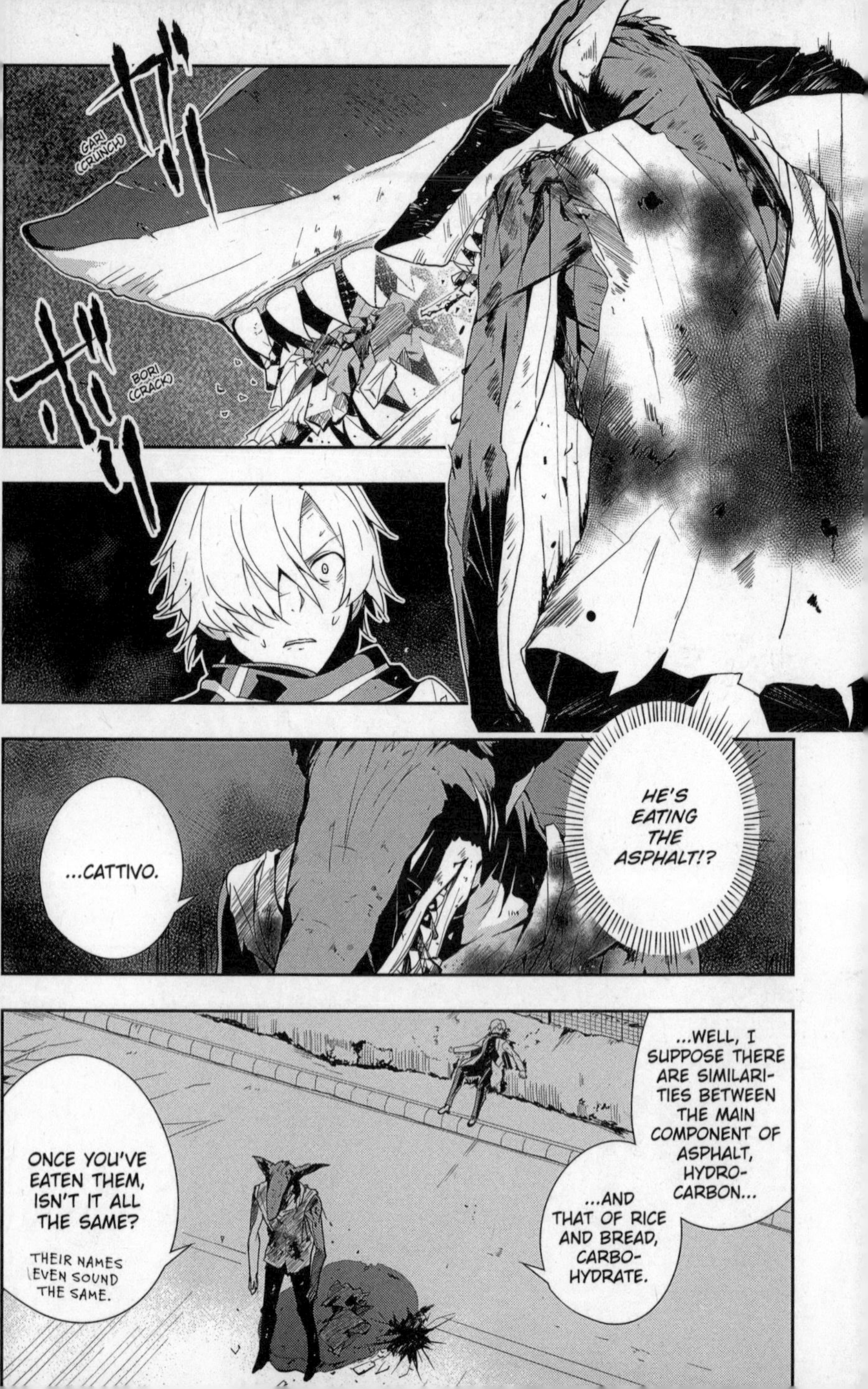
GARI (CRUNCH)
BORI (CRACK)
HE'S EATING THE ASPHALT!?
...CATTIVO.
...WELL, I SUPPOSE THERE ARE SIMILARI-TIES BETWEEN THE MAIN COMPONENT OF ASPHALT, HYDRO-CARBON...
...AND THAT OF RICE AND BREAD, CARBO-HYDRATE.
ONCE YOU'VE EATEN THEM, ISN'T IT ALL THE SAME?
THEIR NAMES EVEN SOUND THE SAME.

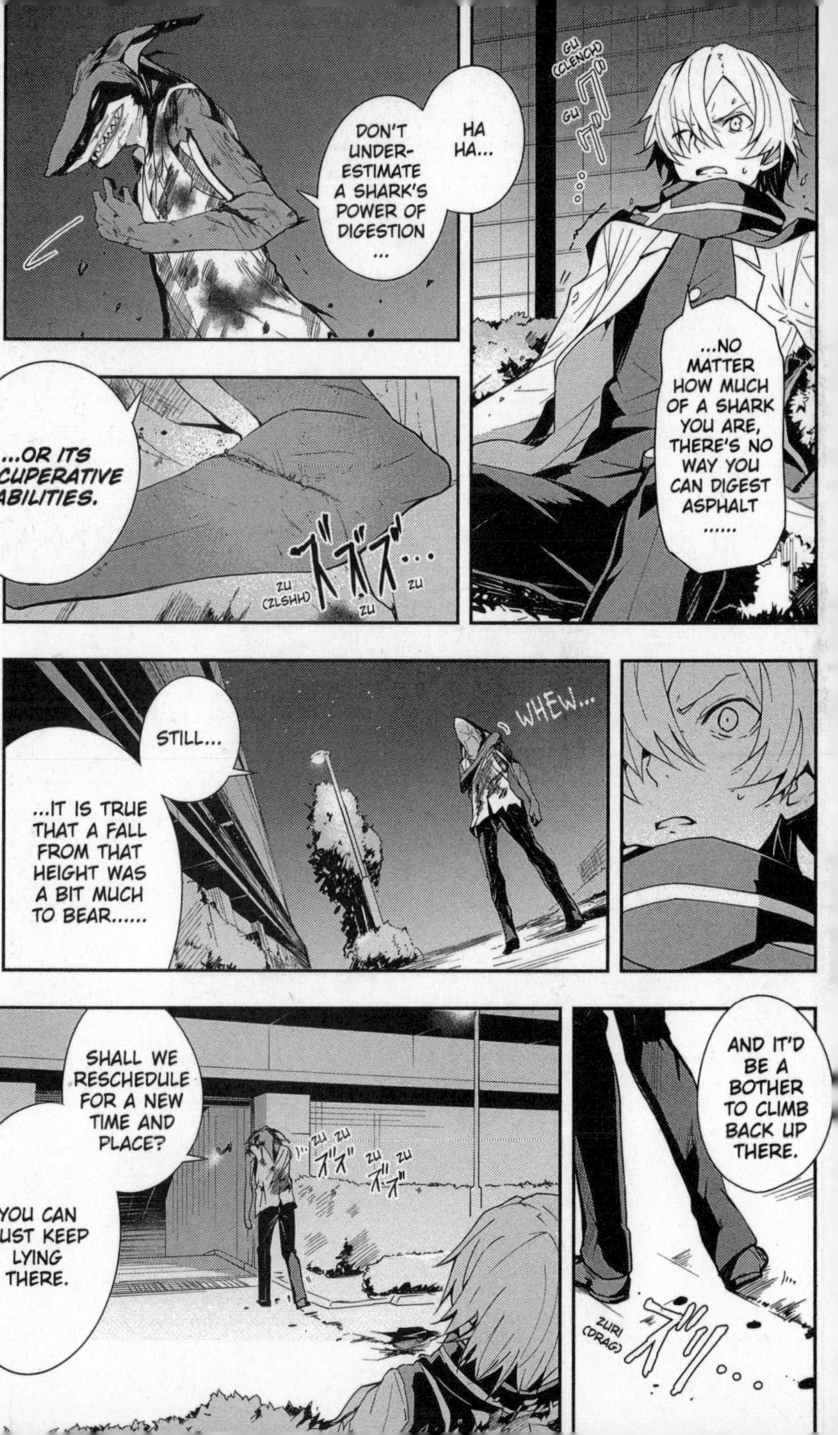
GU (CLENCH) GU...
...NO MATTER HOW MUCH OF A SHARK YOU ARE, THERE'S NO WAY YOU CAN DIGEST ASPHALT ......
HA HA...
DON'T UNDER-ESTIMATE A SHARK'S POWER OF DIGESTION ...
...OR ITS RECUPERATIVE ABILITIES.
ZU (ZLSHH) ZU ZU...
WHEW...
STILL...
...IT IS TRUE THAT A FALL FROM THAT HEIGHT WAS A BIT MUCH TO BEAR......
AND IT'D BE A BOTHER TO CLIMB BACK UP THERE.
ZURI (DRAG)...
ZU ZU ZU ZU
SHALL WE RESCHEDULE FOR A NEW TIME AND PLACE?
YOU CAN JUST KEEP LYING THERE.

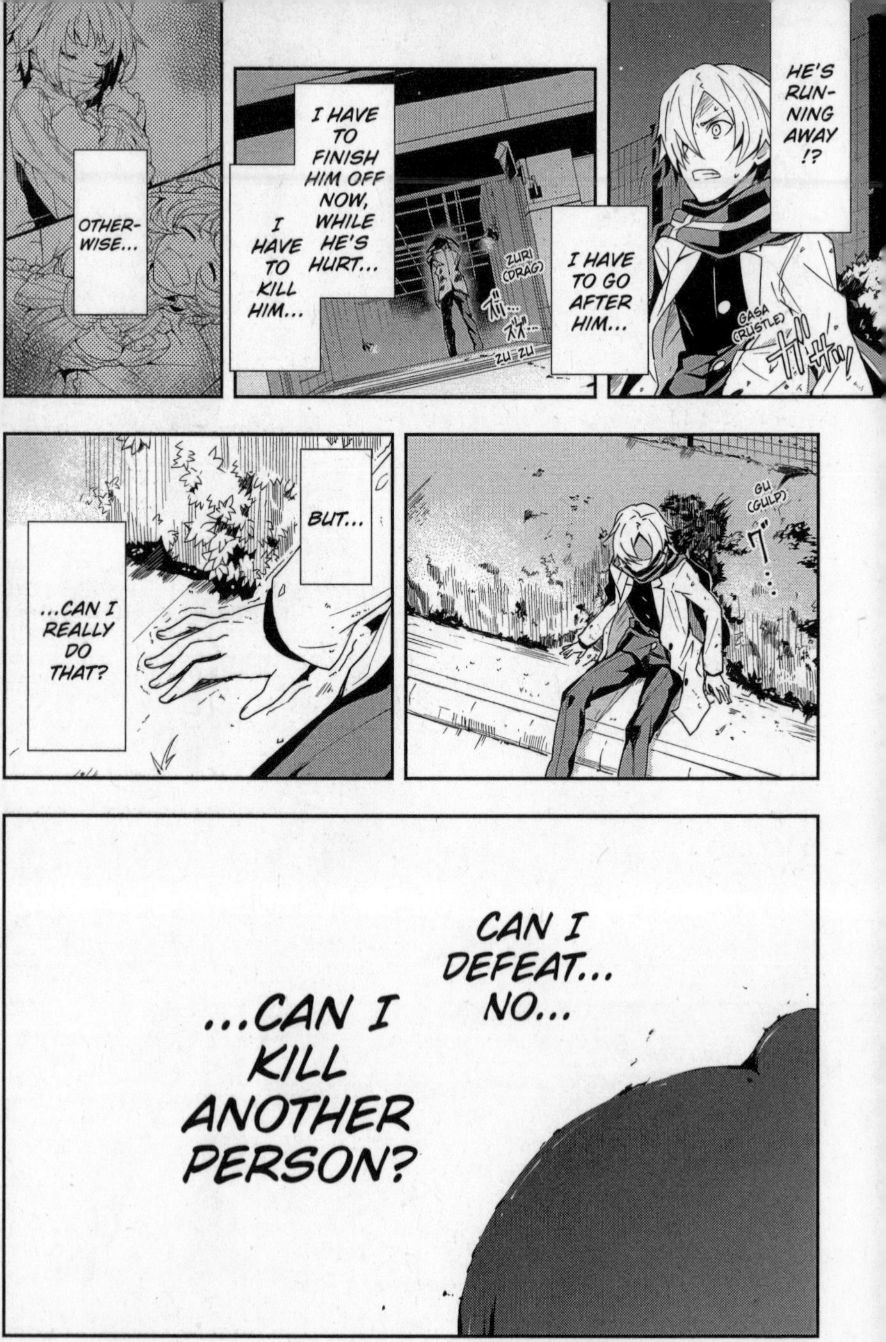
HE'S RUN-NING AWAY!?
GASA (RUSTLE)
I HAVE TO GO AFTER HIM...
ZURI (DRAG)
ZU ZU
I HAVE TO FINISH HIM OFF NOW, WHILE HE'S HURT...
I HAVE TO KILL HIM...
OTHER-WISE...
GU (GULP)
BUT...
...CAN I REALLY DO THAT?
CAN I DEFEAT... NO...
...CAN I KILL ANOTHER PERSON?

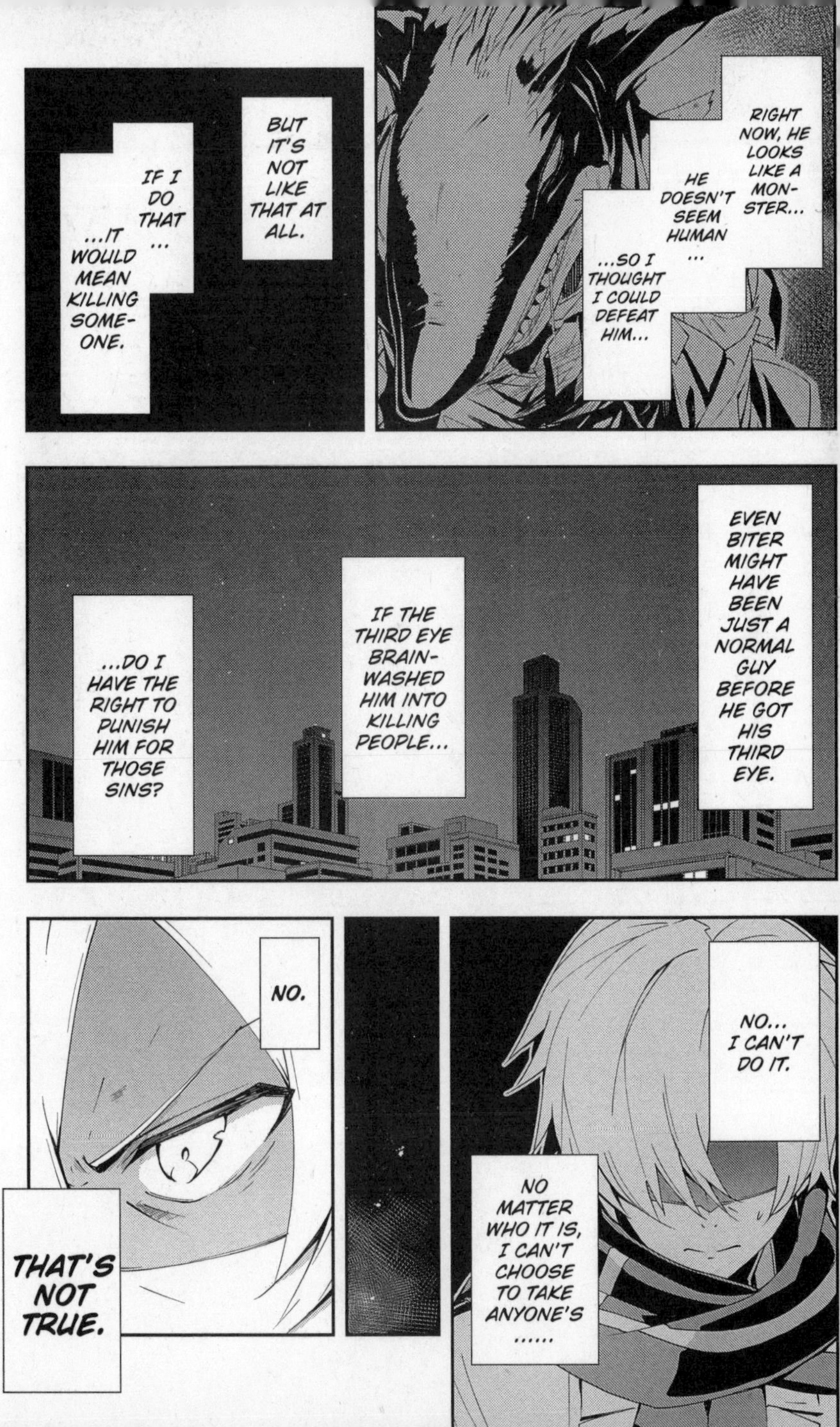
RIGHT NOW, HE LOOKS LIKE A MON-STER...
HE DOESN'T SEEM HUMAN...
...SO I THOUGHT I COULD DEFEAT HIM...
BUT IT'S NOT LIKE THAT AT ALL.
IF I DO THAT...
...IT WOULD MEAN KILLING SOME-ONE.
EVEN BITER MIGHT HAVE BEEN JUST A NORMAL GUY BEFORE HE GOT HIS THIRD EYE.
IF THE THIRD EYE BRAIN-WASHED HIM INTO KILLING PEOPLE...
...DO I HAVE THE RIGHT TO PUNISH HIM FOR THOSE SINS?
NO... I CAN'T DO IT.
NO MATTER WHO IT IS, I CAN'T CHOOSE TO TAKE ANYONE'S ......
NO.
THAT'S NOT TRUE.

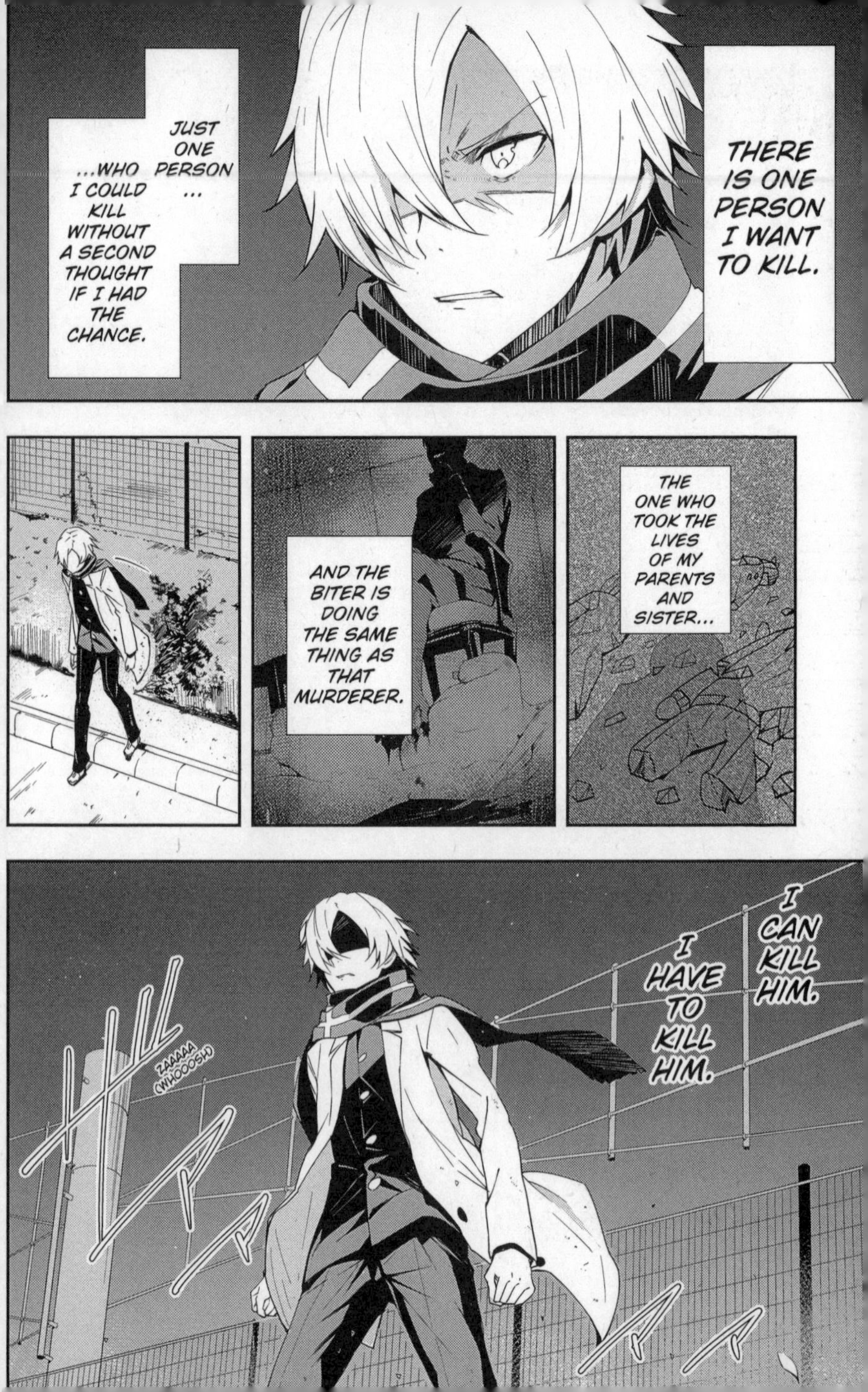
THERE IS ONE PERSON I WANT TO KILL.
JUST ONE PERSON...
...WHO I COULD KILL WITHOUT A SECOND THOUGHT IF I HAD THE CHANCE.
THE ONE WHO TOOK THE LIVES OF MY PARENTS AND SISTER...
AND THE BITER IS DOING THE SAME THING AS THAT MURDERER.
I CAN KILL HIM.
I HAVE TO KILL HIM.
ZAAAAA (WHOOOSH)

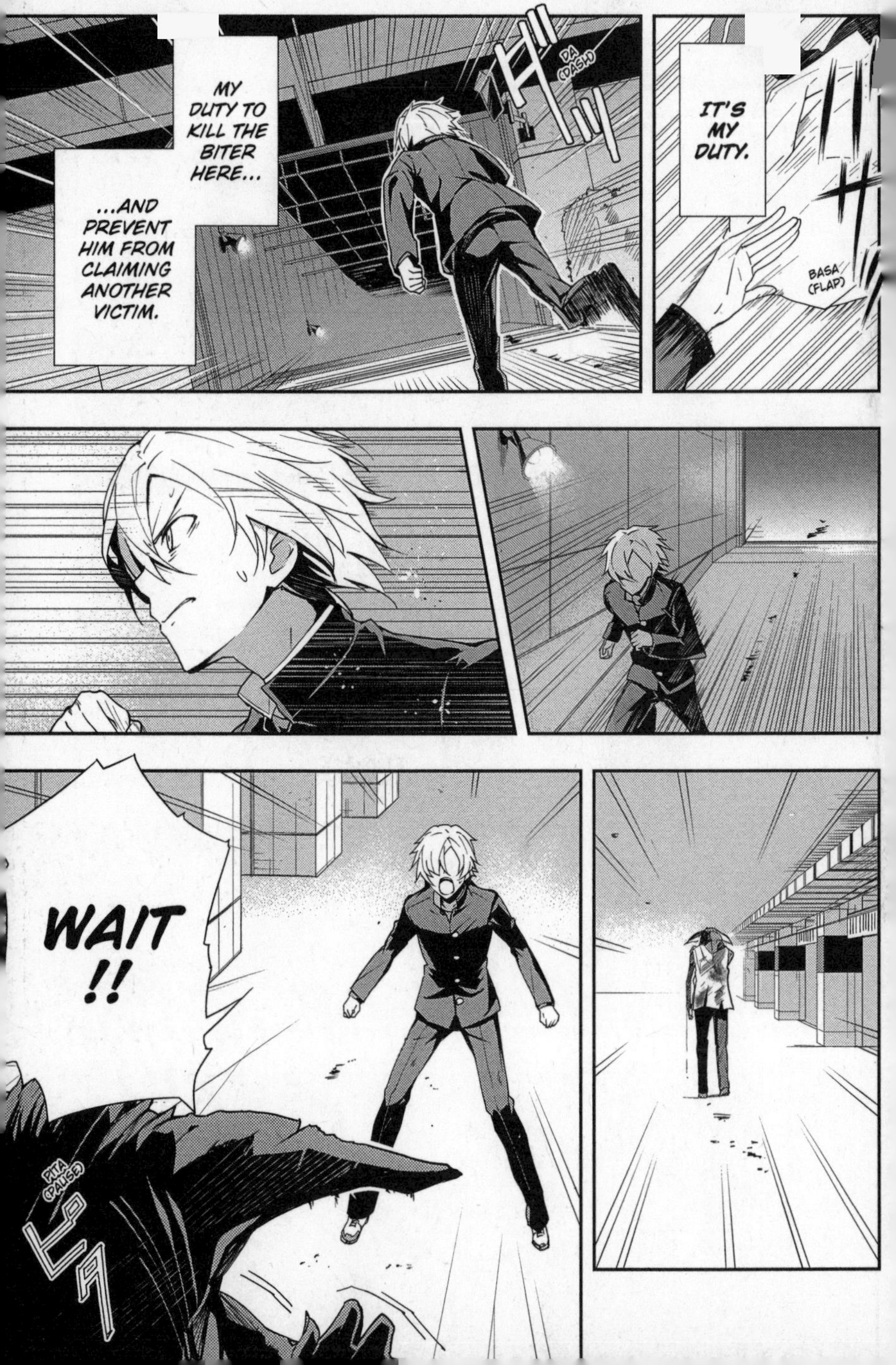
IT'S MY DUTY.
BASA (FLAP)
DA (DASH)
MY DUTY TO KILL THE BITER HERE...
...AND PREVENT HIM FROM CLAIMING ANOTHER VICTIM.
WAIT!!
PITA (PAUSE)
ピタ

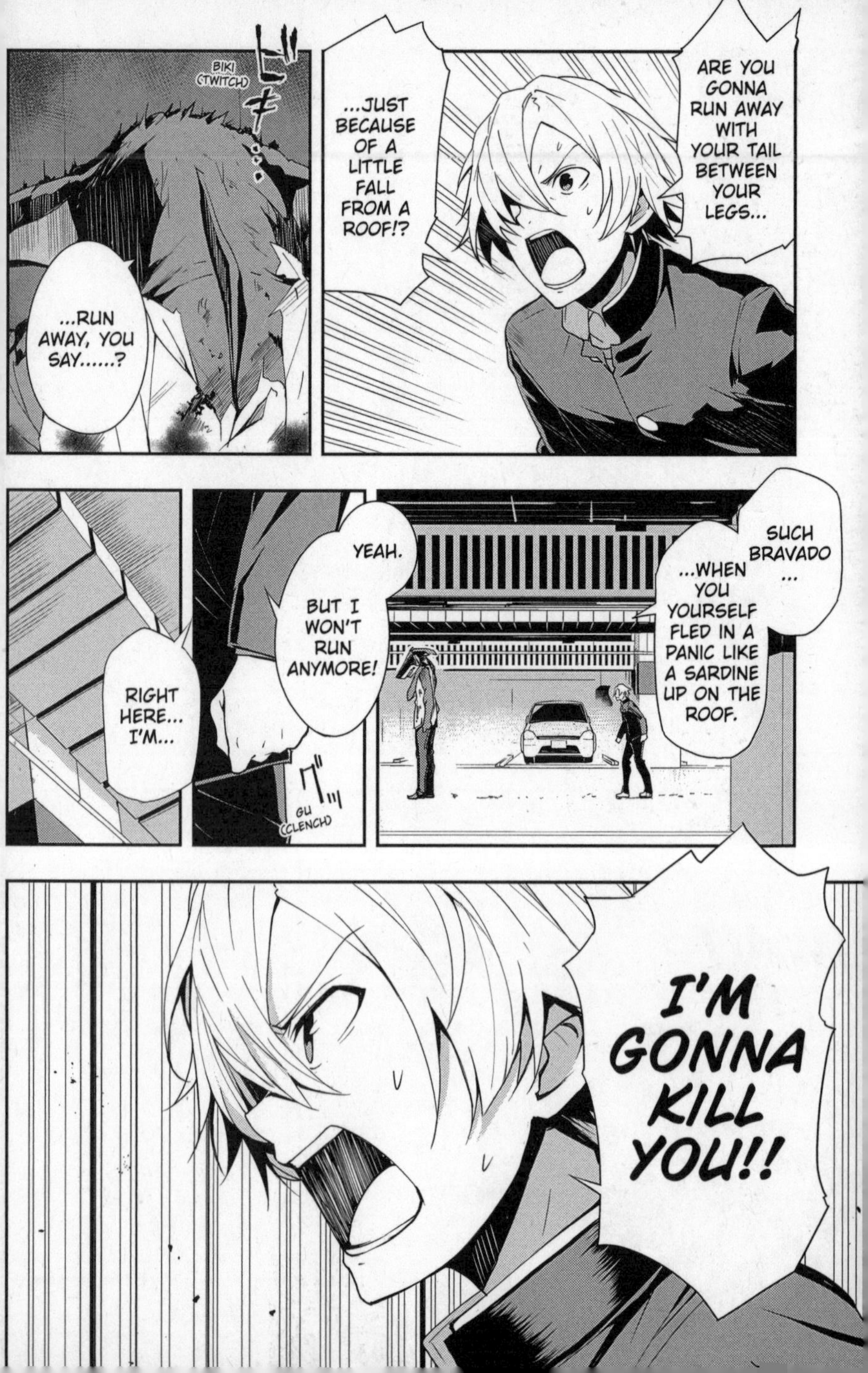
ARE YOU GONNA RUN AWAY WITH YOUR TAIL BETWEEN YOUR LEGS...
...JUST BECAUSE OF A LITTLE FALL FROM A ROOF!?
BIKI (TWITCH)
...RUN AWAY, YOU SAY......?
SUCH BRAVADO ...
...WHEN YOU YOURSELF FLED IN A PANIC LIKE A SARDINE UP ON THE ROOF.
YEAH.
BUT I WON'T RUN ANYMORE!
GU (CLENCH)
RIGHT HERE... I'M...
I'M GONNA KILL YOU!!

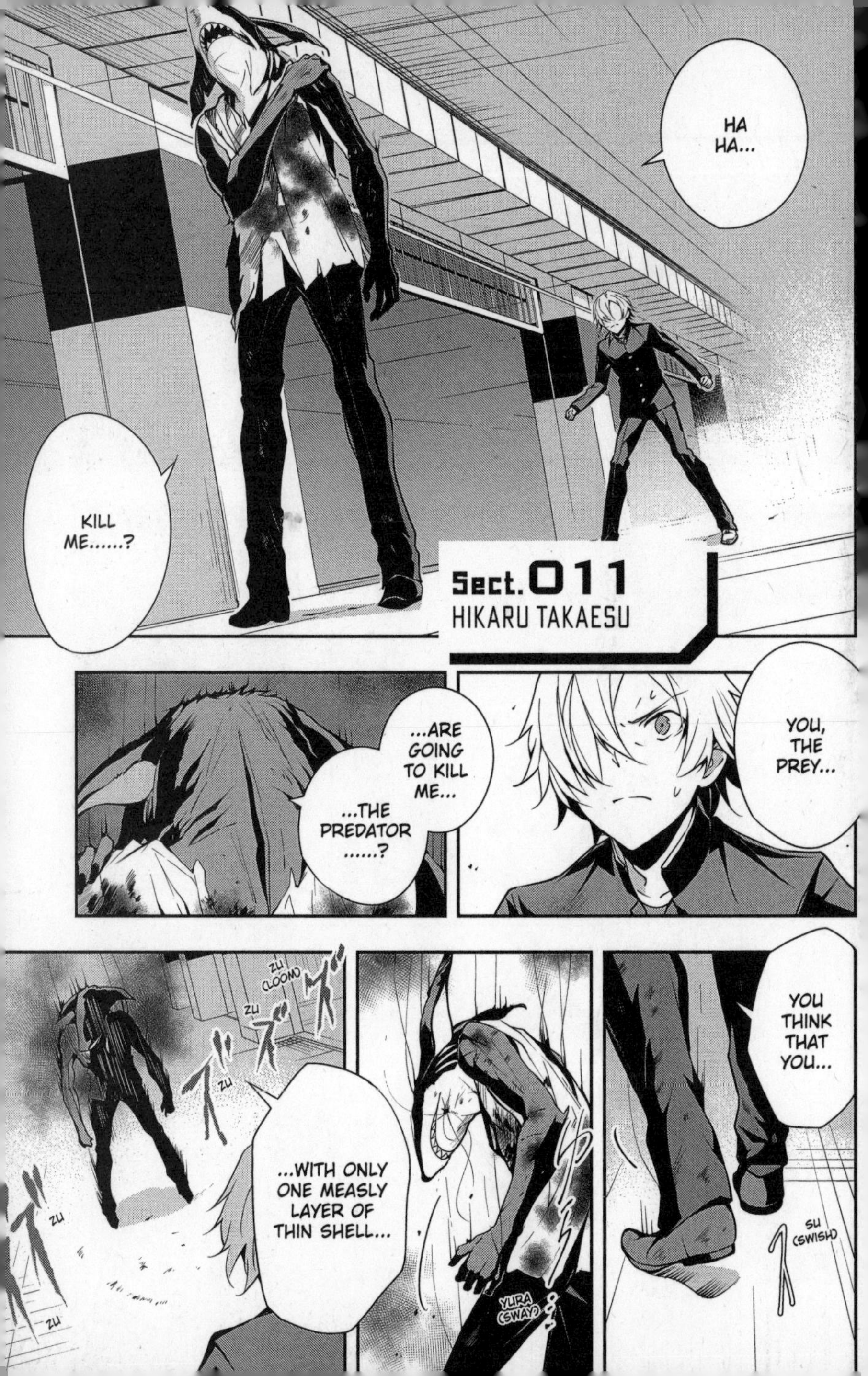
HA HA...
KILL ME......?
Sect. 011
HIKARU TAKAESU
YOU, THE PREY...
...ARE GOING TO KILL ME...
...THE PREDATOR ......?
YOU THINK THAT YOU...
SU (SWISH)
YURA (SWAY)
...WITH ONLY ONE MEASLY LAYER OF THIN SHELL...
ZU (LOOM)
ZU
ZU
ZU
ZU

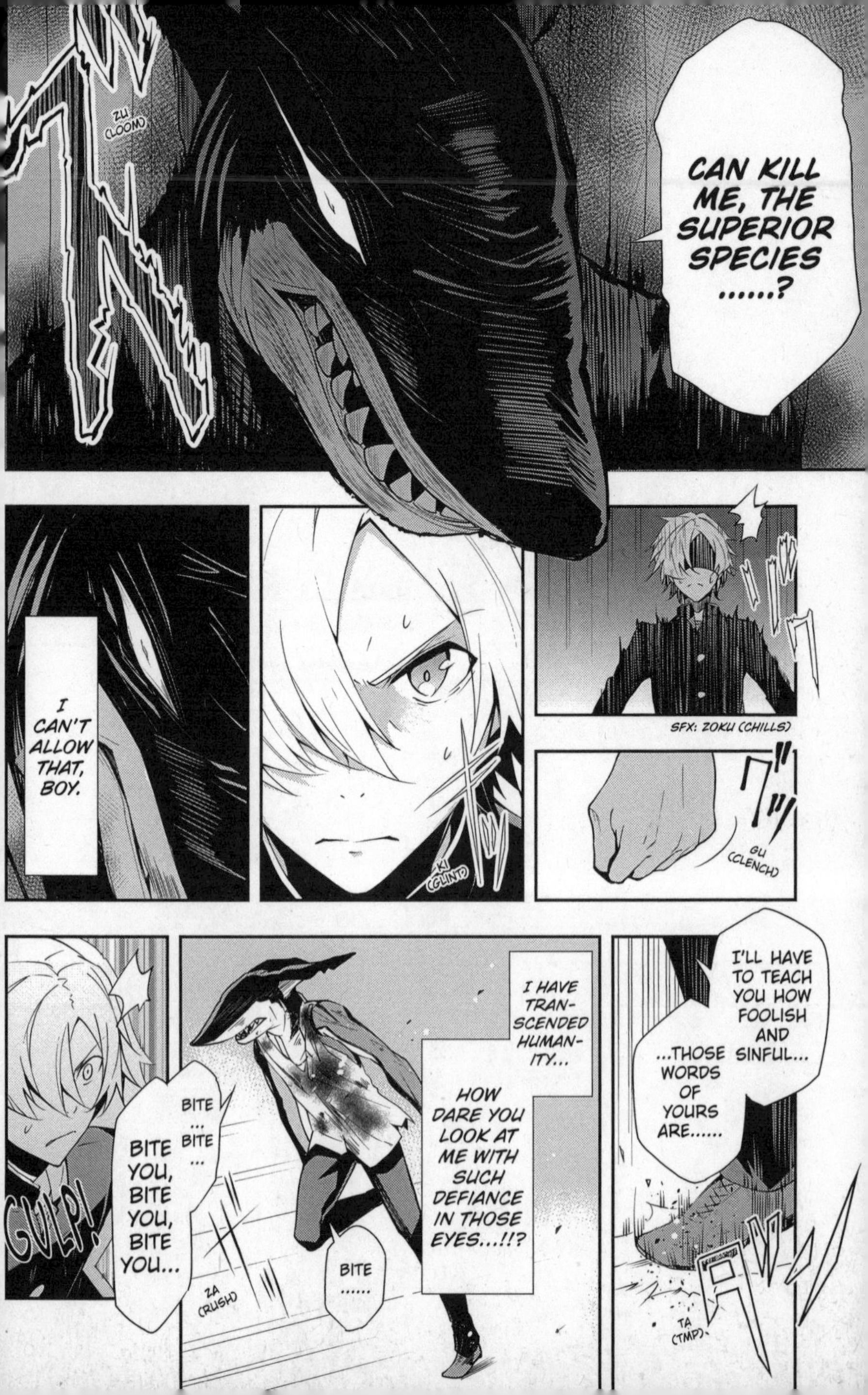
CAN KILL ME, THE SUPERIOR SPECIES ......?
ZU (LOOM)
SFX: ZOKU (CHILLS)
GU (CLENCH)
KI (GLINT)
I CAN'T ALLOW THAT, BOY.
I'LL HAVE TO TEACH YOU HOW FOOLISH AND SINFUL...
...THOSE WORDS OF YOURS ARE......
TA (TMP)
I HAVE TRAN-SCENDED HUMAN-ITY...
HOW DARE YOU LOOK AT ME WITH SUCH DEFIANCE IN THOSE EYES...!!?
BITE ......
ZA (RUSH)
BITE ... BITE ...
BITE YOU, BITE YOU, BITE YOU...
GULP!

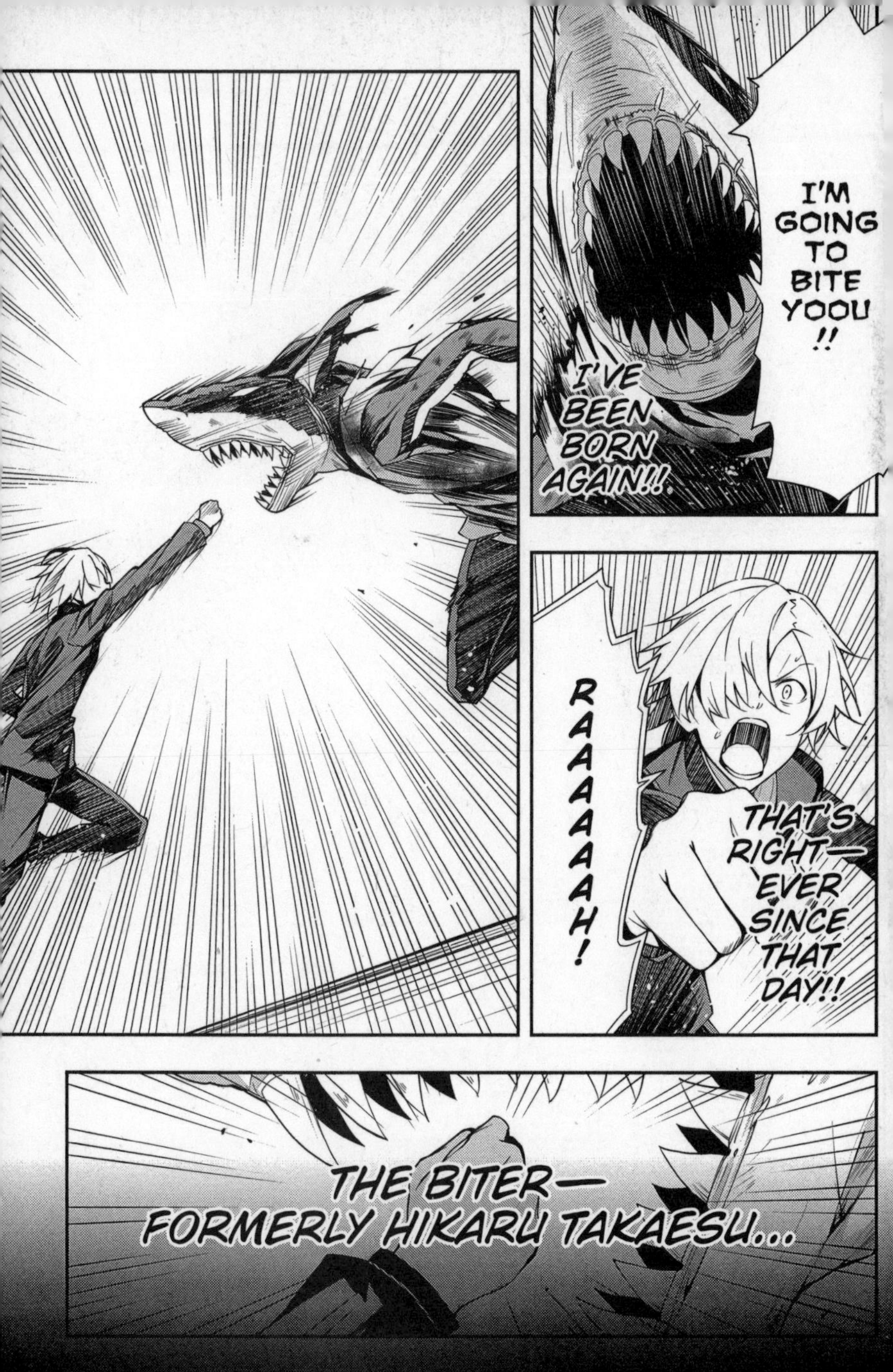
I'M GOING TO BITE YOOU!!
I'VE BEEN BORN AGAIN!!
THAT'S RIGHT—EVER SINCE THAT DAY!!
RAAAAAAAH!
THE BITER—FORMERLY HIKARU TAKAESU...

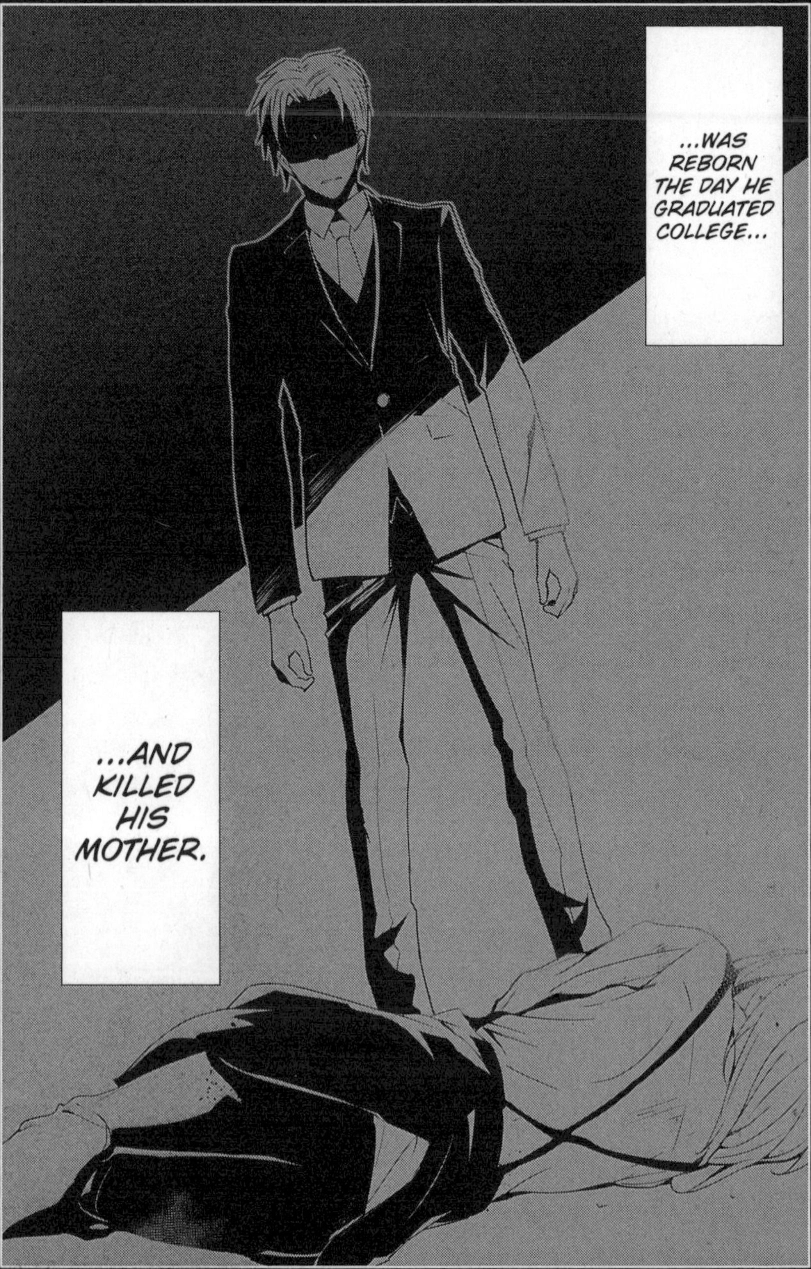
...WAS REBORN THE DAY HE GRADUATED COLLEGE...
...AND KILLED HIS MOTHER.

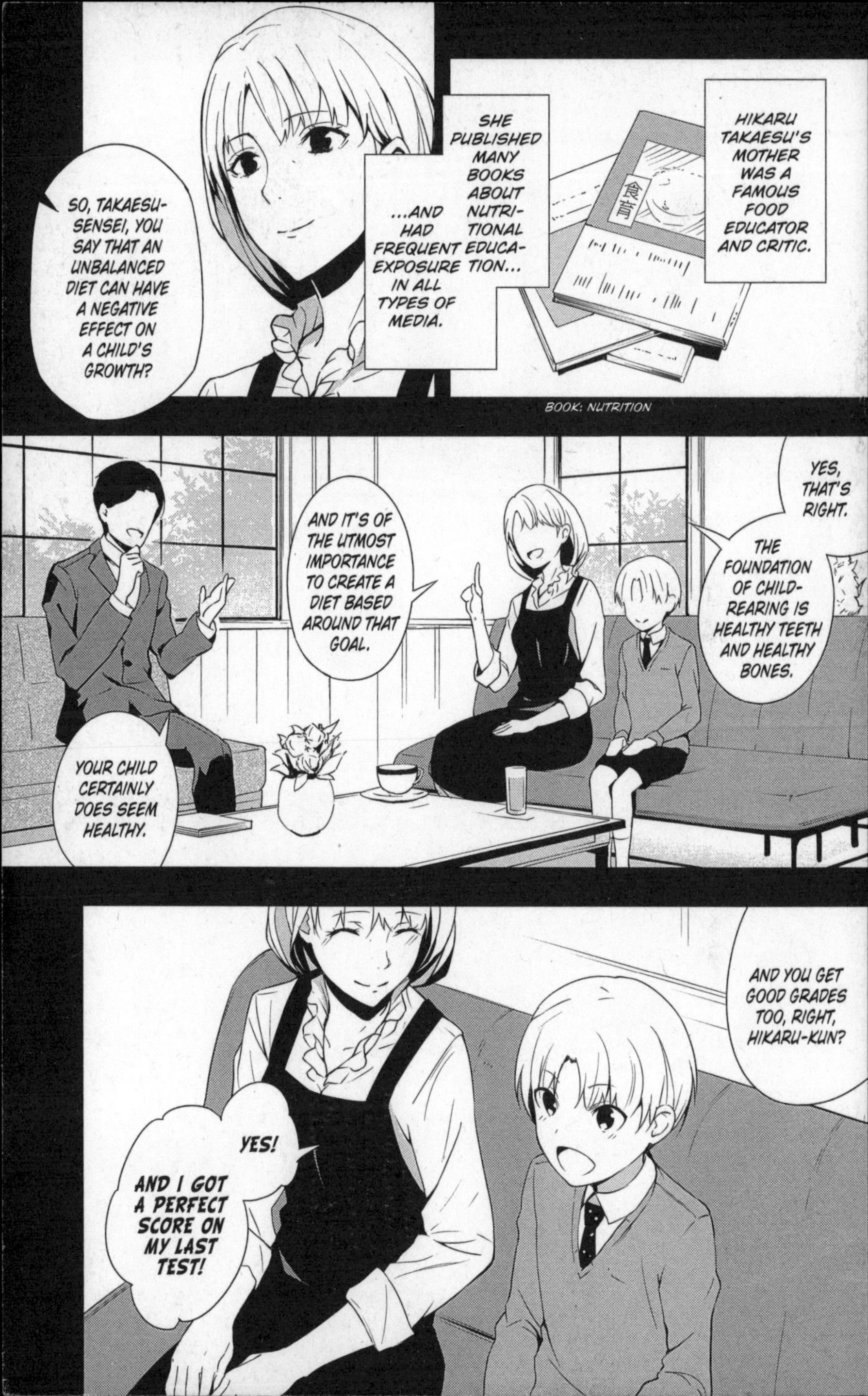
HIKARU TAKAESU'S MOTHER WAS A FAMOUS FOOD EDUCATOR AND CRITIC.
食育
SHE PUBLISHED MANY BOOKS ABOUT NUTRITIONAL EDUCATION...
...AND HAD FREQUENT EXPOSURE IN ALL TYPES OF MEDIA.
SO, TAKAESU-SENSEI, YOU SAY THAT AN UNBALANCED DIET CAN HAVE A NEGATIVE EFFECT ON A CHILD'S GROWTH?
BOOK: NUTRITION
YES, THAT'S RIGHT.
THE FOUNDATION OF CHILD-REARING IS HEALTHY TEETH AND HEALTHY BONES.
AND IT'S OF THE UTMOST IMPORTANCE TO CREATE A DIET BASED AROUND THAT GOAL.
YOUR CHILD CERTAINLY DOES SEEM HEALTHY.
AND YOU GET GOOD GRADES TOO, RIGHT, HIKARU-KUN?
YES!
AND I GOT A PERFECT SCORE ON MY LAST TEST!

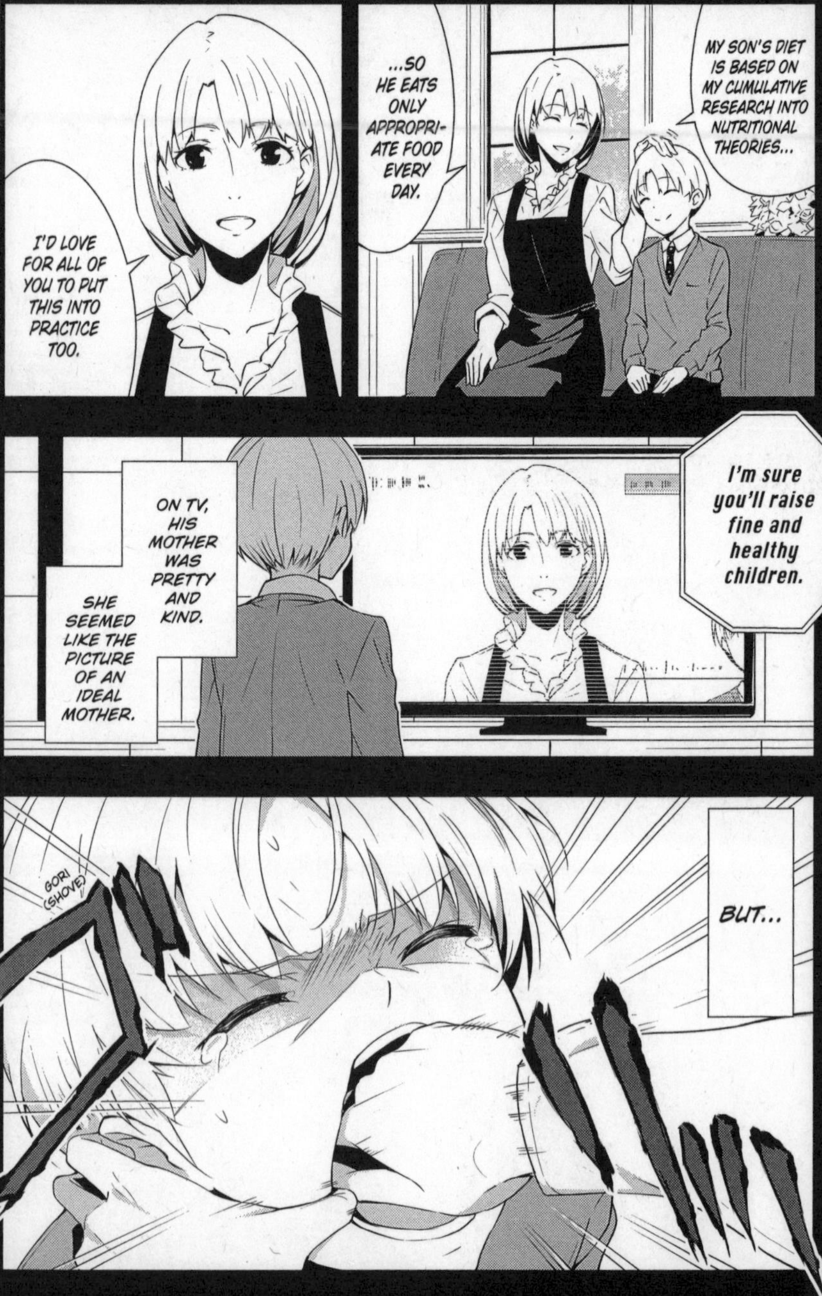
MY SON'S DIET IS BASED ON MY CUMULATIVE RESEARCH INTO NUTRITIONAL THEORIES...
...SO HE EATS ONLY APPROPRIATE FOOD EVERY DAY.
I'D LOVE FOR ALL OF YOU TO PUT THIS INTO PRACTICE TOO.
I'm sure you'll raise fine and healthy children.
ON TV, HIS MOTHER WAS PRETTY AND KIND.
SHE SEEMED LIKE THE PICTURE OF AN IDEAL MOTHER.
BUT...
GORI (SHOVE)

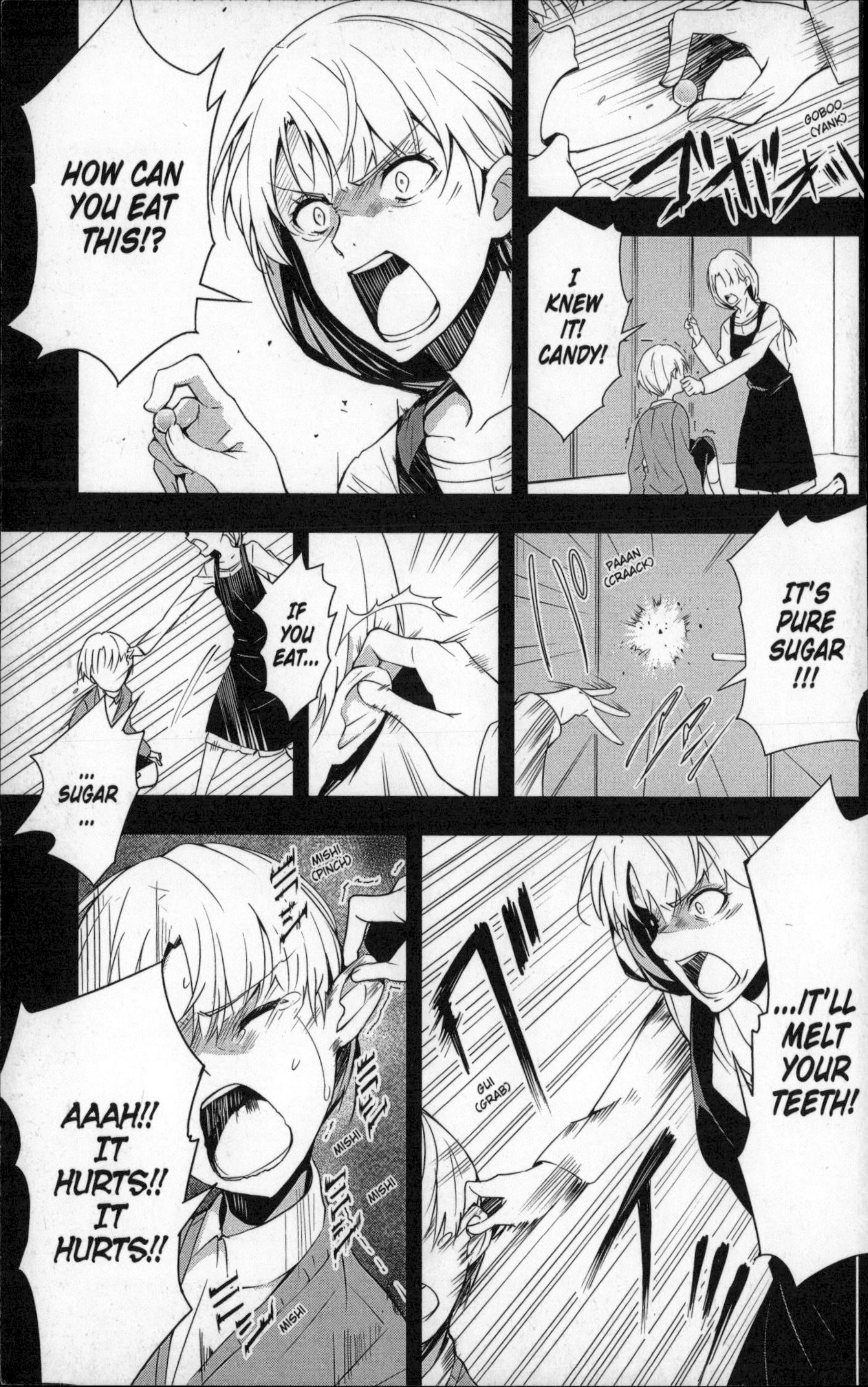
GOBOO (YANK)
I KNEW IT! CANDY!
HOW CAN YOU EAT THIS!?
PAAAN (CRAACK)
IT'S PURE SUGAR!!!
IF YOU EAT...
... SUGAR ...
...IT'LL MELT YOUR TEETH!
GUI (GRAB)
MISHI (PINCH)
MISHI
MISHI
MISHI
AAAH!! IT HURTS!! IT HURTS!!

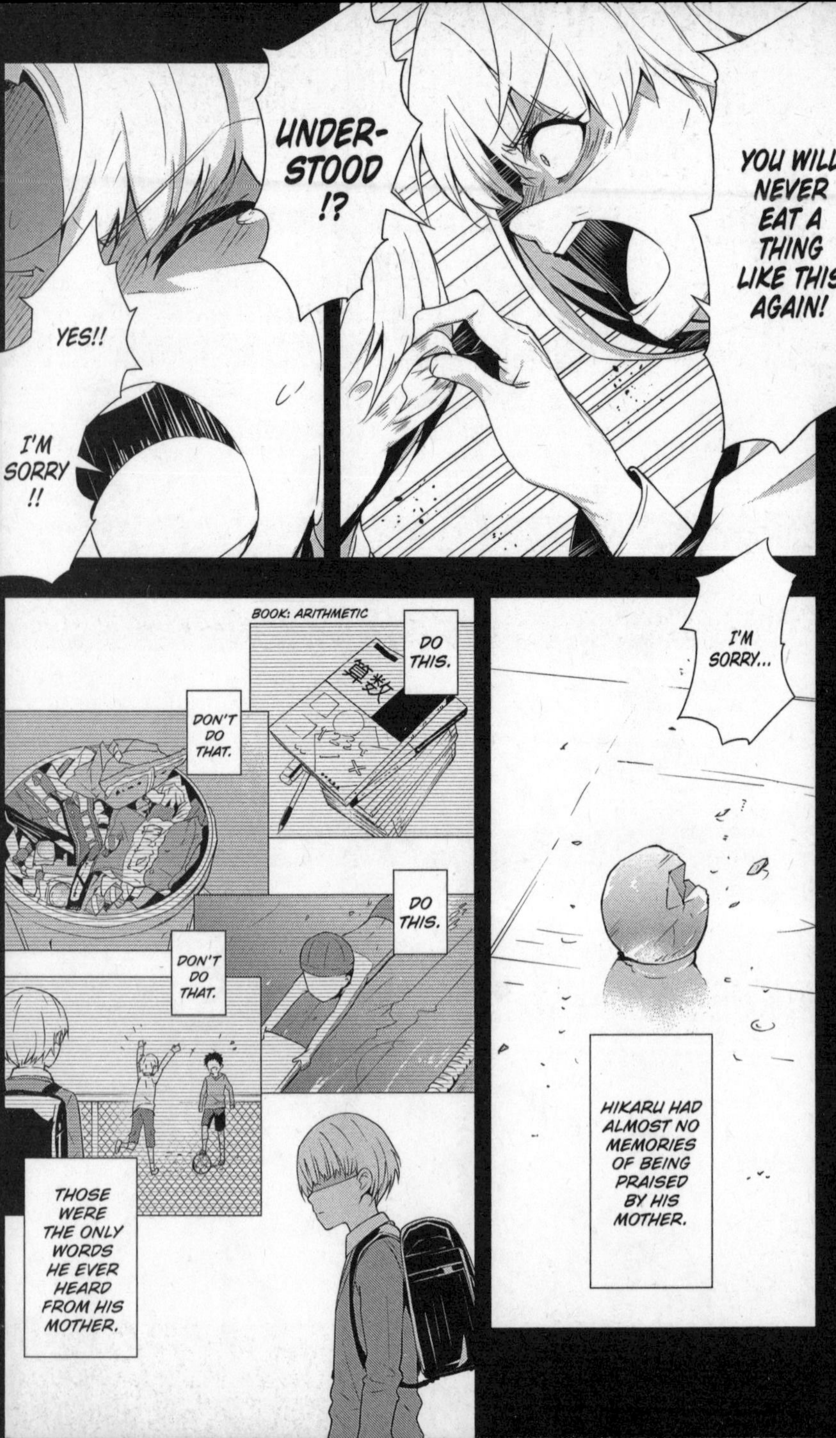
YOU WILL NEVER EAT A THING LIKE THIS AGAIN!
UNDER-STOOD !?
YES!!
I'M SORRY !!
I'M SORRY...
HIKARU HAD ALMOST NO MEMORIES OF BEING PRAISED BY HIS MOTHER.
BOOK: ARITHMETIC
DO THIS.
DON'T DO THAT.
DO THIS.
DON'T DO THAT.
THOSE WERE THE ONLY WORDS HE EVER HEARD FROM HIS MOTHER.

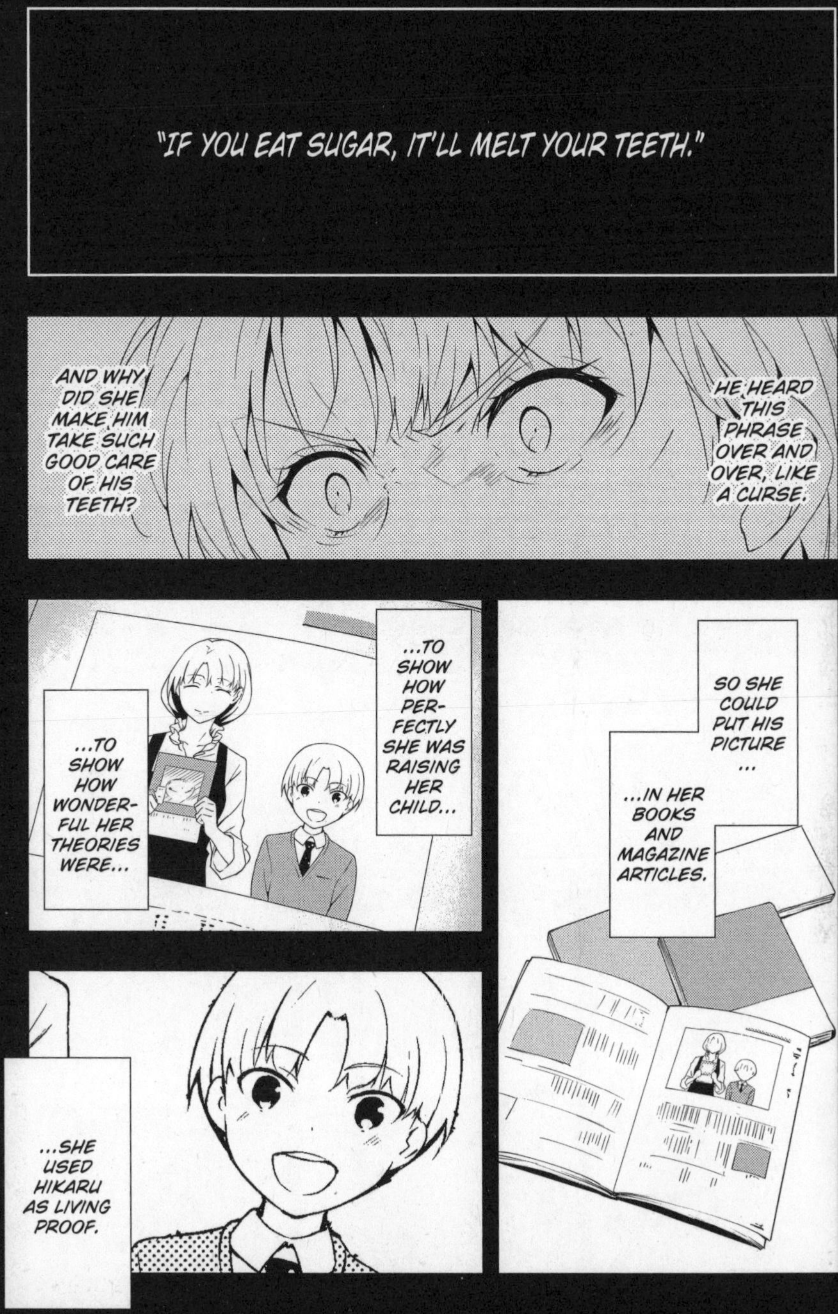
"IF YOU EAT SUGAR, IT'LL MELT YOUR TEETH."
HE HEARD THIS PHRASE OVER AND OVER, LIKE A CURSE.
AND WHY DID SHE MAKE HIM TAKE SUCH GOOD CARE OF HIS TEETH?
SO SHE COULD PUT HIS PICTURE ...
...IN HER BOOKS AND MAGAZINE ARTICLES.
...TO SHOW HOW PERFECTLY SHE WAS RAISING HER CHILD...
...TO SHOW HOW WONDERFUL HER THEORIES WERE...
...SHE USED HIKARU AS LIVING PROOF.

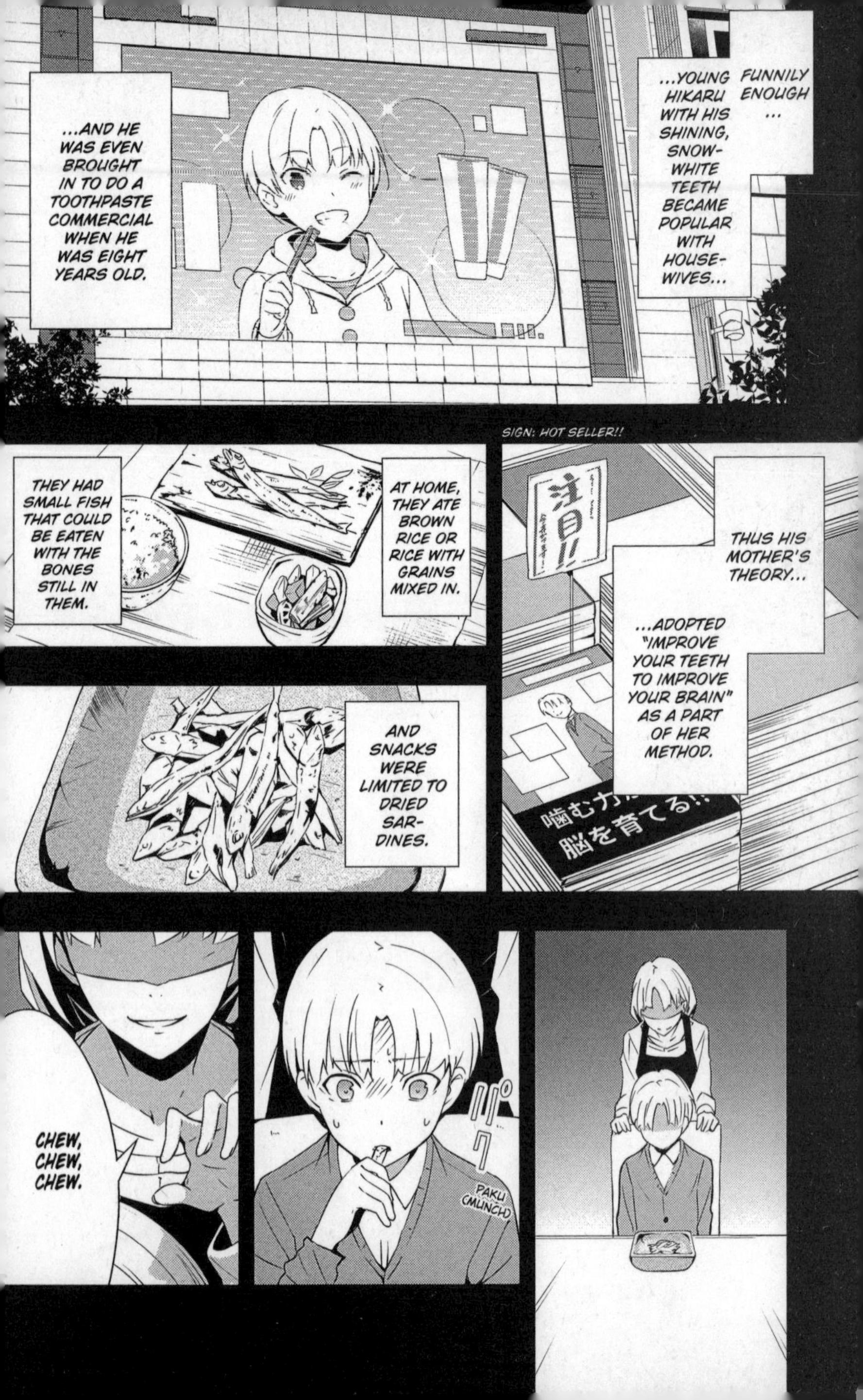
FUNNILY ENOUGH...
...YOUNG HIKARU WITH HIS SHINING, SNOW-WHITE TEETH BECAME POPULAR WITH HOUSE-WIVES...
...AND HE WAS EVEN BROUGHT IN TO DO A TOOTHPASTE COMMERCIAL WHEN HE WAS EIGHT YEARS OLD.
SIGN: HOT SELLER!!
注目!!
THUS HIS MOTHER'S THEORY...
...ADOPTED "IMPROVE YOUR TEETH TO IMPROVE YOUR BRAIN" AS A PART OF HER METHOD.
噛む力
脳を育てる!!
AT HOME, THEY ATE BROWN RICE OR RICE WITH GRAINS MIXED IN.
THEY HAD SMALL FISH THAT COULD BE EATEN WITH THE BONES STILL IN THEM.
AND SNACKS WERE LIMITED TO DRIED SARDINES.
...
パク
PAKU (MUNCH)
CHEW, CHEW, CHEW.

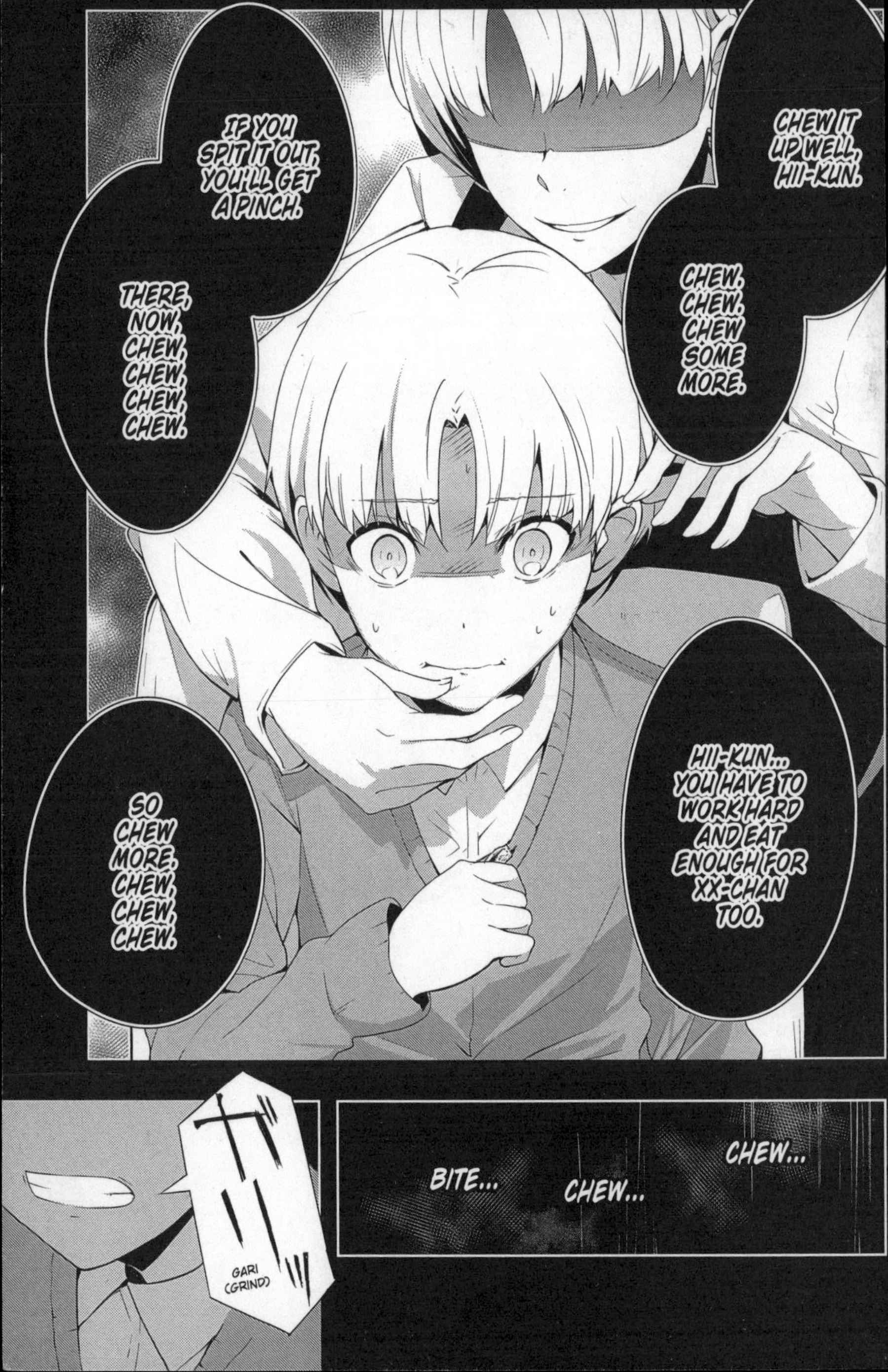
CHEW IT UP WELL, HII-KUN.
IF YOU SPIT IT OUT, YOU'LL GET A PINCH.
CHEW. CHEW. CHEW SOME MORE.
THERE, NOW, CHEW, CHEW, CHEW, CHEW.
HII-KUN... YOU HAVE TO WORK HARD AND EAT ENOUGH FOR XX-CHAN TOO.
SO CHEW MORE, CHEW, CHEW, CHEW.
CHEW...
CHEW...
BITE...
GARI (GRIND)

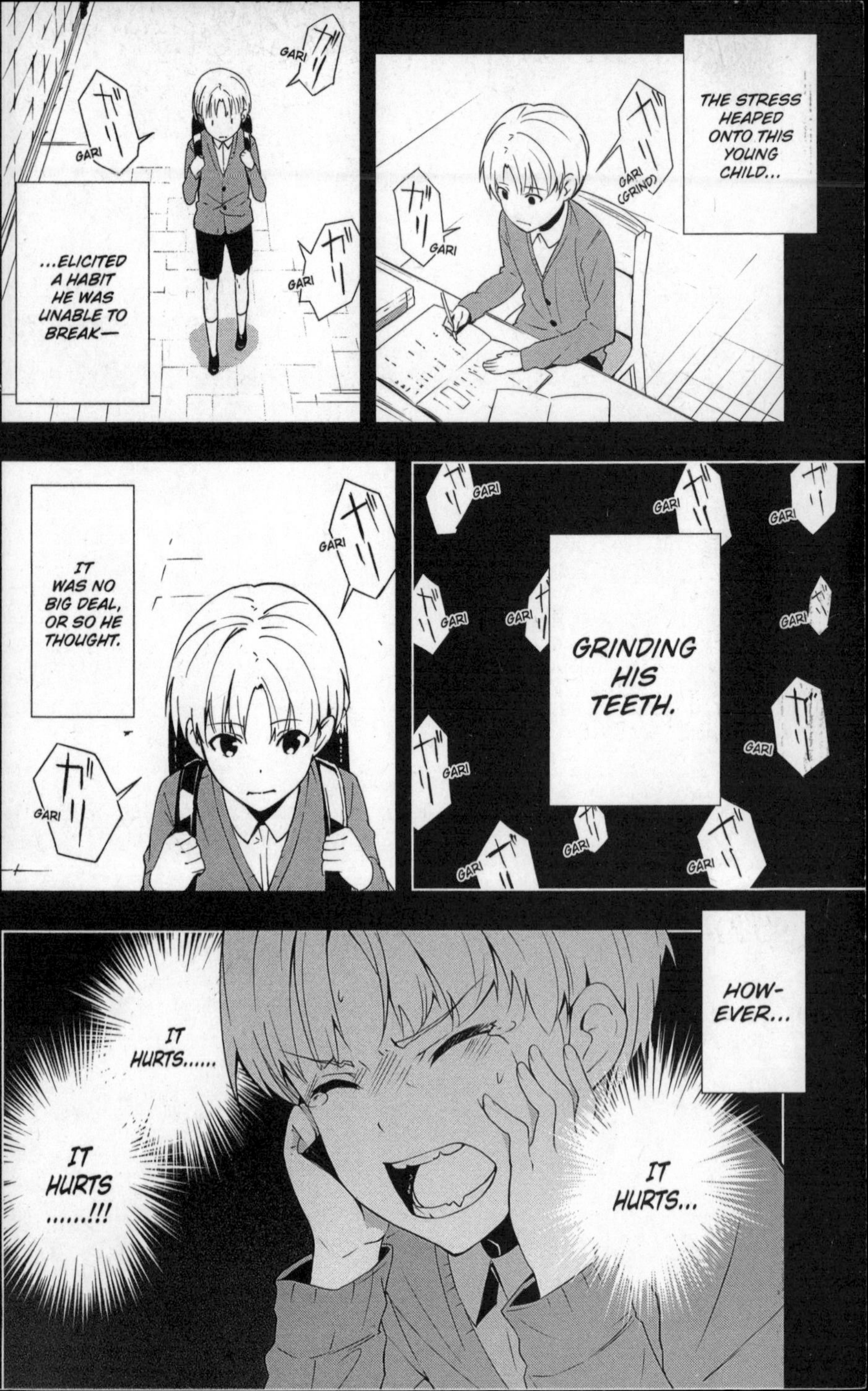
THE STRESS HEAPED ONTO THIS YOUNG CHILD...
GARI (GRIND)
GARI
...ELICITED A HABIT HE WAS UNABLE TO BREAK—
GARI
GARI
GARI
GRINDING HIS TEETH.
GARI
GARI
GARI
GARI
GARI
GARI
GARI
GARI
GARI
GARI
GARI
IT WAS NO BIG DEAL, OR SO HE THOUGHT.
GARI
GARI
HOW-EVER...
IT HURTS...
IT HURTS......
IT HURTS ......!!!

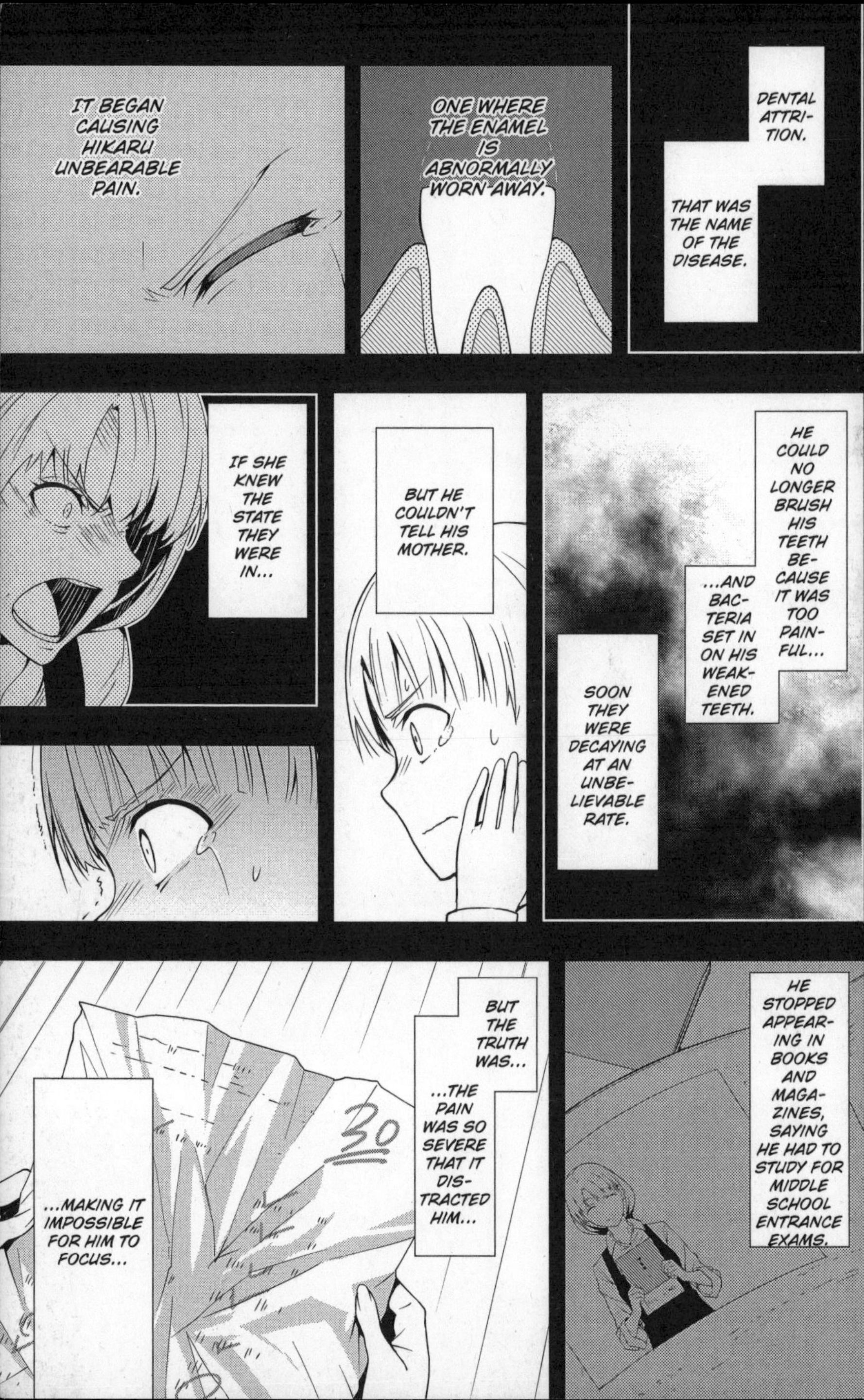
DENTAL ATTRITION.
THAT WAS THE NAME OF THE DISEASE.
ONE WHERE THE ENAMEL IS ABNORMALLY WORN AWAY.
IT BEGAN CAUSING HIKARU UNBEARABLE PAIN.
HE COULD NO LONGER BRUSH HIS TEETH BECAUSE IT WAS TOO PAINFUL...
...AND BACTERIA SET IN ON HIS WEAKENED TEETH.
SOON THEY WERE DECAYING AT AN UNBELIEVABLE RATE.
BUT HE COULDN'T TELL HIS MOTHER.
IF SHE KNEW THE STATE THEY WERE IN...
HE STOPPED APPEARING IN BOOKS AND MAGAZINES, SAYING HE HAD TO STUDY FOR MIDDLE SCHOOL ENTRANCE EXAMS.
BUT THE TRUTH WAS...
...THE PAIN WAS SO SEVERE THAT IT DISTRACTED HIM...
30
...MAKING IT IMPOSSIBLE FOR HIM TO FOCUS...

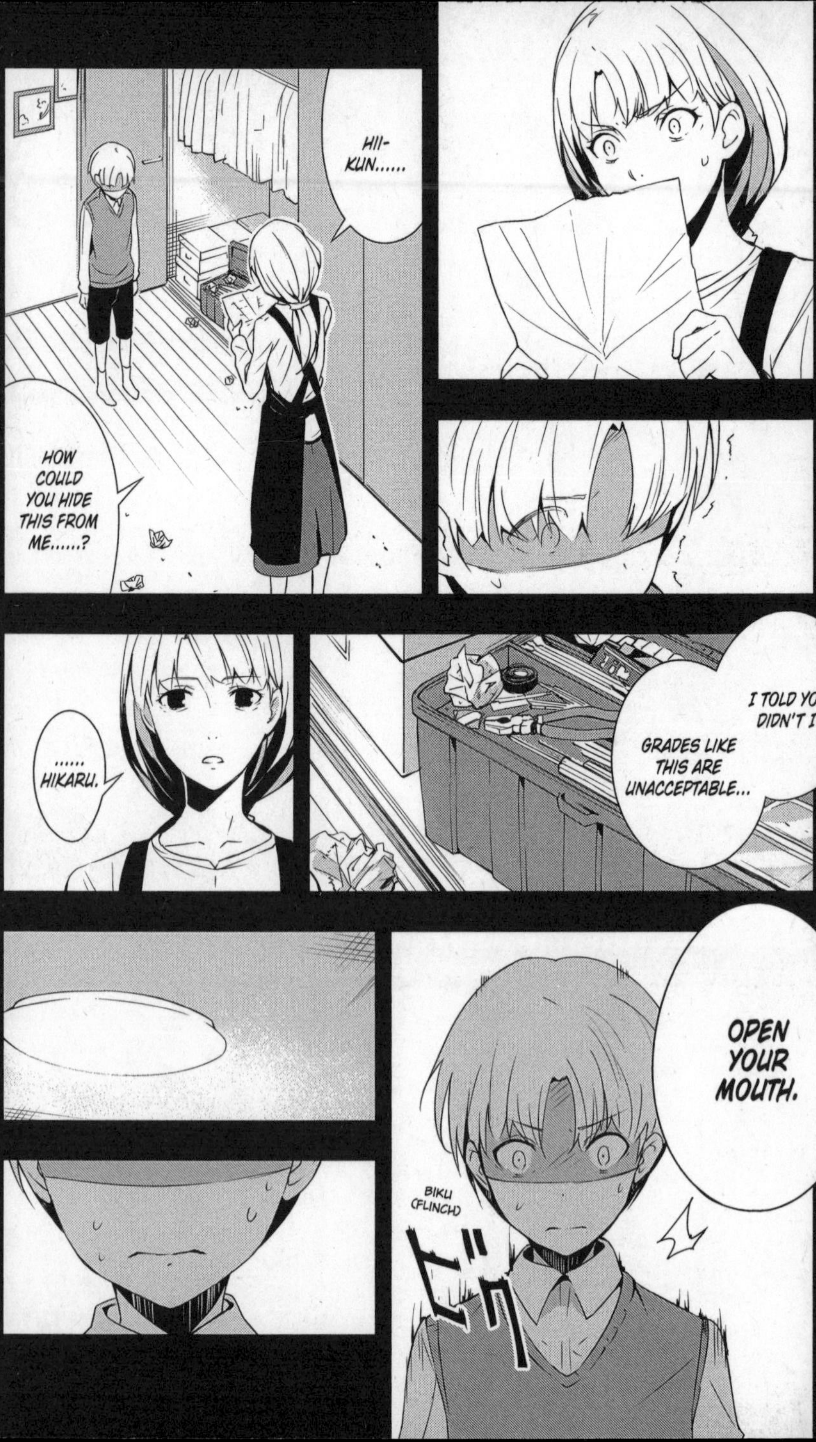
HII-KUN......
HOW COULD YOU HIDE THIS FROM ME......?
I TOLD YOU, DIDN'T I?
GRADES LIKE THIS ARE UNACCEPTABLE...
...... HIKARU.
OPEN YOUR MOUTH.
BIKU (FLINCH)

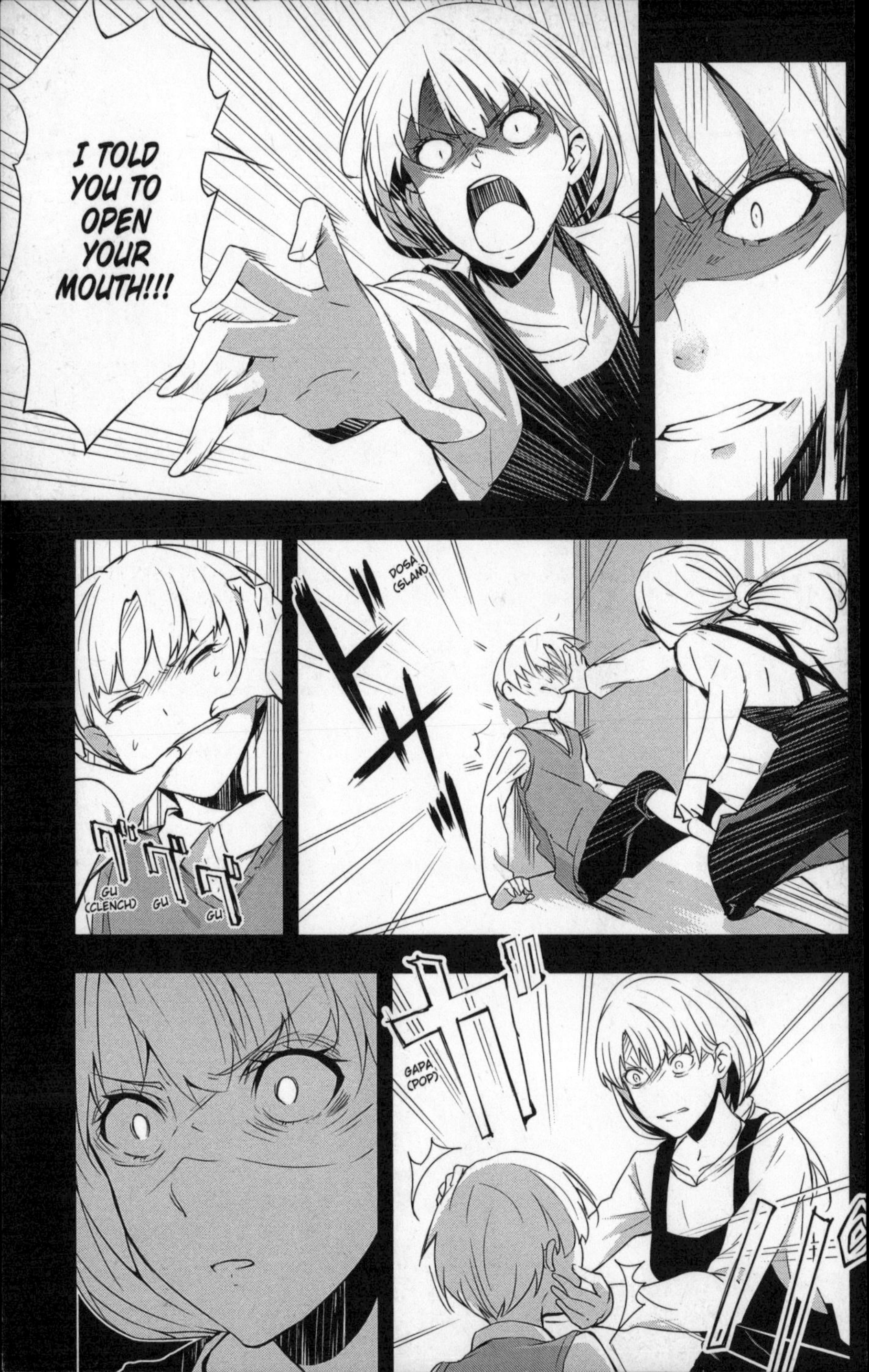
I TOLD YOU TO OPEN YOUR MOUTH!!!
DOSA (SLAM)
GU (CLENCH) GU GU
GAPA (POP)

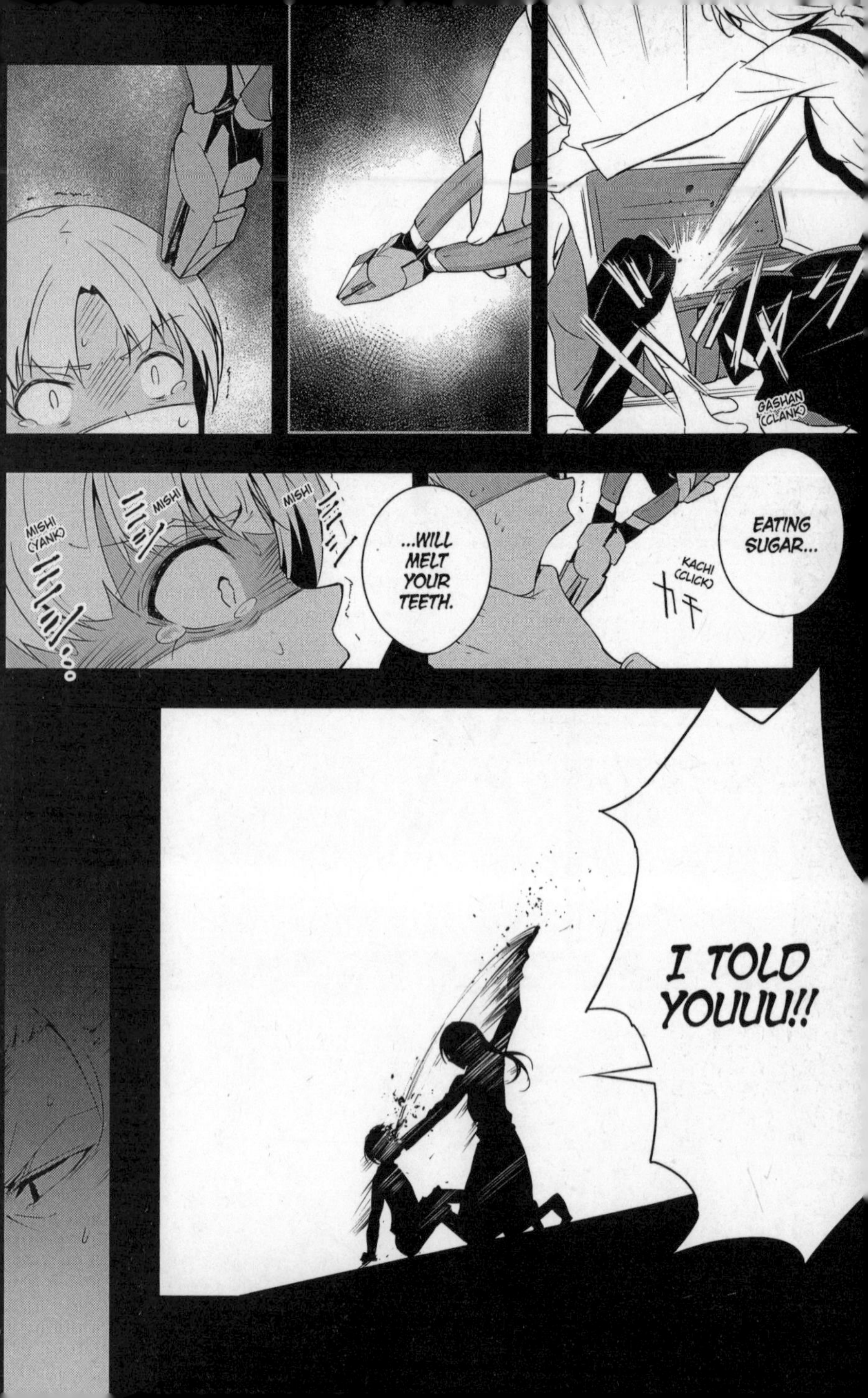
GASHAN (CLANK)
EATING SUGAR...
KACHI (CLICK)
カチ
...WILL MELT YOUR TEETH.
MISHI
MISHI
MISHI (YANK)
I TOLD YOUUU!!

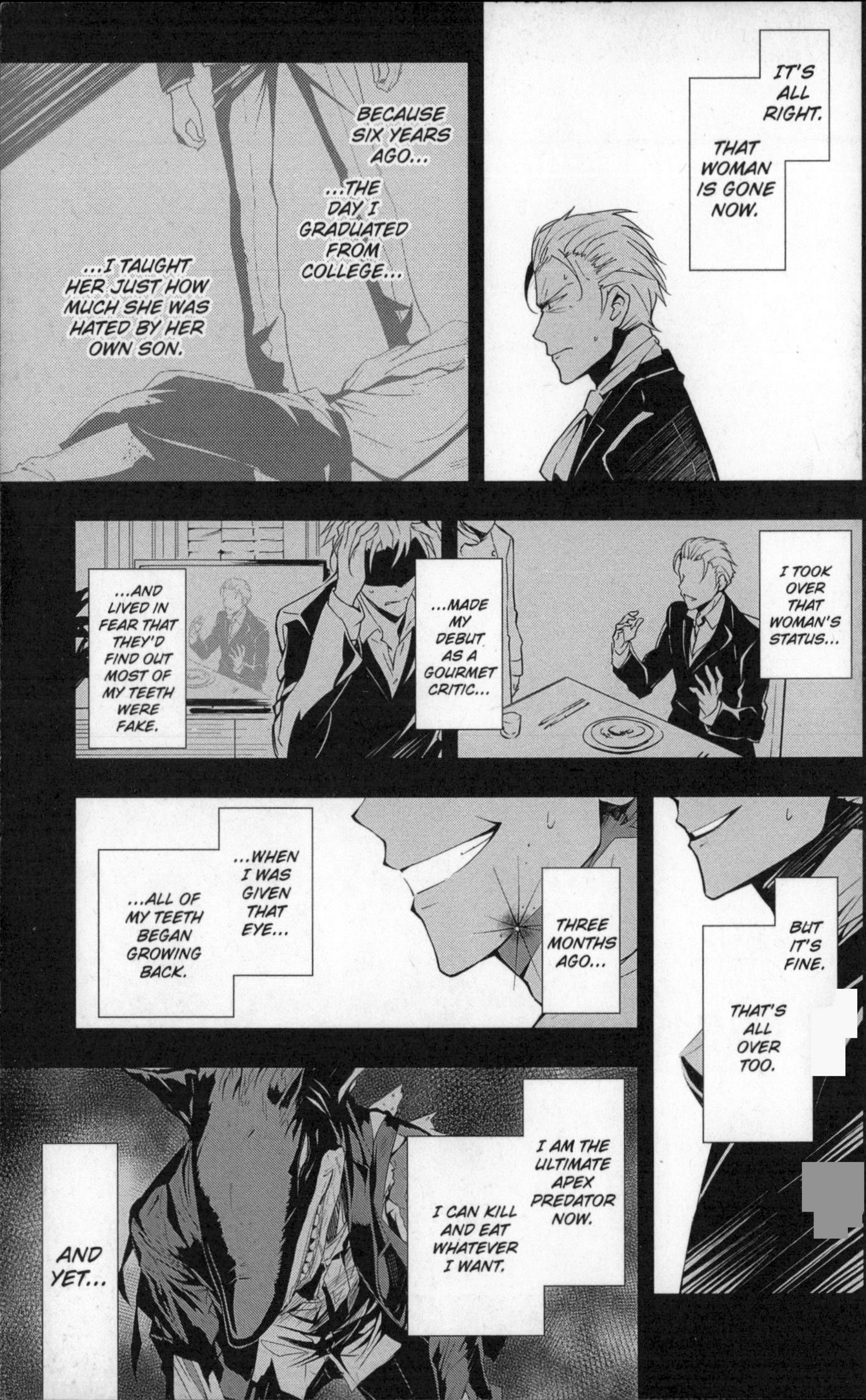
IT'S ALL RIGHT.
THAT WOMAN IS GONE NOW.
BECAUSE SIX YEARS AGO...
...THE DAY I GRADUATED FROM COLLEGE...
...I TAUGHT HER JUST HOW MUCH SHE WAS HATED BY HER OWN SON.
I TOOK OVER THAT WOMAN'S STATUS...
...MADE MY DEBUT AS A GOURMET CRITIC...
...AND LIVED IN FEAR THAT THEY'D FIND OUT MOST OF MY TEETH WERE FAKE.
BUT IT'S FINE.
THAT'S ALL OVER TOO.
THREE MONTHS AGO...
...WHEN I WAS GIVEN THAT EYE...
...ALL OF MY TEETH BEGAN GROWING BACK.
I AM THE ULTIMATE APEX PREDATOR NOW.
I CAN KILL AND EAT WHATEVER I WANT.
AND YET...

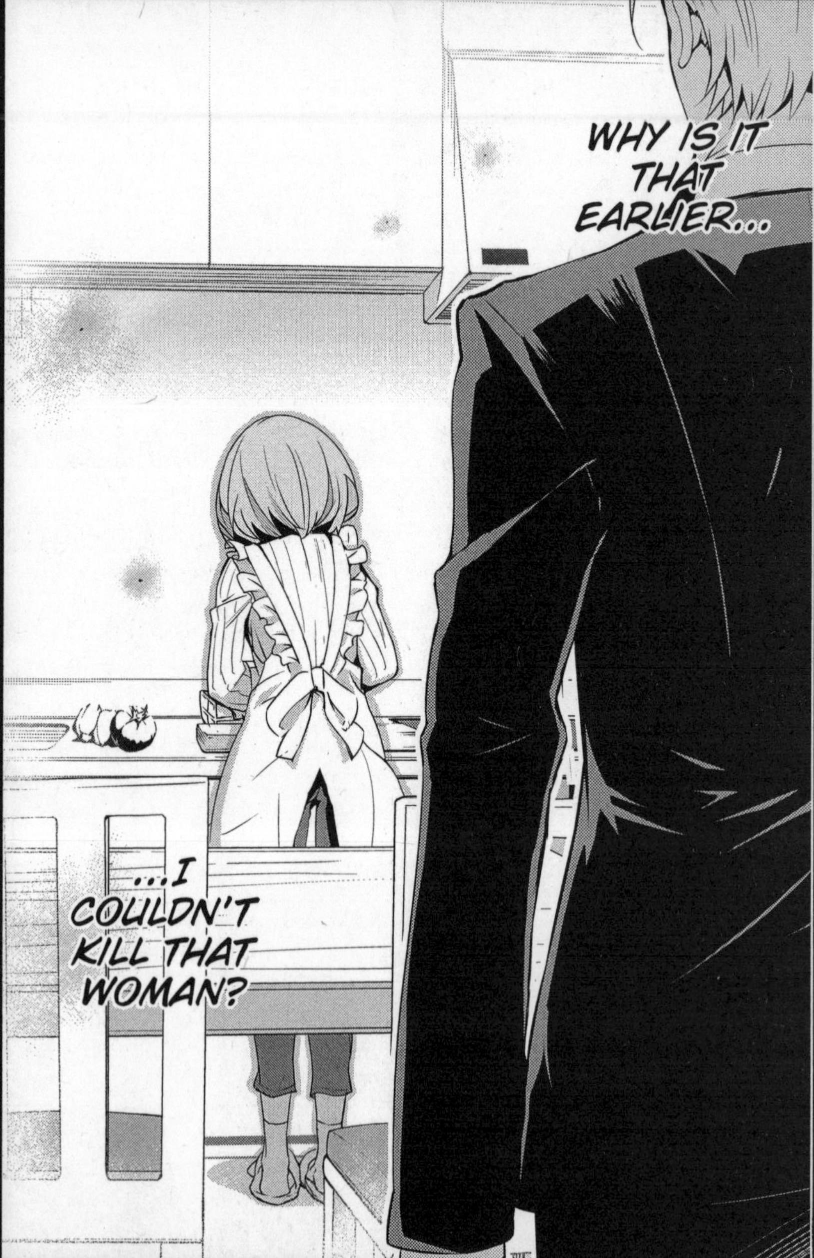
WHY IS IT THAT EARLIER...
...I COULDN'T KILL THAT WOMAN?

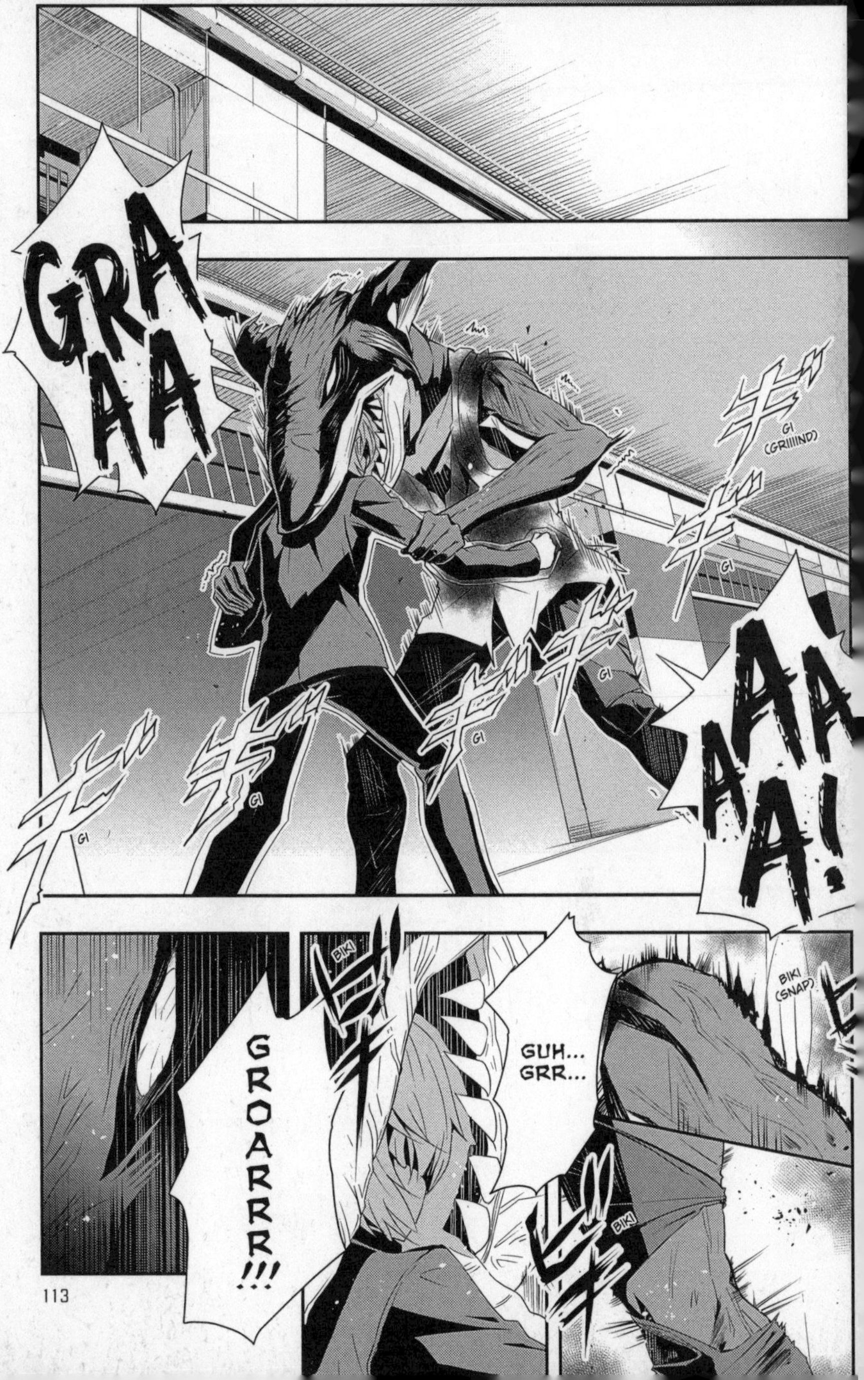
GI (GRIIIND)
GI
GRAAA
AAAAA!
GI
GI
GI
GI
BIKI (SNAP)
GUH... GRR...
BIKI
GROARRR!!!
BIKI

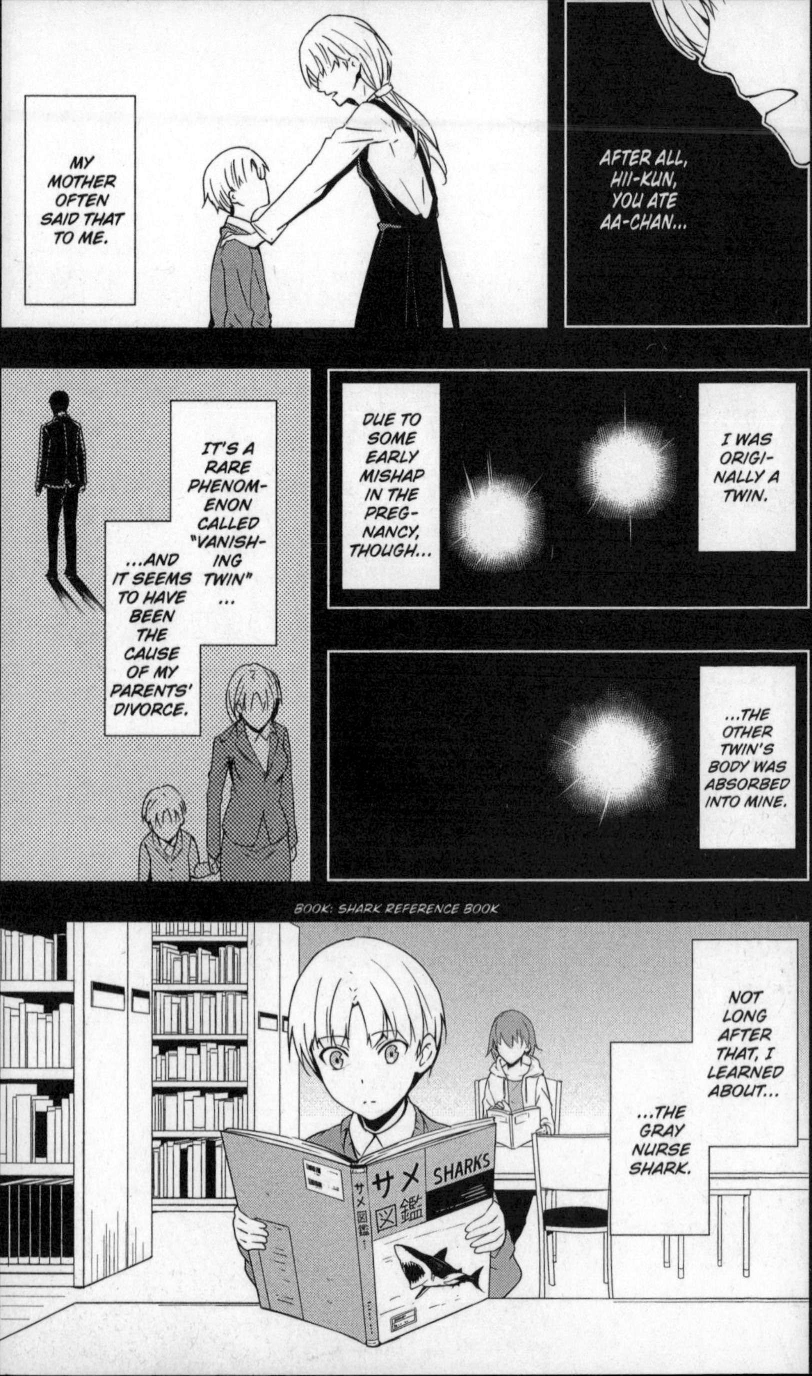
AFTER ALL, HII-KUN, YOU ATE AA-CHAN...
MY MOTHER OFTEN SAID THAT TO ME.
I WAS ORIGINALLY A TWIN.
DUE TO SOME EARLY MISHAP IN THE PREGNANCY, THOUGH...
...THE OTHER TWIN'S BODY WAS ABSORBED INTO MINE.
IT'S A RARE PHENOMENON CALLED "VANISHING TWIN"...
...AND IT SEEMS TO HAVE BEEN THE CAUSE OF MY PARENTS' DIVORCE.
BOOK: SHARK REFERENCE BOOK
NOT LONG AFTER THAT, I LEARNED ABOUT...
...THE GRAY NURSE SHARK.
サメ図鑑
SHARKS
サメ図鑑

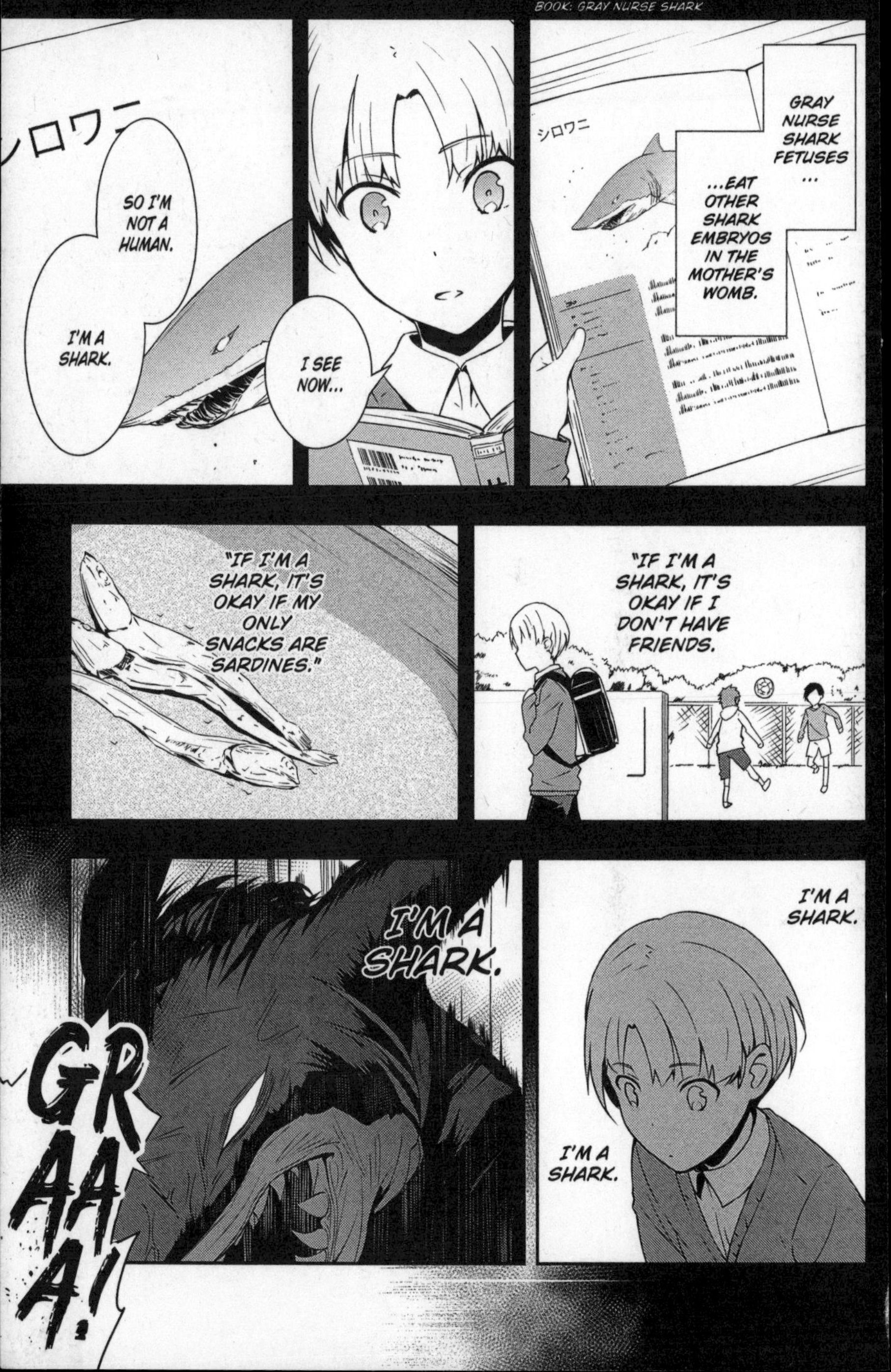
BOOK: GRAY NURSE SHARK
シロワニ
GRAY NURSE SHARK FETUSES...
...EAT OTHER SHARK EMBRYOS IN THE MOTHER'S WOMB.
I SEE NOW...
シロワニ
SO I'M NOT A HUMAN.
I'M A SHARK.
"IF I'M A SHARK, IT'S OKAY IF I DON'T HAVE FRIENDS.
"IF I'M A SHARK, IT'S OKAY IF MY ONLY SNACKS ARE SARDINES."
I'M A SHARK.
I'M A SHARK.
I'M A SHARK.
GRAAAA!

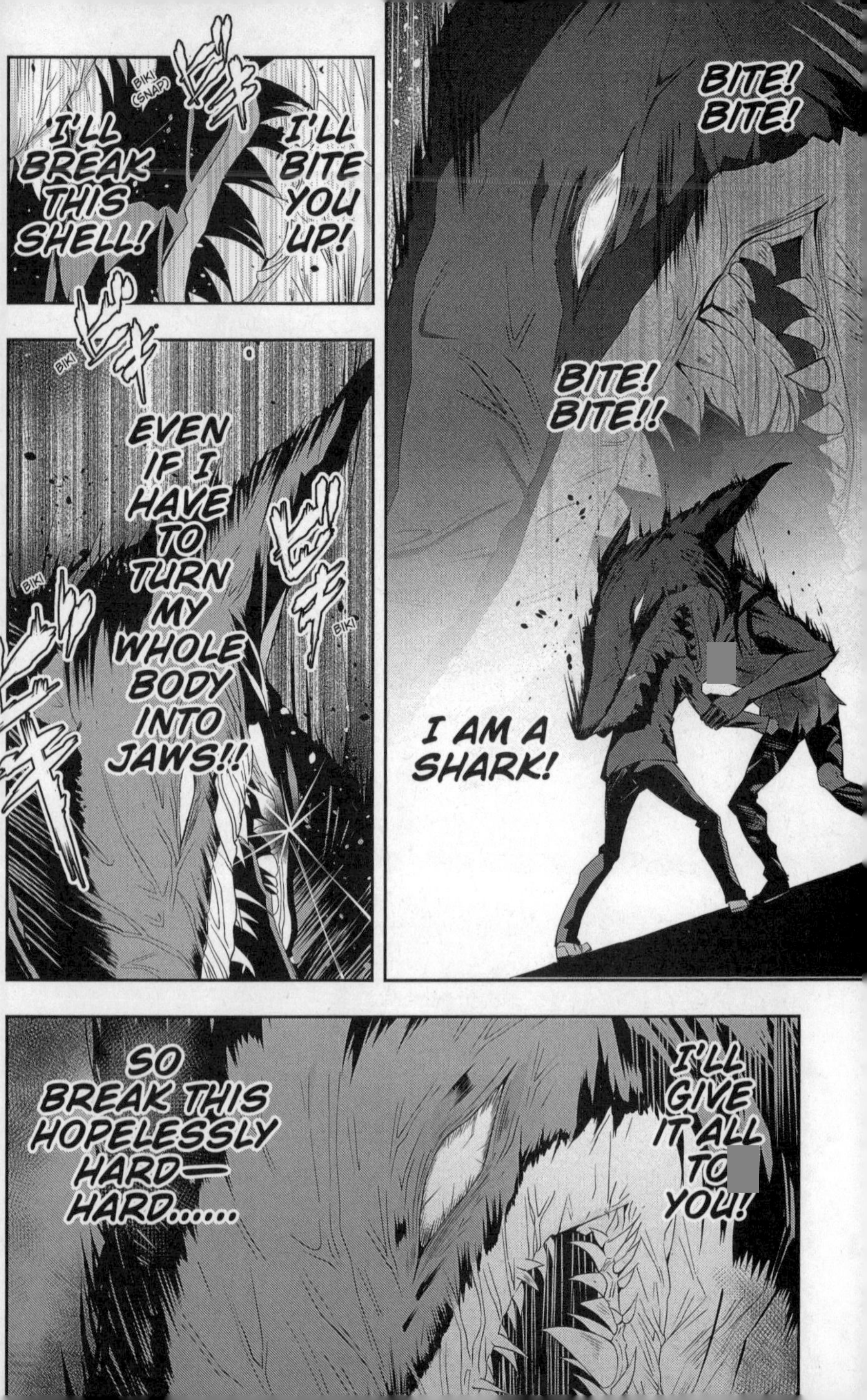
BITE! BITE!
BITE! BITE!!
I AM A SHARK!
I'LL BITE YOU UP!
I'LL BREAK THIS SHELL!
BIKI (SNAP)
BIKI
EVEN IF I HAVE TO TURN MY WHOLE BODY INTO JAWS!!
BIKI
BIKI
I'LL GIVE IT ALL TO YOU!
SO BREAK THIS HOPELESSLY HARD—
HARD......

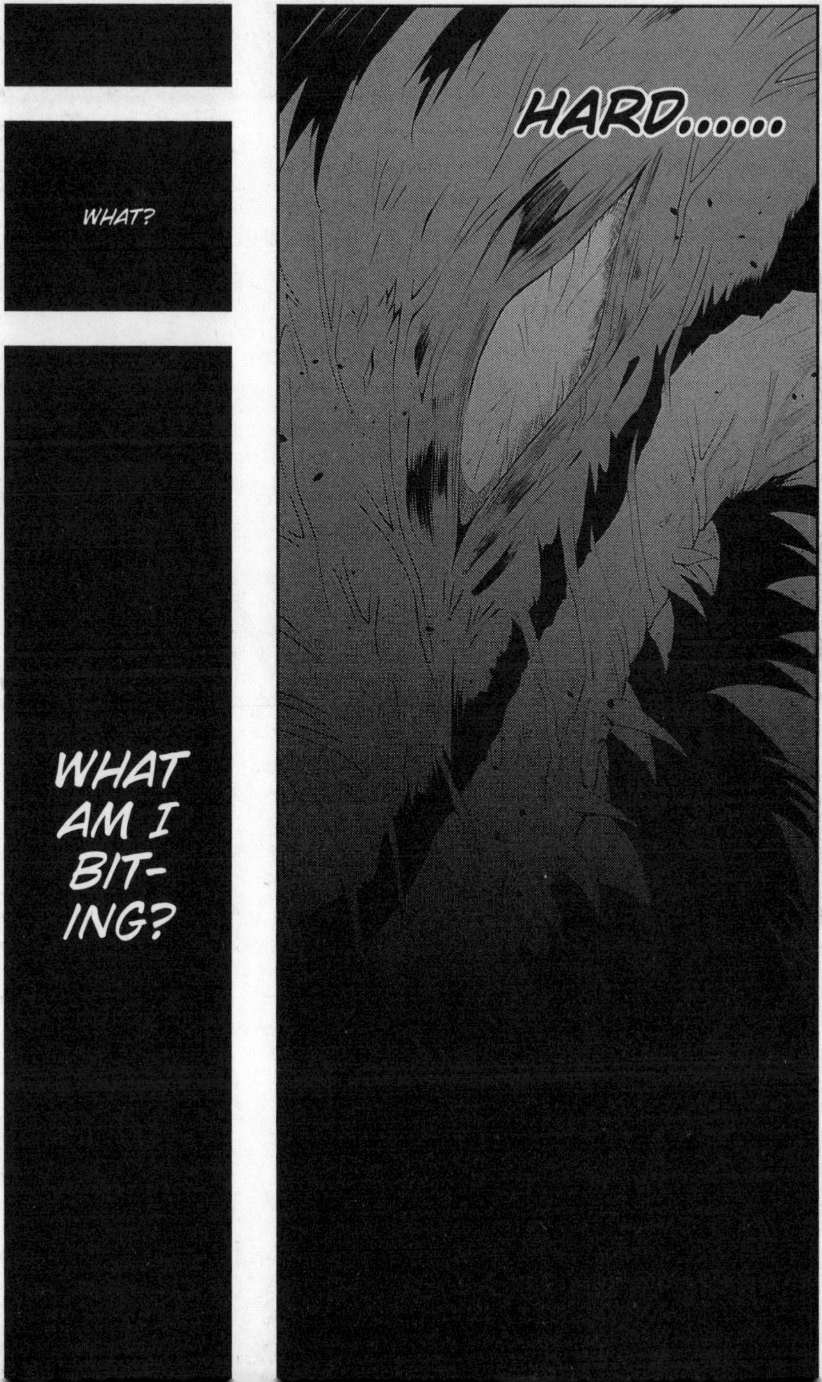
HARD......
WHAT?
WHAT AM I BIT-ING?

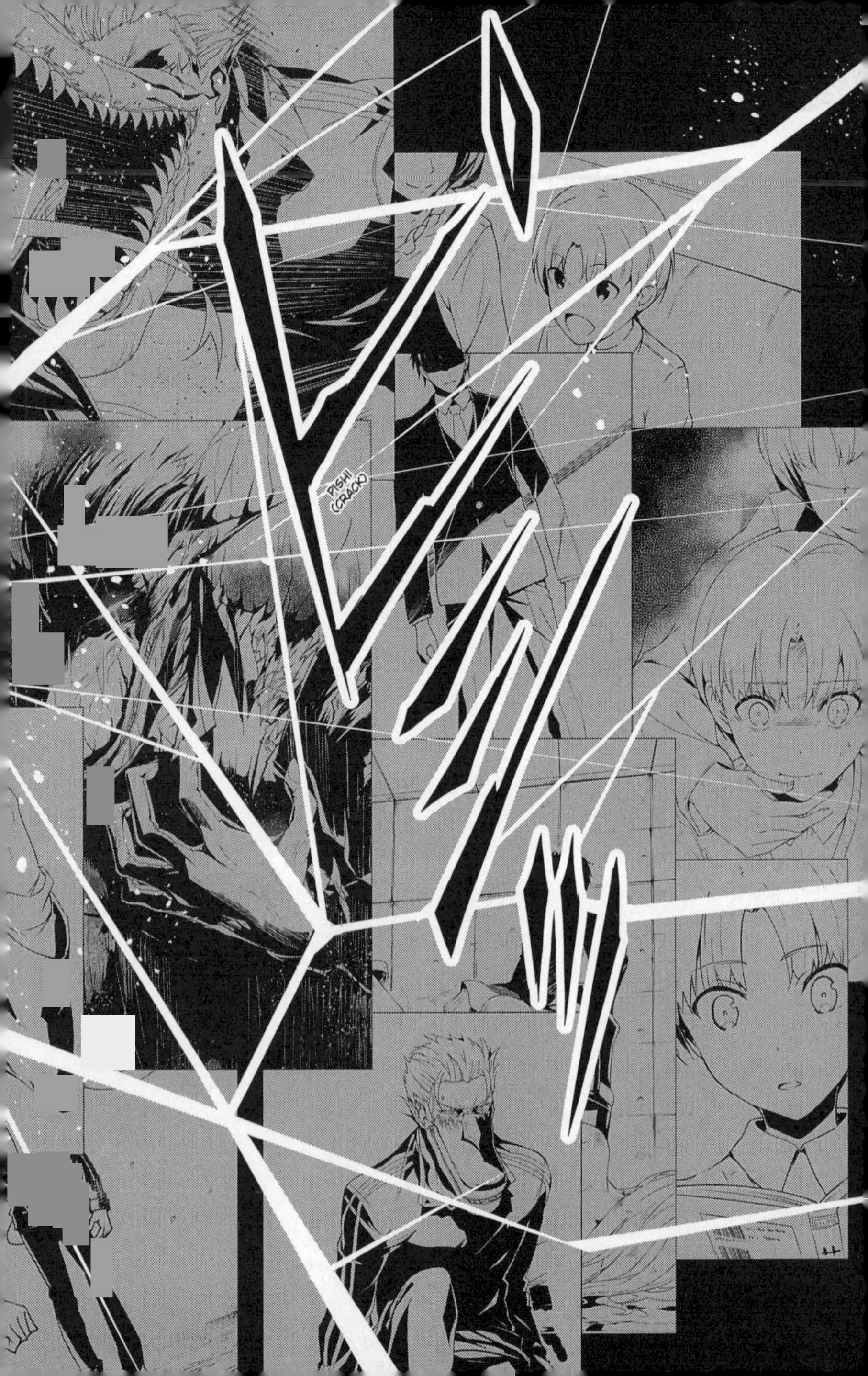
PISHI
(CRACK)

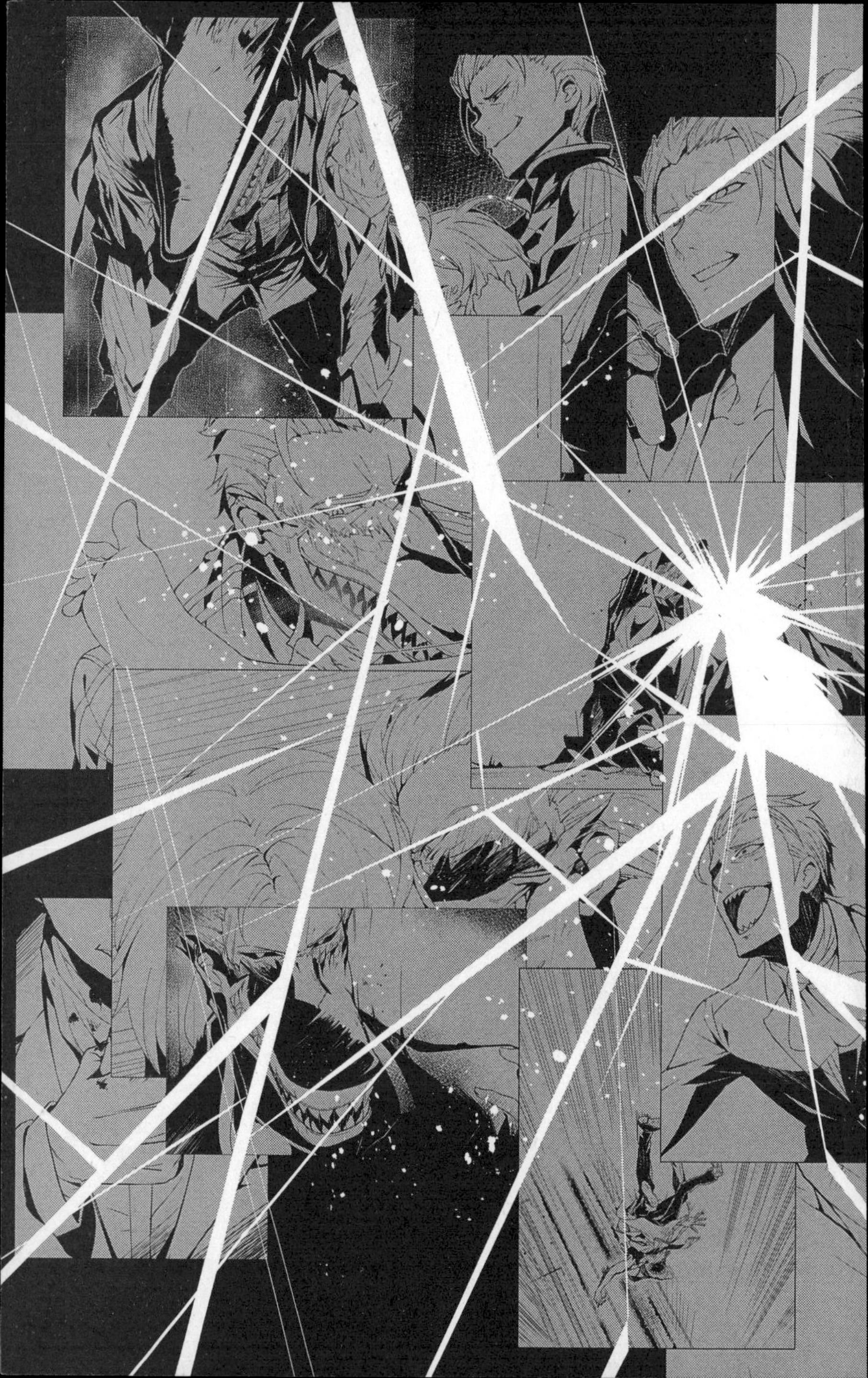

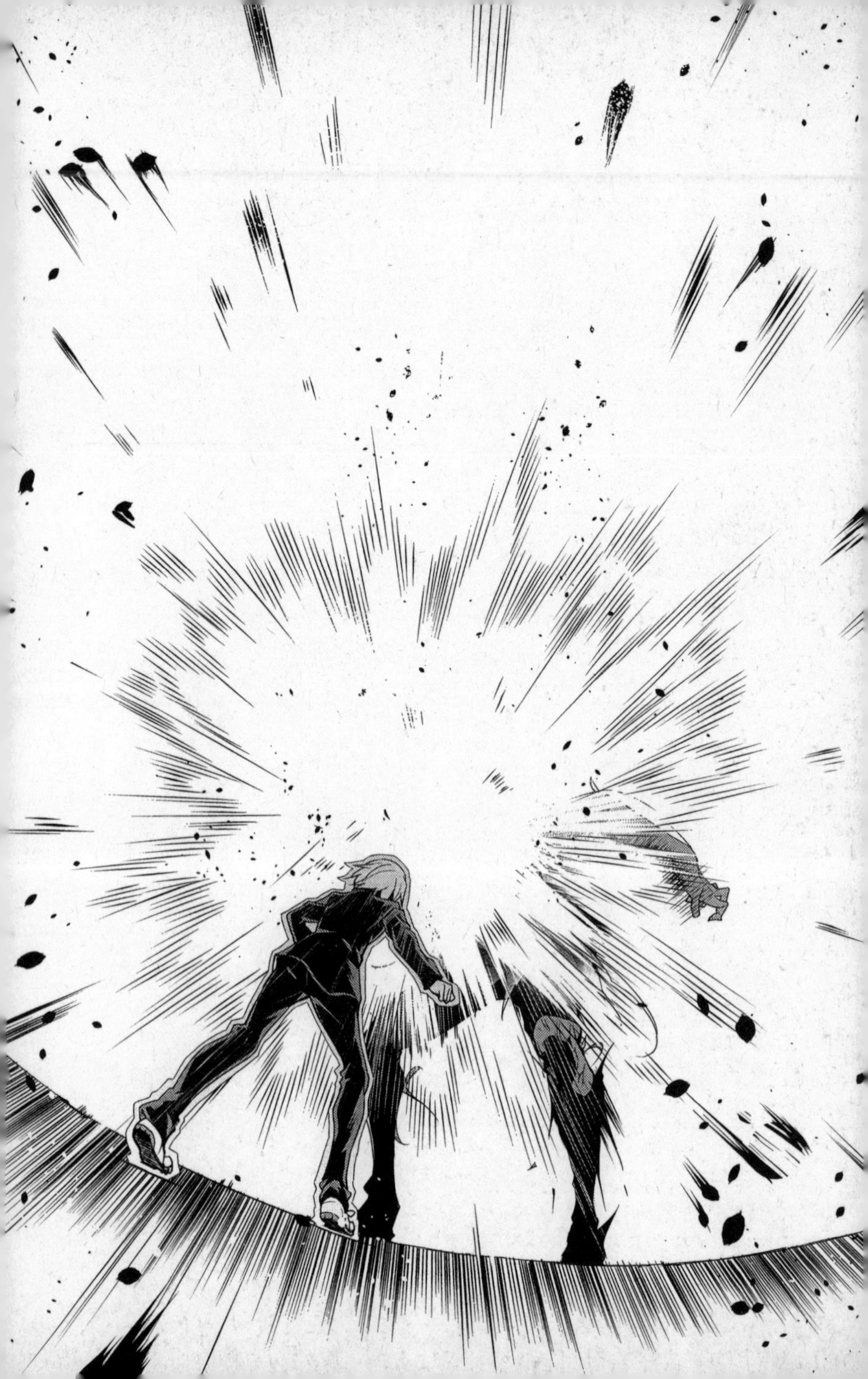

THE ISOLATOR
realization of
absolute solitude

Sect. 012
RUNAWAY

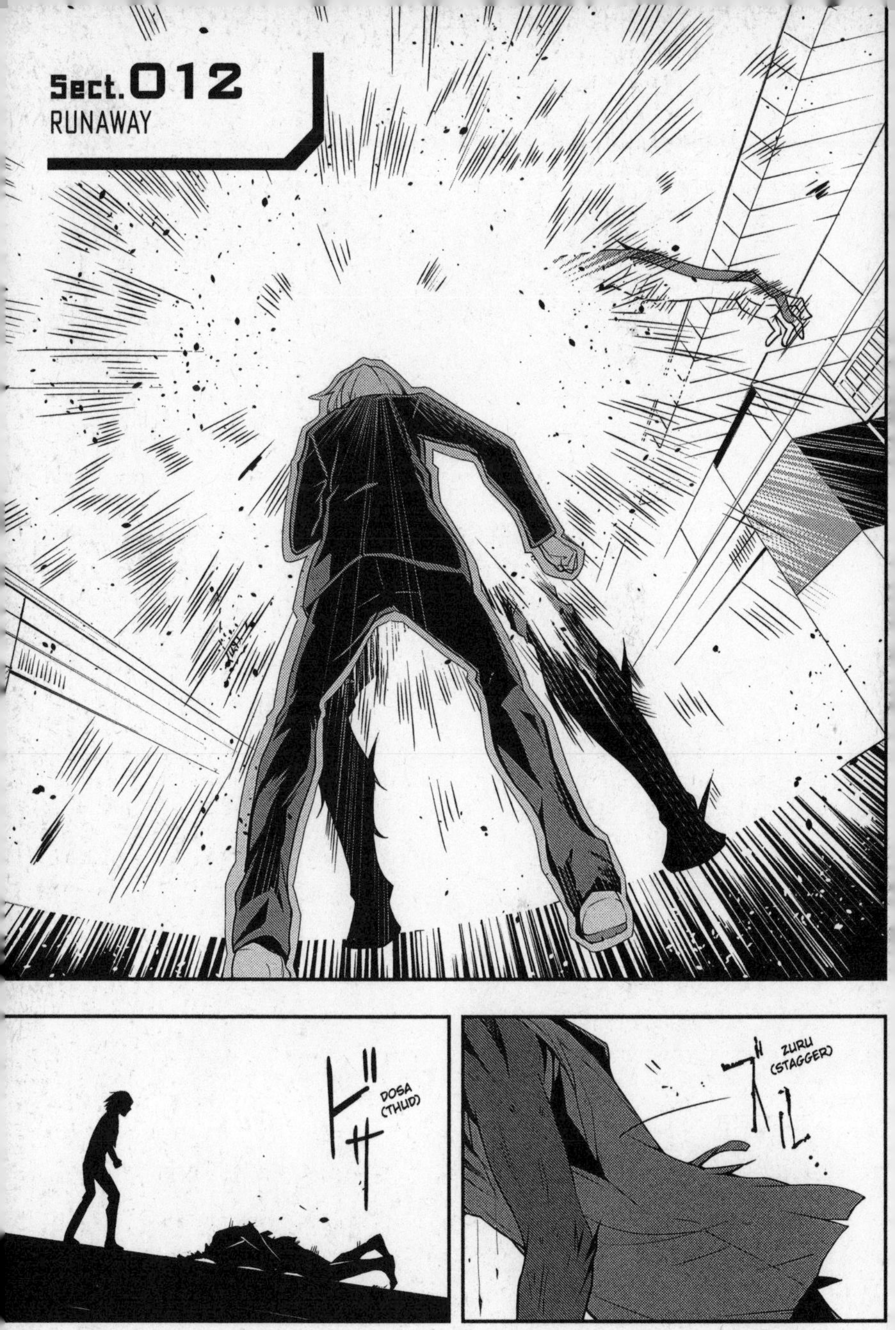
ZURU (STAGGER)
DOSA (THUD)

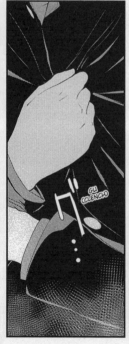

GU
(CLENCH)

POTA
(DRIP)

POTA

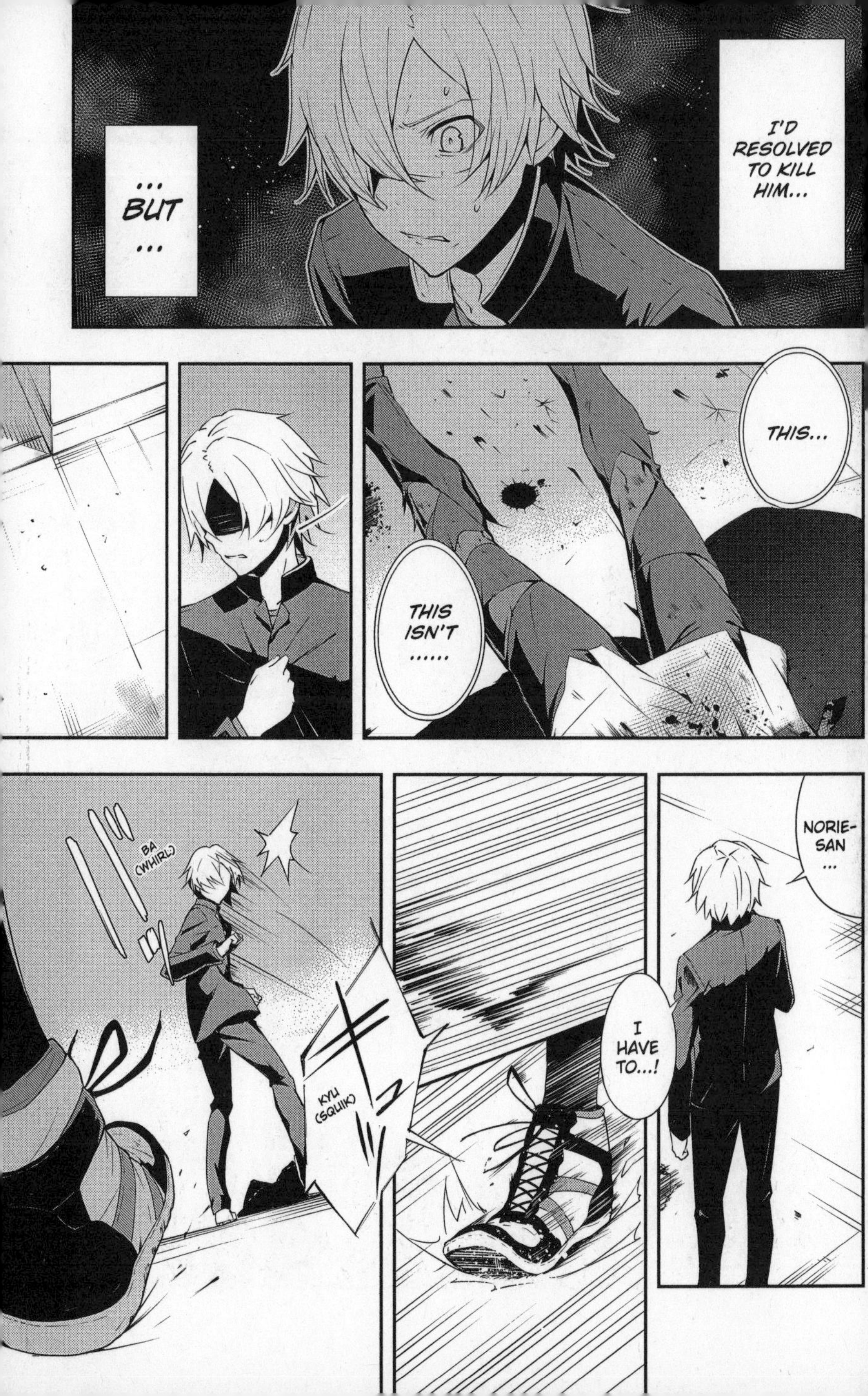
I'D RESOLVED TO KILL HIM...
...BUT...
THIS...
THIS ISN'T ......
NORIE-SAN...
I HAVE TO...!
KYU (SQUIK)
BA (WHIRL)

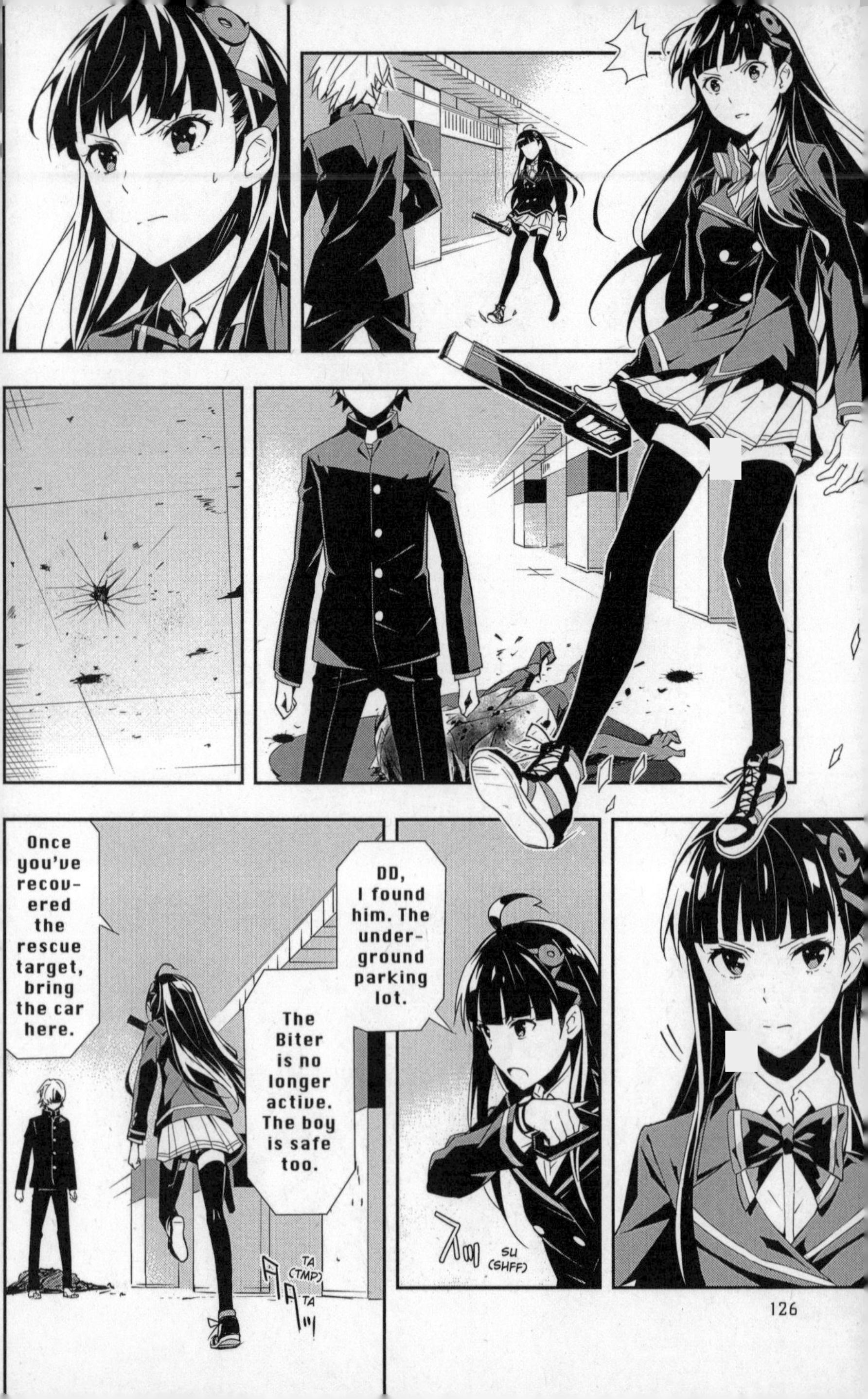
SU (SHFF)
DD, I found him. The underground parking lot.
The Biter is no longer active. The boy is safe too.
Once you've recovered the rescue target, bring the car here.
TA (TMP)
TA

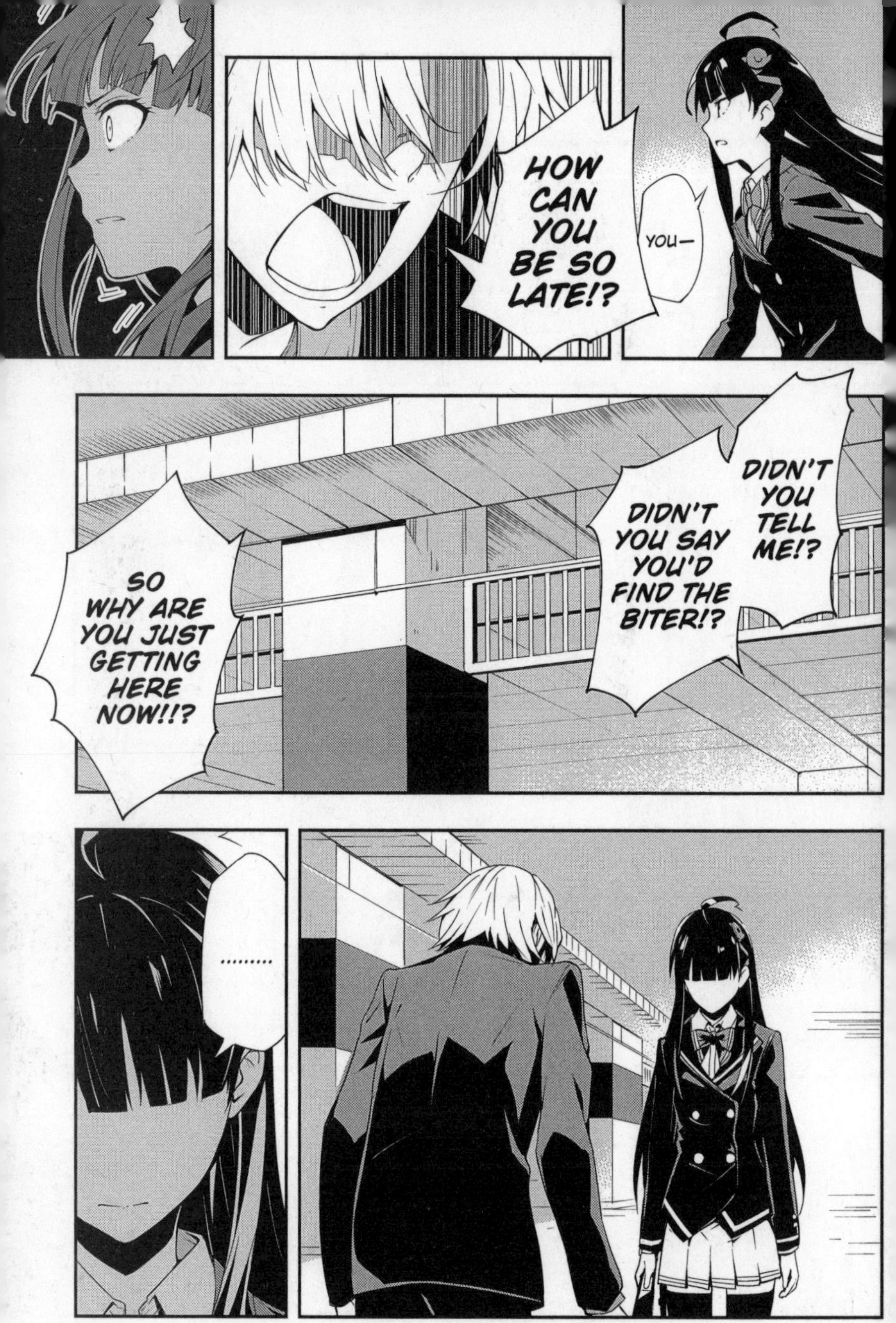
YOU—
HOW CAN YOU BE SO LATE!?
DIDN'T YOU TELL ME!?
DIDN'T YOU SAY YOU'D FIND THE BITER!?
SO WHY ARE YOU JUST GETTING HERE NOW!!?
....

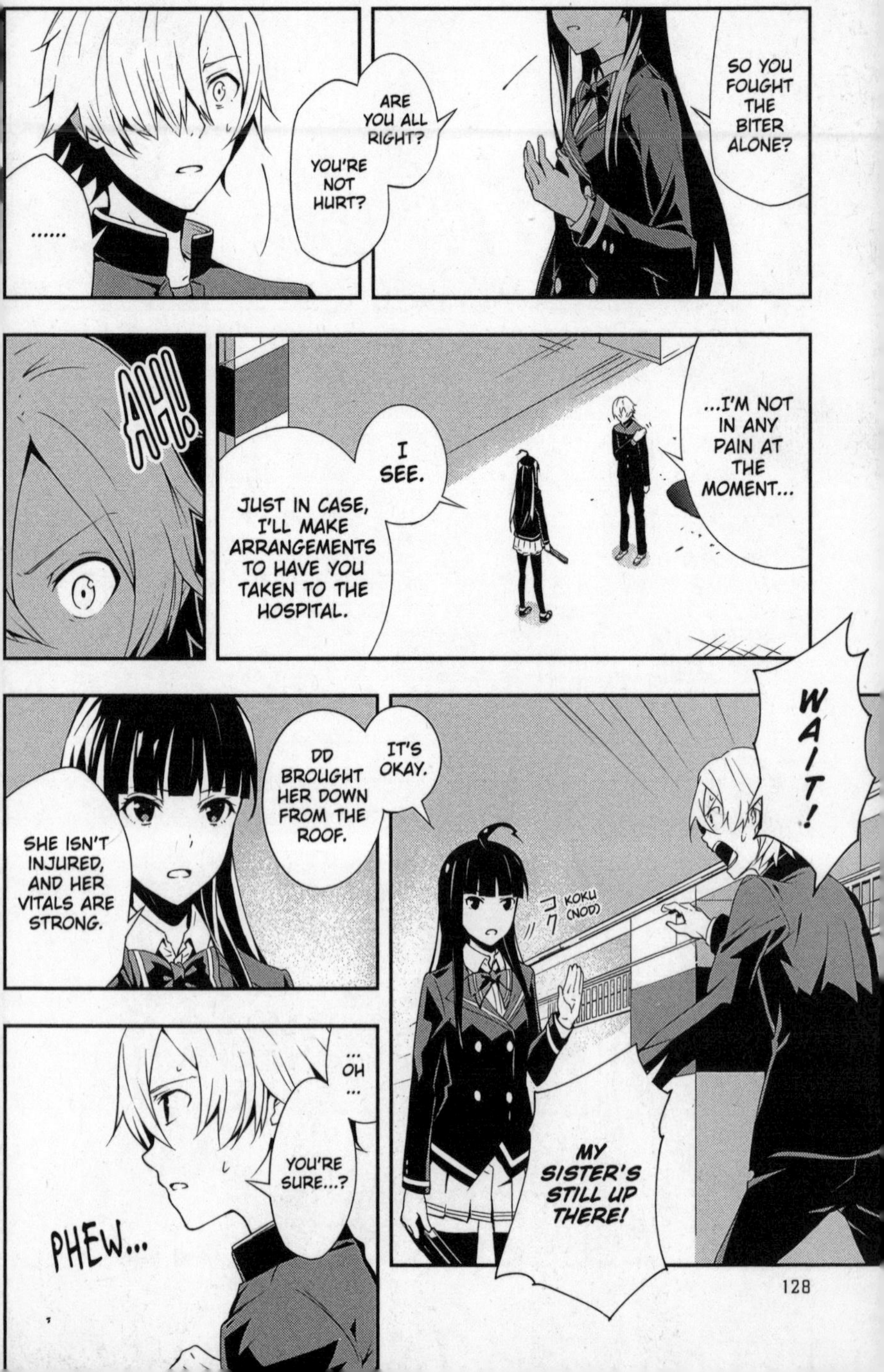
SO YOU FOUGHT THE BITER ALONE?
ARE YOU ALL RIGHT?
YOU'RE NOT HURT?
......
...I'M NOT IN ANY PAIN AT THE MOMENT...
I SEE.
JUST IN CASE, I'LL MAKE ARRANGEMENTS TO HAVE YOU TAKEN TO THE HOSPITAL.
AH!
WAIT!
MY SISTER'S STILL UP THERE!
KOKU (NOD)
IT'S OKAY.
DD BROUGHT HER DOWN FROM THE ROOF.
SHE ISN'T INJURED, AND HER VITALS ARE STRONG.
...OH...
YOU'RE SURE...?
PHEW...

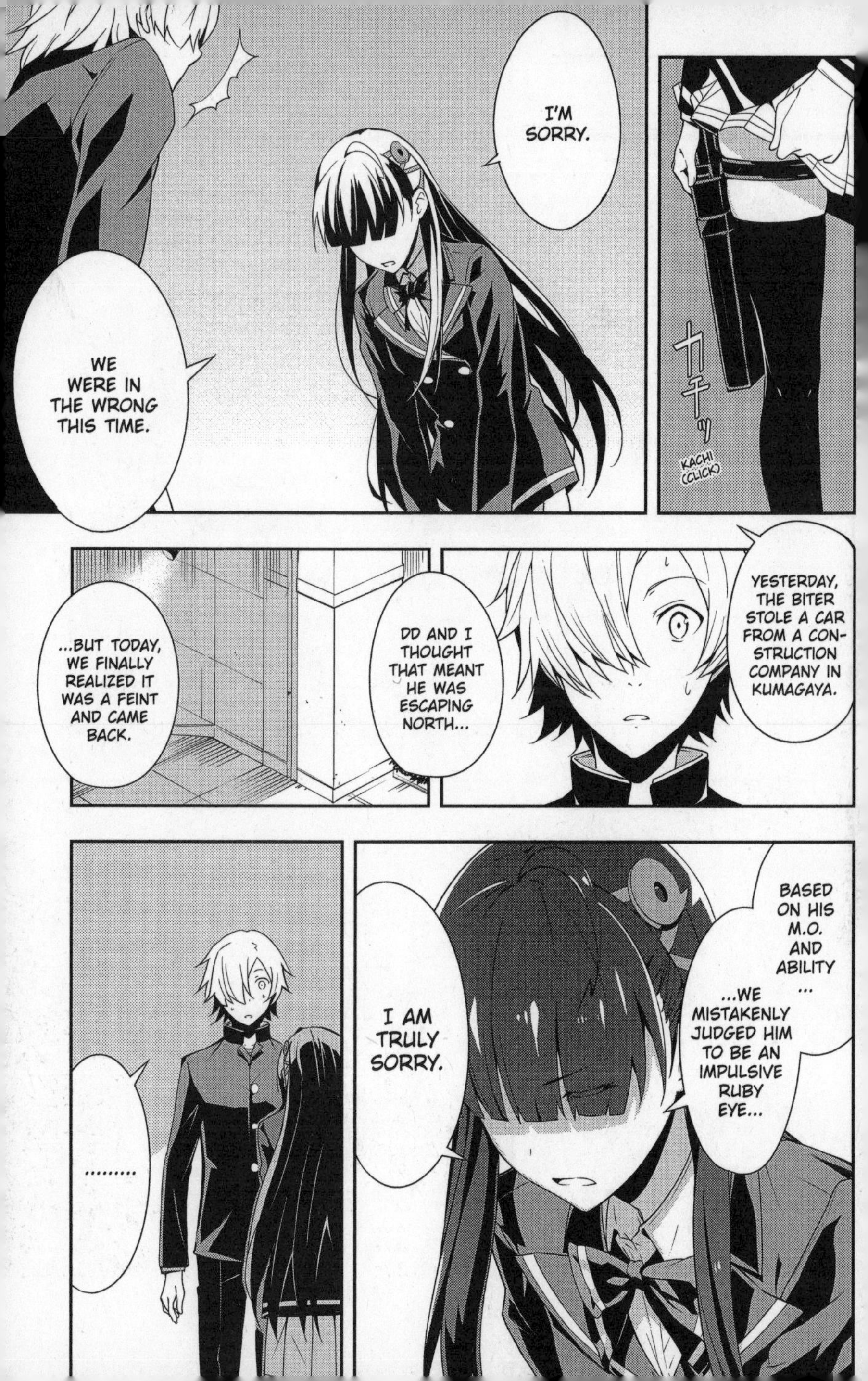
カチッ
KACHI (CLICK)
I'M SORRY.
WE WERE IN THE WRONG THIS TIME.
YESTERDAY, THE BITER STOLE A CAR FROM A CON-STRUCTION COMPANY IN KUMAGAYA.
DD AND I THOUGHT THAT MEANT HE WAS ESCAPING NORTH...
...BUT TODAY, WE FINALLY REALIZED IT WAS A FEINT AND CAME BACK.
BASED ON HIS M.O. AND ABILITY ...
...WE MISTAKENLY JUDGED HIM TO BE AN IMPULSIVE RUBY EYE...
I AM TRULY SORRY.
....

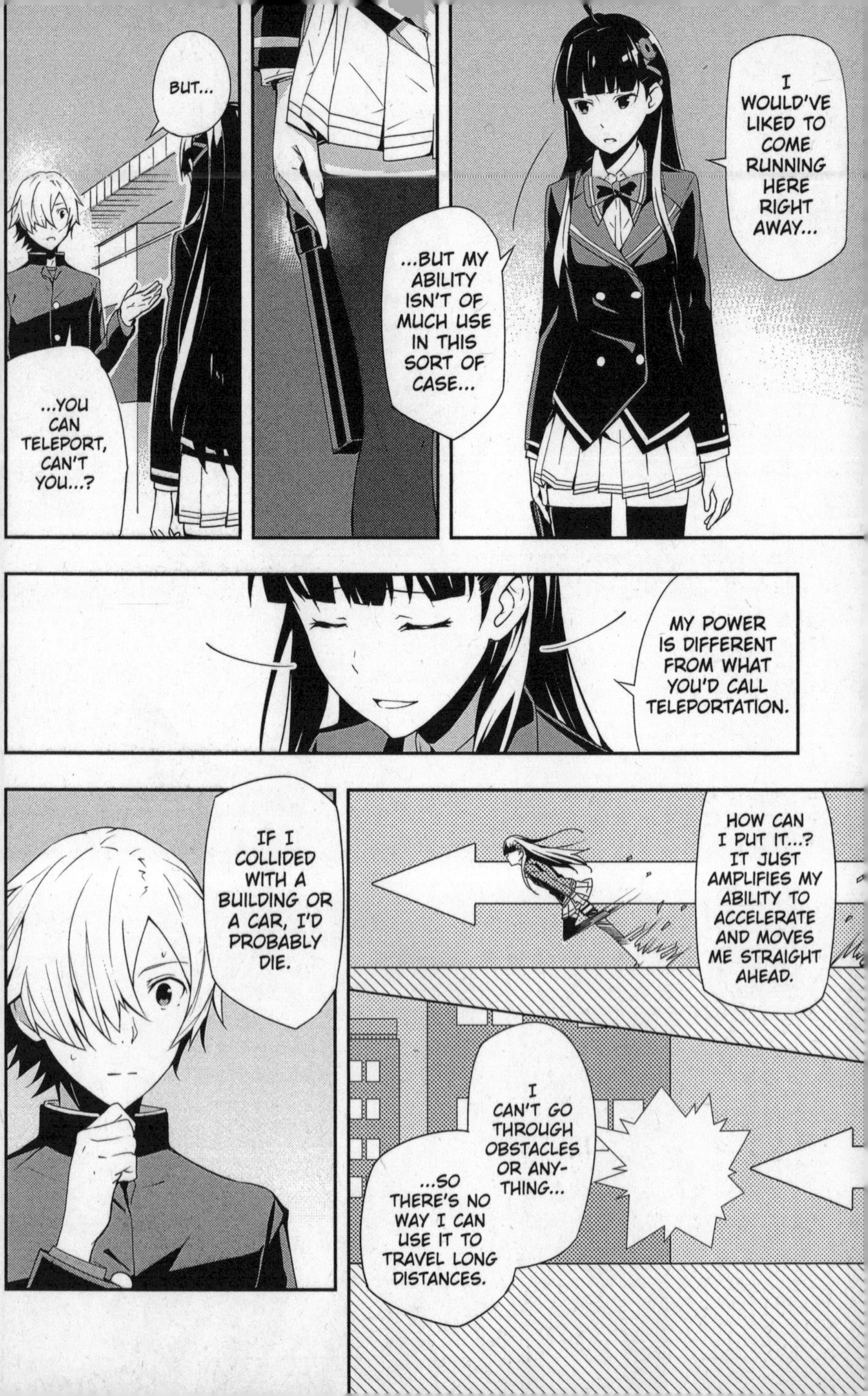
I WOULD'VE LIKED TO COME RUNNING HERE RIGHT AWAY...
...BUT MY ABILITY ISN'T OF MUCH USE IN THIS SORT OF CASE...
BUT...
...YOU CAN TELEPORT, CAN'T YOU...?
MY POWER IS DIFFERENT FROM WHAT YOU'D CALL TELEPORTATION.
HOW CAN I PUT IT...? IT JUST AMPLIFIES MY ABILITY TO ACCELERATE AND MOVES ME STRAIGHT AHEAD.
I CAN'T GO THROUGH OBSTACLES OR ANY-THING...
...SO THERE'S NO WAY I CAN USE IT TO TRAVEL LONG DISTANCES.
IF I COLLIDED WITH A BUILDING OR A CAR, I'D PROBABLY DIE.

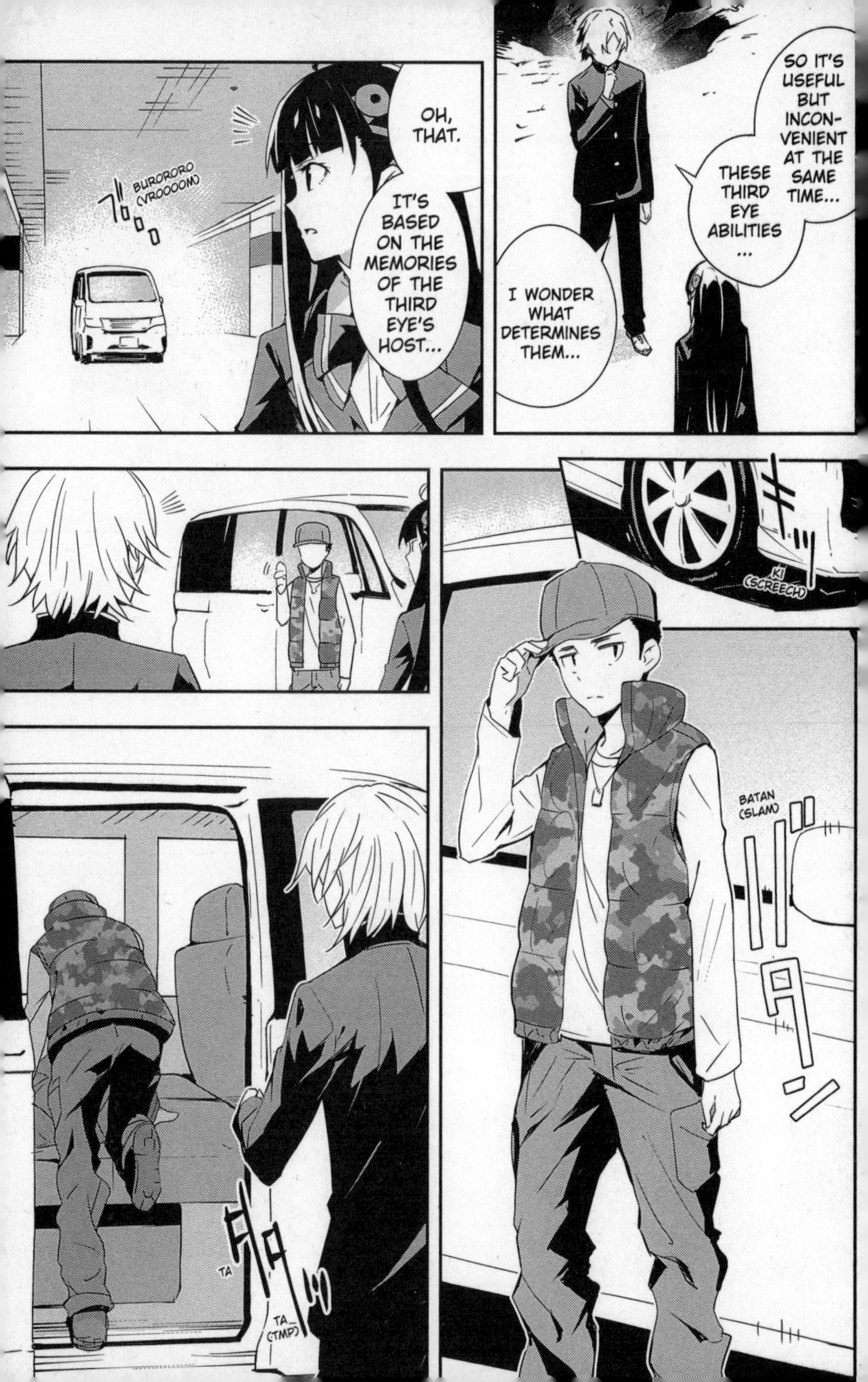
SO IT'S USEFUL BUT INCON-VENIENT AT THE SAME TIME...
THESE THIRD EYE ABILITIES...
I WONDER WHAT DETERMINES THEM...
OH, THAT.
IT'S BASED ON THE MEMORIES OF THE THIRD EYE'S HOST...
BURORORO (VROOOOM)
KI (SCREECH)
BATAN (SLAM)
TA
TA_ (TMP)

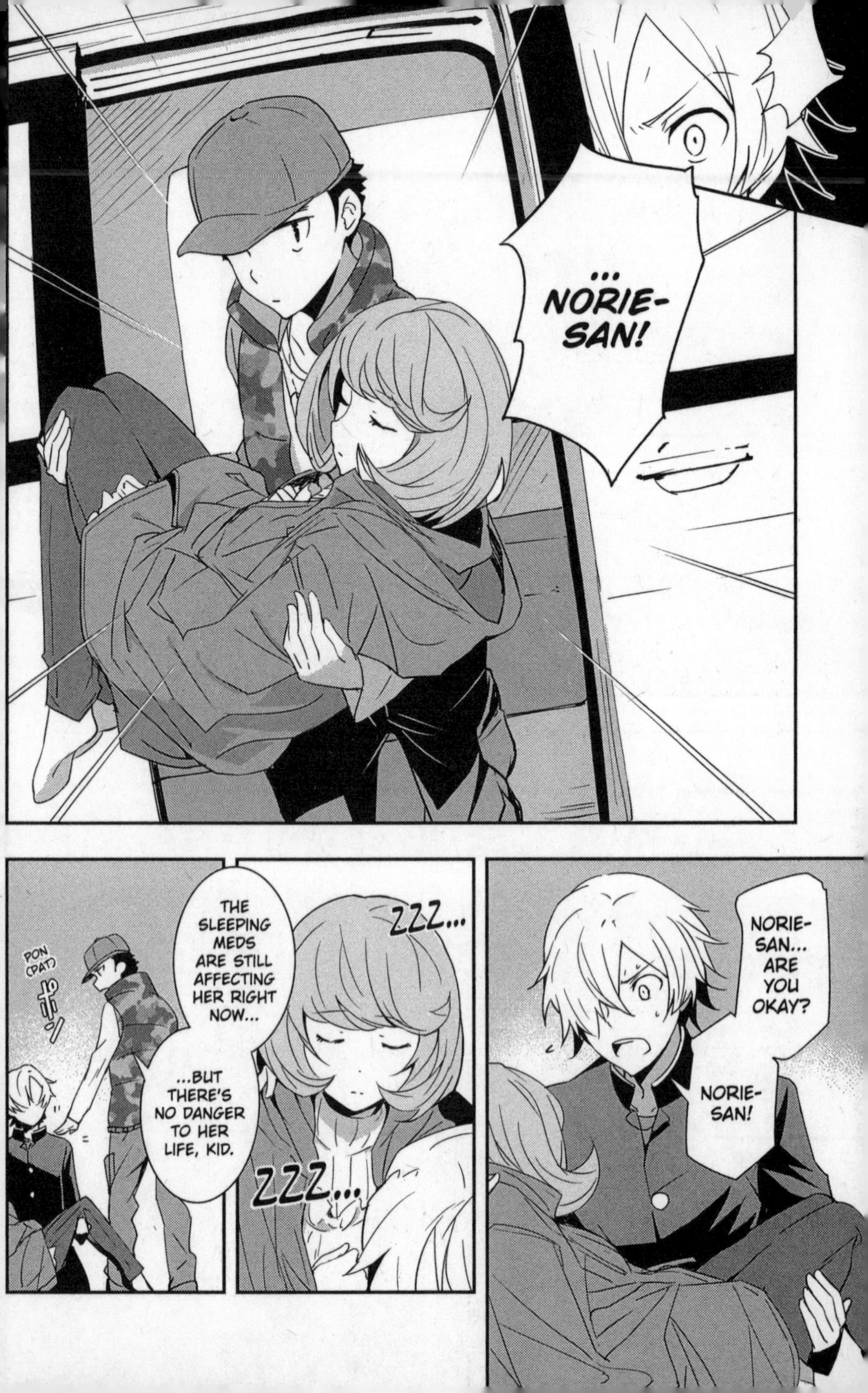
...NORIE-SAN!
NORIE-SAN... ARE YOU OKAY?
NORIE-SAN!
ZZZ...
THE SLEEPING MEDS ARE STILL AFFECTING HER RIGHT NOW...
...BUT THERE'S NO DANGER TO HER LIFE, KID.
ZZZ...
PON (PAT)

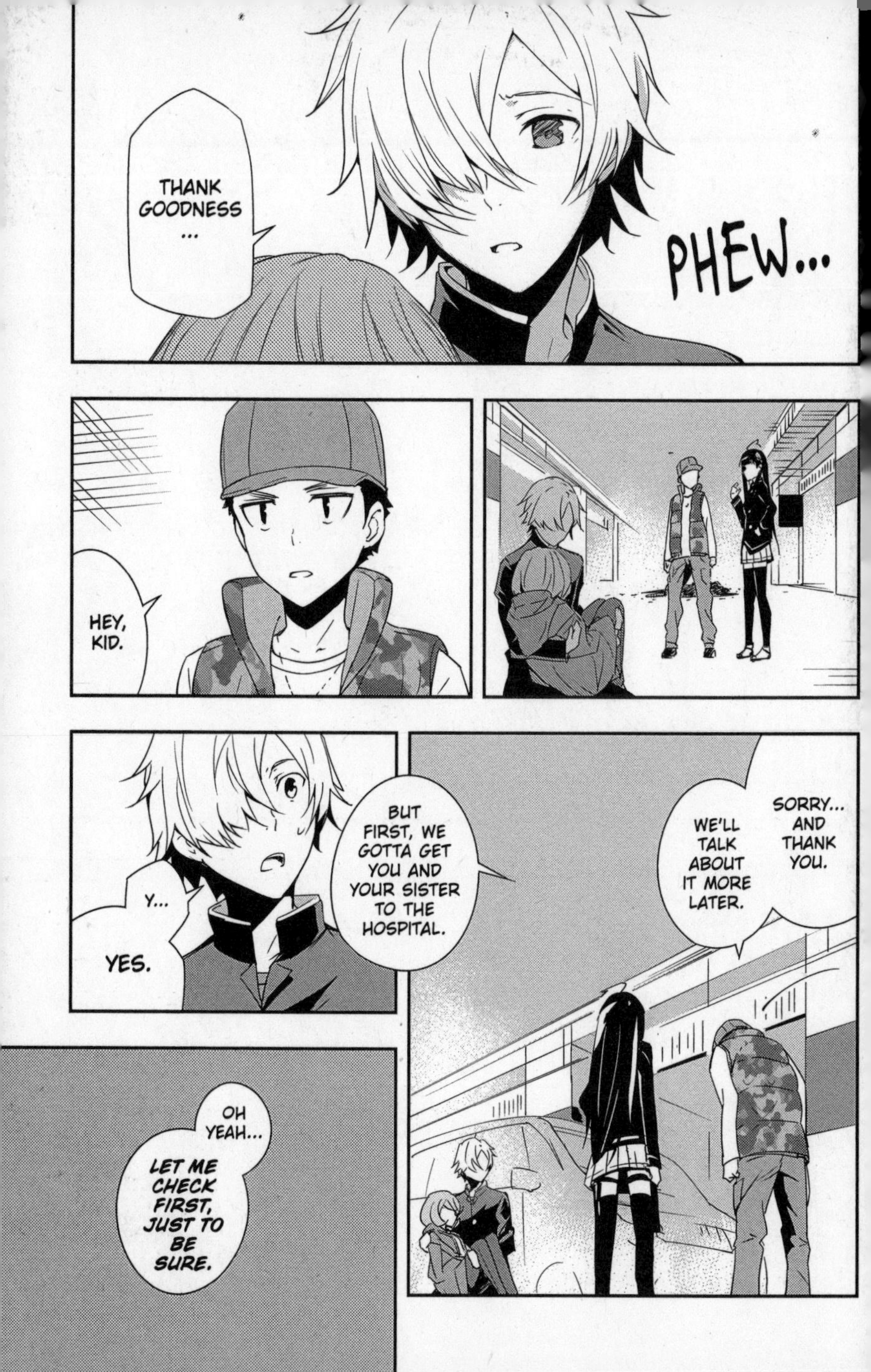
PHEW...
THANK GOODNESS ...
HEY, KID.
SORRY... AND THANK YOU.
WE'LL TALK ABOUT IT MORE LATER.
BUT FIRST, WE GOTTA GET YOU AND YOUR SISTER TO THE HOSPITAL.
Y... YES.
OH YEAH... LET ME CHECK FIRST, JUST TO BE SURE.

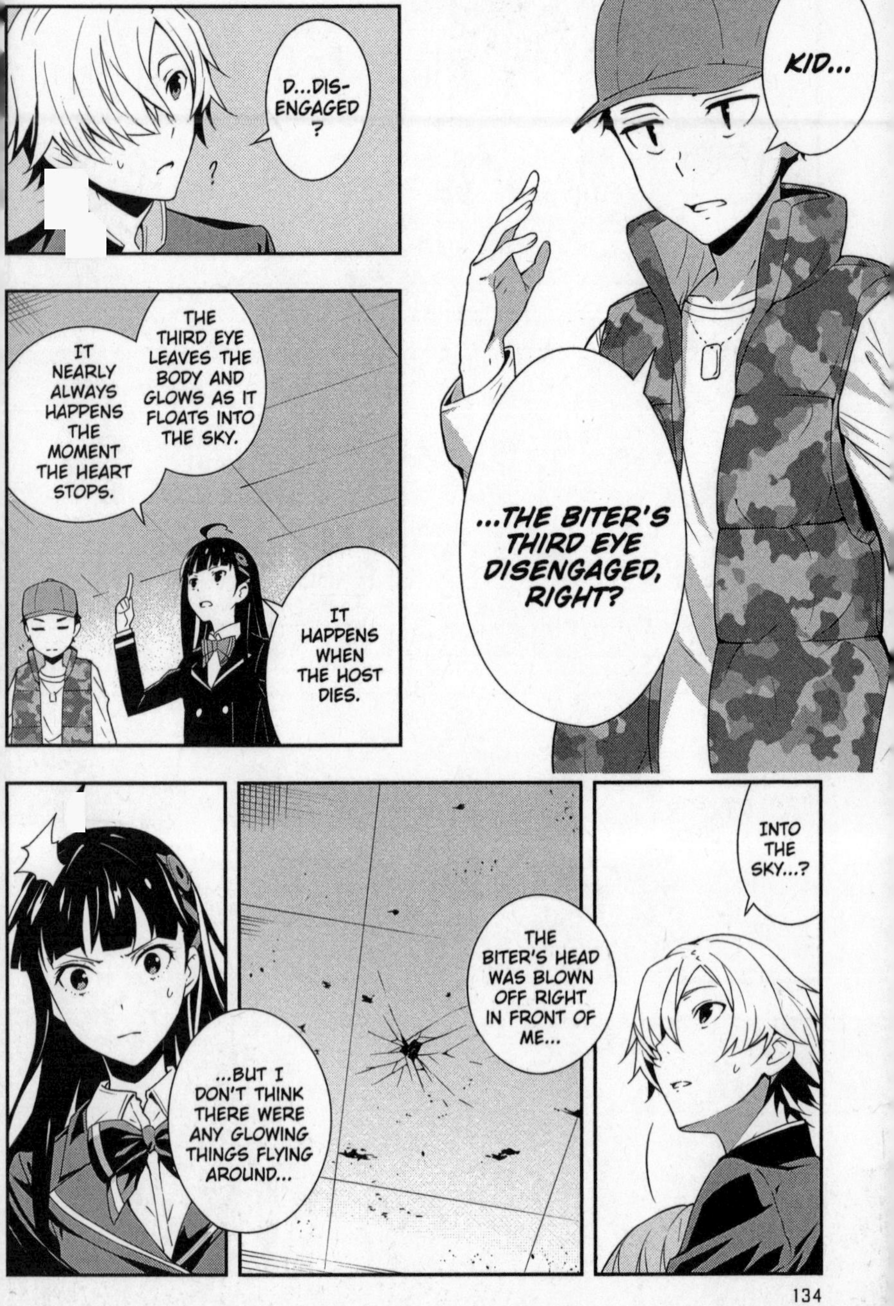
KID...
...THE BITER'S THIRD EYE DISENGAGED, RIGHT?
D...DIS-ENGAGED?
IT HAPPENS WHEN THE HOST DIES.
THE THIRD EYE LEAVES THE BODY AND GLOWS AS IT FLOATS INTO THE SKY.
IT NEARLY ALWAYS HAPPENS THE MOMENT THE HEART STOPS.
INTO THE SKY...?
THE BITER'S HEAD WAS BLOWN OFF RIGHT IN FRONT OF ME...
...BUT I DON'T THINK THERE WERE ANY GLOWING THINGS FLYING AROUND...

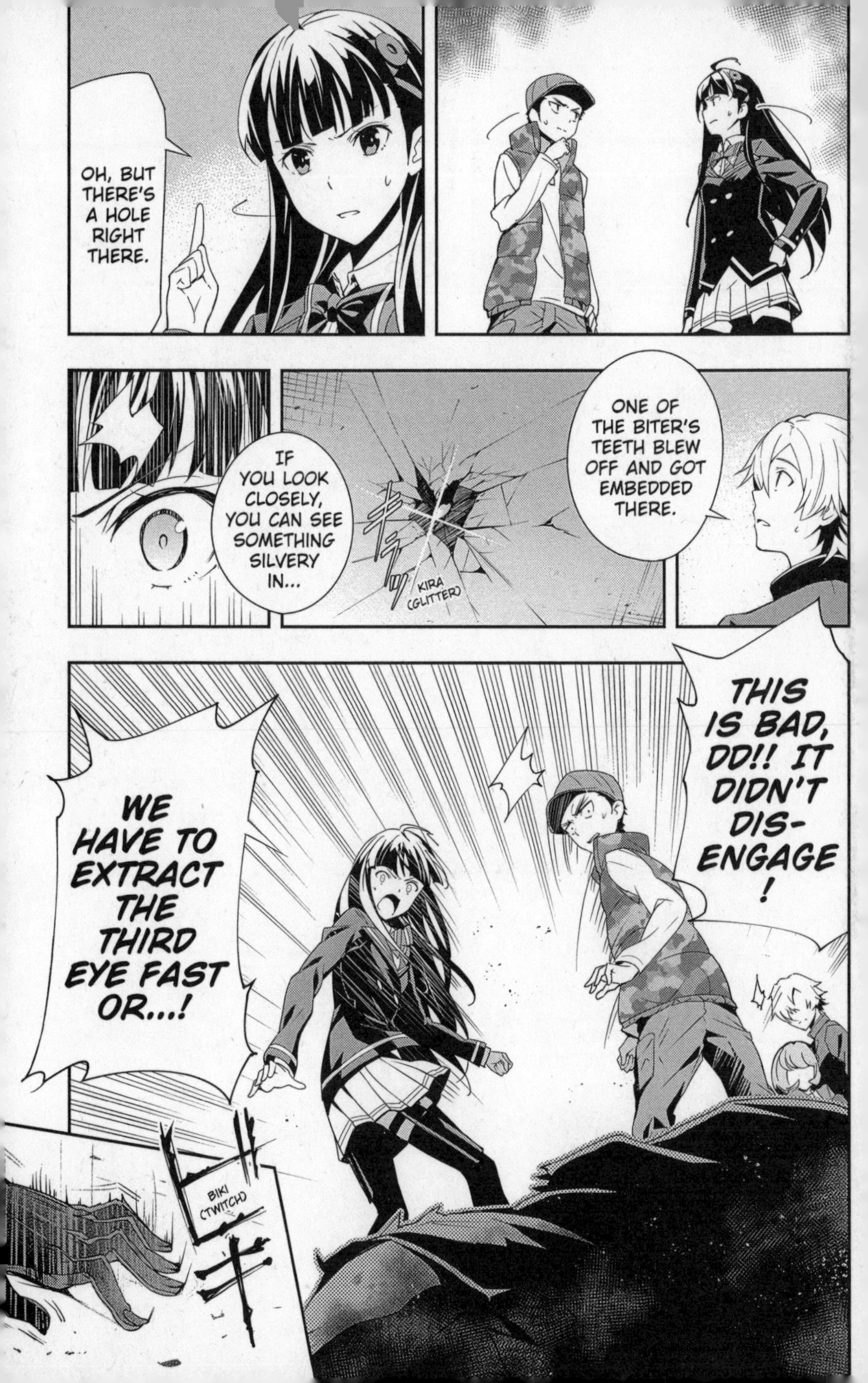
OH, BUT THERE'S A HOLE RIGHT THERE.
ONE OF THE BITER'S TEETH BLEW OFF AND GOT EMBEDDED THERE.
IF YOU LOOK CLOSELY, YOU CAN SEE SOMETHING SILVERY IN...
KIRA (GLITTER)
THIS IS BAD, DD!! IT DIDN'T DIS-ENGAGE!
WE HAVE TO EXTRACT THE THIRD EYE FAST OR...!
BIKI (TWITCH)

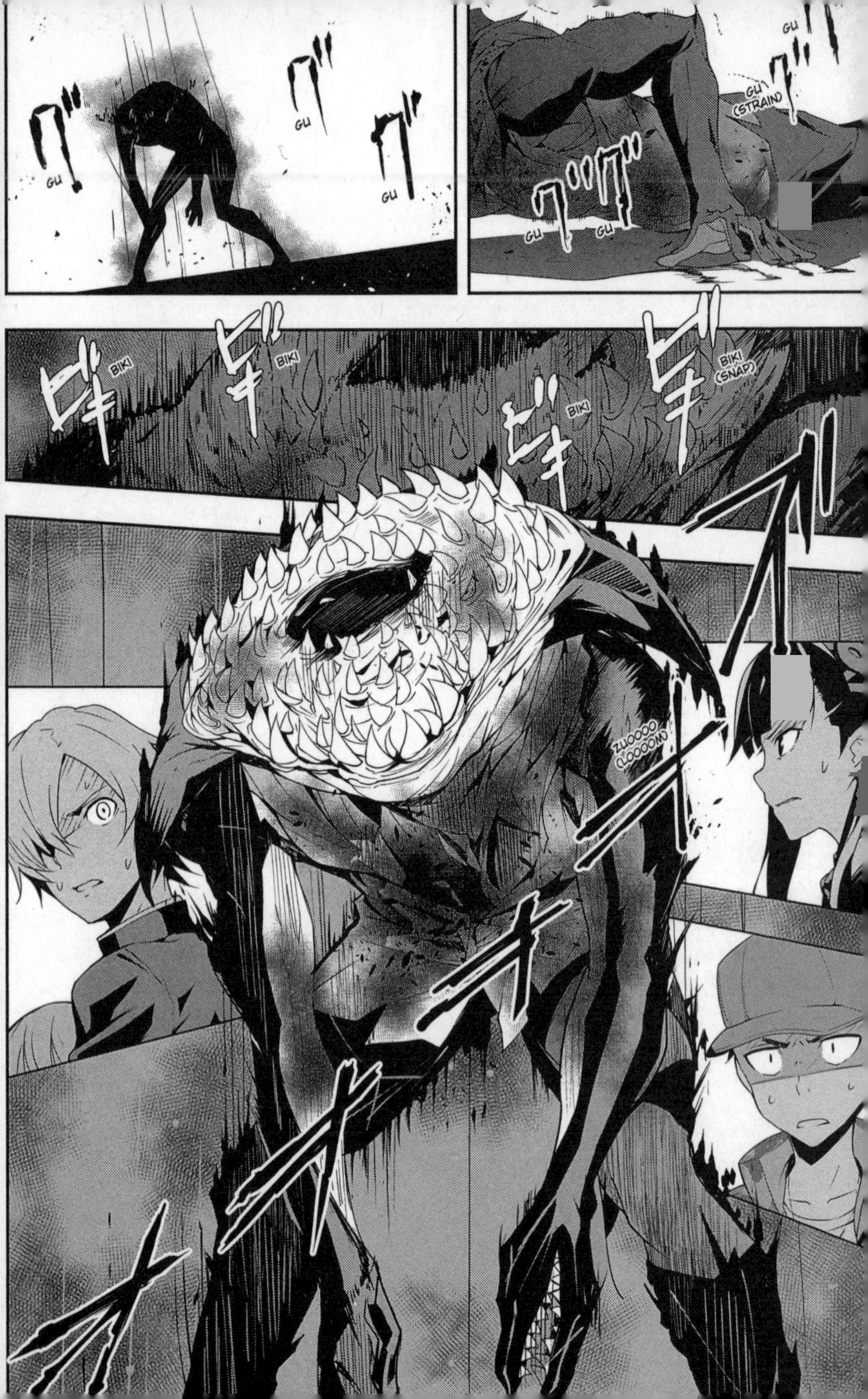
GU
GU (STRAIN)
GU
GU
GU
GU
GU
BIKI (SNAP)
BIKI
BIKI
BIKI
ZUOOOO (LOOOOM)

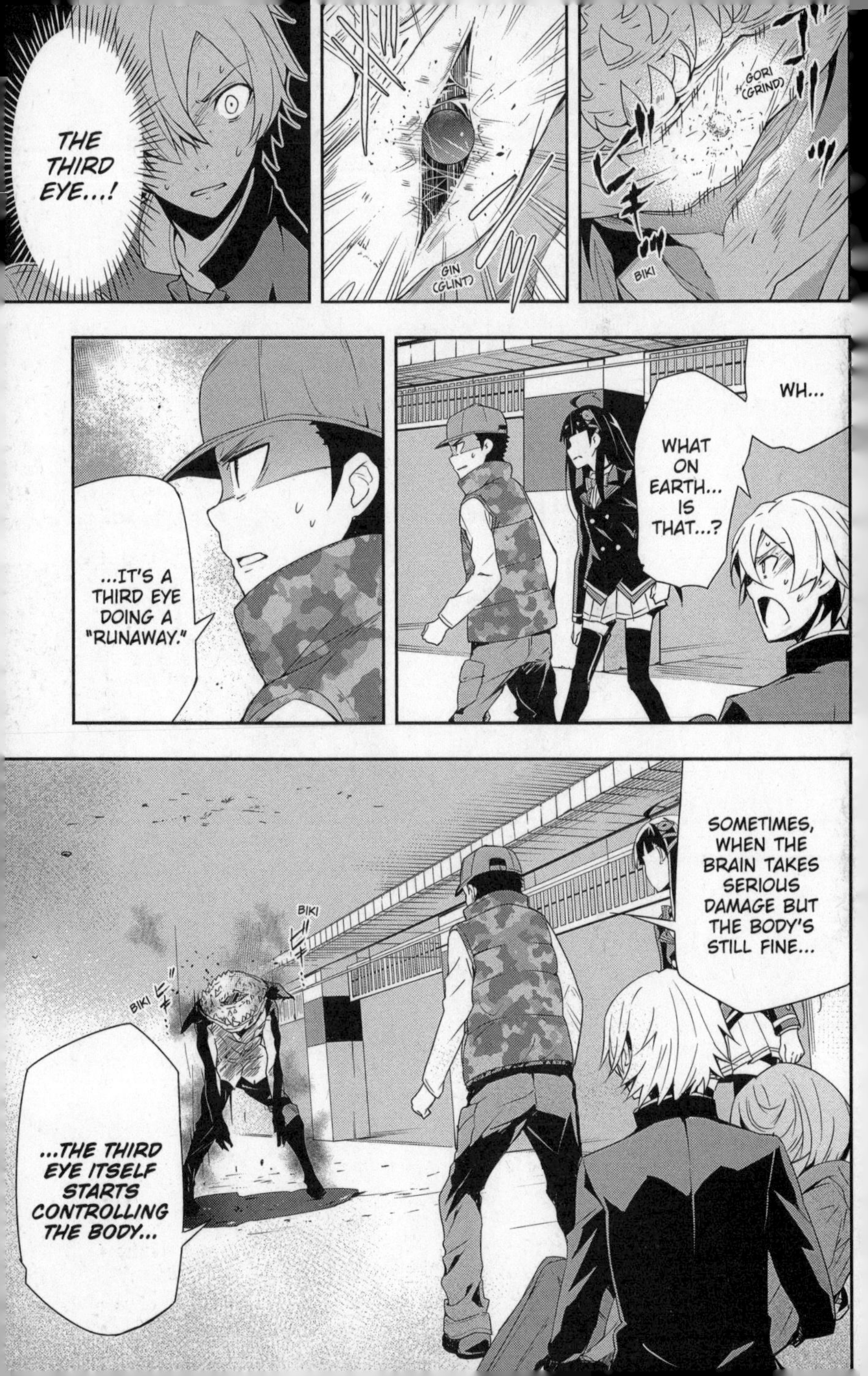
GORI (GRIND)
BIKI
GIN (GLINT)
THE THIRD EYE...!
WH...
WHAT ON EARTH... IS THAT...?
...IT'S A THIRD EYE DOING A "RUNAWAY."
SOMETIMES, WHEN THE BRAIN TAKES SERIOUS DAMAGE BUT THE BODY'S STILL FINE...
BIKI
BIKI
...THE THIRD EYE ITSELF STARTS CONTROLLING THE BODY...

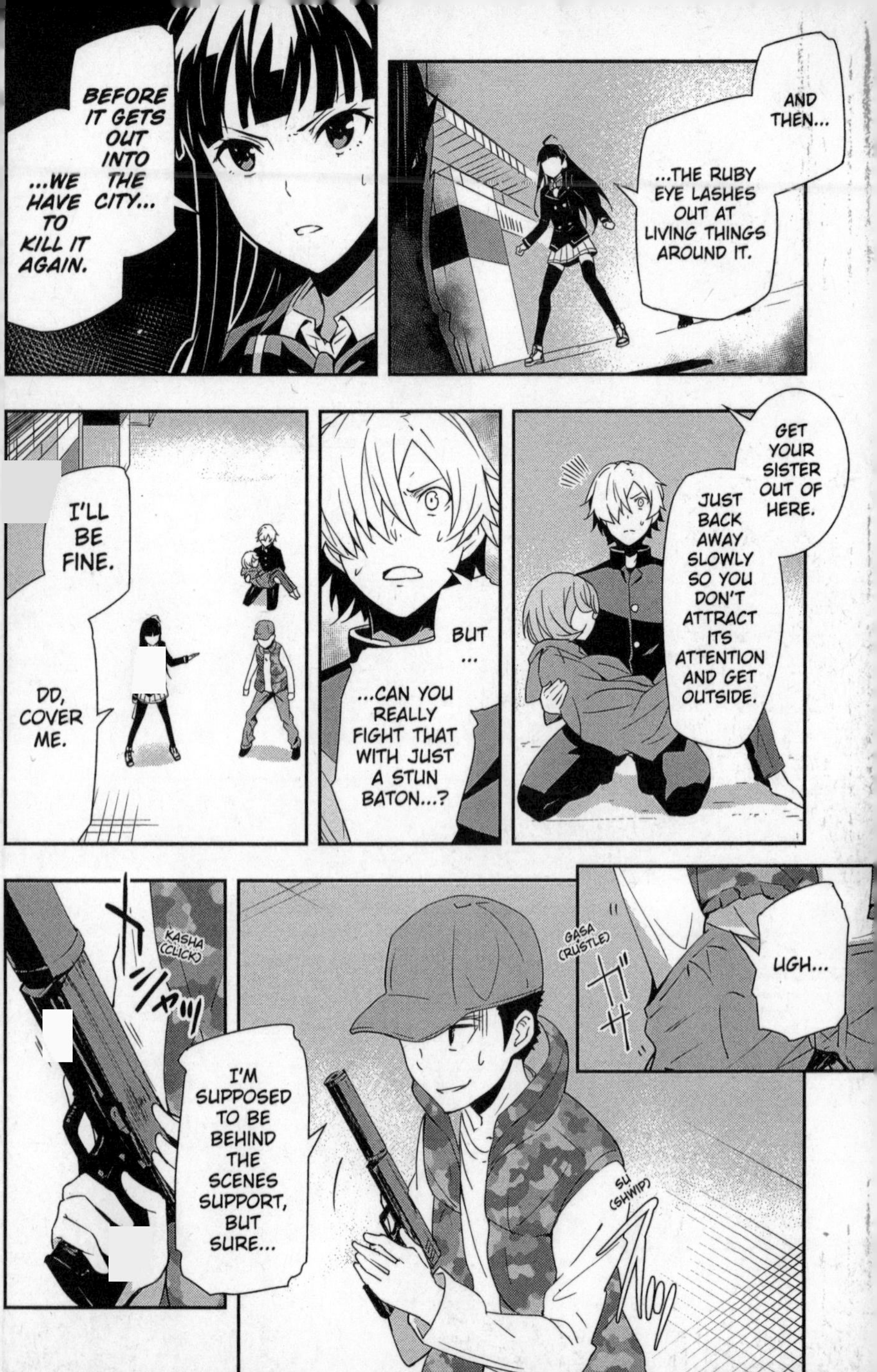
AND THEN...
...THE RUBY EYE LASHES OUT AT LIVING THINGS AROUND IT.
BEFORE IT GETS OUT INTO THE CITY...
...WE HAVE TO KILL IT AGAIN.
GET YOUR SISTER OUT OF HERE.
JUST BACK AWAY SLOWLY SO YOU DON'T ATTRACT ITS ATTENTION AND GET OUTSIDE.
BUT ...
...CAN YOU REALLY FIGHT THAT WITH JUST A STUN BATON...?
I'LL BE FINE.
DD, COVER ME.
GASA (RUSTLE)
UGH...
I'M SUPPOSED TO BE BEHIND THE SCENES SUPPORT, BUT SURE...
SU (SHWIP)
KASHA (CLICK)

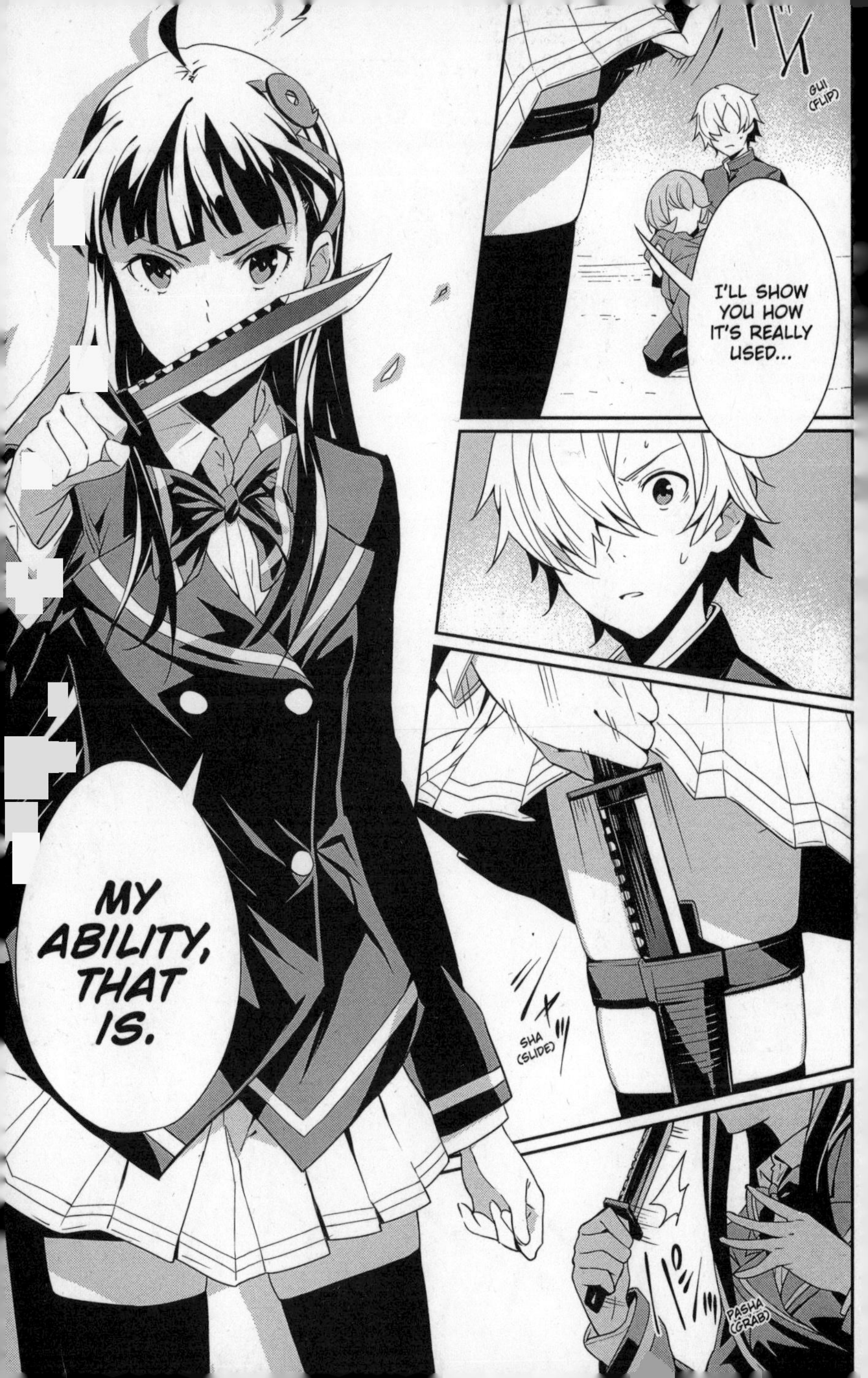
GUI (FLIP)
I'LL SHOW YOU HOW IT'S REALLY USED...
SHA (SLIDE)
PASHA (GRAB)
MY ABILITY, THAT IS.

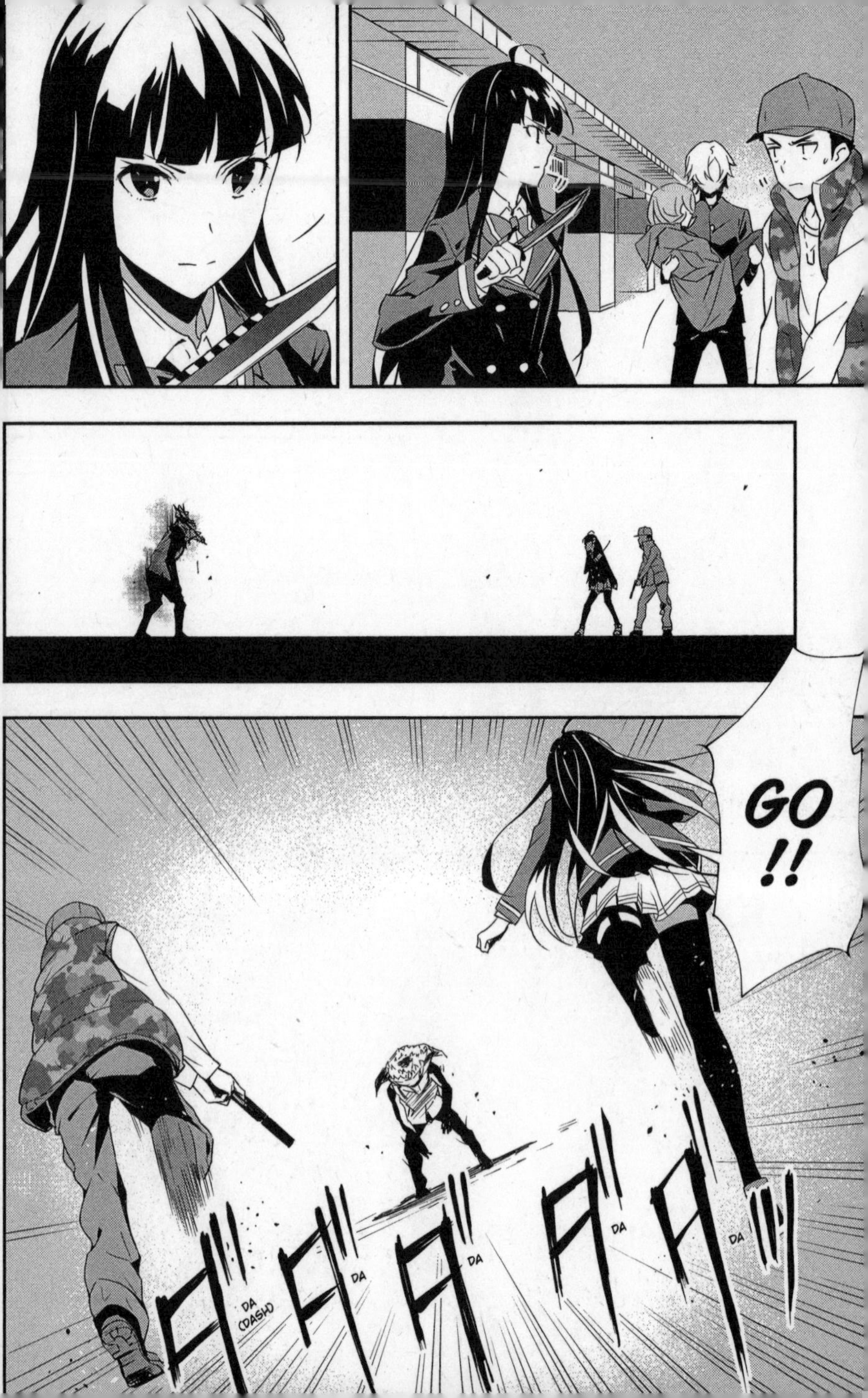
GO !!
DA
DA
DA
DA
DA (DASH)

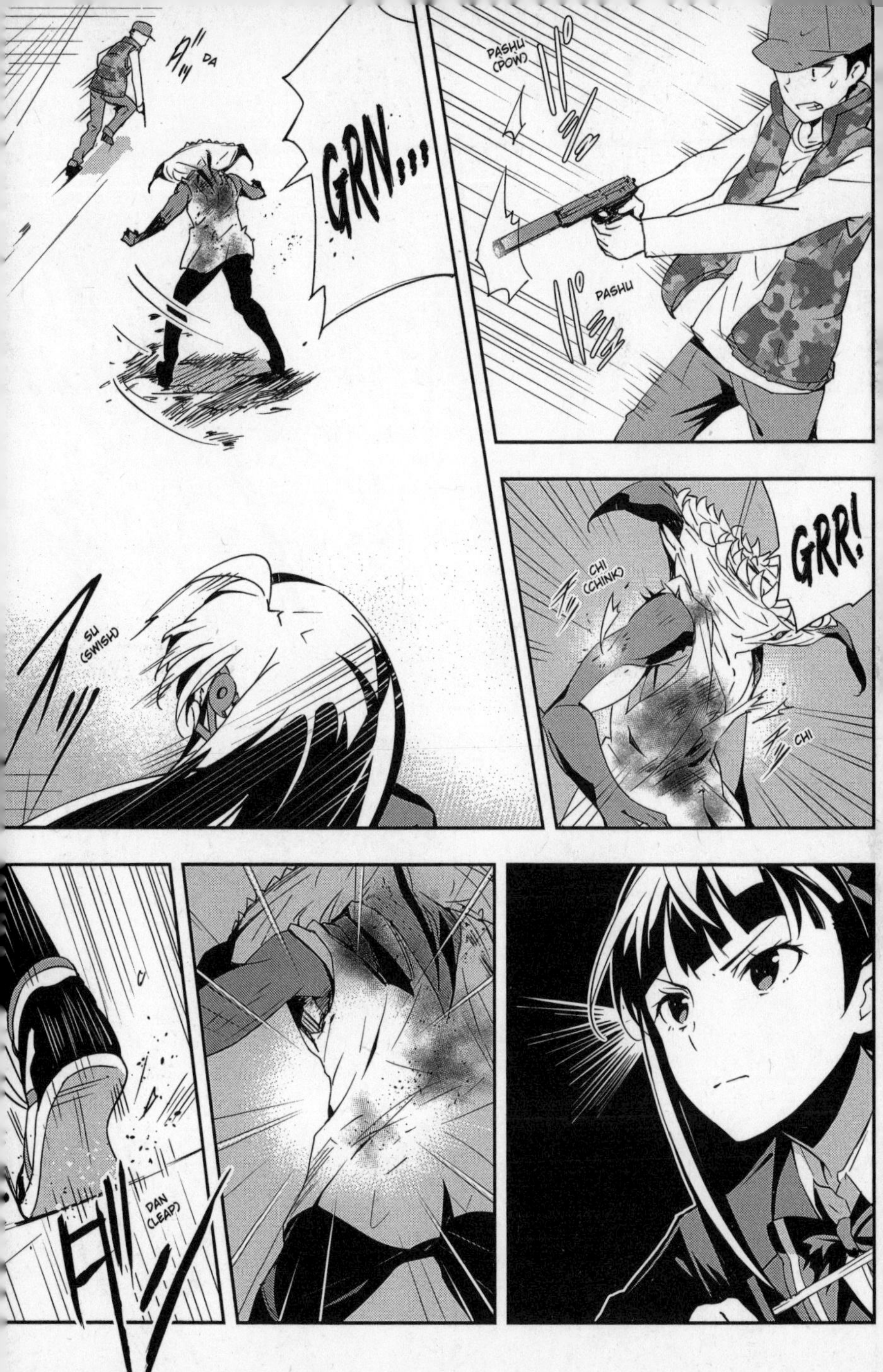
PASHU
(POW)
PASHU
DA
GRN...
GRR!
CHI
(CHINK)
CHI
SU
(SWISH)
DAN
(LEAP)

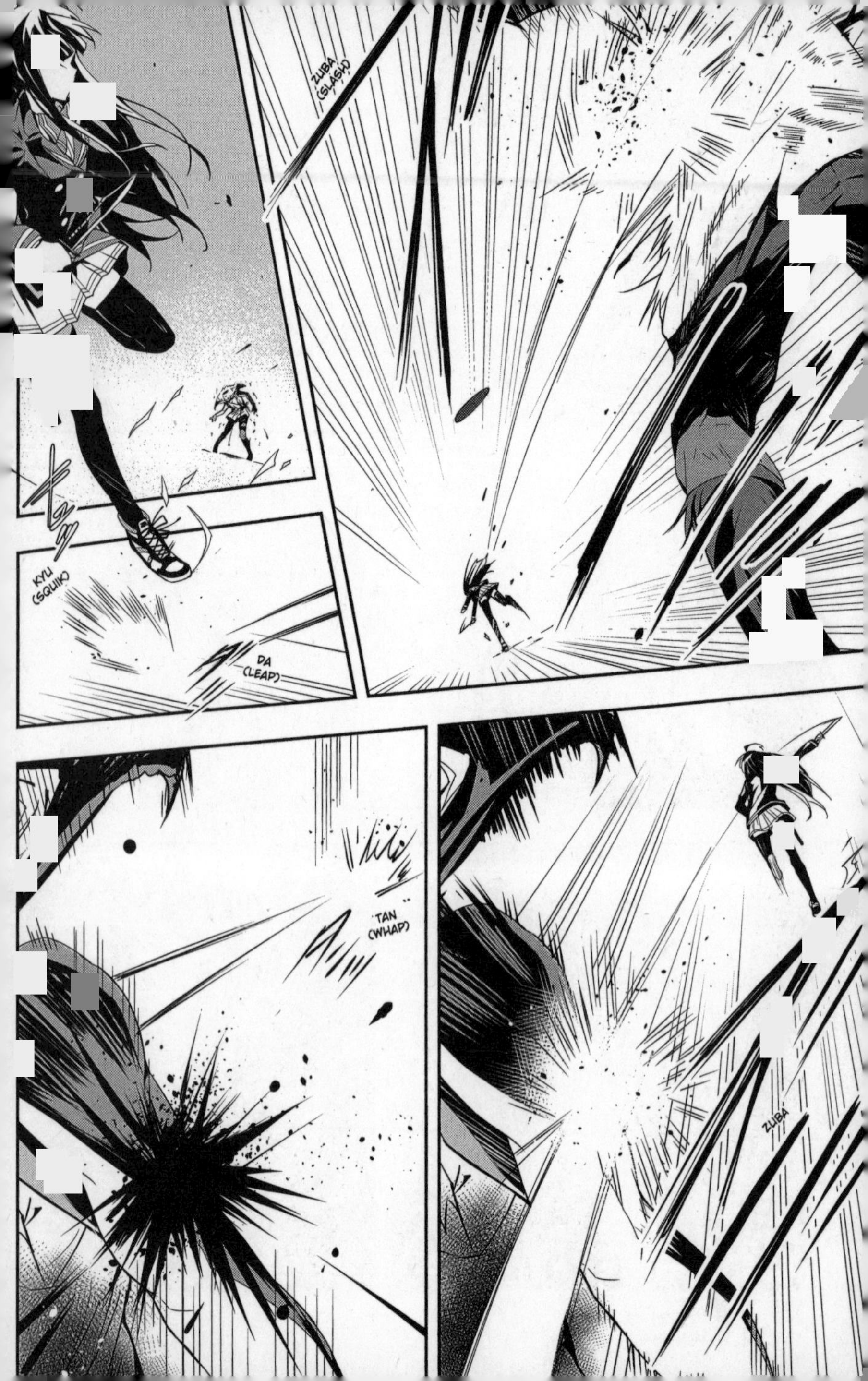
ZUBA
(SLASH)
KYU
(SQUIK)
DA
(LEAP)
ZUBA
TAN
(WHAP)

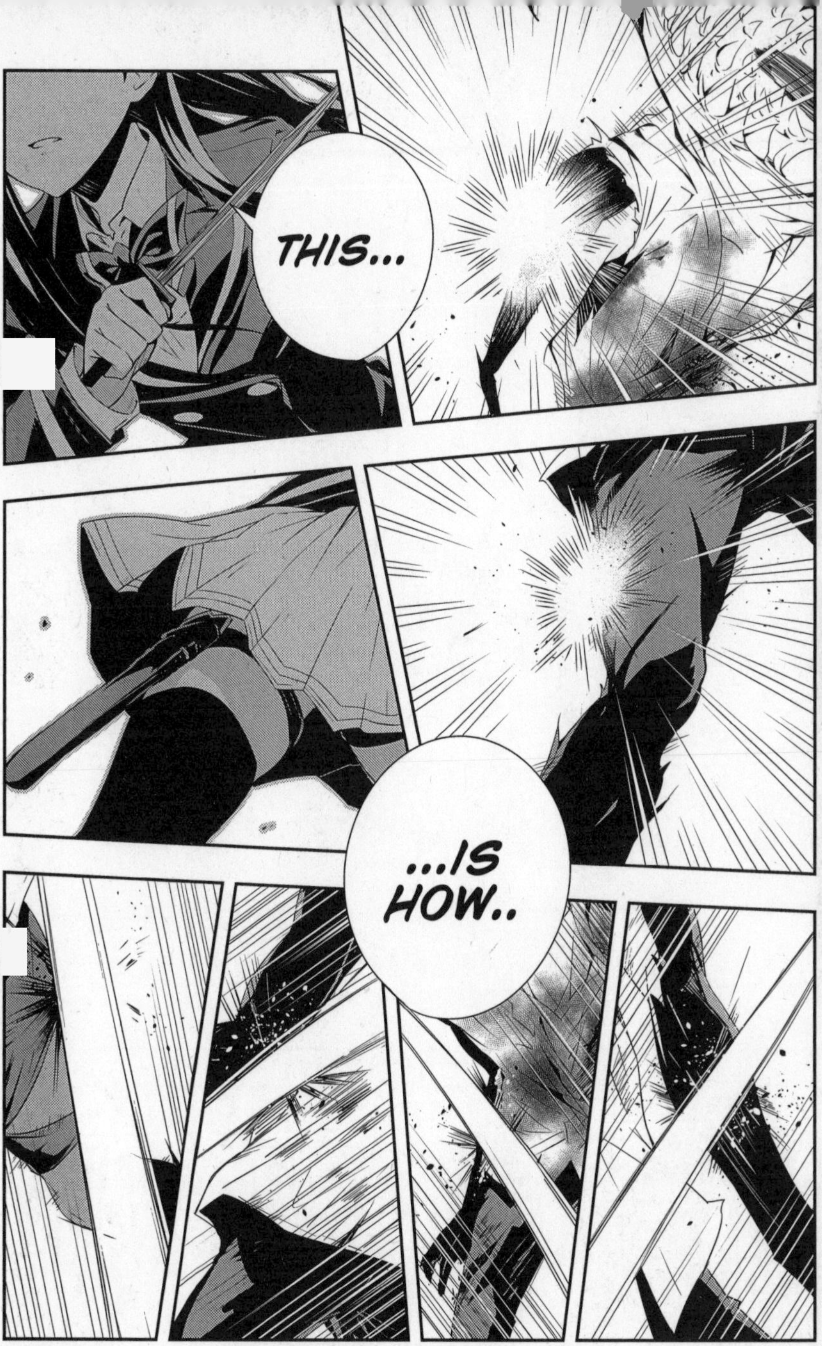
THIS...
...IS HOW..

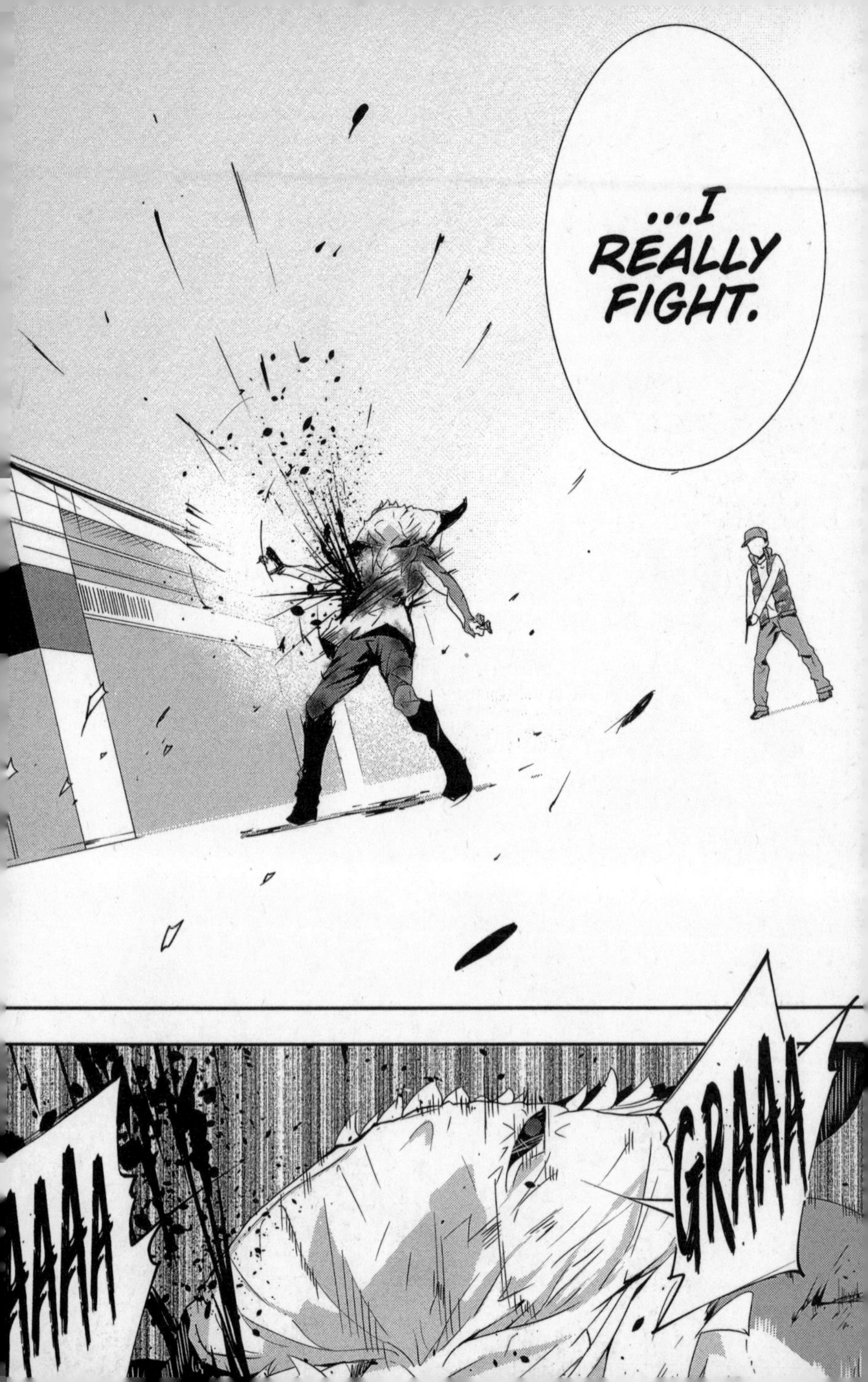
...I REALLY FIGHT.
GRAAA
AAAA

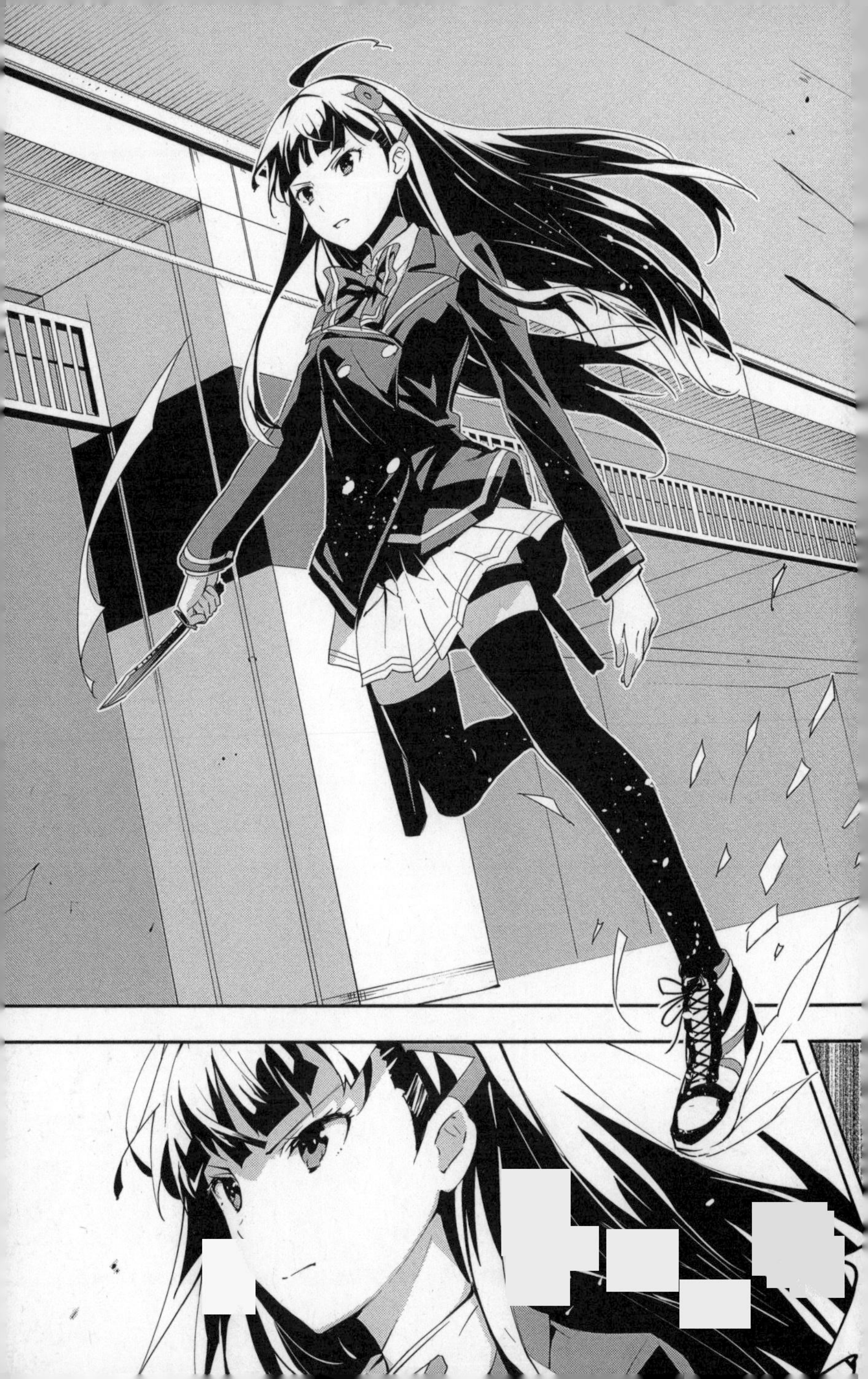

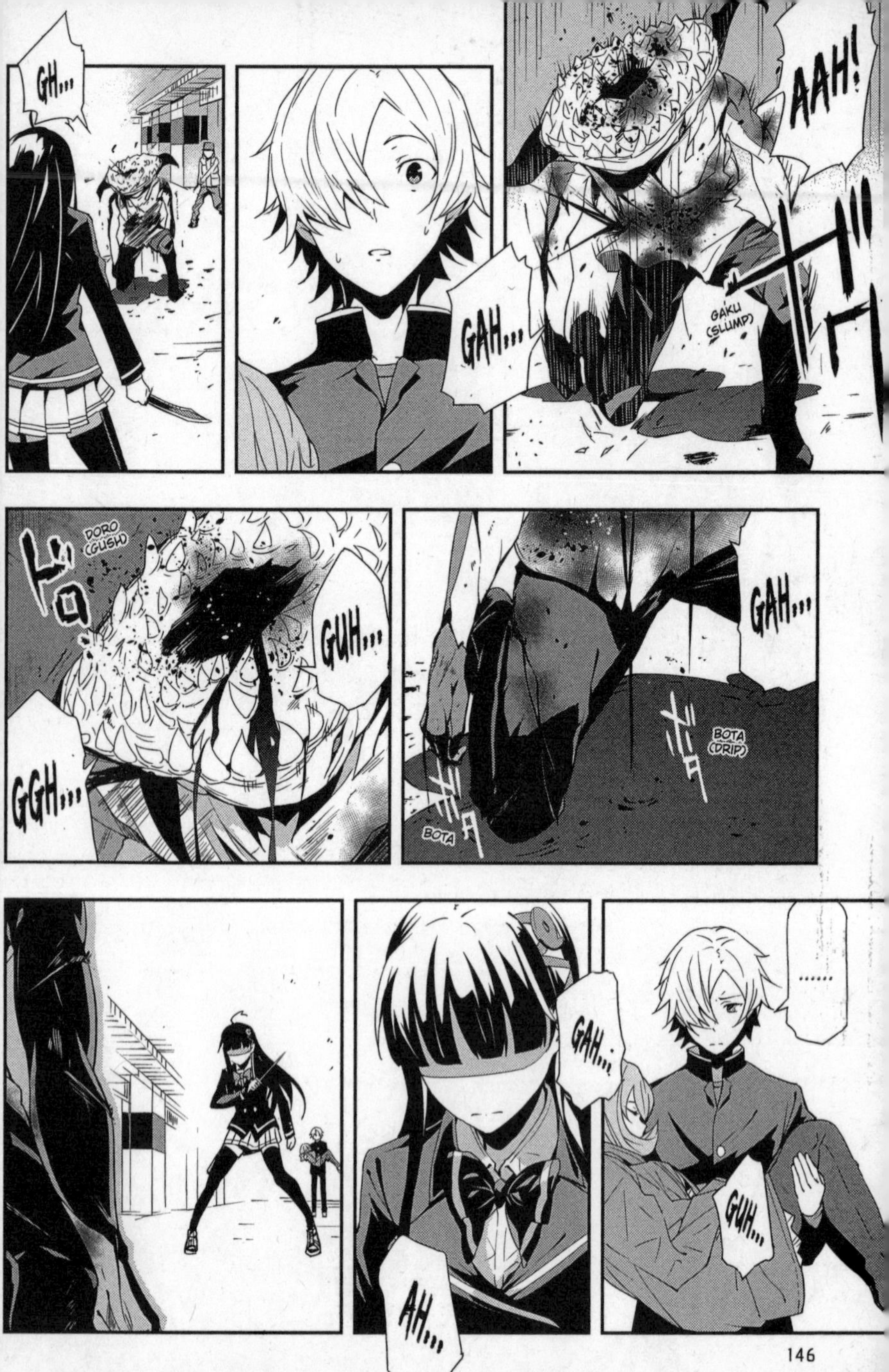
AAH!
GAKU (SLUMP)
GAH...
GH...
GAH...
BOTA (DRIP)
BOTA
DORO (GUSH)
GUH...
GGH...
......
GUH...
GAH...
AH...

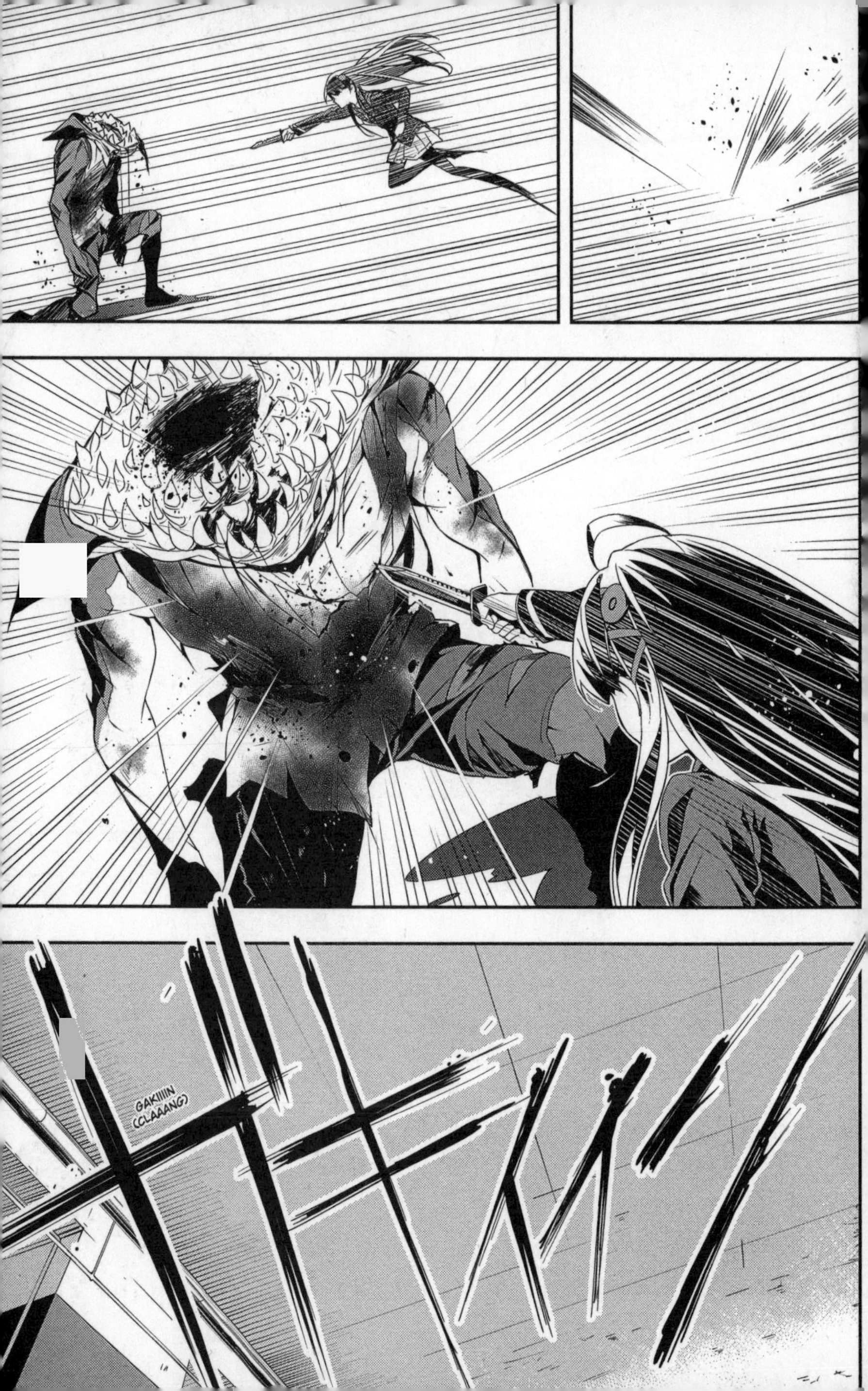
GAKIIIIN
(CLAAANG)

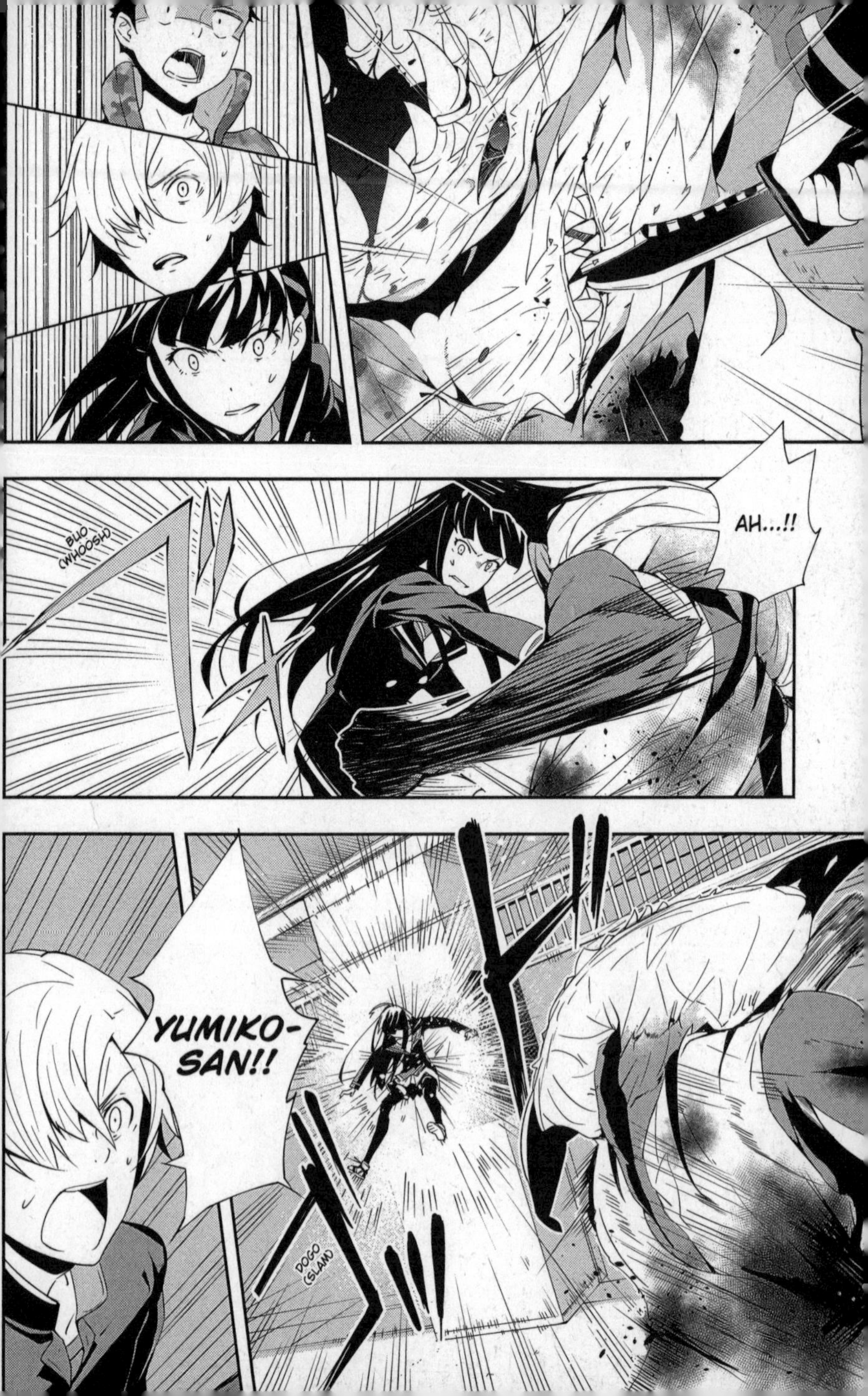
AH...!!
BUO (WHOOSH)
YUMIKO-SAN!!
DOGO (SLAM)

THE ISOLATOR
realization of
absolute solitude

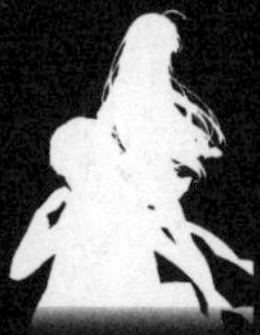

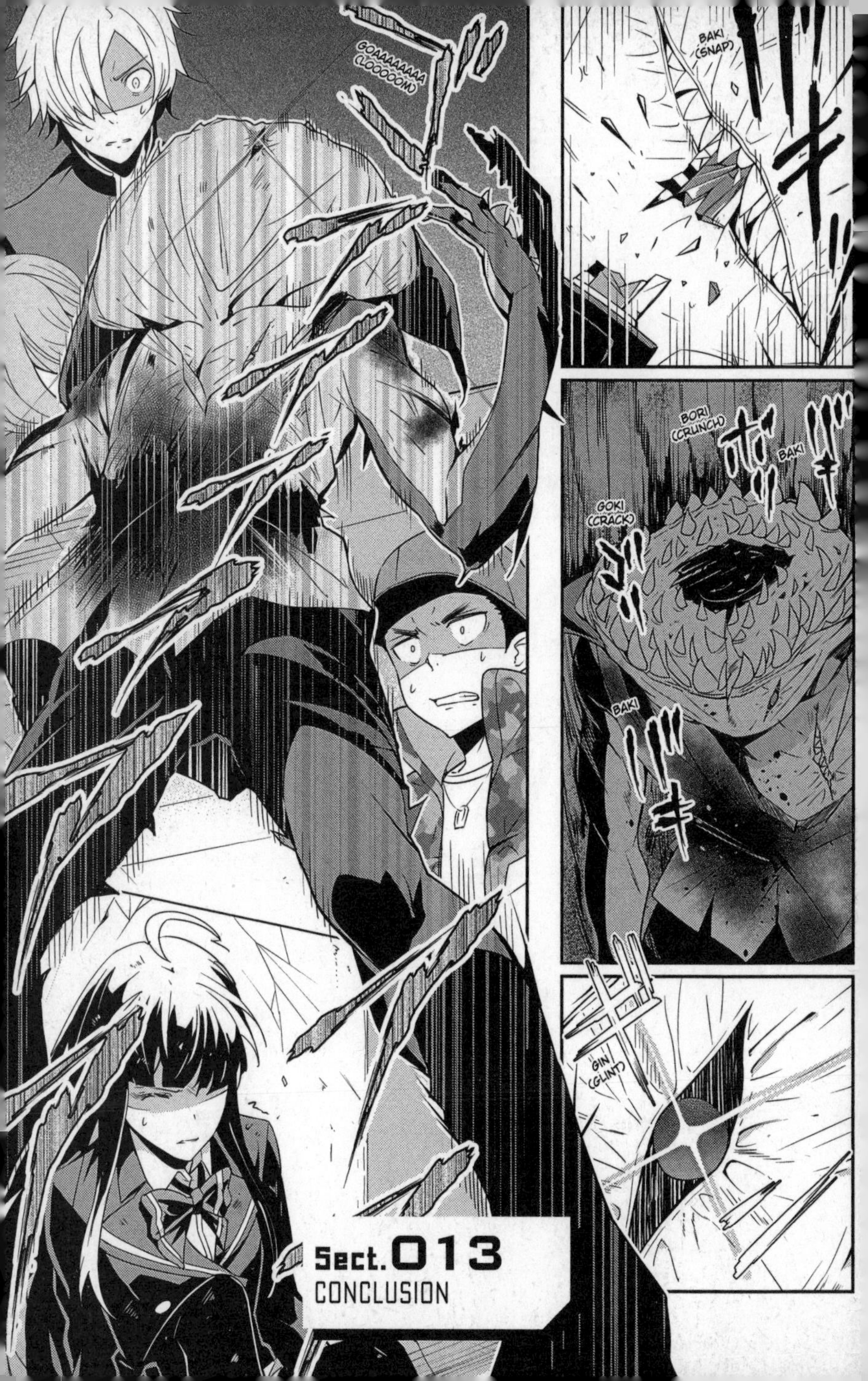
BAKI
(SNAP)
BORI
(CRUNCH)
BAKI
GOKI
(CRACK)
BAKI
GIN
(GLINT)
GOAAAAAAAA
(LOOOOOM)
Sect. 013
CONCLUSION

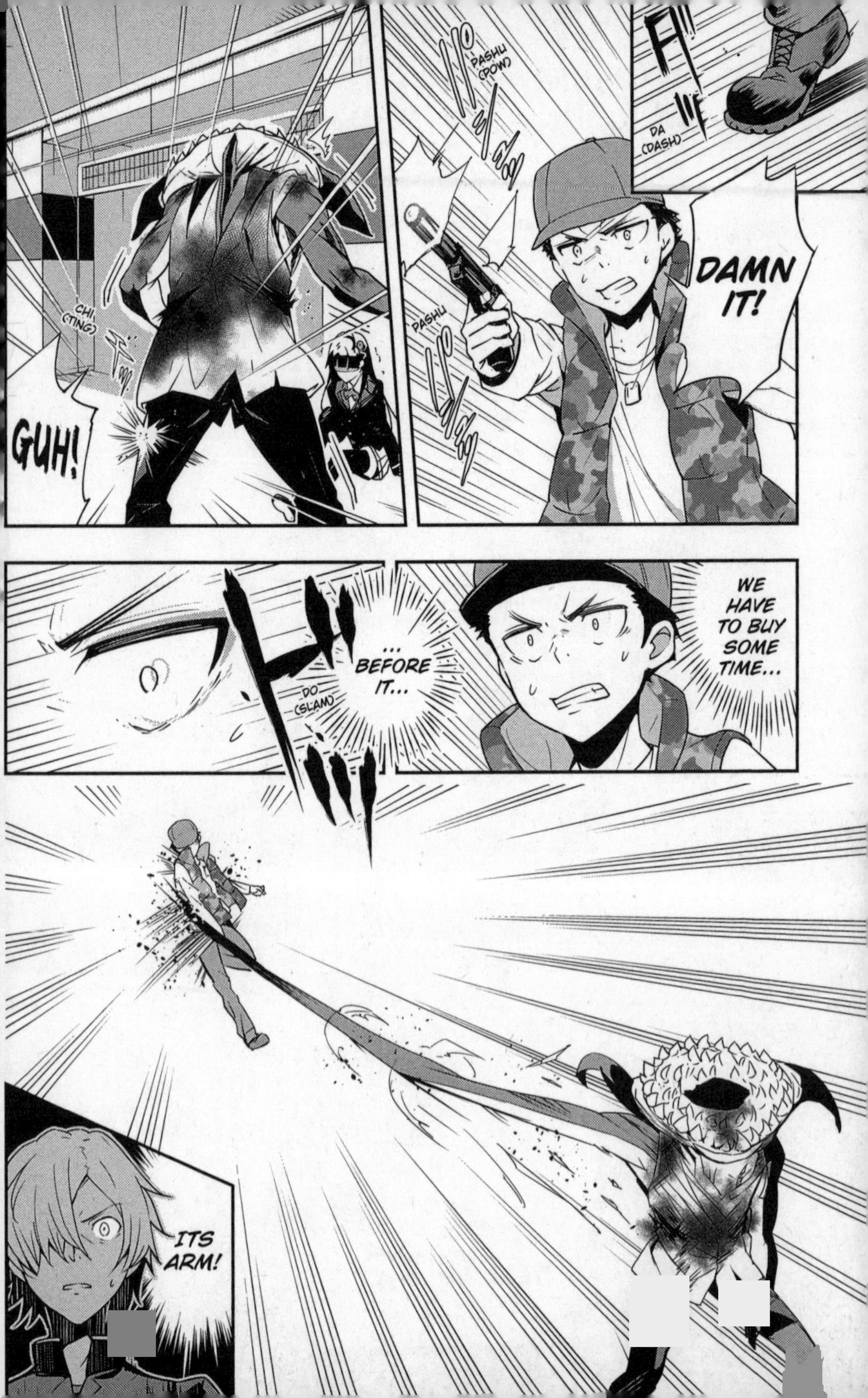
DA (DASH)
DAMN IT!
PASHU (POW)
PASHU
CHI (TING)
GUH!
WE HAVE TO BUY SOME TIME...
... BEFORE IT...
DO (SLAM)
ITS ARM!

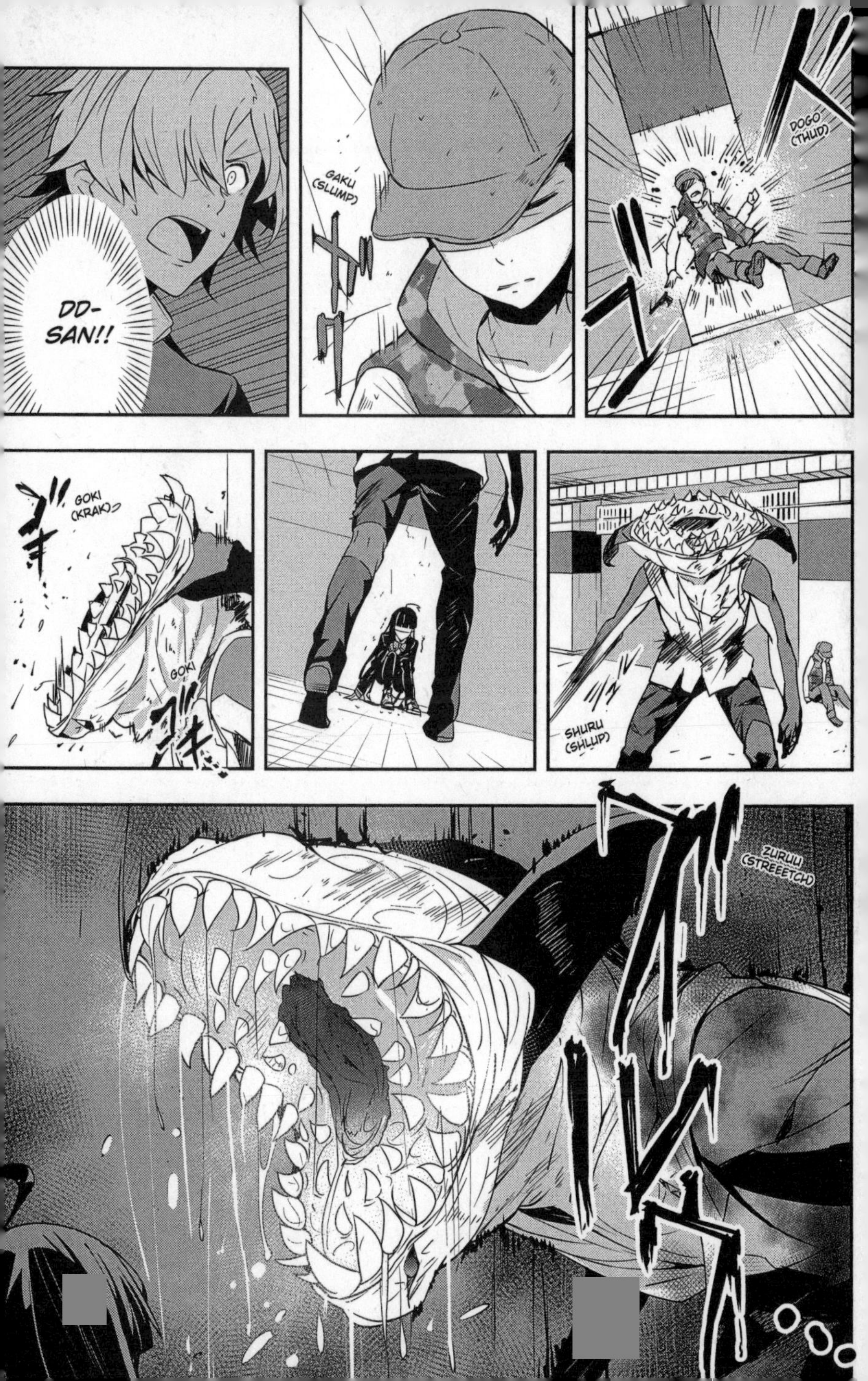
DOGO (THUD)
GAKU (SLUMP)
DD-SAN!!
SHURU (SHLUP)
GOKI (KRAK)
GOKI
ZURUU (STREEETCH)

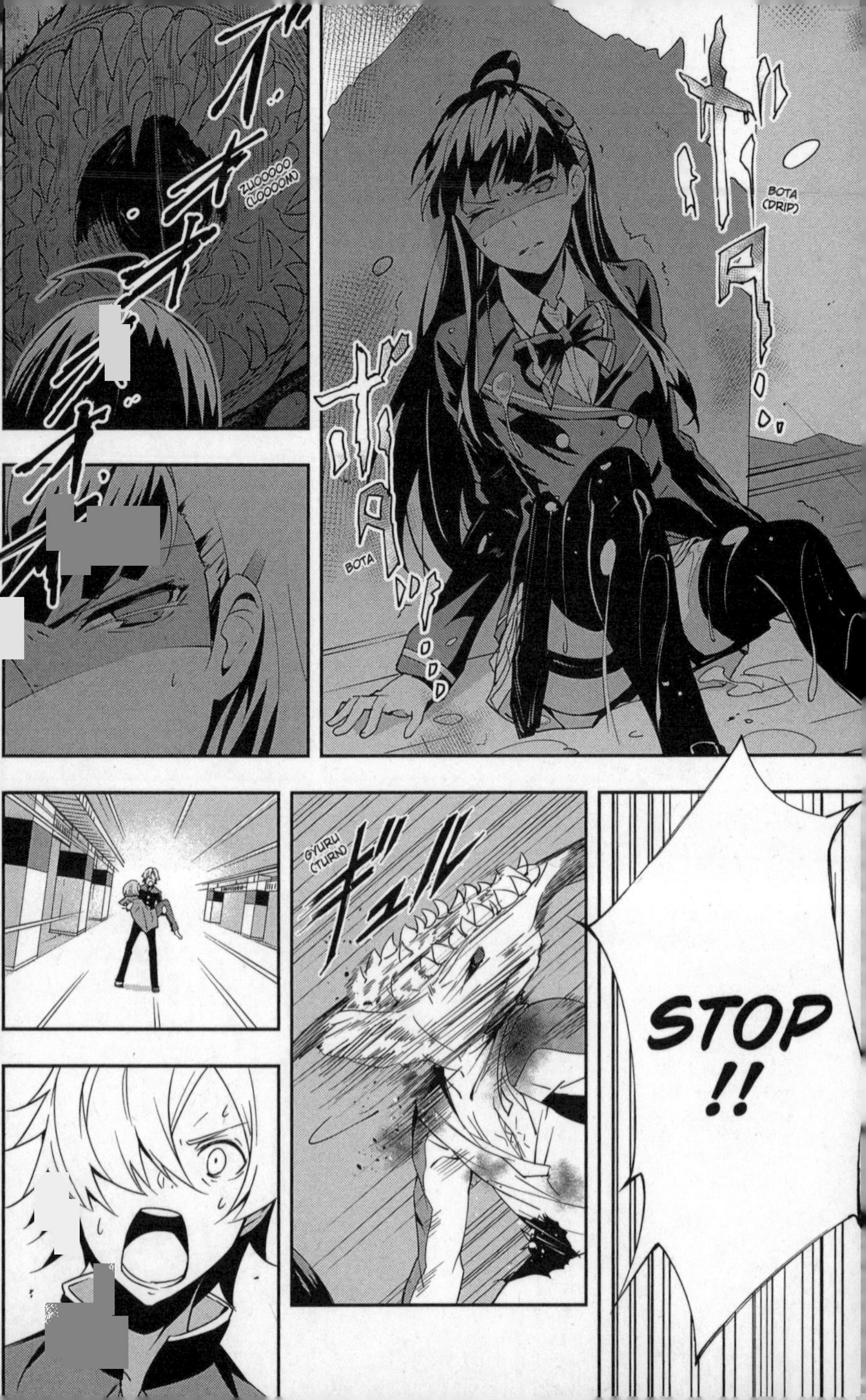
BOTA (DRIP)
BOTA
ZUOOOOO (WOOOOO)
STOP !!
GYURU (TURN)

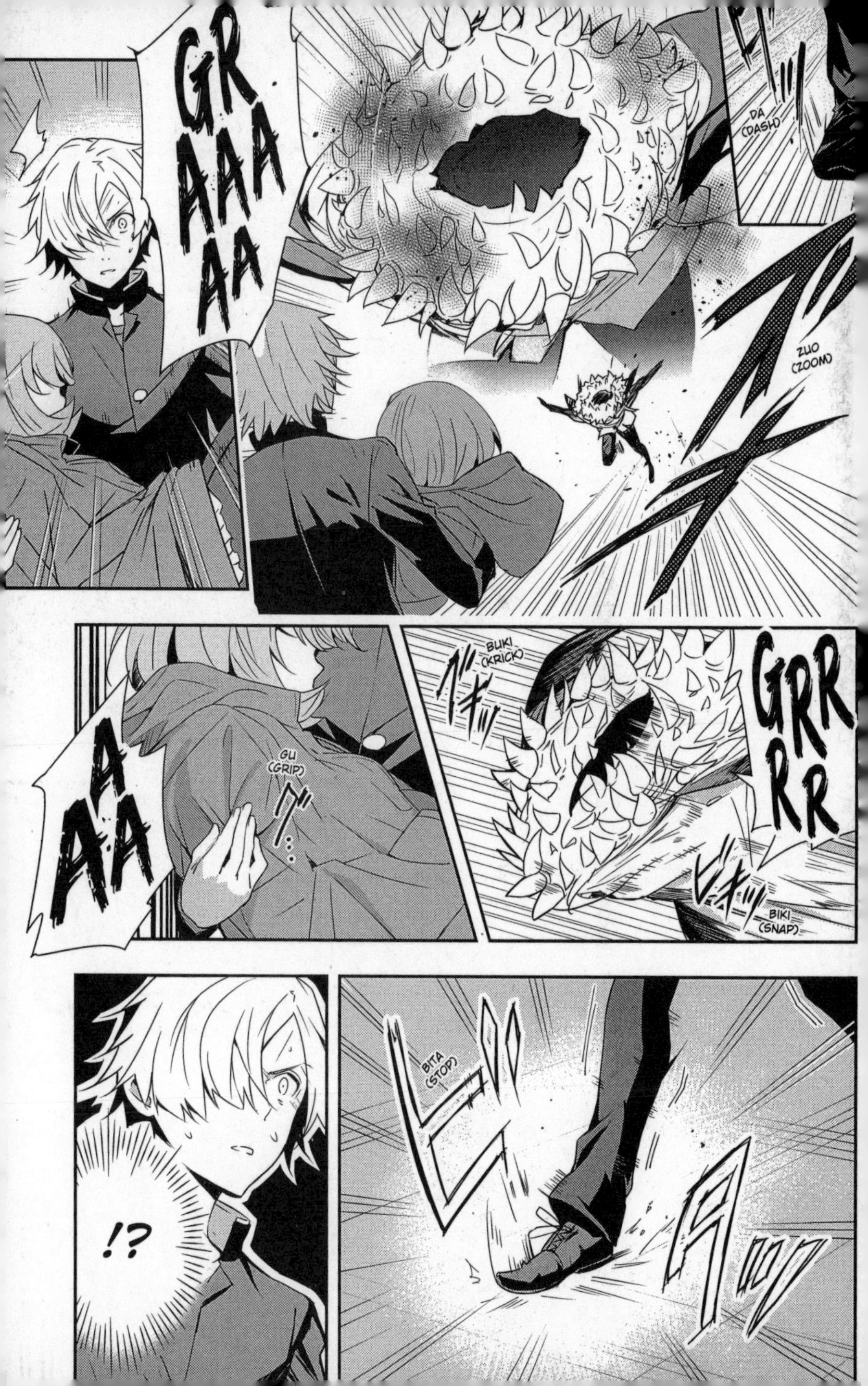
DA (DASH)
ZUO (ZOOM)
GRAAAAA
BUKI (KRICK)
GRRRR
BIKI (SNAP)
GU (GRIP)
AAAA
BITA (STOP)
!?

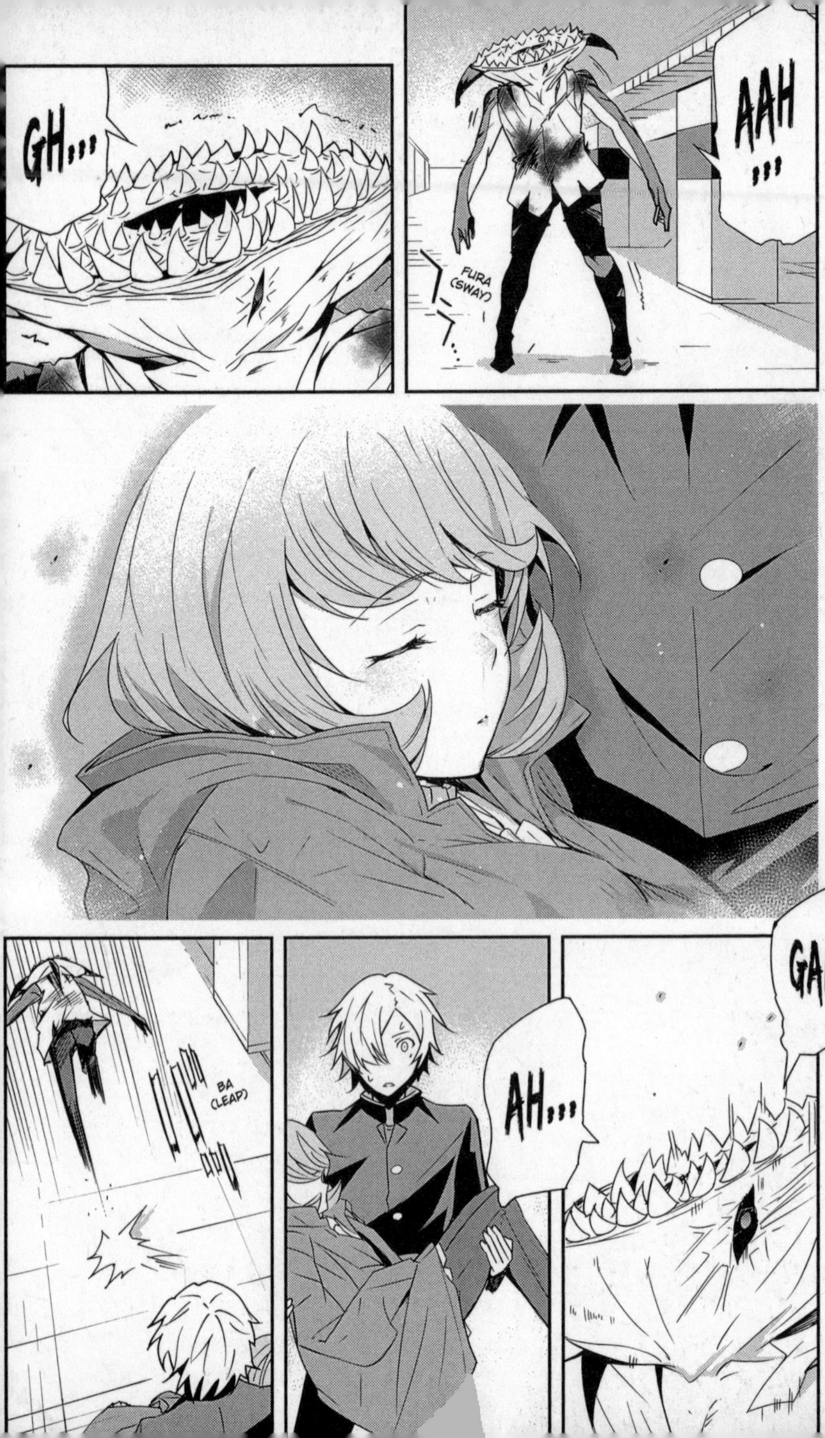

AAH...
FURA (SWAY)
GH...
GAH.
AH...
BA (LEAP)

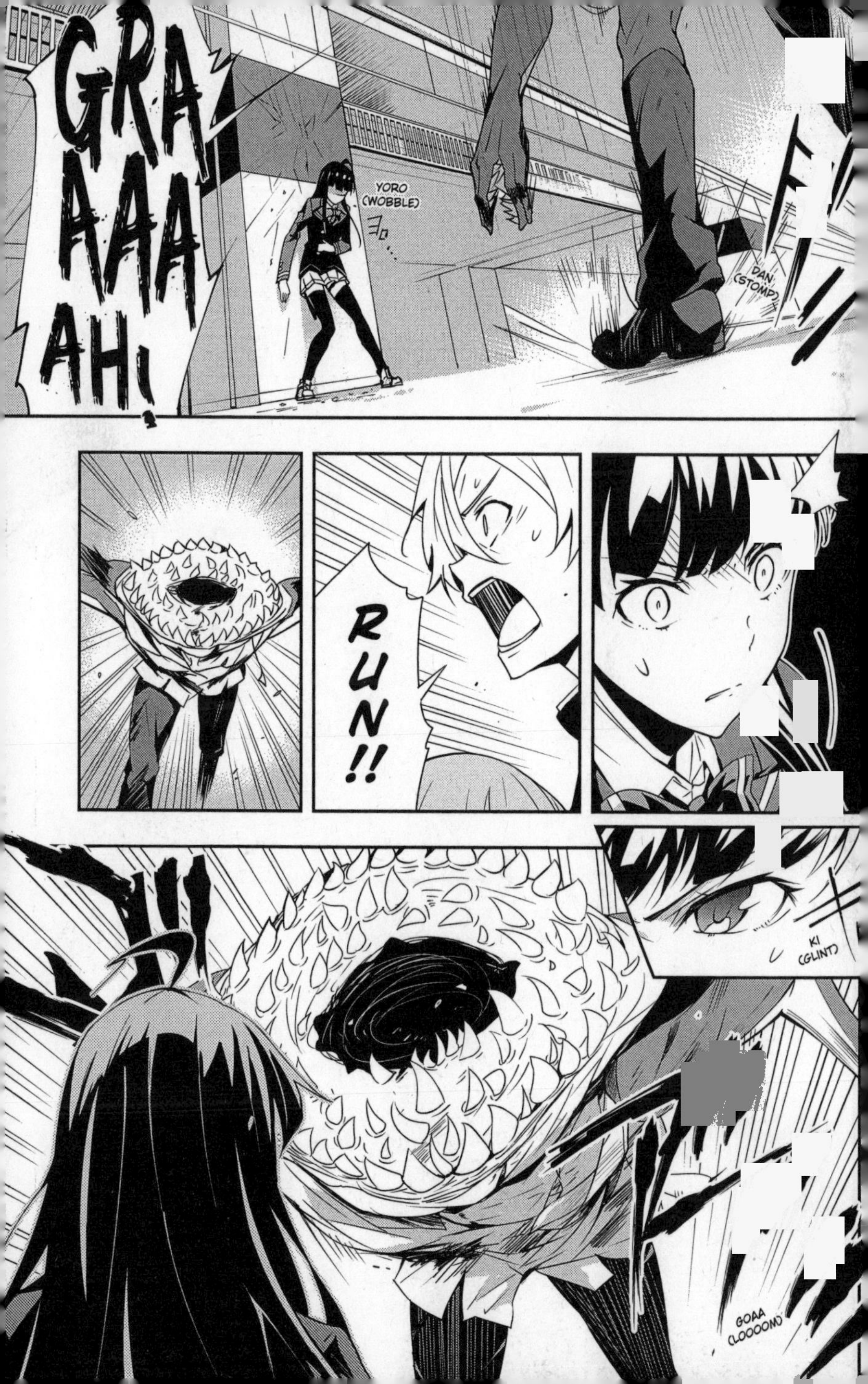
DAN (STOMP)
YORO (WOBBLE)
ヨロ…
GRAAAAAAAAH!
RUN!!
KI (GLINT)
GOAA (LOOOOM)

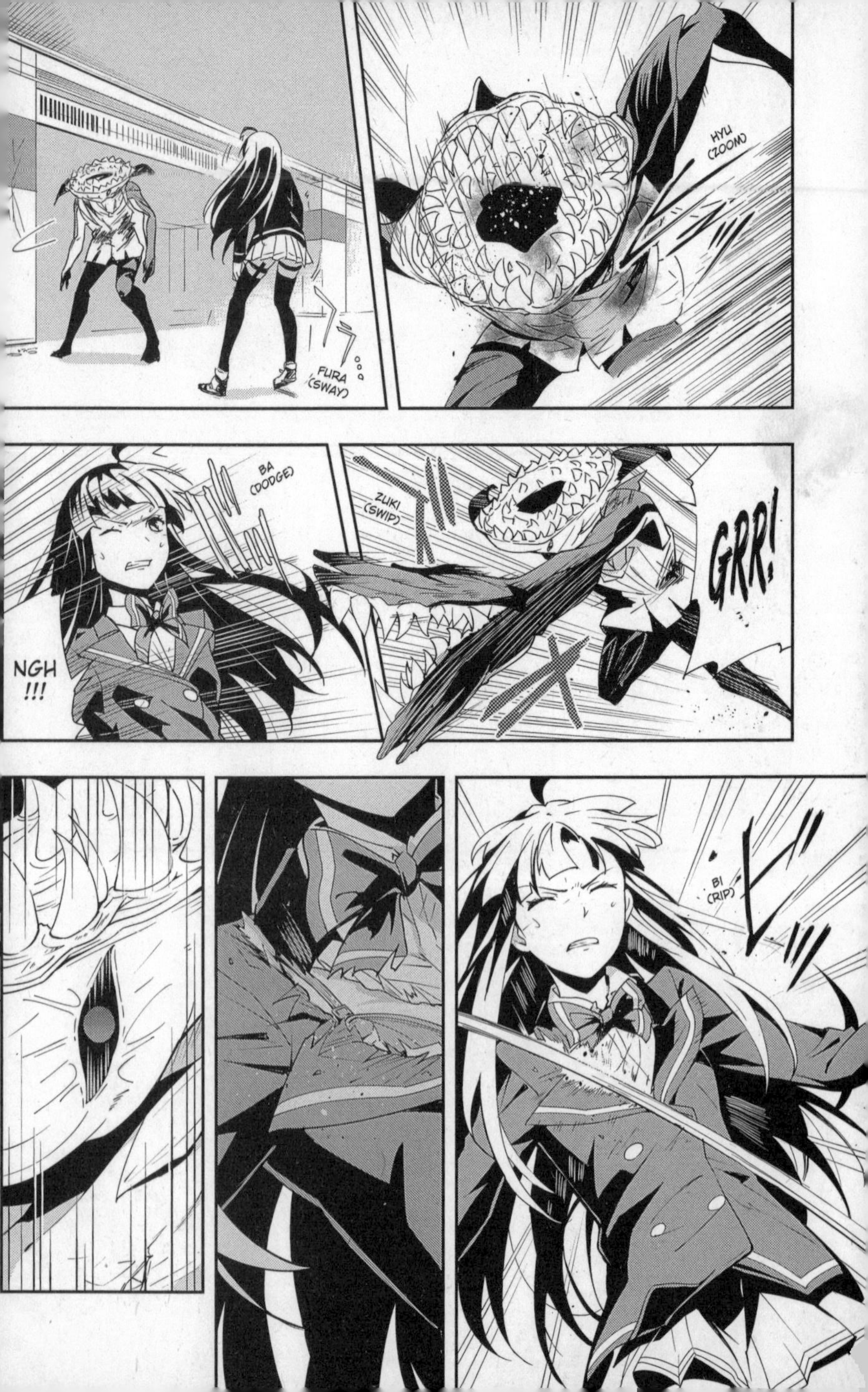
HYU (ZOOM)
FURA (SWAY)
ZUKI (SWIP)
GRR!
BA (DODGE)
NGH !!!
BI (RIP)

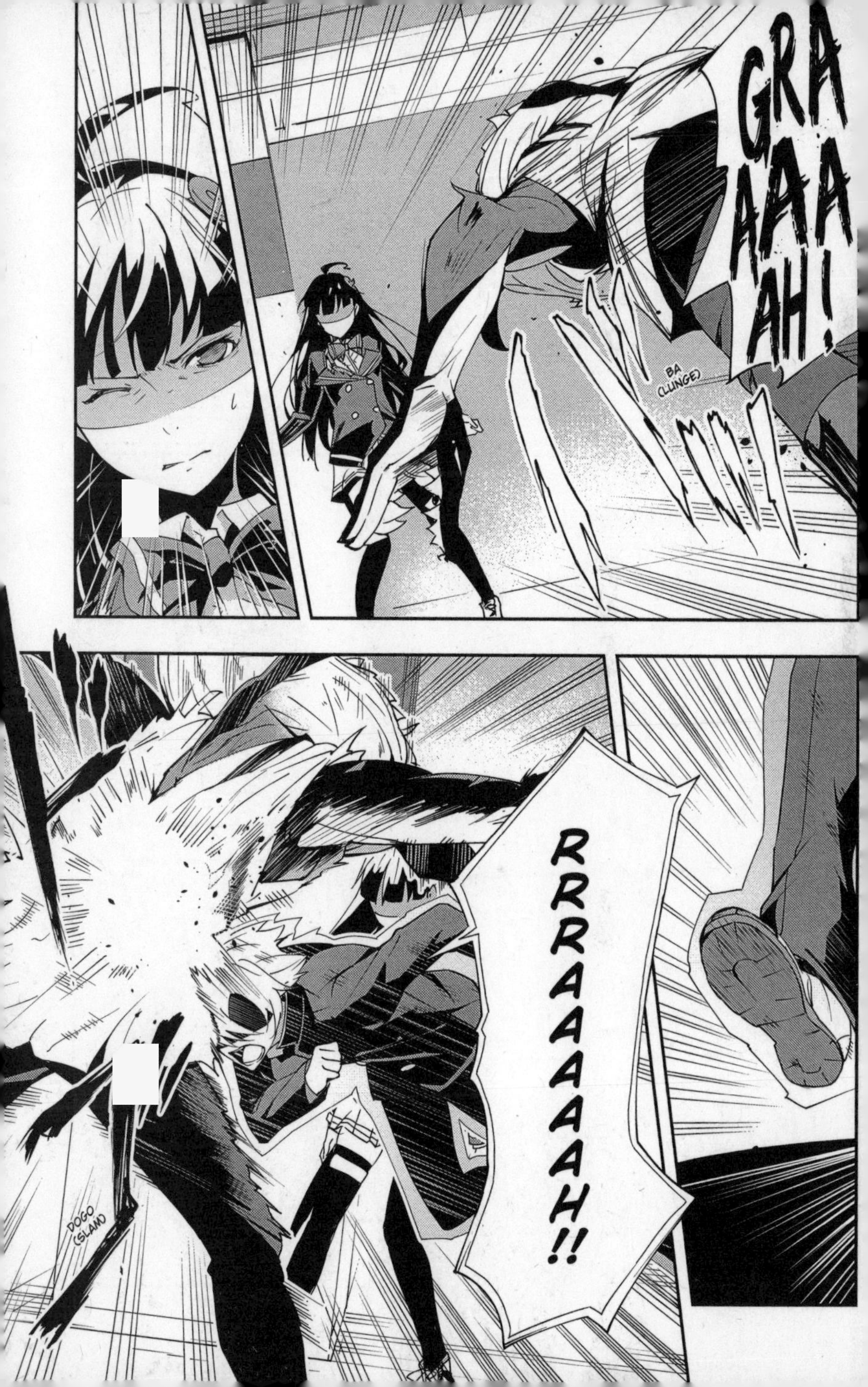
GRAAAAAAAAH!
BA (LUNGE)
RRRAAAAAH!!
DOGO (SLAM)

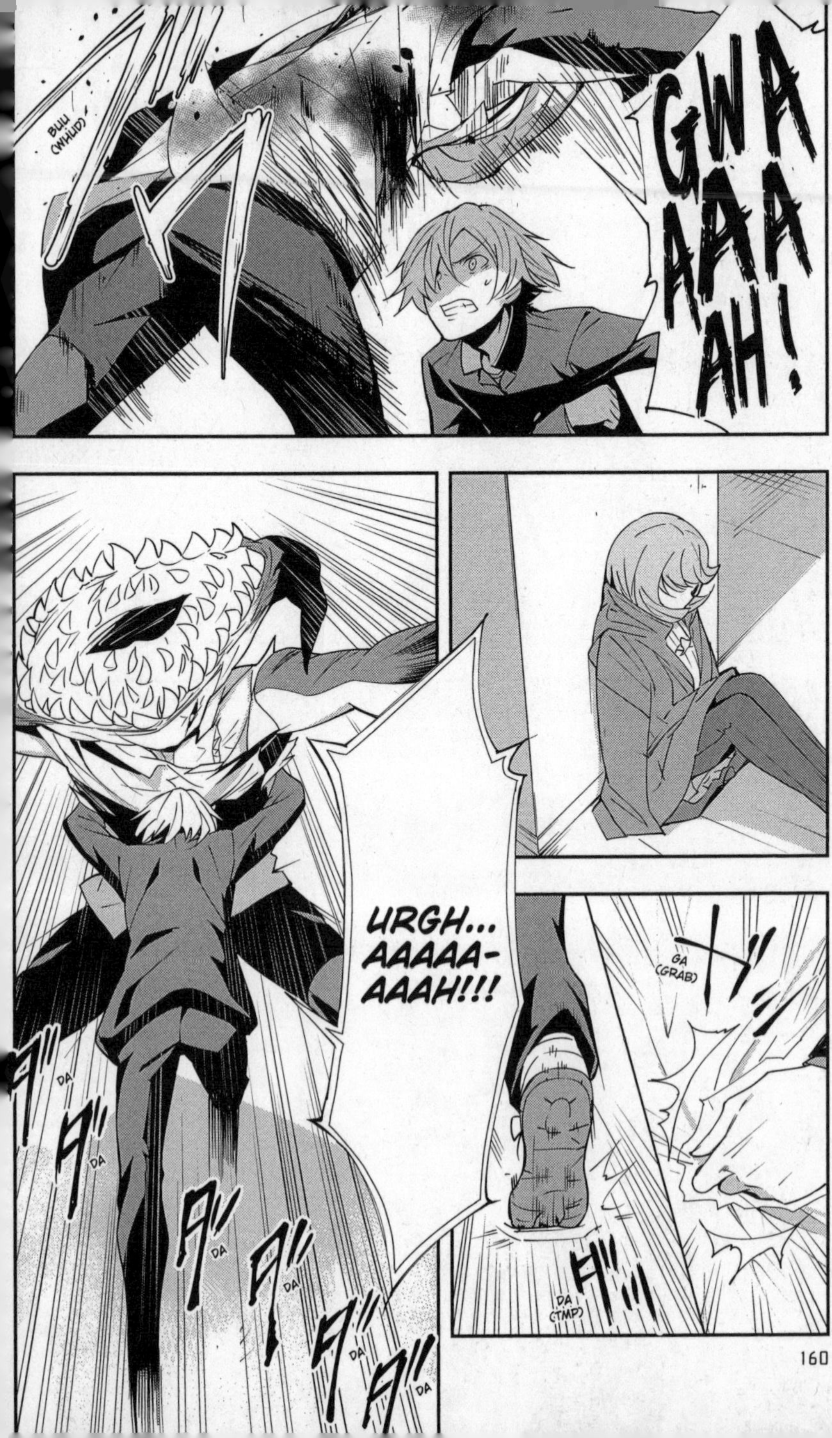
GWAAAAAAH!
BUU (WHUD)
GA (GRAB)
DA (TMP)
URGH... AAAAA-AAAH!!!
DA
DA
DA
DA
DA
DA

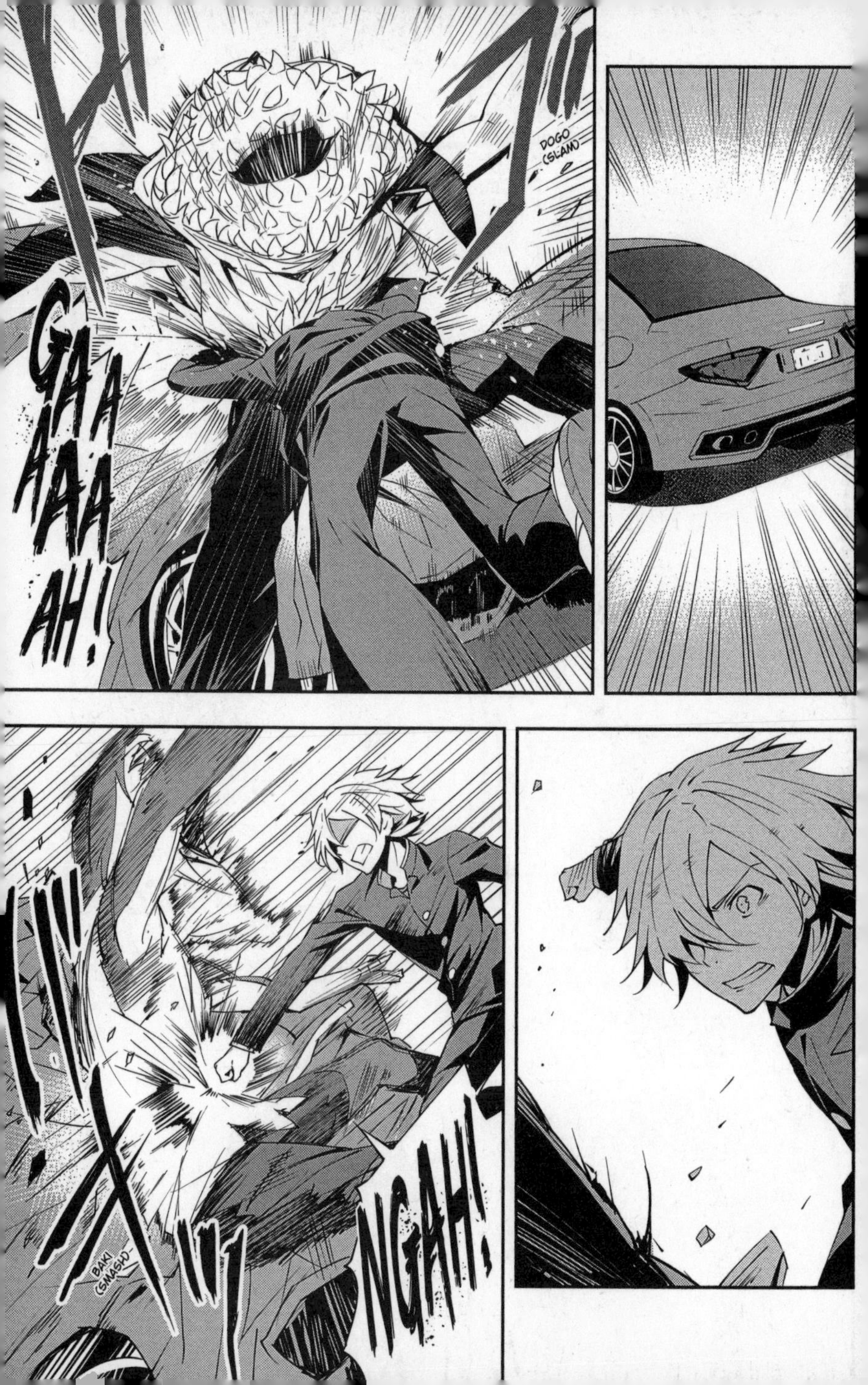
DOGO (SLAM)
GAAAAAAAH!
NGAH!
BAKI (SMASH)

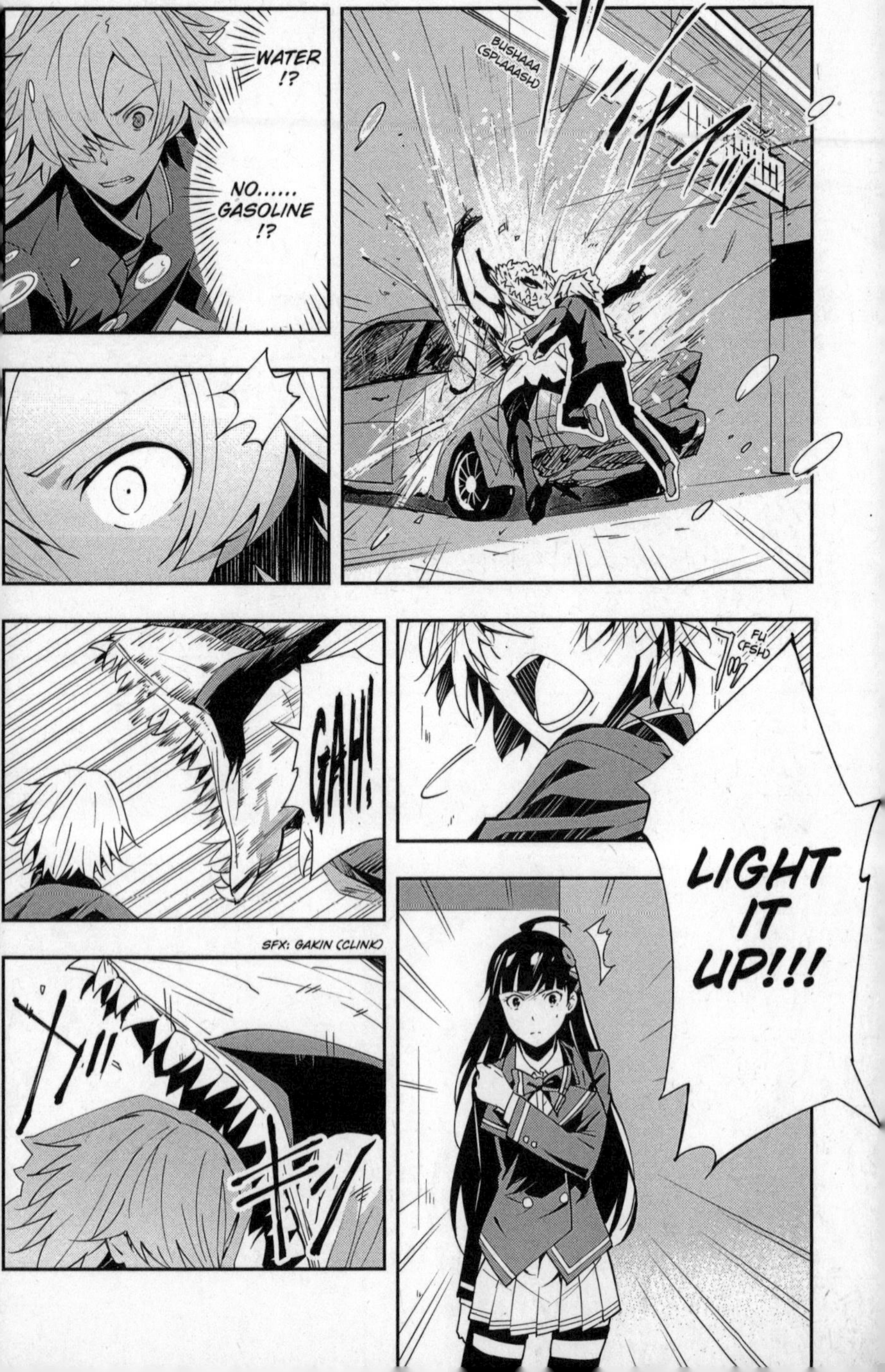
BUSHAAA (SPLAAASH)
WATER !?
NO...... GASOLINE !?
FU (FSHD)
LIGHT IT UP!!!
GAH!
SFX: GAKIN (CLINK)

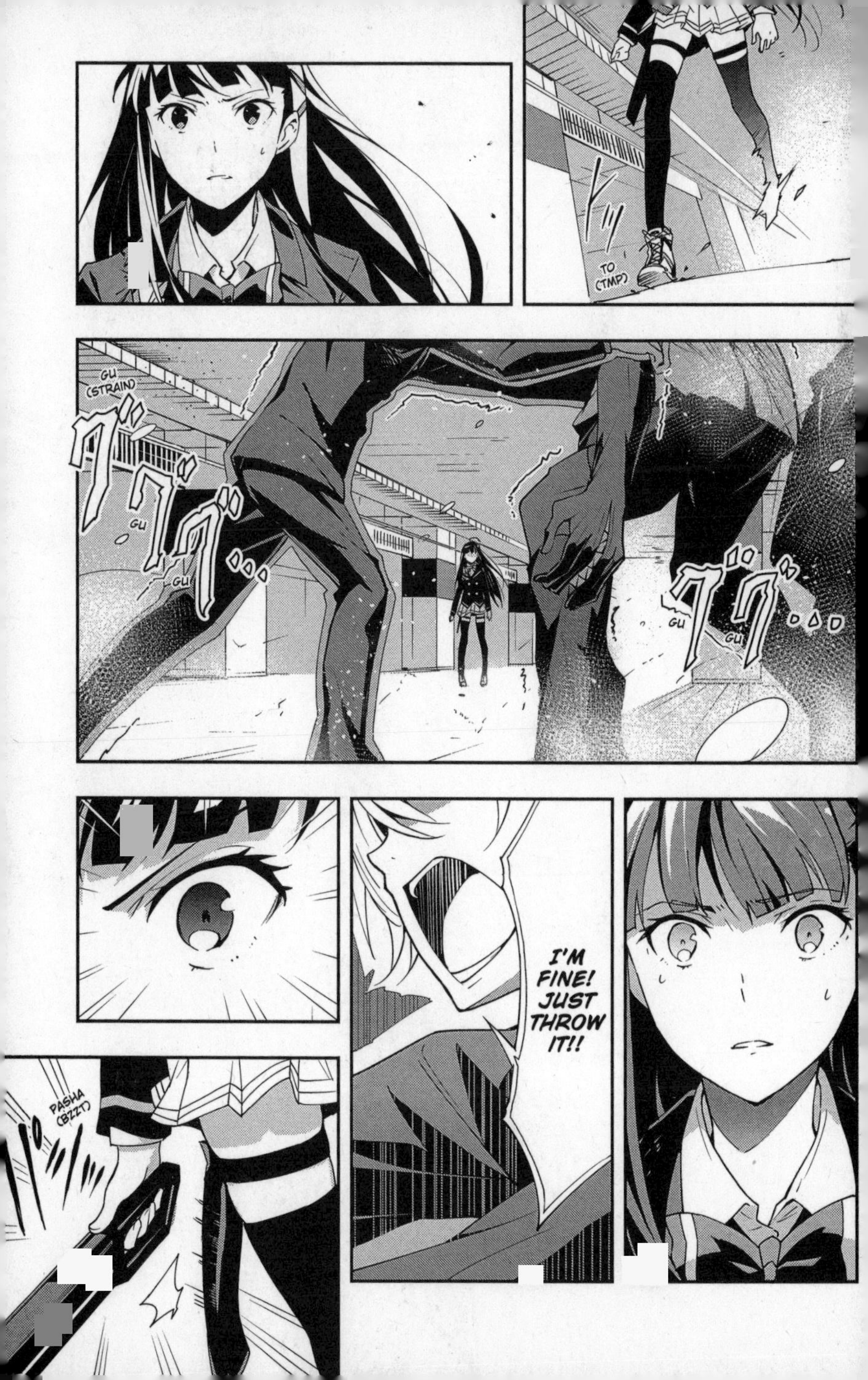
TO (TMP)
GU
GU
GU (STRAIN)
GU
GU
I'M FINE! JUST THROW IT!!
PASHA (BZZT)

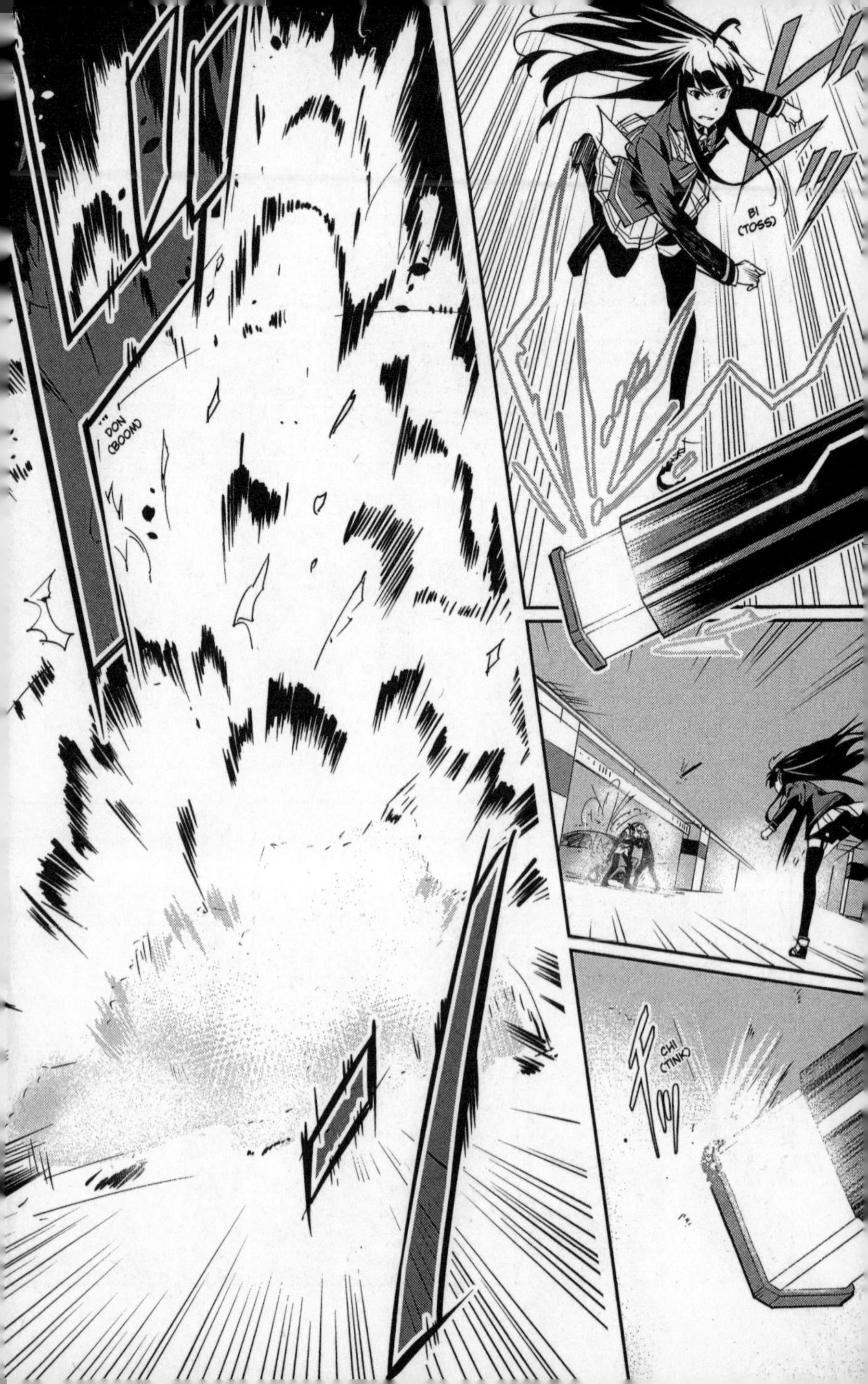
BI (TOSS)
CHI (TINK)
... DON (BOOM)

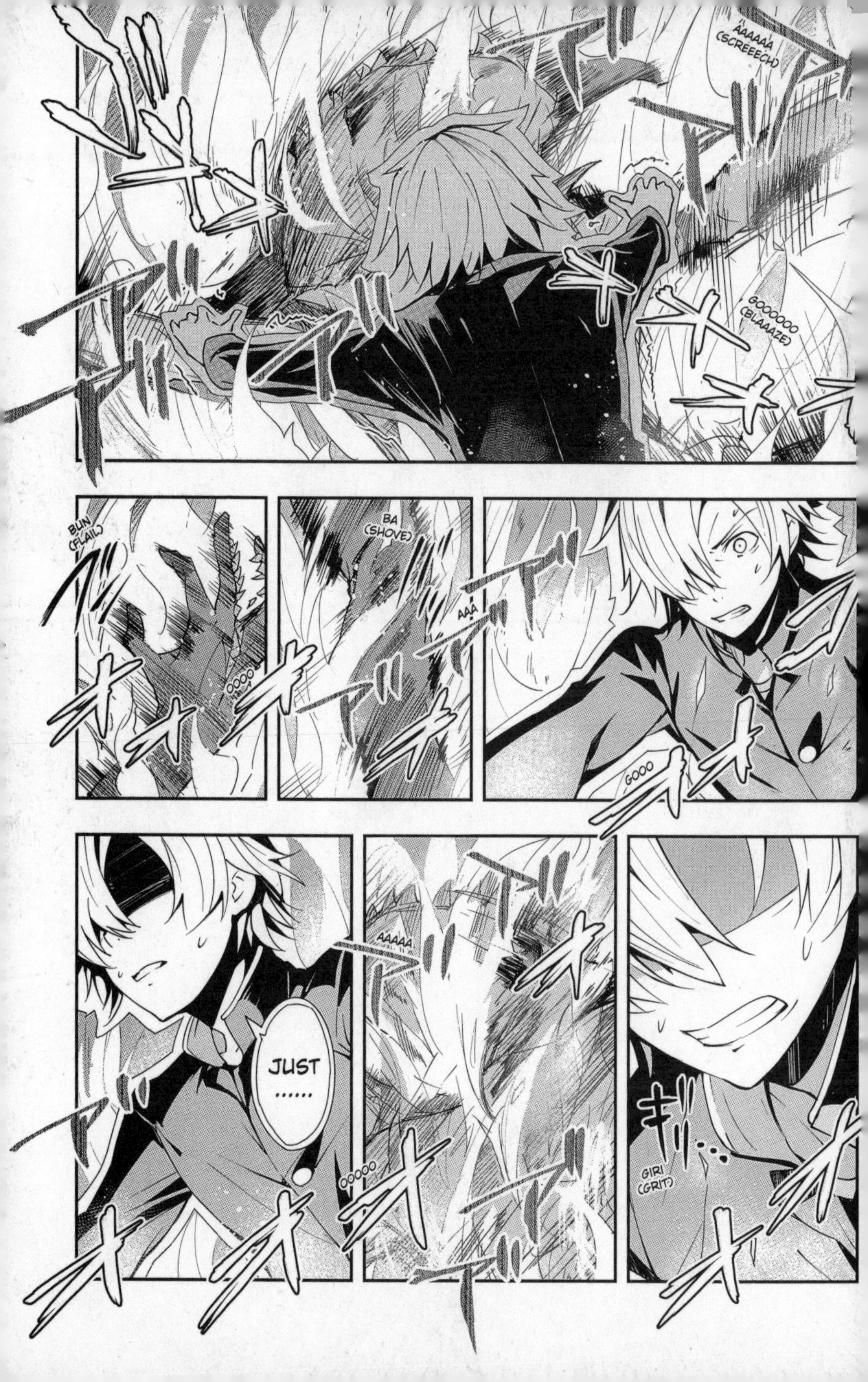

ÁAAAAA (SCREEECH)
GOOOOOO (BLAAAZE)
GOOO
AAA
BA (SHOVE)
OOOO
BUN (FLAIL)
GIRI (GRIT)
AAAAA
OOOOO
JUST ......

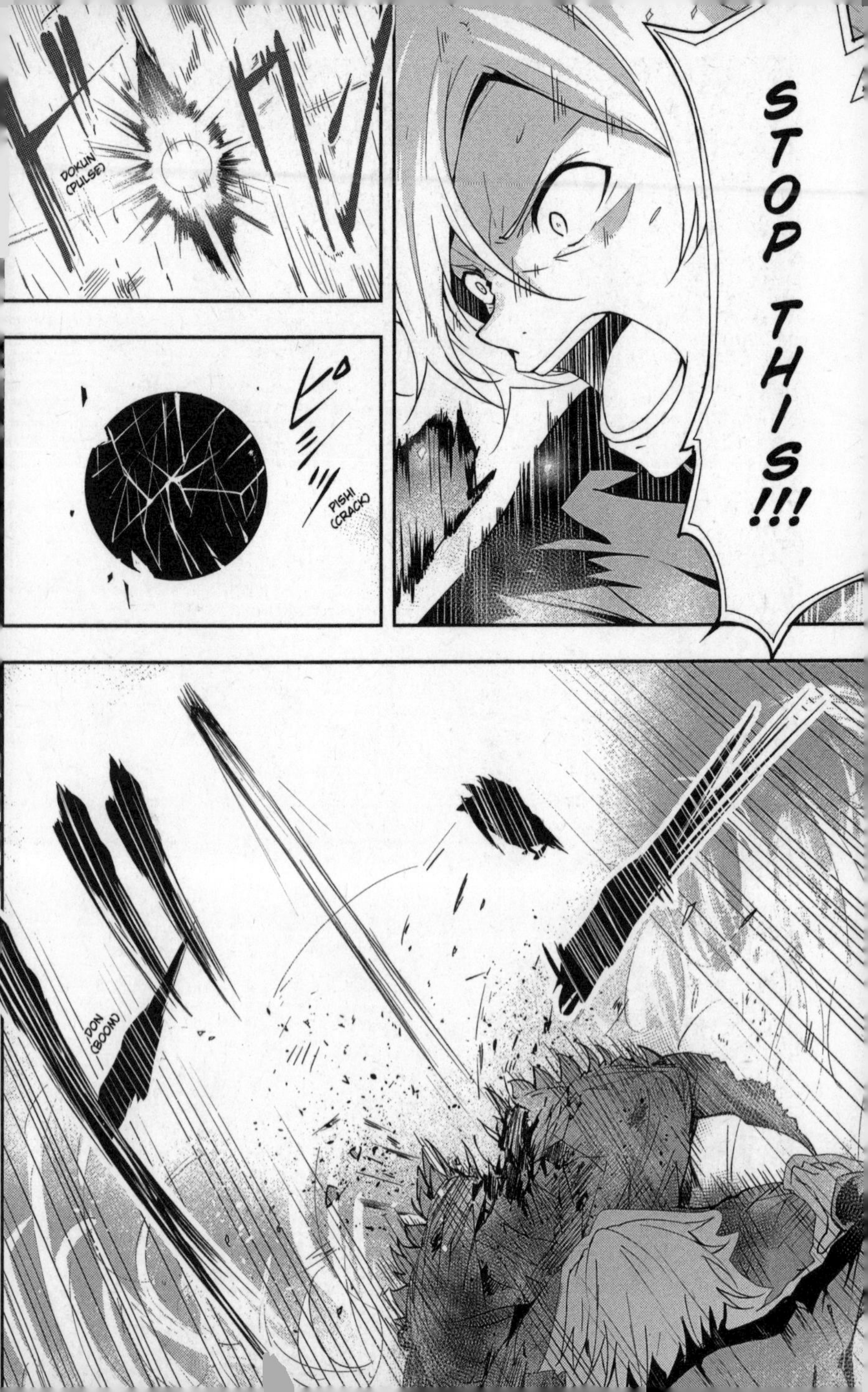
STOP THIS!!!
DOKUN (PULSE)
PISHI (CRACK)
DON (BOOM)

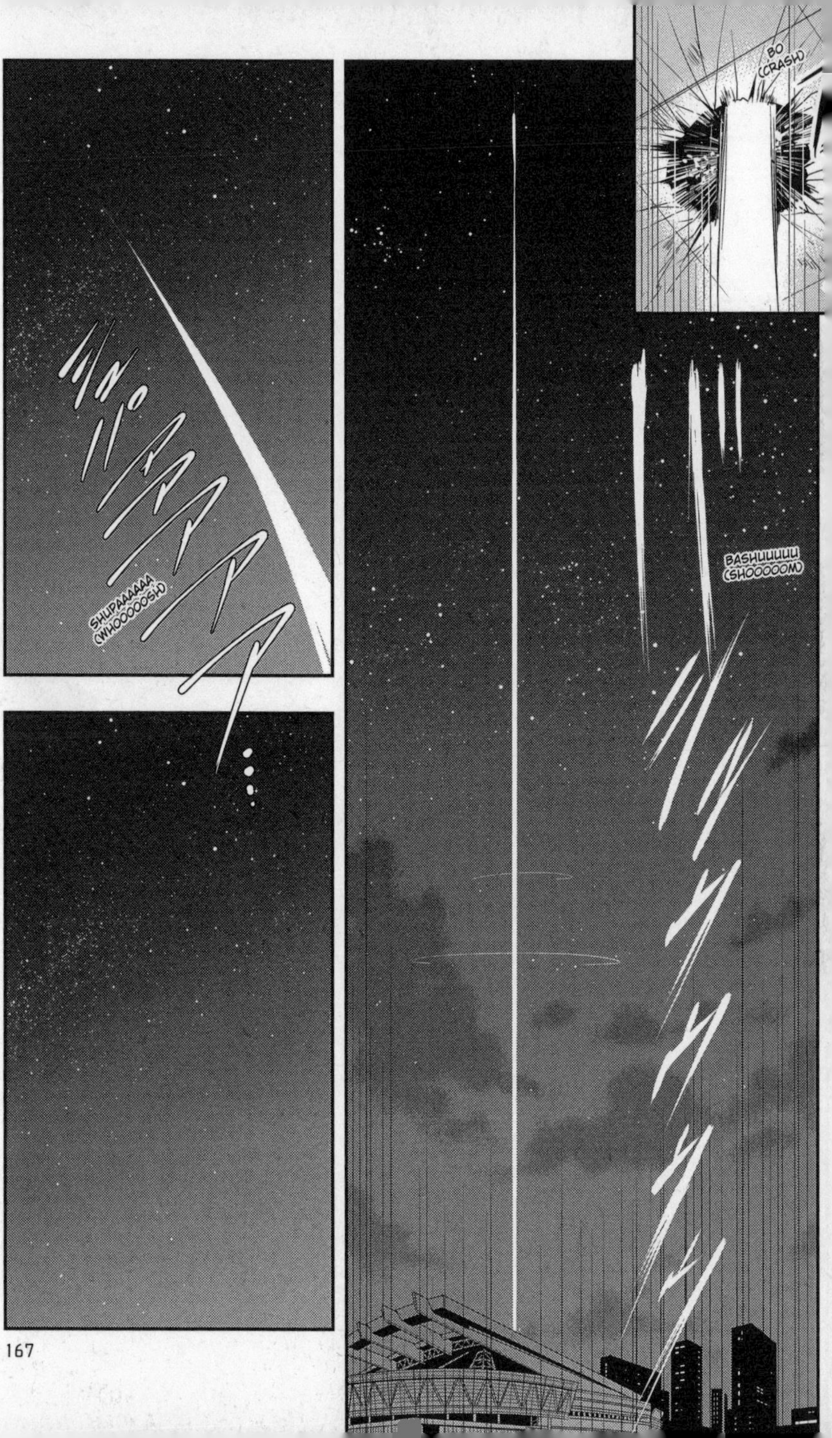
BO (CRASH)
BASHUUUUU (SHOOOOOM)
SHUPAAAAA (WHOOOOOSH)

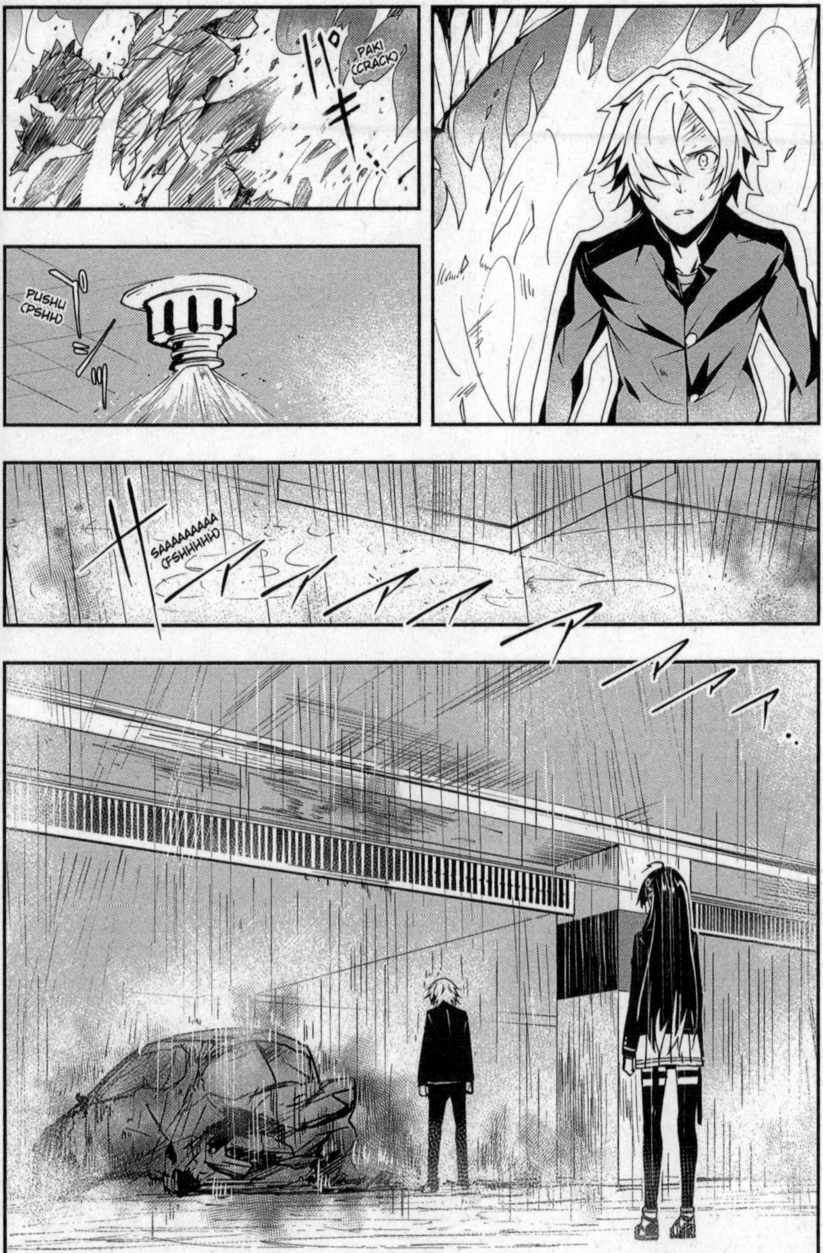
PAKI
(CRACK)
PUSHU
(PSHH)
SAAAAAAAAA
(FSHHHHH)

THE ISOLATOR
realization of
absolute solitude

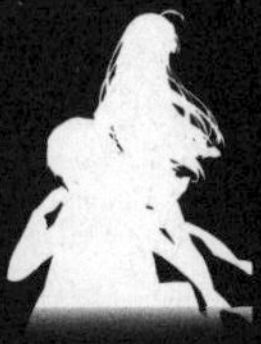

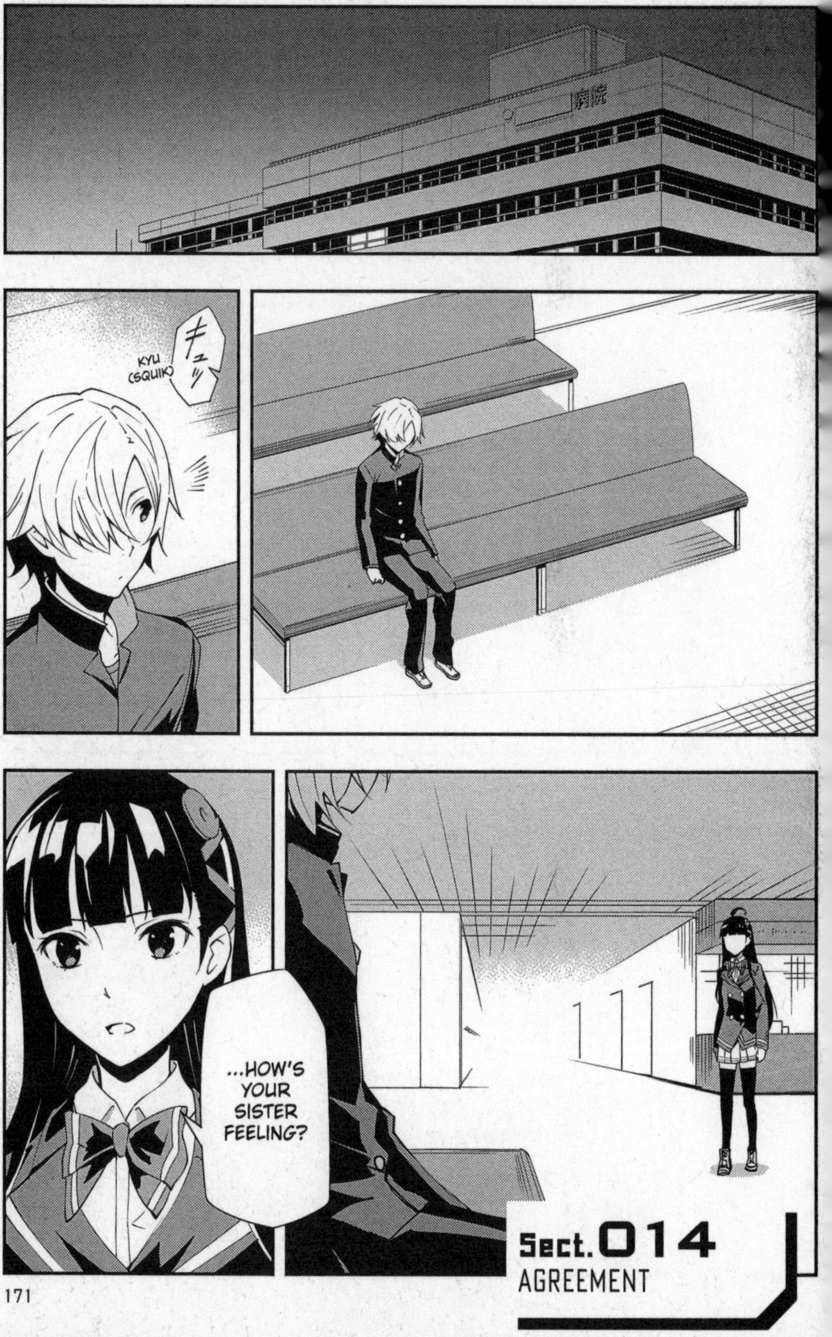
病院
キュッ
KYU (SQUIK)
...HOW'S YOUR SISTER FEELING?

Sect. 014
AGREEMENT

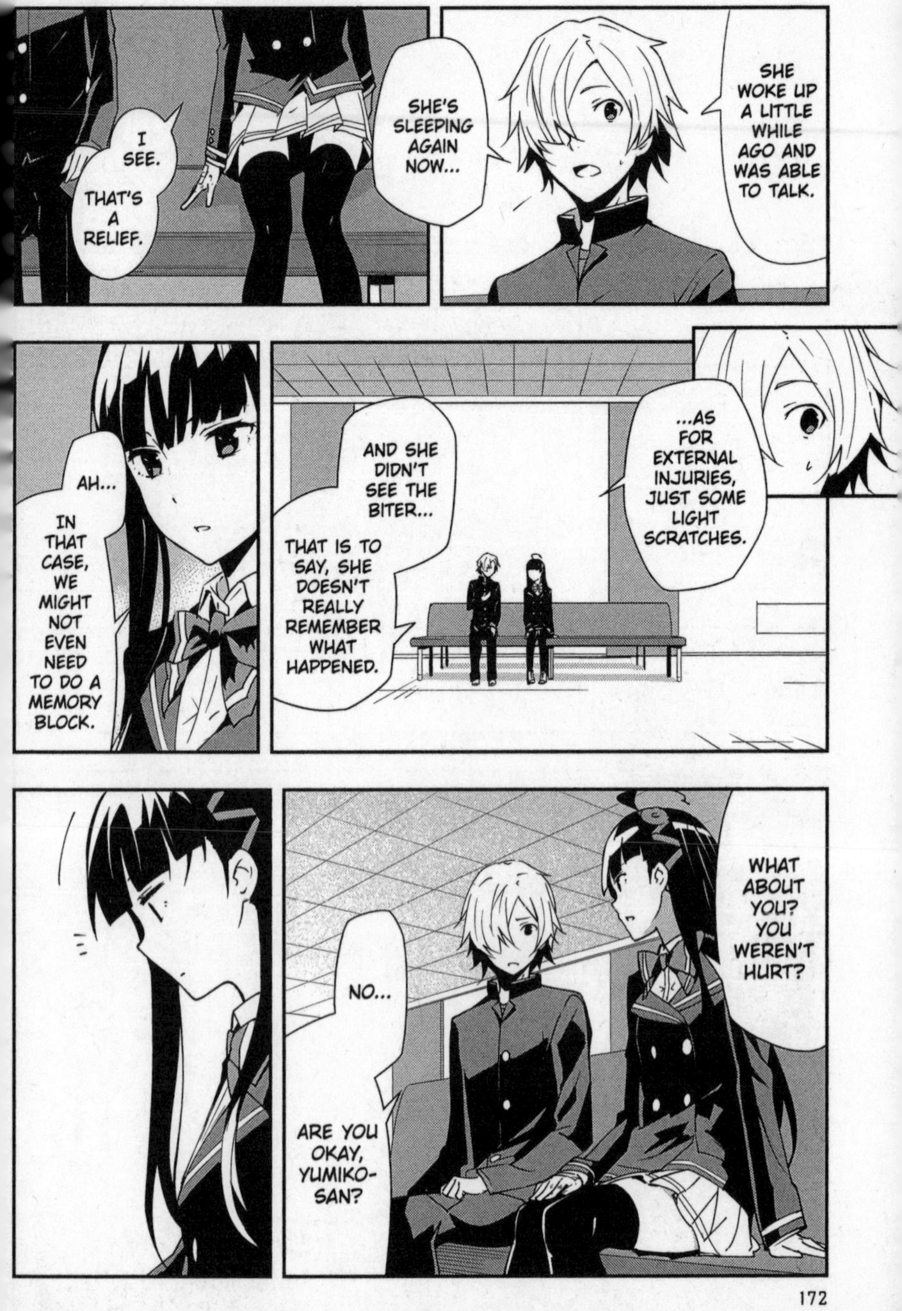
SHE WOKE UP A LITTLE WHILE AGO AND WAS ABLE TO TALK.
SHE'S SLEEPING AGAIN NOW...
I SEE.
THAT'S A RELIEF.
...AS FOR EXTERNAL INJURIES, JUST SOME LIGHT SCRATCHES.
AND SHE DIDN'T SEE THE BITER...
THAT IS TO SAY, SHE DOESN'T REALLY REMEMBER WHAT HAPPENED.
AH...
IN THAT CASE, WE MIGHT NOT EVEN NEED TO DO A MEMORY BLOCK.
WHAT ABOUT YOU? YOU WEREN'T HURT?
NO...
ARE YOU OKAY, YUMIKO-SAN?

"PERFECTLY NORMAL" ...?

DD AND I ARE FINE.

THIS LEVEL OF DAMAGE IS PERFECTLY NORMAL.

... YEAH.

SIGN: B WING / EXIT

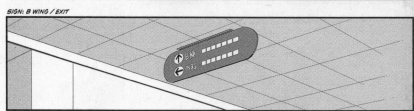

B棟
出口

...WHEN THE BITER TRIED TO KILL NORIE-SAN AND ME......

THAT TIME...

...HE LOOKED AT NORIE-SAN, AND...

HOW SHOULD I PUT IT...?

IT WAS LIKE HE HESITATED.

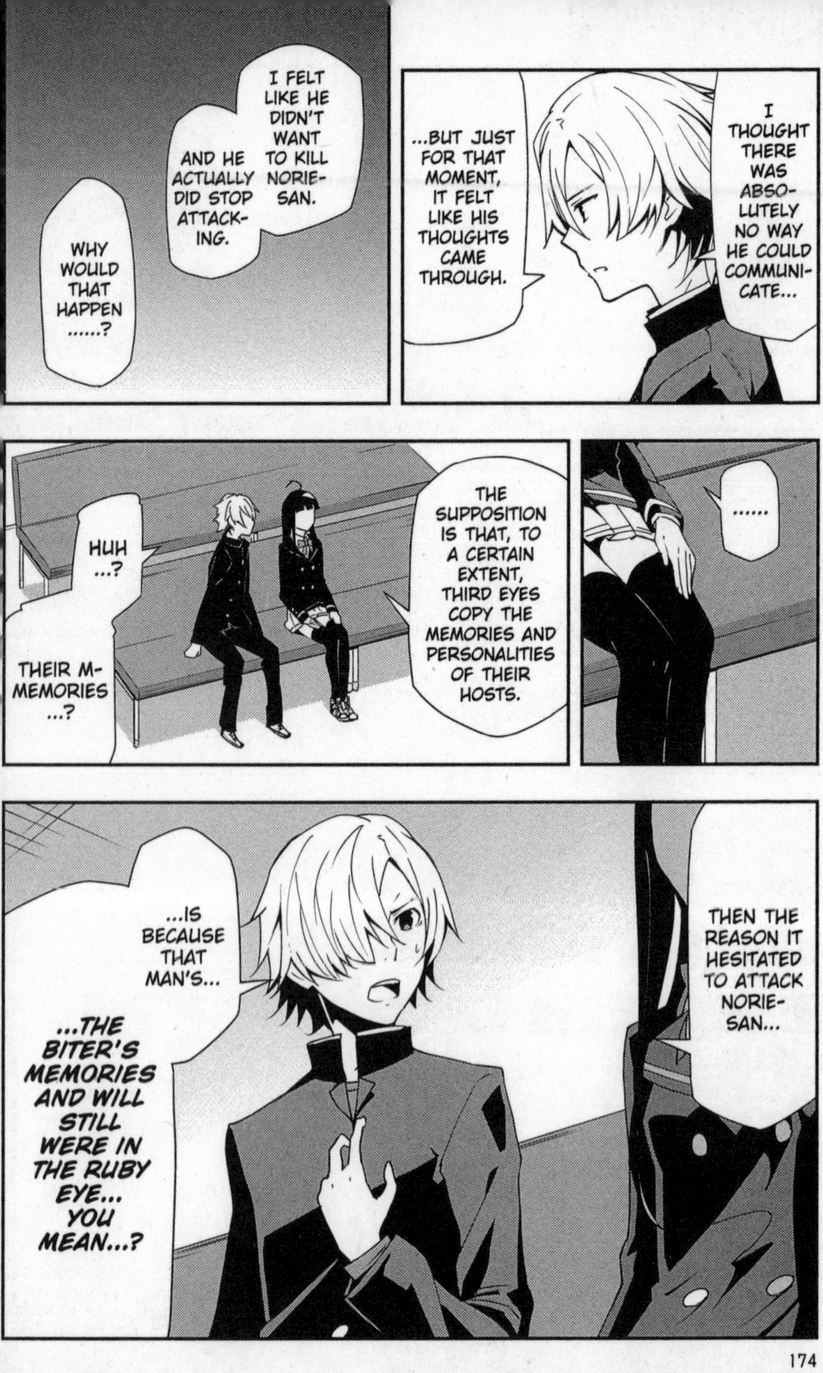
I THOUGHT THERE WAS ABSOLUTELY NO WAY HE COULD COMMUNICATE...
...BUT JUST FOR THAT MOMENT, IT FELT LIKE HIS THOUGHTS CAME THROUGH.
I FELT LIKE HE DIDN'T WANT TO KILL NORIE-SAN.
AND HE ACTUALLY DID STOP ATTACKING.
WHY WOULD THAT HAPPEN ......?
......
THE SUPPOSITION IS THAT, TO A CERTAIN EXTENT, THIRD EYES COPY THE MEMORIES AND PERSONALITIES OF THEIR HOSTS.
HUH ...?
THEIR M-MEMORIES ...?
THEN THE REASON IT HESITATED TO ATTACK NORIE-SAN...
...IS BECAUSE THAT MAN'S...
...THE BITER'S MEMORIES AND WILL STILL WERE IN THE RUBY EYE... YOU MEAN...?

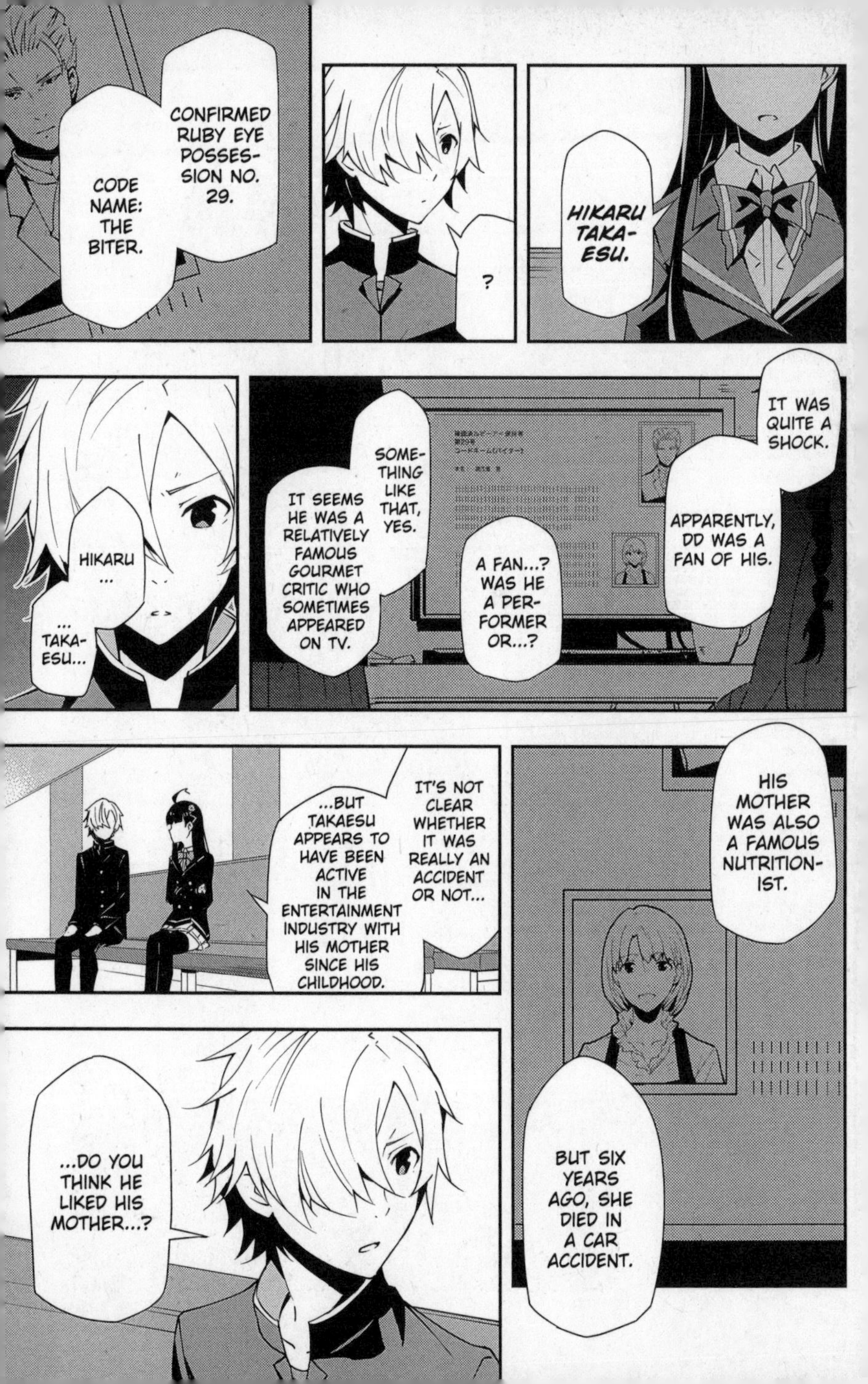
HIKARU TAKAESU.
?
CONFIRMED RUBY EYE POSSESSION NO. 29.
CODE NAME: THE BITER.
IT WAS QUITE A SHOCK.
APPARENTLY, DD WAS A FAN OF HIS.
A FAN...? WAS HE A PERFORMER OR...?
SOMETHING LIKE THAT, YES.
IT SEEMS HE WAS A RELATIVELY FAMOUS GOURMET CRITIC WHO SOMETIMES APPEARED ON TV.
HIKARU ...
... TAKAESU...
HIS MOTHER WAS ALSO A FAMOUS NUTRITIONIST.
BUT SIX YEARS AGO, SHE DIED IN A CAR ACCIDENT.
IT'S NOT CLEAR WHETHER IT WAS REALLY AN ACCIDENT OR NOT...
...BUT TAKAESU APPEARS TO HAVE BEEN ACTIVE IN THE ENTERTAINMENT INDUSTRY WITH HIS MOTHER SINCE HIS CHILDHOOD.
...DO YOU THINK HE LIKED HIS MOTHER...?

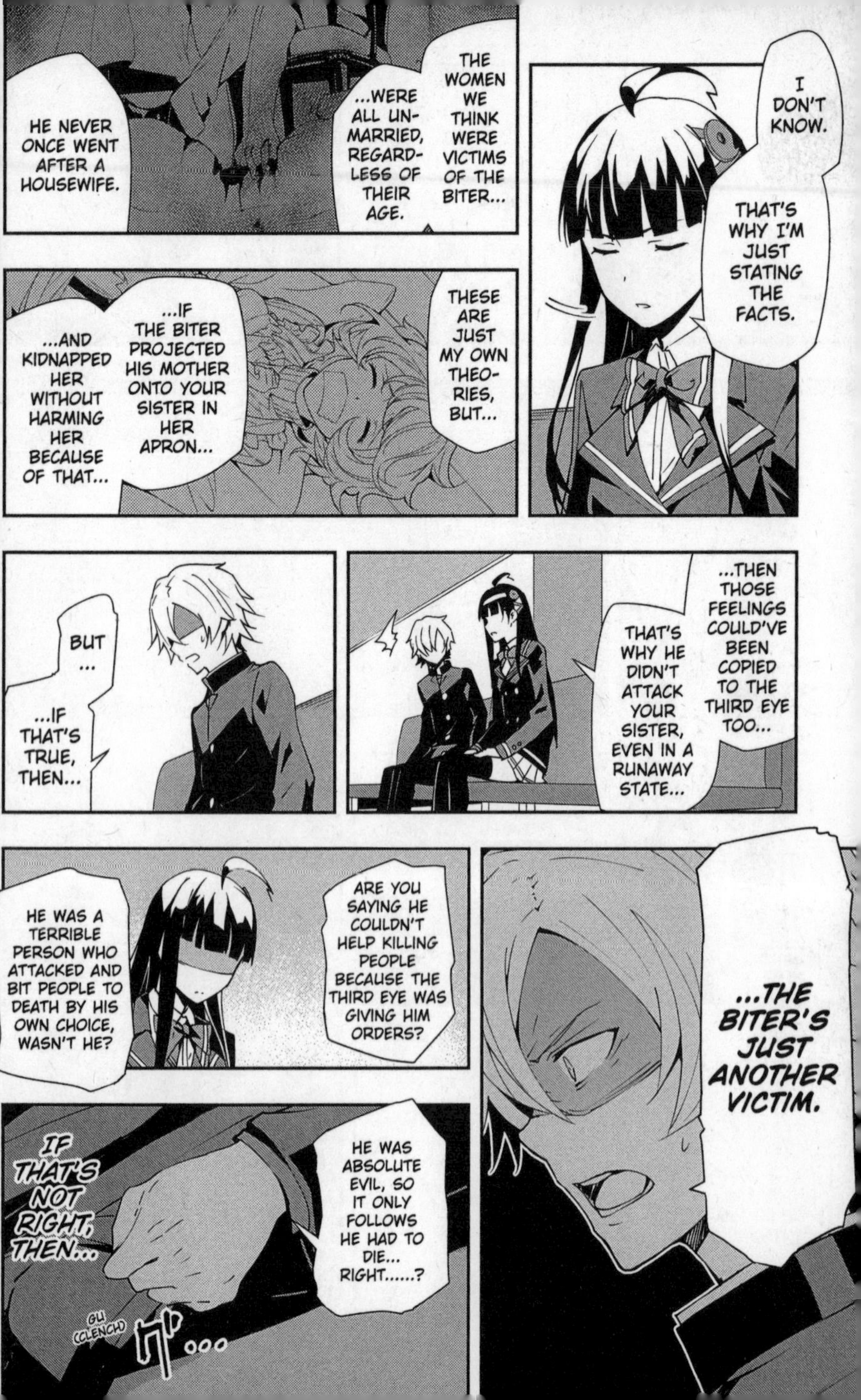
I DON'T KNOW.
THAT'S WHY I'M JUST STATING THE FACTS.
THE WOMEN WE THINK WERE VICTIMS OF THE BITER...
...WERE ALL UN-MARRIED, REGARD-LESS OF THEIR AGE.
HE NEVER ONCE WENT AFTER A HOUSEWIFE.
THESE ARE JUST MY OWN THEO-RIES, BUT...
...IF THE BITER PROJECTED HIS MOTHER ONTO YOUR SISTER IN HER APRON...
...AND KIDNAPPED HER WITHOUT HARMING HER BECAUSE OF THAT...
...THEN THOSE FEELINGS COULD'VE BEEN COPIED TO THE THIRD EYE TOO...
THAT'S WHY HE DIDN'T ATTACK YOUR SISTER, EVEN IN A RUNAWAY STATE...
BUT...
...IF THAT'S TRUE, THEN...
...THE BITER'S JUST ANOTHER VICTIM.
ARE YOU SAYING HE COULDN'T HELP KILLING PEOPLE BECAUSE THE THIRD EYE WAS GIVING HIM ORDERS?
HE WAS A TERRIBLE PERSON WHO ATTACKED AND BIT PEOPLE TO DEATH BY HIS OWN CHOICE, WASN'T HE?
HE WAS ABSOLUTE EVIL, SO IT ONLY FOLLOWS HE HAD TO DIE... RIGHT......?
IF THAT'S NOT RIGHT, THEN...
GU (CLENCH)

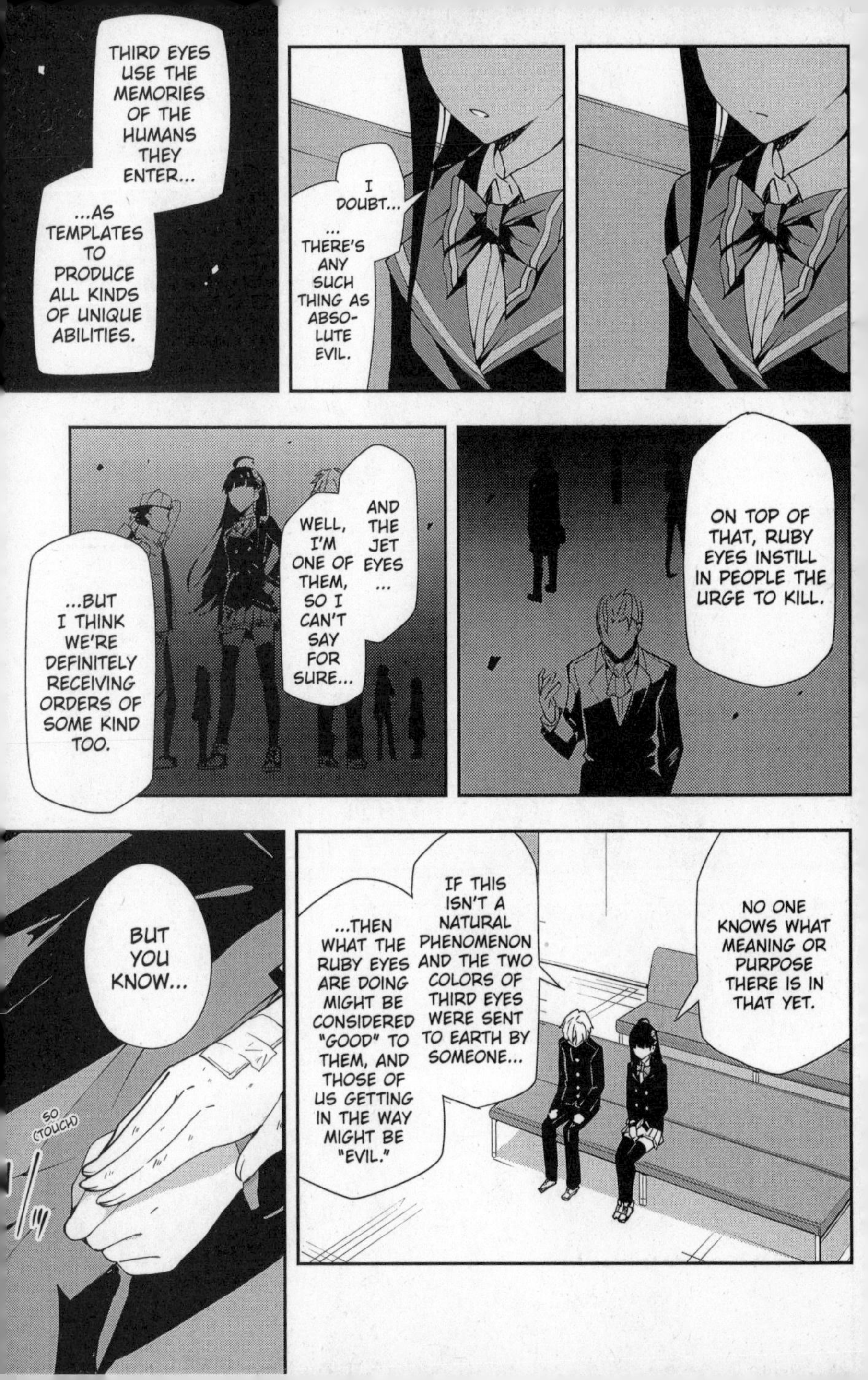
I DOUBT...
... THERE'S ANY SUCH THING AS ABSOLUTE EVIL.
THIRD EYES USE THE MEMORIES OF THE HUMANS THEY ENTER...
...AS TEMPLATES TO PRODUCE ALL KINDS OF UNIQUE ABILITIES.
ON TOP OF THAT, RUBY EYES INSTILL IN PEOPLE THE URGE TO KILL.
AND THE JET EYES...
WELL, I'M ONE OF THEM, SO I CAN'T SAY FOR SURE...
...BUT I THINK WE'RE DEFINITELY RECEIVING ORDERS OF SOME KIND TOO.
NO ONE KNOWS WHAT MEANING OR PURPOSE THERE IS IN THAT YET.
IF THIS ISN'T A NATURAL PHENOMENON AND THE TWO COLORS OF THIRD EYES WERE SENT TO EARTH BY SOMEONE...
...THEN WHAT THE RUBY EYES ARE DOING MIGHT BE CONSIDERED "GOOD" TO THEM, AND THOSE OF US GETTING IN THE WAY MIGHT BE "EVIL."
BUT YOU KNOW...
SO (TOUCH)

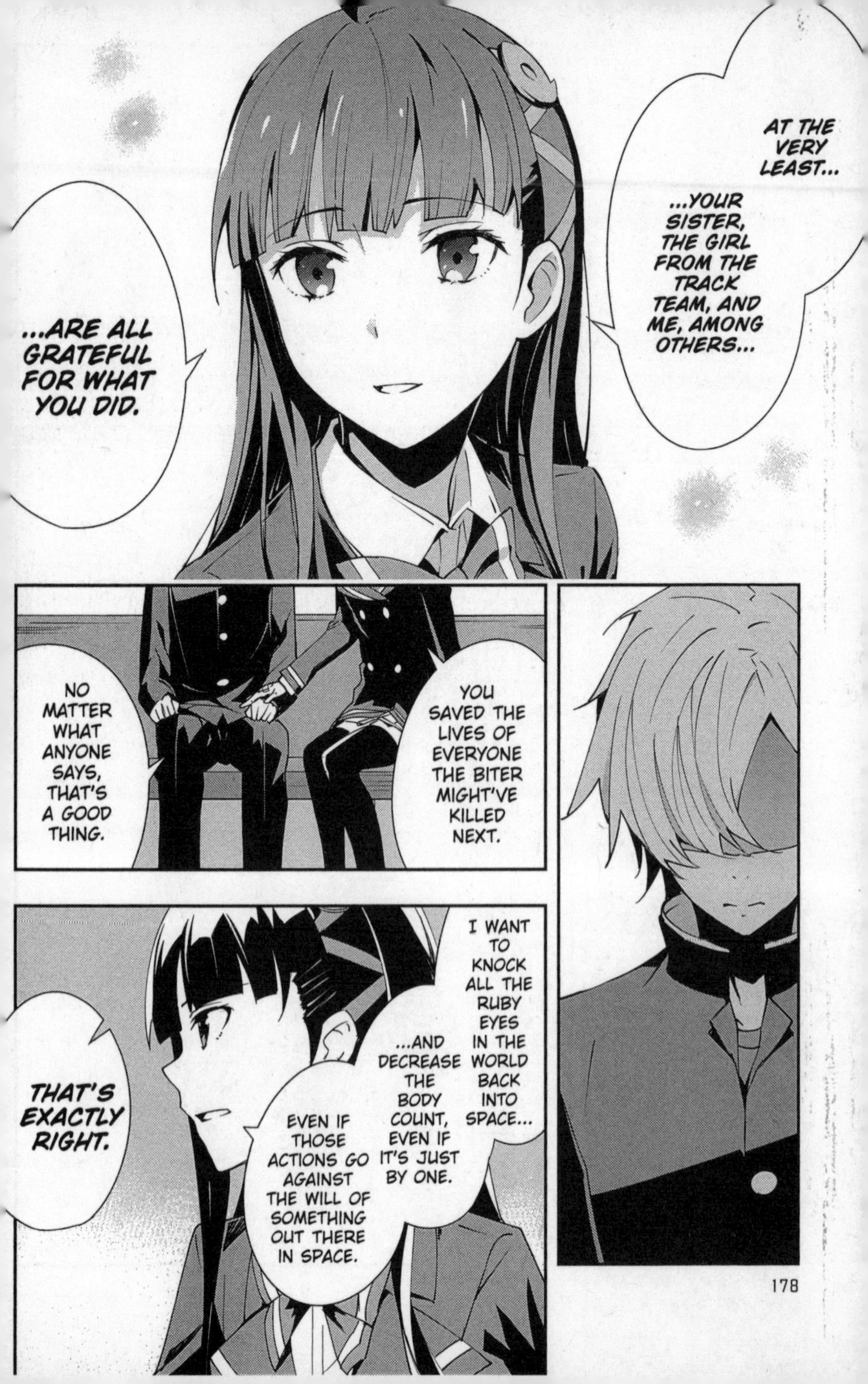
AT THE VERY LEAST...
...YOUR SISTER, THE GIRL FROM THE TRACK TEAM, AND ME, AMONG OTHERS...
...ARE ALL GRATEFUL FOR WHAT YOU DID.
YOU SAVED THE LIVES OF EVERYONE THE BITER MIGHT'VE KILLED NEXT.
NO MATTER WHAT ANYONE SAYS, THAT'S A GOOD THING.
I WANT TO KNOCK ALL THE RUBY EYES IN THE WORLD BACK INTO SPACE...
...AND DECREASE THE BODY COUNT, EVEN IF IT'S JUST BY ONE.
EVEN IF THOSE ACTIONS GO AGAINST THE WILL OF SOMETHING OUT THERE IN SPACE.
THAT'S EXACTLY RIGHT.

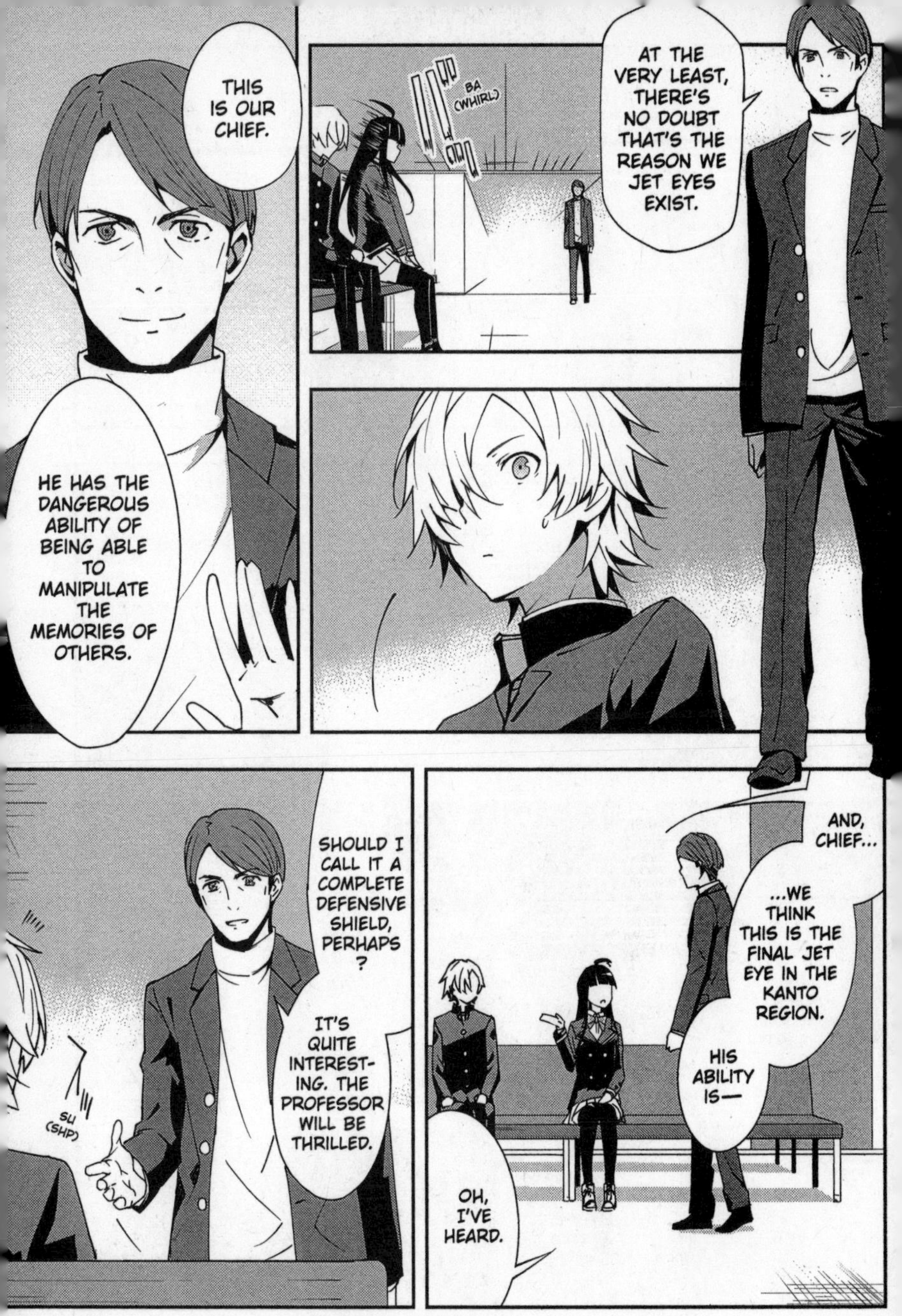
AT THE VERY LEAST, THERE'S NO DOUBT THAT'S THE REASON WE JET EYES EXIST.
BA (WHIRL)
THIS IS OUR CHIEF.
HE HAS THE DANGEROUS ABILITY OF BEING ABLE TO MANIPULATE THE MEMORIES OF OTHERS.
AND, CHIEF...
...WE THINK THIS IS THE FINAL JET EYE IN THE KANTO REGION.
HIS ABILITY IS—
OH, I'VE HEARD.
SHOULD I CALL IT A COMPLETE DEFENSIVE SHIELD, PERHAPS?
IT'S QUITE INTERESTING. THE PROFESSOR WILL BE THRILLED.
SU (SHP)

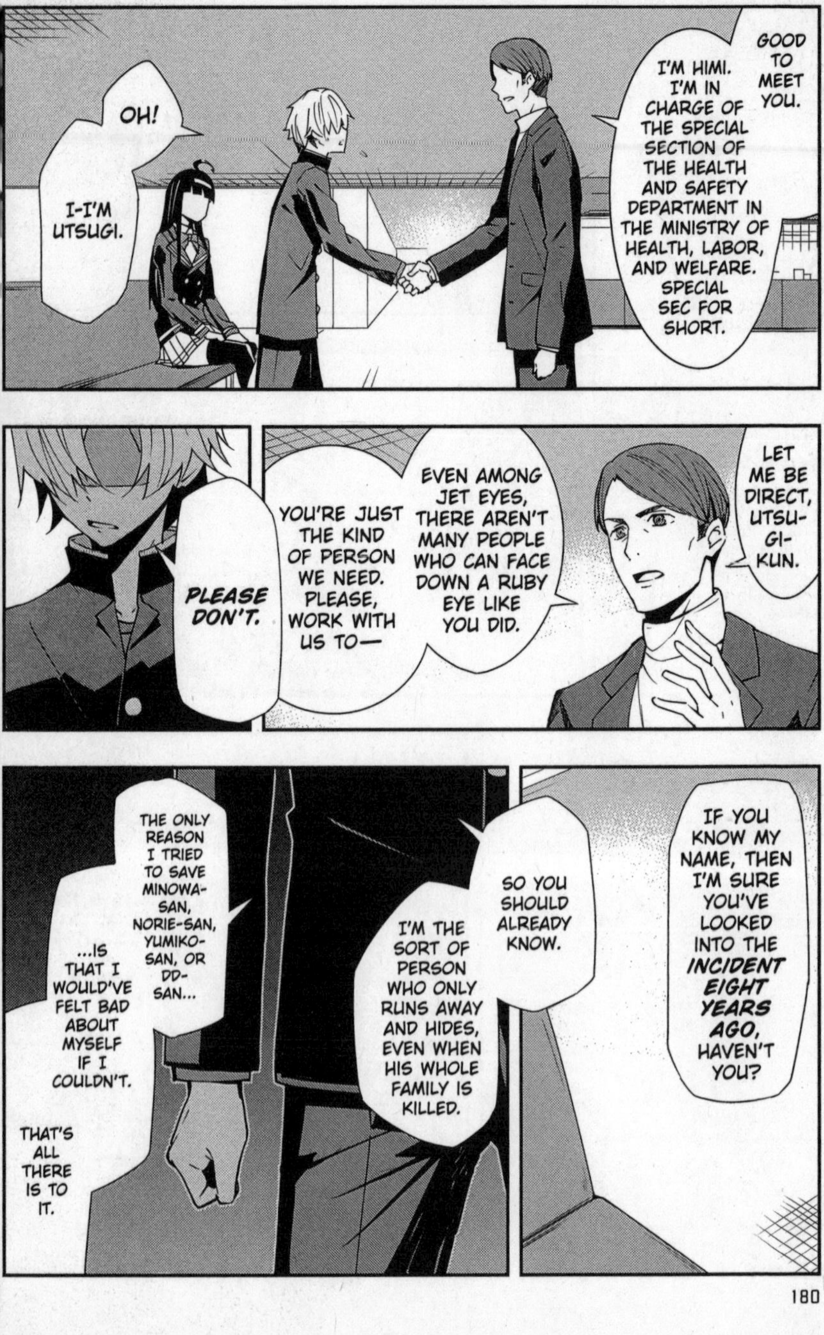
GOOD TO MEET YOU.
I'M HIMI. I'M IN CHARGE OF THE SPECIAL SECTION OF THE HEALTH AND SAFETY DEPARTMENT IN THE MINISTRY OF HEALTH, LABOR, AND WELFARE. SPECIAL SEC FOR SHORT.
OH!
I-I'M UTSUGI.
LET ME BE DIRECT, UTSU-GI-KUN.
EVEN AMONG JET EYES, THERE AREN'T MANY PEOPLE WHO CAN FACE DOWN A RUBY EYE LIKE YOU DID.
YOU'RE JUST THE KIND OF PERSON WE NEED. PLEASE, WORK WITH US TO—
PLEASE DON'T.
IF YOU KNOW MY NAME, THEN I'M SURE YOU'VE LOOKED INTO THE *INCIDENT EIGHT YEARS AGO*, HAVEN'T YOU?
SO YOU SHOULD ALREADY KNOW.
I'M THE SORT OF PERSON WHO ONLY RUNS AWAY AND HIDES, EVEN WHEN HIS WHOLE FAMILY IS KILLED.
THE ONLY REASON I TRIED TO SAVE MINOWA-SAN, NORIE-SAN, YUMIKO-SAN, OR DD-SAN...
...IS THAT I WOULD'VE FELT BAD ABOUT MYSELF IF I COULDN'T.
THAT'S ALL THERE IS TO IT.

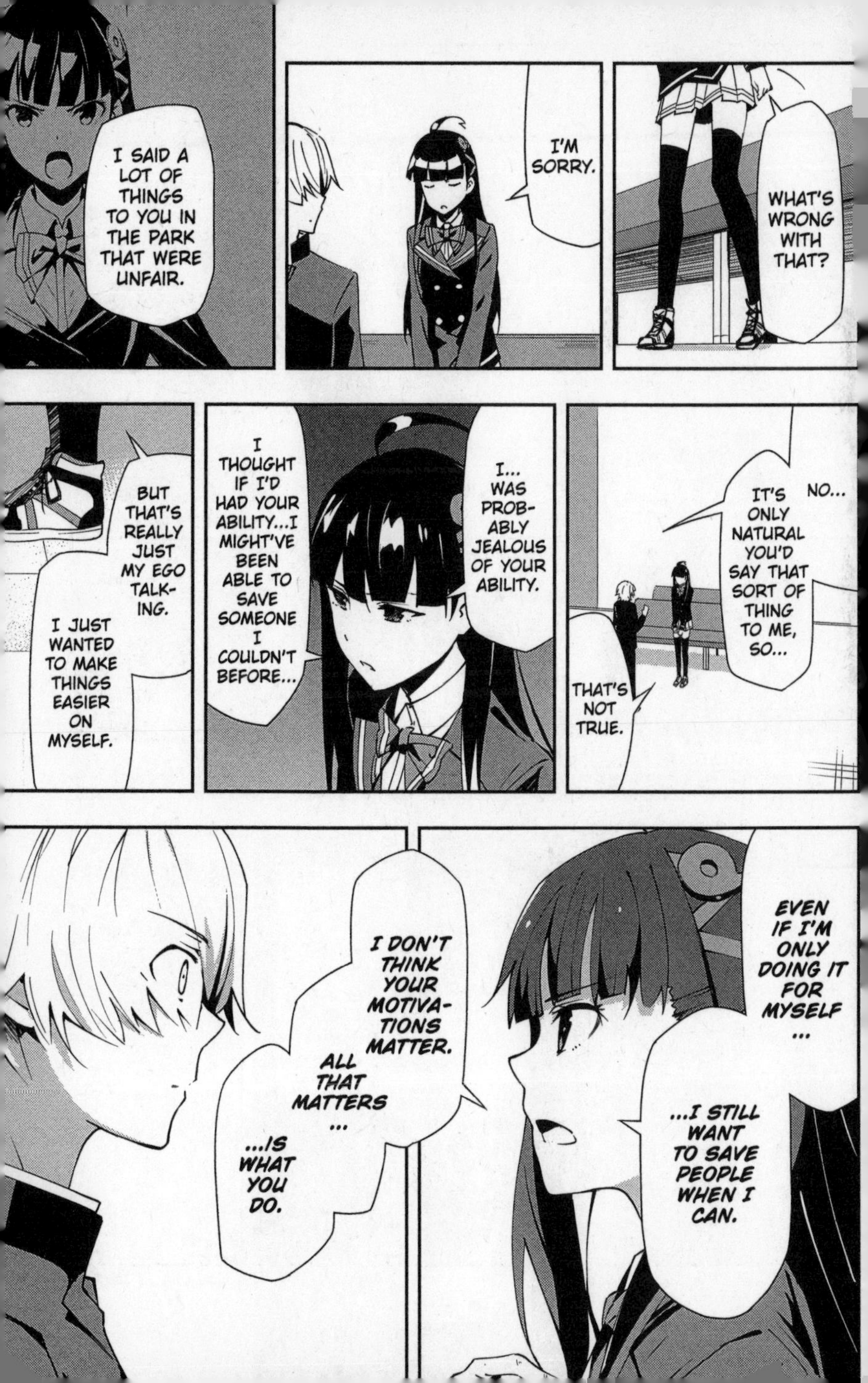
WHAT'S WRONG WITH THAT?
I'M SORRY.
I SAID A LOT OF THINGS TO YOU IN THE PARK THAT WERE UNFAIR.
NO...
IT'S ONLY NATURAL YOU'D SAY THAT SORT OF THING TO ME, SO...
THAT'S NOT TRUE.
I... WAS PROB-ABLY JEALOUS OF YOUR ABILITY.
I THOUGHT IF I'D HAD YOUR ABILITY...I MIGHT'VE BEEN ABLE TO SAVE SOMEONE I COULDN'T BEFORE...
BUT THAT'S REALLY JUST MY EGO TALK-ING.
I JUST WANTED TO MAKE THINGS EASIER ON MYSELF.
EVEN IF I'M ONLY DOING IT FOR MYSELF...
...I STILL WANT TO SAVE PEOPLE WHEN I CAN.
I DON'T THINK YOUR MOTIVA-TIONS MATTER.
ALL THAT MATTERS...
...IS WHAT YOU DO.

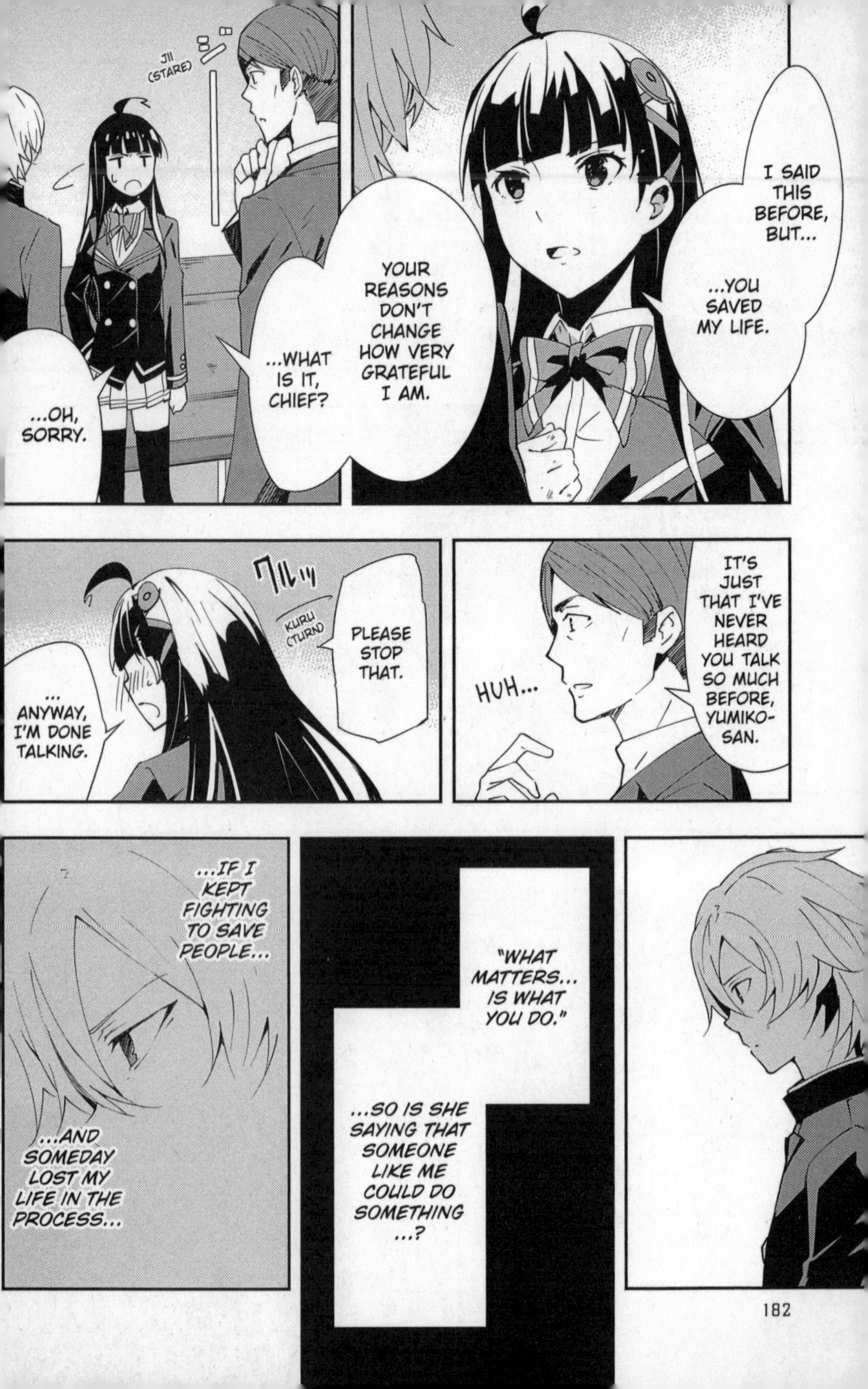
I SAID THIS BEFORE, BUT...
...YOU SAVED MY LIFE.
YOUR REASONS DON'T CHANGE HOW VERY GRATEFUL I AM.
JII (STARE)
...WHAT IS IT, CHIEF?
...OH, SORRY.
IT'S JUST THAT I'VE NEVER HEARD YOU TALK SO MUCH BEFORE, YUMIKO-SAN.
HUH...
クルッ
KURU (TURN)
PLEASE STOP THAT.
...ANYWAY, I'M DONE TALKING.
"WHAT MATTERS... IS WHAT YOU DO."
...SO IS SHE SAYING THAT SOMEONE LIKE ME COULD DO SOMETHING ...?
...IF I KEPT FIGHTING TO SAVE PEOPLE...
...AND SOMEDAY LOST MY LIFE IN THE PROCESS...

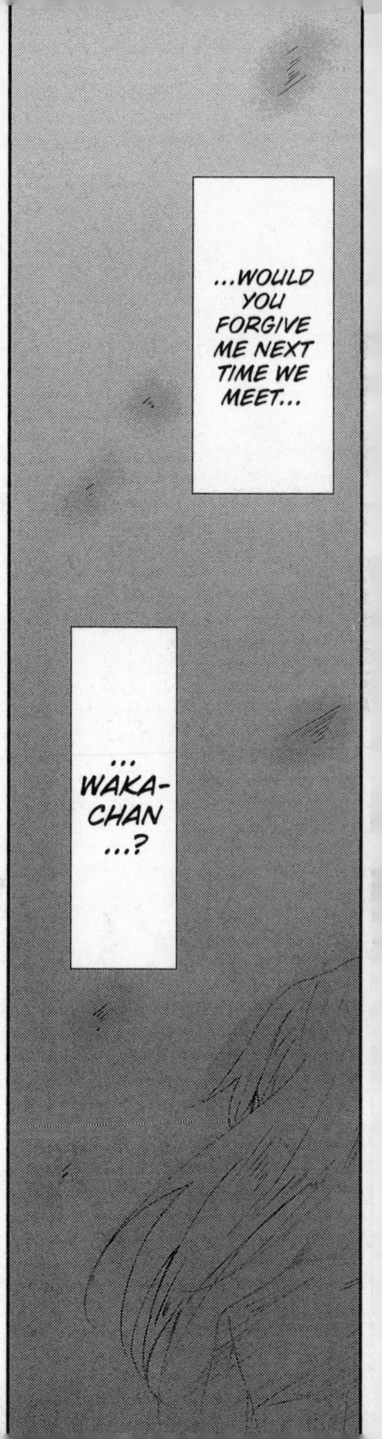
...WOULD YOU FORGIVE ME NEXT TIME WE MEET...
...WAKA-CHAN...?

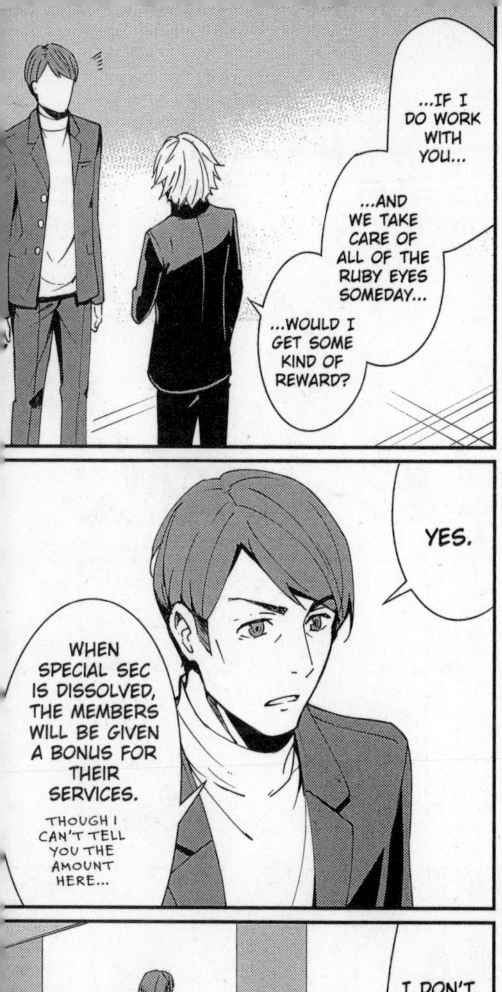
...IF I DO WORK WITH YOU...
...AND WE TAKE CARE OF ALL OF THE RUBY EYES SOMEDAY...
...WOULD I GET SOME KIND OF REWARD?
YES.
WHEN SPECIAL SEC IS DISSOLVED, THE MEMBERS WILL BE GIVEN A BONUS FOR THEIR SERVICES.
THOUGH I CAN'T TELL YOU THE AMOUNT HERE...
I DON'T NEED A SINGLE YEN.
BUT WHEN EVERYTHING IS OVER, I WANT TO USE YOUR ABILITY.
?

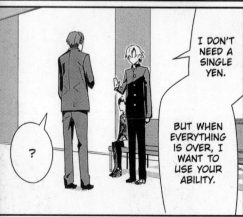

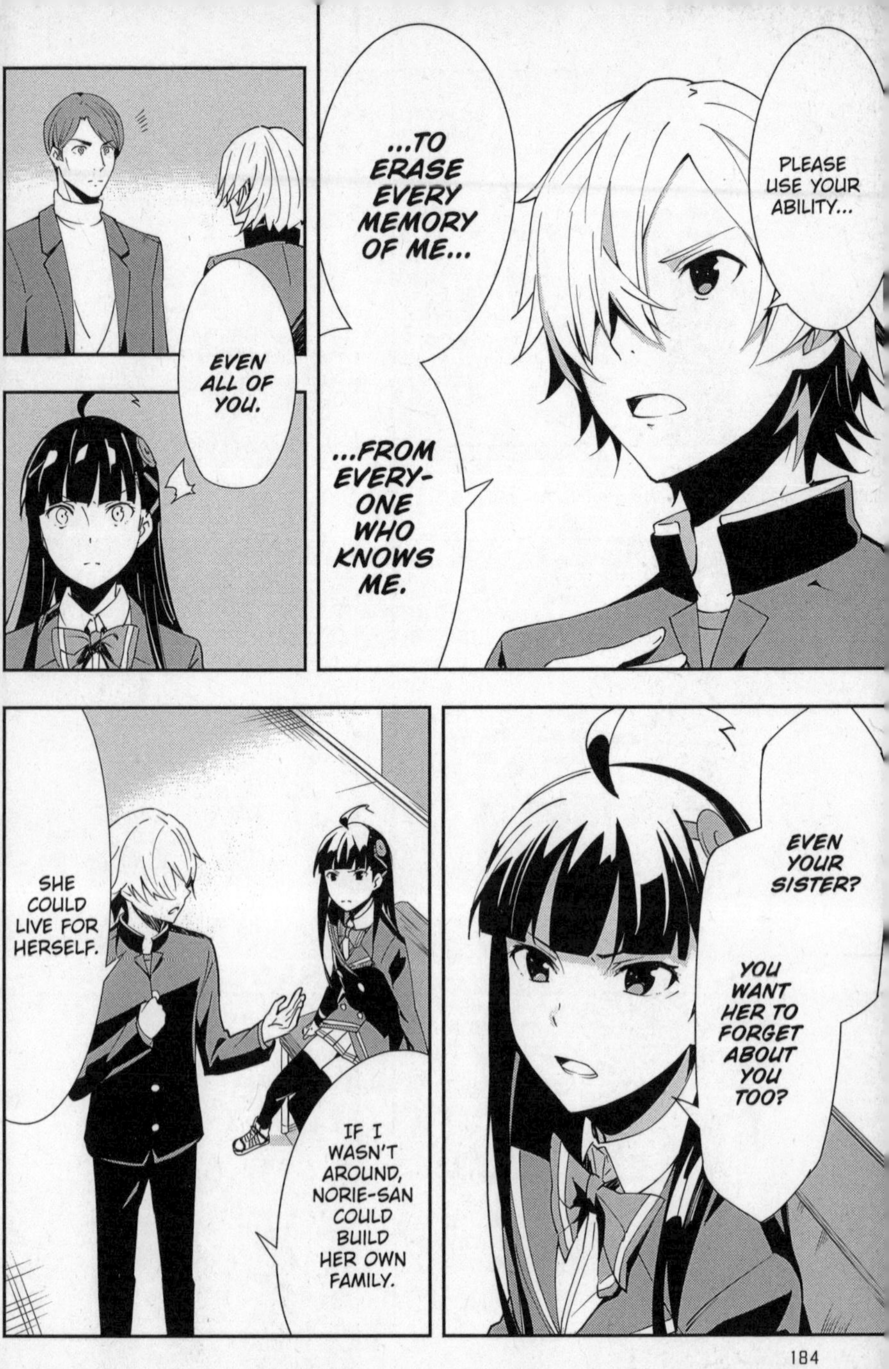
PLEASE USE YOUR ABILITY...
...TO ERASE EVERY MEMORY OF ME...
...FROM EVERY-ONE WHO KNOWS ME.
EVEN ALL OF YOU.
EVEN YOUR SISTER?
YOU WANT HER TO FORGET ABOUT YOU TOO?
IF I WASN'T AROUND, NORIE-SAN COULD BUILD HER OWN FAMILY.
SHE COULD LIVE FOR HERSELF.

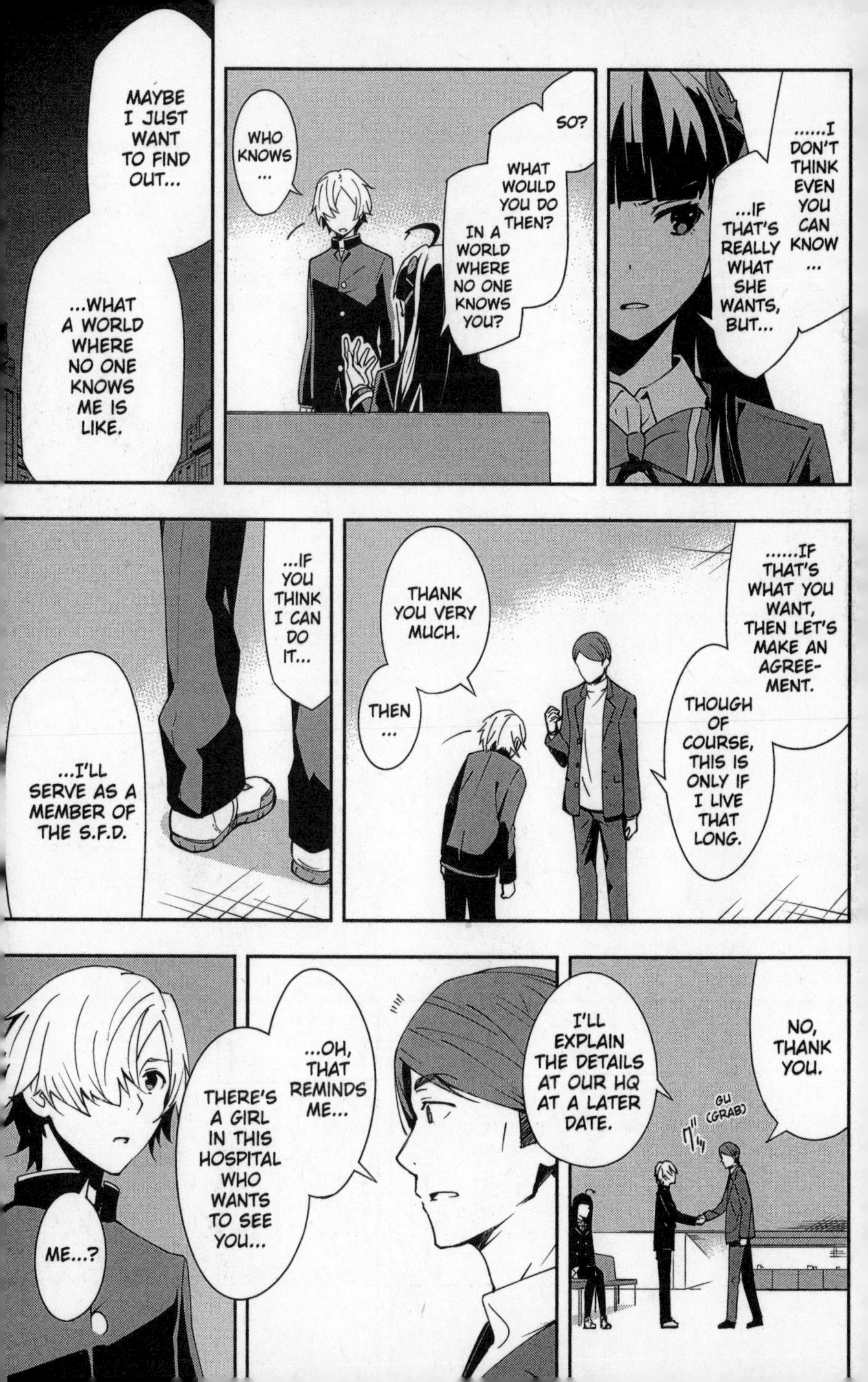
......I DON'T THINK EVEN YOU CAN KNOW ...
...IF THAT'S REALLY WHAT SHE WANTS, BUT...
SO?
WHAT WOULD YOU DO THEN?
IN A WORLD WHERE NO ONE KNOWS YOU?
WHO KNOWS ...
MAYBE I JUST WANT TO FIND OUT...
...WHAT A WORLD WHERE NO ONE KNOWS ME IS LIKE.
......IF THAT'S WHAT YOU WANT, THEN LET'S MAKE AN AGREE-MENT.
THOUGH OF COURSE, THIS IS ONLY IF I LIVE THAT LONG.
THANK YOU VERY MUCH.
THEN ...
...IF YOU THINK I CAN DO IT...
...I'LL SERVE AS A MEMBER OF THE S.F.D.
NO, THANK YOU.
I'LL EXPLAIN THE DETAILS AT OUR HQ AT A LATER DATE.
GU (GRAB)
...OH, THAT REMINDS ME...
THERE'S A GIRL IN THIS HOSPITAL WHO WANTS TO SEE YOU...
ME...?

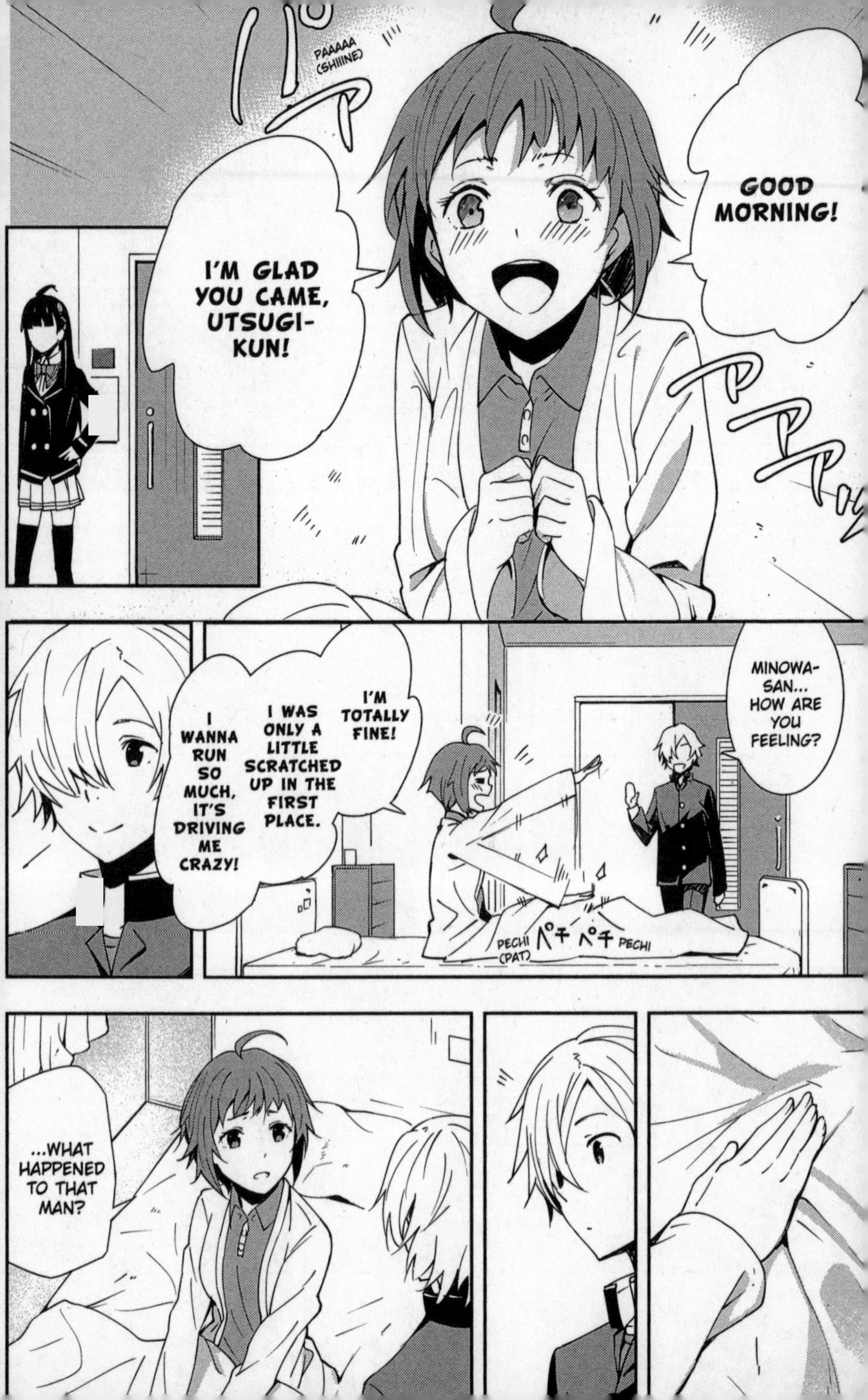
GOOD MORNING!
PAAAAA (SHIIINE)
I'M GLAD YOU CAME, UTSUGI-KUN!
MINOWA-SAN... HOW ARE YOU FEELING?
I'M TOTALLY FINE!
I WAS ONLY A LITTLE SCRATCHED UP IN THE FIRST PLACE.
I WANNA RUN SO MUCH, IT'S DRIVING ME CRAZY!
PECHI (PAT) ペチ ペチ PECHI
...WHAT HAPPENED TO THAT MAN?

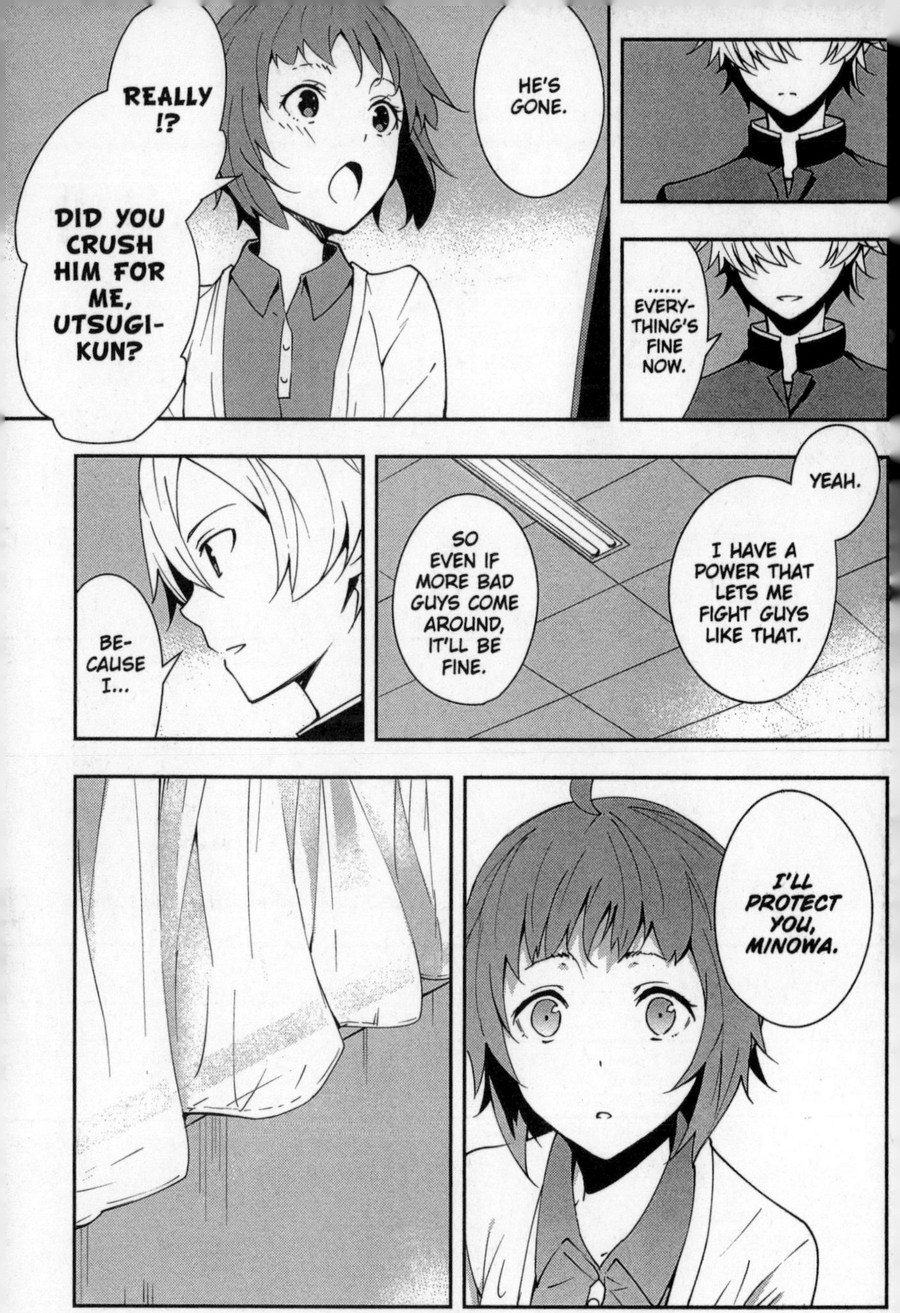

...... EVERYTHING'S FINE NOW.
HE'S GONE.
REALLY!?
DID YOU CRUSH HIM FOR ME, UTSUGI-KUN?
YEAH.
I HAVE A POWER THAT LETS ME FIGHT GUYS LIKE THAT.
SO EVEN IF MORE BAD GUYS COME AROUND, IT'LL BE FINE.
BECAUSE I...
I'LL PROTECT YOU, MINOWA.

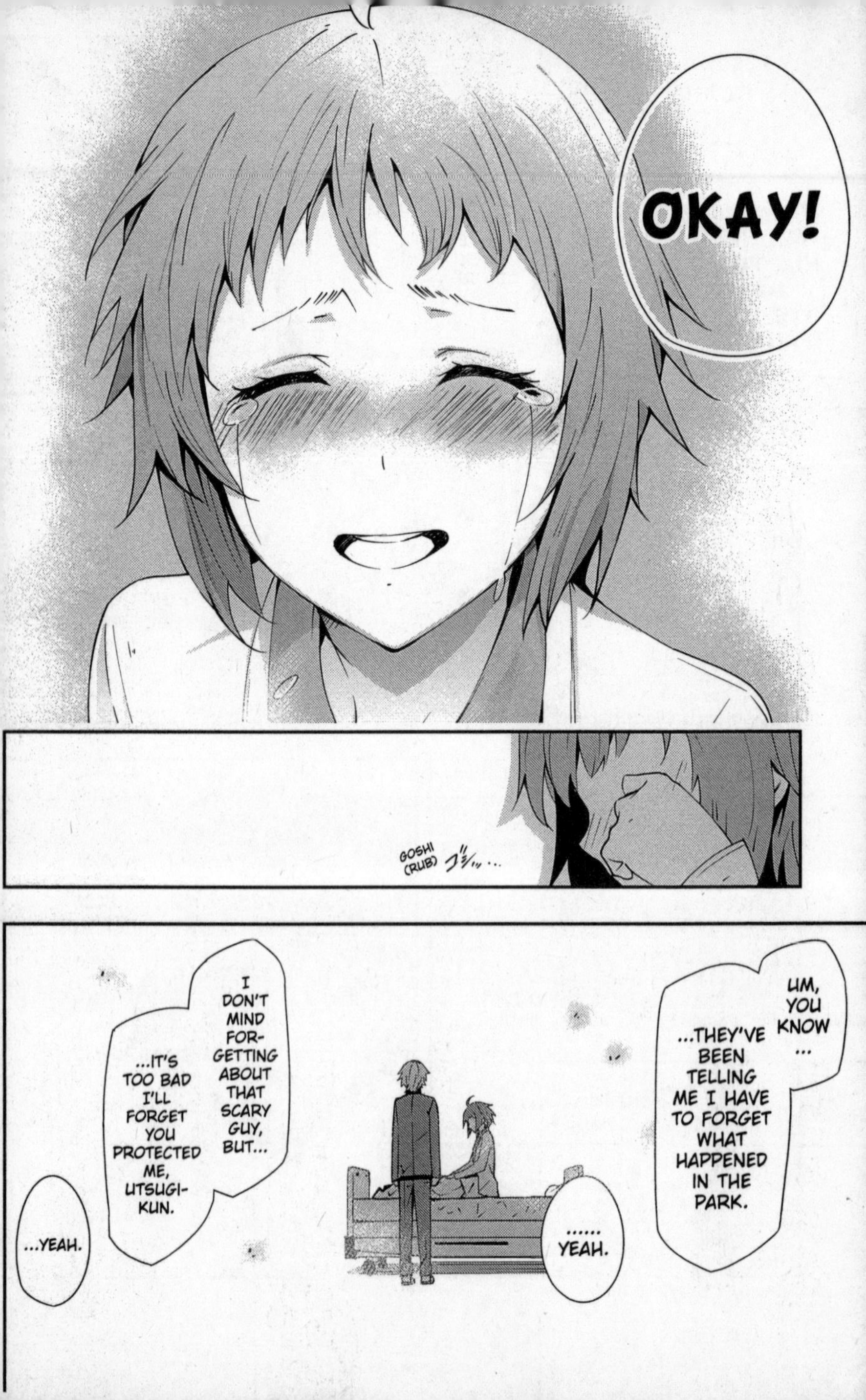
OKAY!
GOSHI (RUB)
UM, YOU KNOW ...
...THEY'VE BEEN TELLING ME I HAVE TO FORGET WHAT HAPPENED IN THE PARK.
...... YEAH.
I DON'T MIND FORGETTING ABOUT THAT SCARY GUY, BUT...
...IT'S TOO BAD I'LL FORGET YOU PROTECTED ME, UTSUGI-KUN.
...YEAH.

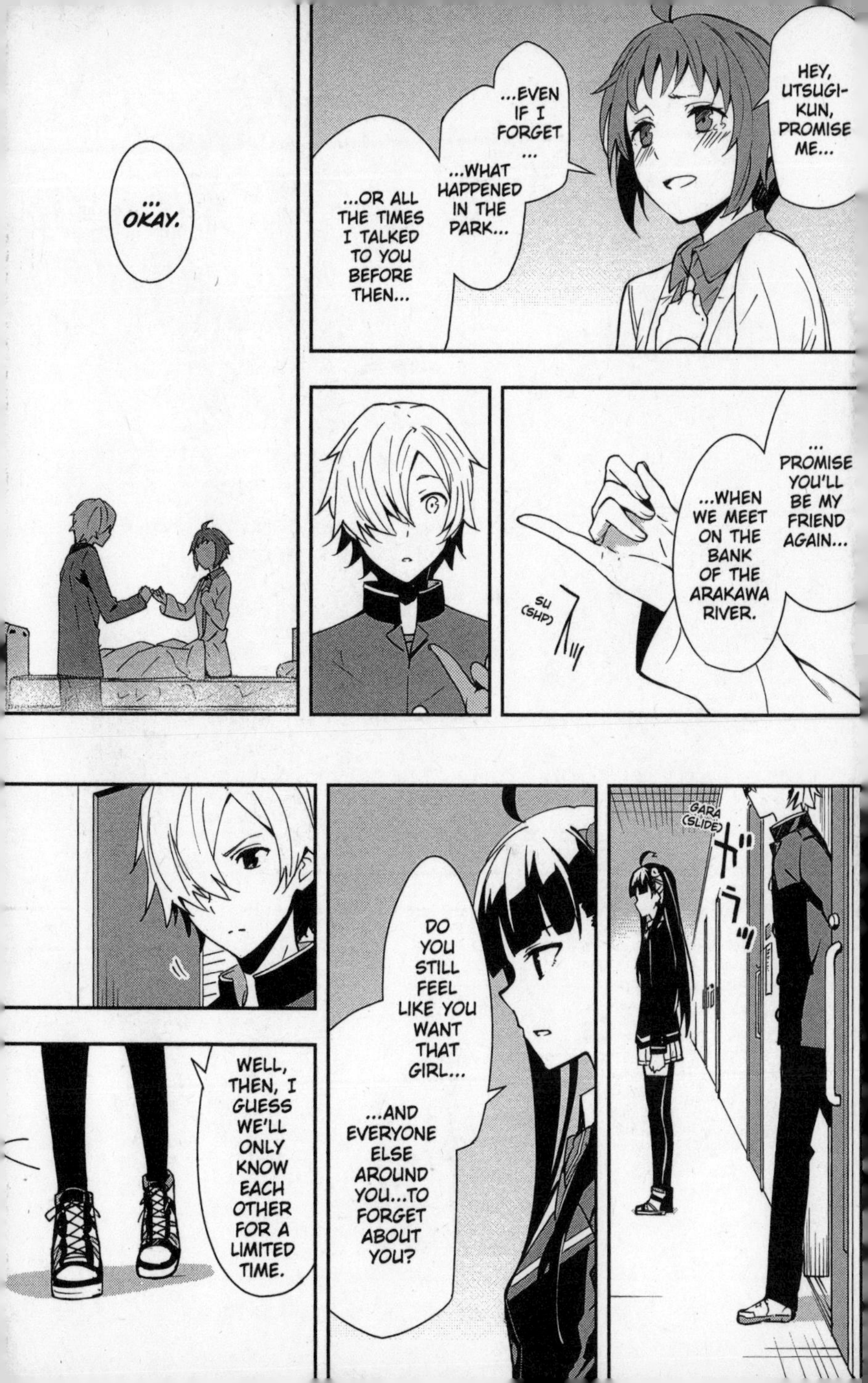
HEY, UTSUGI-KUN, PROMISE ME...
...EVEN IF I FORGET...
...WHAT HAPPENED IN THE PARK...
...OR ALL THE TIMES I TALKED TO YOU BEFORE THEN...
...PROMISE YOU'LL BE MY FRIEND AGAIN...
...WHEN WE MEET ON THE BANK OF THE ARAKAWA RIVER.
SU (SHP)
... OKAY.
GARA (SLIDE)
DO YOU STILL FEEL LIKE YOU WANT THAT GIRL...
...AND EVERYONE ELSE AROUND YOU...TO FORGET ABOUT YOU?
WELL, THEN, I GUESS WE'LL ONLY KNOW EACH OTHER FOR A LIMITED TIME.

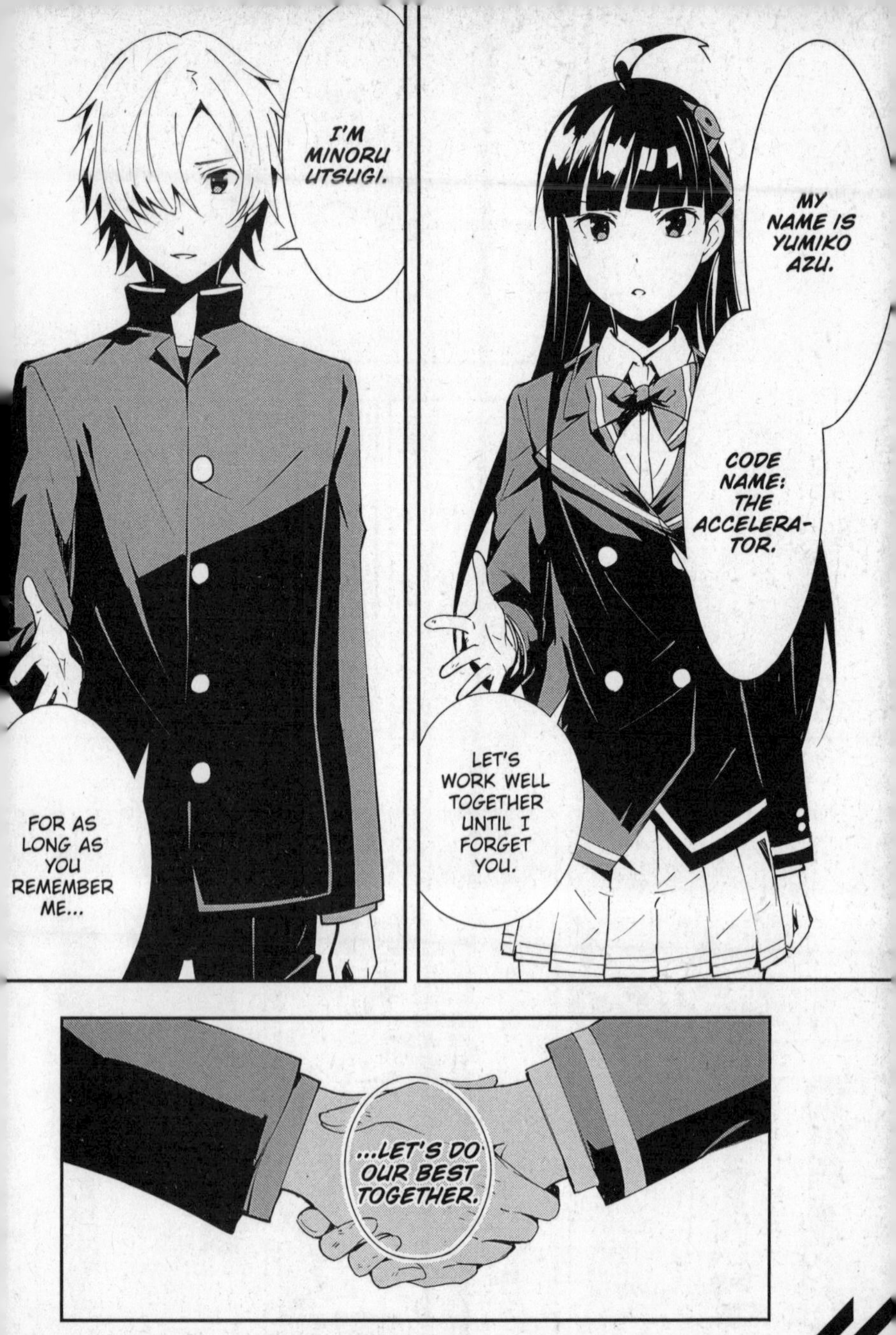
MY NAME IS YUMIKO AZU.
CODE NAME: THE ACCELERATOR.
LET'S WORK WELL TOGETHER UNTIL I FORGET YOU.
I'M MINORU UTSUGI.
FOR AS LONG AS YOU REMEMBER ME...
...LET'S DO OUR BEST TOGETHER.

To be continued...

THE ISOLATOR
realization of
absolute solitude

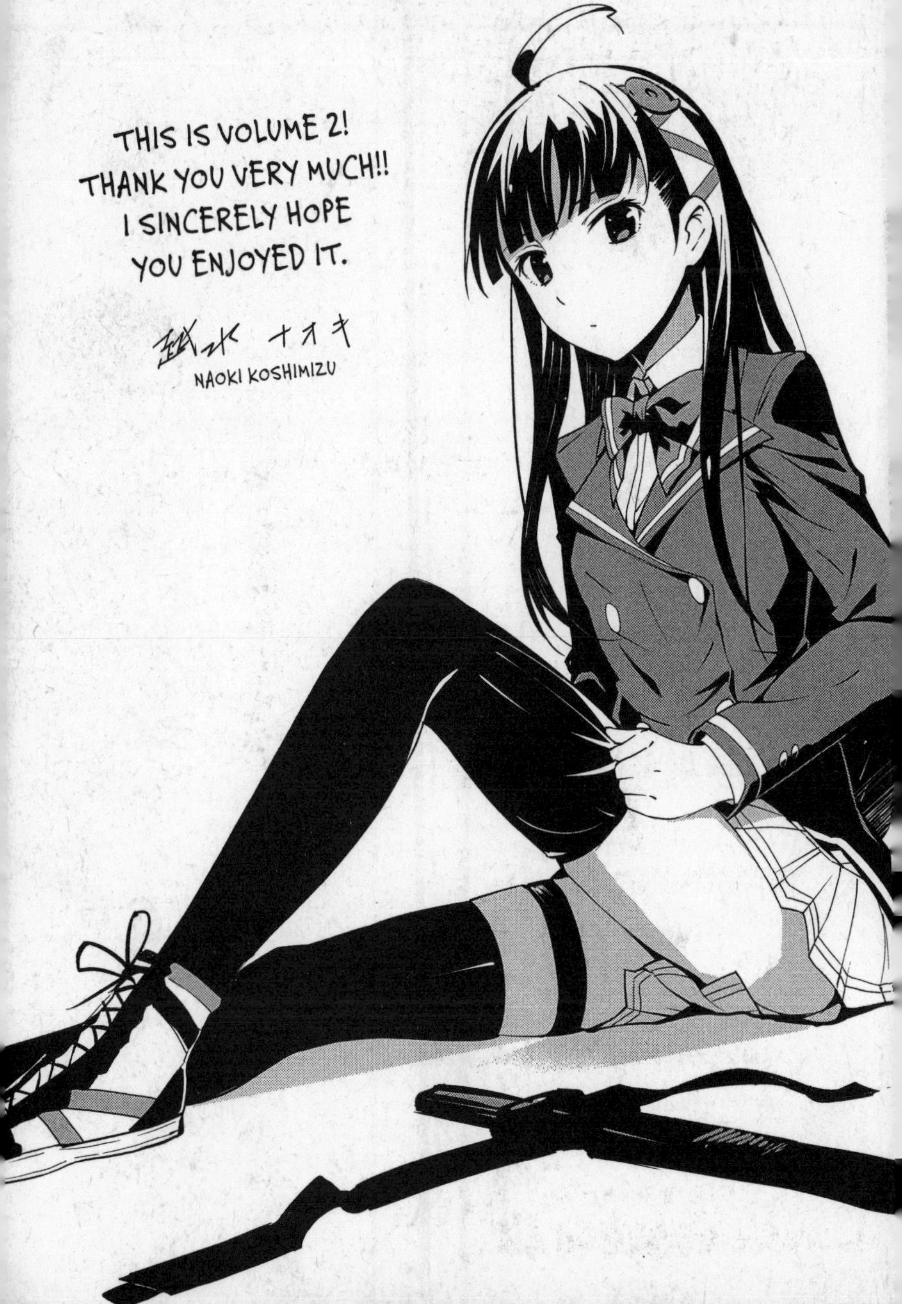
THIS IS VOLUME 2!
THANK YOU VERY MUCH!!
I SINCERELY HOPE
YOU ENJOYED IT.
越水 ナオキ
NAOKI KOSHIMIZU

THE ISOLATOR 2

Art: NAOKI KOSHIMIZU

Original Story: REKI KAWAHARA

Character Design: SHIMEJI

Translation: JENNY McKEON

Lettering: XIAN MICHELE LEE AND SCOTT BRANDON JONES

THE ISOLATOR Volume 2
© REKI KAWAHARA/NAOKI KOSHIMIZU 2016
All rights reserved.
Edited by ASCII MEDIA WORKS
First published in Japan in 2016 by KADOKAWA CORPORATION, Tokyo.
English translation rights arranged with KADOKAWA CORPORATION, Tokyo,
through Tuttle-Mori Agency, Inc., Tokyo.

English translation © 2017 by Yen Press, LLC.

Yen Press
1290 Avenue of the Americas
New York, NY 10104

Visit us at yenpress.com • facebook.com/yenpress • twitter.com/yenpress •
yenpress.tumblr.com • instagram.com/yenpress

First Yen Press Edition: November 2017

Yen Press is an imprint of Yen Press, LLC.
The Yen Press name and logo are trademarks of Yen Press, LLC.

The publisher is not responsible for websites
(or their content) that are not owned by the publisher.

Library of Congress Control Number: 2016958581

ISBNs: 978-0-316-43976-3 (paperback)
        978-1-975-30108-8 (ebook)

10 9 8 7 6 5 4 3 2 1

BVG

Printed in the United States of America